Spring
advisor
college

Health + Safety pg 279

Ch 13 Pg
217 →

ch 19
pg 351 →

NAFSA's Guide To

Education Abroad

For Advisers And Administrators

Second Edition

D0898443

NAFSA's Guide To

Education Abroad

For Advisers And Administrators

Second Edition

Edited by
William Hoffa and
John Pearson

NAFSA Association of International Educators
Washington, D.C.

NAFSA Association of International Educators promotes the exchange of students and scholars to and from the United States. The Association sets and upholds standards of good practice and provides professional education and training that strengthen institutional programs and services related to international educational exchange. NAFSA provides a forum for discussion of issues and a network for sharing information as it seeks to increase awareness of and support for international education in higher education, in government, and in the community.

Library of Congress Cataloging-in-Publication Data

NAFSA's guide to education abroad for advisers and administrators
   edited by William Hoffa and John Pearson. -- 2nd ed.
    492 pp.
   Includes bibliographical references and index.
   ISBN 0-912207-75-2
   1. Foreign study—Handbooks, manuals, etc. 2. American students—Travel—Handbooks, manuals, etc. 3. College students—Travel—Handbooks, manuals, etc. 4. Faculty advisors—Handbooks, manuals, etc. 5. College administrators—Handbooks, manuals, etc.
I. Hoffa, William. II. Pearson, John, 1948– . III. NAFSA: Association of International Educators (Washington, D.C.)

LB2376.N26   1997   97-125
370.19'62—dc21   CIP

Contents

Part One Education Abroad And American Higher Education

Part Three Program Development And Evaluation

Appendixes and Index

Publisher's Acknowledgments

Education abroad is done well and variously across the country and around the world. Embodying that variety in this volume has required extensive collaboration among authors and between authors and editors. We are gratified that the collaborative approach appears to have worked. By design, the chapters in this volume, with one exception, have at least two authors. That design reflects our attempt to tap into the wide range of professional experience that exists in the field of education abroad.

It is our hope that *NAFSA's Guide to Education Abroad for Advisers and Administrators* will continue to serve as the basic text in our vital and burgeoning field. To help make that hope a reality, the editors of this volume strove to unify the text and to give it a consistent tone, no easy assignment when dealing with contributions from two score practitioners, each gifted with a singular voice and strong views on matters of professional importance. Imposing consistency over individuality is never an easy process, but we believe that the effort has maximized the value of this volume as a key educational tool in NAFSA's professional development program.

The fact that we have identified our authors as "contributors" in this edition, as in the first, reflects the collaborative, integrative approach described above.

Most of the team that produced the first edition returned to contribute again to the second. The names of those who did not, but of whose contribution to the first edition a substantial portion remains in the second, appear at the beginning of each chapter along with the names of their colleagues who participated in the new work of producing the second edition. We would be remiss if we did not also recall here Marvin Slind's work as coeditor of the first edition. Preoccupied with his teaching duties in the Department of History at Washington State University, Marv elected not to participate in this revision, but the popularity of the first edition stands as a testament to his contribution.

The editors join me in thanking the following individuals who contributed in various ways to the text of this edition:

- Juan Arroyo, Cornell University (Chapter 9)
- Jane Cary, Princeton University (Chapter 9)
- Stephen Cooper, Louisiana State University (Chapter 9)
- Carol Dickerman, University of Michigan (Chapter 12)
- Mary Anne Grant, International Student Exchange Program (Chapter 9)
- Art Neisberg, SECUSS-L list manager (Chapter 7)
- Kerry O'Connor, Foothill College (Chapter 19)
- Lisa Park, Stanford University (Chapters 6 and 7)
- Paul Primak, Oregon State System of Higher Education (Chapter 11)
- John Sommer, School for International Training (Chapter 12)
- My Yarabinec, San Francisco State University (Chapter 11).

Finally, Bill Hoffa and John Pearson are the kind of editors publishers count themselves lucky to have. Their knowledge of education abroad runs wide and deep, and they have a real knack for bringing out the best in their collaborators. The profession owes them a debt of gratitude.

—Steven Kennedy
Director of Publications
NAFSA: Association of International Educators

Introduction to the Revised Edition

In 1975 NAFSA published *The SECUSSA Sourcebook: A Guide for Advisors of U.S. Students Planning an Overseas Experience.* This pioneering book grew out of the professional excitement and interchange of ideas among 50 representatives from U.S. colleges and universities across the country, plus other professional educators from the Experiment in International Living/School for International Training, the Council on International Educational Exchange, the Institute of International Education, and the U.S. Office of Education, who had attended a December 1974 workshop held on the campus of the Experiment/SIT in Brattleboro, Vermont. The workshop was sponsored by the then-new NAFSA Section on U.S. Students Abroad (SECUSSA), and the costs were largely underwritten by a grant from the Carnegie Corporation of New York and Educational Programmes Abroad, Brighton, England.

In the *Sourcebook's* preface, editor Judy Frank expressed her hope that the book represented "the first steps toward professionalizing the field of advising U.S. students who wish an overseas experience." Denying that the *Sourcebook* contained the final word on advising students, she envisioned a "constant reevaluation and change" in professional training and knowledge in the years ahead. As Frank predicted, "constant reevaluation and change" indeed took place over the next two decades, and most of the professional concerns identified in 1975 became perennial. The *Sourcebook* remains for those who can find a copy a repository of sound insight and useful advice, coupled with an inspired vision of the value of living and learning abroad. Especially noteworthy are its sections on cross-cultural training, the importance of language learning, and experiential education.

The *Sourcebook* was followed four years later by another collective effort, *Study Abroad: A Handbook for Advisers and Administrators*, also published by NAFSA. This work invited its readers to turn to it for "information, points of view, practices, alternatives, suggestions, and cautions." This professional counsel was presented in outline form—unlike the *Sourcebook*, which is composed of individual essays. Recognizing that its audience worked in diverse institutions, or in similar institutions in different phases of internationalization, the *Handbook* offered numerous levels of guidance and tried to be "descriptive rather than prescriptive."

Whereas the *Sourcebook* centered somewhat broadly on "the overseas experience," the *Handbook* centered more on study abroad and offered less pedagogy. The *Handbook* acknowledged the clear historical trend during the 1960s and 1970s (which continued through the 1980s and is only just now being challenged) toward formal, academic, credit-bearing programs sponsored directly by American colleges and universities, somewhat at the expense of other forms of international education. The *Handbook* also addressed the fact that advisers and administrators are likely to be employed by academic institutions, and that most students need credit and often financial assistance for their time abroad.

The *Sourcebook* and the *Handbook* were both concerned with the ongoing issues for advisers, administrators, and institutions: the place of overseas study in its institutional context and in American higher education; the diverse roles and responsibilities of advisers and administrators; how to evaluate programs and advise students; how to plan, implement, and promote programs; how to prepare students for their time abroad and their return; how to assess and award academic credit; and how to provide adequate financial aid, to mention just a few areas of lasting concern.

Viewed from the realities of the late 1980s and early 1990s, however, much had changed in the field of international education since the *Sourcebook* and the *Handbook* were written. The professional practice of advising and administration had evolved into something considerably more complex and demanding; student opportunities had multiplied dramatically; many more types of institutions were supporting education abroad in some form; and the national mood and economy, as well as world events, had significantly altered the climate of support for international education. What was required of practitioners and institutions, in order to provide the best advice, services, and support that students and institutions required, was seen as more substantial than ever before. In short, the dimensions of the field had become greatly enlarged, its terrain more varied. Hence, the need was seen by many SECUSSA members for a more current and inclusive guide to the field.

The first edition of *NAFSA's Guide to Education Abroad for Advisers and Administrators* (1993) was begun as an updated version of *The SECUSSA Sourcebook*. It provided a broad perspective on most important issues and practices that make up the current field of education abroad. Like the *Sourcebook* and *Handbook,* its contents represented a collaborative effort on the part of many education abroad professionals.

The book's audience has included (1) newcomers in search of an inclusive, introductory overview of the variety of professional thought and practice on advising and programming; (2) mid-level professionals whose institutional responsibilities have shifted or expanded; and (3) seasoned practitioners in need of new information, points of comparative reference, or an expanded perspective. Each chapter acknowledged that there are a huge variety of workable approaches to education abroad. The hope was that this approach would offer something of interest to nearly everyone, whatever their experience, position, or institution.

Of special note was its use of the operative term "education abroad" rather than "study abroad." Although most practitioners are employed by academic institutions and most of their work concerns credit-bearing study programs for undergraduates, NAFSA has long supported a broad range of overseas educational opportunities, academic and experiential. After all, SECUSSA stands for the "Section on U.S. Students Abroad," and not, as is often assumed, the "section on U.S. students studying abroad." What might seem a semantic shift was really a recognition of the earliest and broadest principles in the field, namely support for all varieties of living and learning abroad that have genuine and lasting educational value. The term education abroad also expresses the belief that colleges and universities have an obligation to be proactive in their support of this wide range of activities.

When we were approached to edit a second edition of *NAFSA's Guide to Education Abroad,* we were of course delighted. The call demonstrated to us that (1) the first edition had met its aims and pleased its readers, and (2) there existed a rationale to update and expand it, given the rapid evolution of developments in the field over only a few short years since it appeared. Although we were disappointed that Marv Slind's new career as a full-time teacher meant that he could not be involved, we looked forward to the challenge of reflecting again with our SECUSSA colleagues on what needed to be added to the first edition and what might have changed in the field since the beginning of the decade.

To a large degree the introduction to the first edition still holds true. The challenges that faced the profession in the early 1990s still exist— some are being met while others remain formidable. Although we remain confident that increased interest in education abroad is evident, both from students and institutions, this interest is not always positive nor even benign.

The economic uncertainties that face much of higher education, have, if anything, increased. The costs simply of attending college continue to spiral upward, and therefore the resolve of a student to pursue an over-seas opportunity may need extra support. Remedies need to be found on both national and institutional levels. During the past year we have fol-lowed, sometimes with despair, the problems with the National Security Education Program, and, as we write, the difficulties with federal inter-pretations of financial aid availability for education abroad. Even fund-ing for the Fulbright programs is being threatened.

On a number of campuses hard questions are being asked regarding the financial implications, to that institution, of study abroad: is study abroad fiscally neutral, or does it in fact drain valuable and finite resources? Does it make fiscal sense to provide the resources to allow open-minded advising for students who are interested in an education-abroad experience, even if the student ends up enrolling in a program sponsored by another institution? Or, to ask this question in a way that hits home to SECUSSAns, will we, as education-abroad professionals, be able to center our counsel on the academic, career, and personal benefits of an overseas experience to each individual student, rather than the cost to the institution?

This degree of uncertainty suggests that all education abroad profes-sionals need to continue to involve themselves in both local and nation-al outreach and advocacy. Our assumptions must remain that the intrin-sic, or even the academic, value of education abroad can no longer be relied on to satisfy university administrators and faculty. National advo-cacy on issues of education abroad by NAFSA, by the SECUSSA leader-ship, by in-the-trenches SECUSSAns, by the Alliance for International Educational and Cultural Exchange, and by other concerned organiza-tions and professionals has increased, of necessity, in recent years. But ongoing local advocacy at the campus level is also needed, in light of these growing questions and doubts.

Proactive advocacy, whether at the national or institutional level, will, we anticipate, become an even more important aspect of the work of the profession. It is ironic that after the decades of work to encourage students to consider an overseas opportunity, we now have to devote time to safeguarding these opportunities. But we do. At the national level, the death of Senator Fulbright, the retirement of stalwart supporters such as Senators Boren and Simon, and the often draconian cost cutting by federal and state legislators that has become part of daily life, means that education abroad will need to find new national and governmental advocates in order to maintain funds that support such programs as Title IV, Fulbright, FIPSE, USIA, and NSEP.

This is, of course, only one side of the coin. The other side is the one of possibilities and progress. Student interest in education abroad appears to be continuing on an upward curve; institutions and programs are making more effort to develop programs that offer new destinations and are relevant to underrepresented groups of students; and new and exciting technological developments enable the exchange of information in a manner only dreamed about when the first edition was published.

The field of education abroad is of necessity developing a more realistic awareness of the accomplishments required to reach the field's highest aspirations and to meet perceived national needs. At the end of the past decade, a spate of important studies and reports on international education compellingly analyzed the current U.S. situation and found it wanting. Among these documents are *Educating for Global Competence* (1988), by the CIEE Advisory Council for International Educational Exchange; *Abroad and Beyond: Patterns in American Overseas Education* (1988), by Craufurd Goodwin and Michael Nacht for IIE; *America in Transition: Report of the Task Force on International Education* (1989), from the National Governor's Association; *International Studies and the Undergraduate* (1989), by Richard Lambert of the National Foreign Language Center for the American Council on Education; *Exchange 2000: International Leadership for the Next Century* (1990), offered by The Liaison Group for International Educational Exchange; and *Getting on With the Task: Report of the National Task Force on Undergraduate Education Abroad* (NAFSA/CIEE/IIE, 1990), the complete text of which appears in the appendix to this volume). To these calls for action can now be added *Educating Americans for a World in Flux: Ten Ground Rules for Internationalizing Higher Education* (1995) from the American Council on Education.

All of these studies contain ambitious and challenging recommendations for international educators, colleges and universities, federal and state governments, U.S. foundations, and the private sector. The recommendations have enlarged the stakes and set a challenging national agenda for the entire field. However, the National Task Force on

Undergraduate Education Abroad perhaps still best summarizes the goals of the above publications when it states what is needed:

- to make undergraduate study and other academically related experiences abroad a higher national priority, with particular reference to such specific needs as increasing financial support, greater diversity of opportunity and program participation, and the assurance of program quality
- to initiate and introduce language in existing legislation that will facilitate and expand undergraduate study abroad, develop new legislation at the state and federal levels, and explore and support nonlegislative, nongovernmental avenues of funding
- to develop an action agenda for the exchange field and the broader higher education community and involve these constituencies in the advocacy and implementation of the Task Force's recommendations.

Because education abroad professionals almost universally accept the recommendations contained in these studies, the question is no longer what direction the field should take at the end of the twentieth century, but how best to work together to implement these goals; to identify, tap, and recycle the requisite resources; and to set a realistic timetable and measure progress. The agreement on goals has never been clearer.

As the past few years have shown, support for education abroad from the U.S. government, as well as from many states, is far from assured. In the view of those of us in the field, such support reflects a recognition that national self-interest is at stake in an ever more global economy and new political order. We have yet, however, to fully convince others of this imperative. The rhetoric of internationalism from our political, business, and campus leaders often remains at variance with concrete achievements and commitments. In a country that has yet to provide equal, democratic access to the best of our domestic educational system, questions of entitlement loom with regard to education abroad. In a country whose history and cultural references, especially during the current century, have been so highly Eurocentric, the reality and significance of other continents and cultures remains too often a mirage. The challenge to international educators is to build on these beginnings and to contribute our knowledge to continued advocacy and progress on our own campuses and in the national arena.

Although it is difficult to suggest that some topics should concern us more than others, we do think that education abroad professionals, during the next few years, will need to give some thought and attention to the following issues:

Goals and Purposes. The discussion about the ultimate rationale and value of education abroad continues without resolution. Do students study overseas primarily for academic reasons related to their home campus goals? Or is study abroad seen by its participants mainly as a means of becoming acquainted with another culture through first-hand exposure? Given the mobility of people and ideas across borders and the growth of global communications, is education abroad now a bicultural, a polycultural, or a transcultural experience? Are students seeking mainly the opportunity to become more independent and informed than the chauvinism of America sometimes allows? Does study abroad indeed represent the career enhancement it is claimed to be, in relation to the global job market? How important are nonacademic components of study abroad, such as internships and the development of cross-cultural understanding?

There are no clear answers to these questions from campus to campus or across the country generally, and that should come as no surprise. That such issues are being discussed, however, is a healthy sign. Although we as professionals cannot exist without a broad base of commonly held assumptions and goals, it is not a bad thing that different campuses, in keeping with their own institutional missions, define and carry out dramatically different approaches to education abroad programming.

Innovative Program Modes and Models. Education abroad continues to benefit from pressures to diversify itself and to reach out to new academic constituencies and new destinations. More programs than ever go to nontraditional destinations, and more offer different academic and social experiences to students. It is trite to say that the language- and cultural-immersion Junior Year Abroad program is no longer the model—whatever we might think about this development—but it is true. Undergraduate and graduate students now pursue overseas opportunities via a bewildering array of approaches (including independent research, internships, direct enrollment, amd work abroad as well as the many forms of study abroad), from an increasing number of disciplines, and in more and more countries.

Diversity of Participants. There remains a sincere conviction in the field that opportunities for an overseas experience must be made available to students who, heretofore, have not studied abroad in large numbers. This includes not just students from ethnic communities but also students from academic majors without a tradition of education abroad, learning disabled students, physically handicapped students, students who are not in the 18–24 age range, gay and lesbian students, and students who are economically disadvantaged. Although education abroad may have been a little slow in realizing the diversity of the student population, there is no doubt that much is now being to done to provide relevant overseas opportunities to a wider range of students.

Computerization. The developments of electronic communication have been a mixed blessing to many offices where the potential is understood but the resources needed to take full advantage have perhaps been lacking. Nevertheless there is no denying that, of all the topics the first edition dealt with, the application of information technologies was most in need of an update. What is both exciting and disconcerting is that change in this field is exponential. The increasing reliance on electronic communication, either on campus or across the globe, has not been without problems, but it has dramatically affected the way we all communicate and work together. The development of the World Wide Web has changed, forever, how we disseminate and retrieve information and ultimately how we advise students and administer programs.

Data Collection and Analysis. The field continues to improve its data collection, even if there is still a long way to go before we know exactly how many students take part in an education abroad experience and before we can accurately assess the long-range impact their time abroad has had on their work and life. But new leadership at IIE has given better direction to individual campuses on how best to track their students who spend a period of time overseas. It might not be too much to hope that one day the data on U.S. students abroad will be as reliable as those on foreign students in the United States. Such progress is essential. If advocacy is to become part of our working culture, then comprehensive data for individual campuses on all aspects of education abroad will be vital: students studying overseas, working as interns, conducting independent research, or winning scholarship competitions, and, indeed, faculty who are involved in programs such as Fulbright.

Assessment. Evaluations, not just of programs but of services and education abroad offices as units, will be more important in the future; not just to discover, for example, what students think about programs in which they have participated, but also to improve programs and to be able to provide an analysis of such evaluations that can underline the worth of the education abroad office on campus should it be questioned. It is no longer possible to avoid comprehensive assessment; if we do not evaluate, others will. In other words, evaluations are not just useful for what they might tell the office about its work at a particular time, but also for helping us to defend this work in the future.

Cooperation and Consolidation. Education abroad offices can no longer be islands unto themselves. It is now very clear that for study abroad to flourish education abroad offices need to be proactive with faculty, other campus administrative offices, and students. Cooperation across the campus is a theme of this publication and underlines the necessity of local action within the context of what is occurring nationally and internationally.

We hope this new edition not only assists newcomers to the field but also suggests new approaches to those who have been in the field for some time. The authors of the chapters, and others who gave their advice and suggestions in other ways, strongly support the long-established tradition in our field of sharing what we know with each other.

All chapters have been carefully rethought, in some cases by their original contributors, in others by new authors, or by both. Some, it was concluded, have stood the test of time well and needed only minor revision and updating. Others were judged to be in need of a more thorough conceptual overhaul or major updating. These include Chapter 4 on academic credit; Chapter 6 on office resources; Chapter 7 on computerizing; Chapter 10 on advising strategies; Chapter 16 on program designs; and Chapter 17 on work abroad and international careers. Brand new chapters focusing on areas covered only indirectly or not at all in the previous edition include: Chapter 3 on Faculty Roles; Chapter 12 on promoting whole world study abroad; and Chapter 19 on legal issues. In addition, the SECUSSA Bibliography, found in the appendix, has been significantly updated and expanded. The editors wish to thank their many colleagues who have undertaken this important and painstaking work, as well as the SECUSSA leadership and Steven Kennedy of NAFSA Publications, for urging and supporting it.

The following volume is divided into three parts. Chapters 1 through 8 focus on the American institutional contexts of education abroad. This section discusses professional qualifications, opportunities, and responsibilities; training and linkages with colleagues; the place of education abroad operations within institutional structures and values; faculty roles; working with the registrar and financial aid officers to ensure that students qualify for academic credit and financial aid; setting up and furnishing the advising office with the necessary resources and equipment; and the promotion and publicity that may be needed to sell the general idea of education abroad, as well as particular programs.

Part Two, Chapters 9 through 14, centers on advisers and students. It presents a national profile of students who have traditionally gone abroad to study or work, then discusses what an adviser needs to know in order to provide the best counsel and support to students; general strategies and approaches to advising; how to reach out to nontraditional education abroad students; how to encourage students to consider study abroad programs in the whole world; health and safety questions; and effective orientation strategies for preparing students for departure and return.

Part Three, Chapters 15 through 19, centers on program development, administration, and oversight. It presents examples of how three particular programs came into being, and from these examples discusses some general principles of program planning, budgeting, and implementation; explores the academic and economic strengths and drawbacks of a range of different program models, the relative educational merits and advantages of work and study programs, and the many experiential program opportunities that now exist; how to go about assessing quality of programs sponsored by one's own institution and those sponsored by other institutions; and finally on the many legal issues that campuses need to understand and address.

Nearly four centuries ago Francis Bacon noted that "travel, in the younger sort, is a part of education." Whether or not education abroad "travel" is practical and career-related or broad and general, it is germane to the challenges we all face in the globally interdependent future. Enlightened engineers and scientists, businesspeople and economic developers, social workers and environmentalists increasingly understand that to survive, much less thrive, in the world marketplace we all need not merely technical skills, but also the ability to work with our fellow workers in culturally diverse environments.

Finding universal commonalities and principles while learning to value and respect cultural differences has long been the cherished ideal of American liberal and humane higher education. At the close of the current century, education abroad is one way to achieve this ideal and to ensure that its lessons remain of value well into the globalized future. It is our sincere hope and intention that this publication will assist in developing education abroad advising and programming commensurate with the highest professional principles of international educators and is of pragmatic value to the U.S. students and institutions they serve.

—William Hoffa and John Pearson

I

Part One

Education Abroad And American Higher Education

Being An Education Abroad Professional
Contributors: David Larsen, M. Archer Brown, and Susan Ansara

The Education Abroad Office In Its Campus Context
Contributors: Paul DeYoung and Paul Primak

Faculty Roles
Contributors: Bill Barnhart, Tom Ricks, and Paula Spier

Academic Credit
Contributors: Kathleen Sideli and Stephen Cooper

Financial Aid
Contributor: Nancy Stubbs

The Office Library And Resources
Contributors: Margaret Warpeha, Larry Laffrey, Catherine Gamon, Heidi Soneson, and Richard Warzecha

Computerizing Education Abroad Operations
Contributors: Ruth M. Sylte and James L. Buschman

Promotion And Publicity
Contributors: My Yarabinec and Harlan Henson

Being An Education Abroad Professional

Contributors: David Larsen, M. Archer Brown, and Susan Ansara

Whether you are new to the education abroad field, have newly expanded responsibilities, or are an old-timer simply trying to keep up with new developments, you should recognize that you are involved in a dynamic and demanding field within higher education. Your knowledge, skill, and talents will be tested every day. Being a professional means working hard to assimilate and embody the best that others have said and done, as well as following your own best instincts while remaining alert to the special needs of your institution. There are many established networks of information, training, and professional discourse. Taking advantage of these will make your work easier and more enjoyable, and will better prepare you to contribute to the growth and development of our field.

A *profession*, according to the dictionary, is an occupation requiring advanced education and training and involving intellectual skills. A *professional* is, simply, a person who practices a profession. Although professionals serve those who employ them, they are also called upon to serve the profession's ideals. Professions achieve and maintain their integrity through specialized training and certification, establishing and enforcing performance standards, censuring practitioners who depart from accepted practices, and defining criteria for advancement, promotion, awards, and honors. Broadly speaking, this definition applies to physicians, lawyers, engineers, architects, and numerous other professionals. The profession of international education (and, more specifically for the purposes of this book, of education abroad advising and program administration) shares many of the characteristics of other professions, but not all.

Education abroad advising and administration in the United States, like other professions, has come a long way. Over the years it has developed a body of knowledge and theory, some carefully defined standards of conduct, and a body of essential resources. In terms of professional development, the field itself, through organizations like NAFSA: Association of International Educators, contributes to the initial and ongoing training of its members and has organized itself through meetings, publications, and communications networks to share information and perspectives and to develop a professional consensus and community.

The professionalism achieved thus far has developed under the broad umbrella of NAFSA, especially through the work of members of its Section on U.S. Students Abroad (SECUSSA); the Council on International Educational Exchange (CIEE); and the Institute of International Education (IIE). In recent years, the Association of International Education Administrators (AIEA) has emerged as another important contributor to this effort.

Colleges and universities across the country are increasingly calling on the expertise of NAFSA members, along with other international educators, to help them work with students, faculty, and other administrators to accomplish newly defined goals for international and intercultural learning. In other countries, somewhat parallel professional associations—such as the European Association for International Education (EAIE) and others in Mexico, Japan, and Canada—have begun to pay special attention to professional expertise in education abroad advising and program administration.

Until quite recently, entrants into this field seldom undertook formal training in international educational exchange. Now, however, several master's degree programs provide some basic training (for example, at the School for International Training, Lesley College, and elsewhere), and more are being developed for full- and part-time participants. It is still generally true that individuals enter the profession by first securing a position and then developing the specific professional skills they need in their work. In other words, there appears as yet to be no single career-preparation path for education abroad professionals.

For newcomers, a host of backgrounds and experiences in areas as diverse as teaching and scholarship, international travel and study, student development/student services and education administration is generally regarded as relevant. Although each individual may have areas of special strength and expertise—either by virtue of background, specific

4

training, or personal predilection—no one is expert in all the essential areas of this diverse and demanding field. Moreover, the field is constantly expanding, and what sufficed yesterday may be insufficient to meet the challenges of tomorrow.

Because formal training opportunities are rare and the required skills and talents so varied, becoming an education abroad professional is a process of learning by doing. There is, therefore, a practical necessity to learn as much as possible from your colleagues. Practices that might be regarded as piracy in the corporate world are encouraged in education abroad. An insight, a procedure, an information resource, or an approach to a particular program developed and implemented successfully at one institution is more often than not generously shared with others. The general assumption is that when there is innovation, others in the field will hear about it and ask questions. Education abroad advising and administration occur in an arena where questions are always answered with a view to contributing to the development of other professionals and the promotion of belief in the value of education abroad.

Most practitioners used to enter the field on a relatively short-term basis because institutions considered advising and programming responsibilities as adjuncts to other campus assignments. But in recent years more and more aspiring education abroad professionals have purposely selected this career path and acquired the relevant training.

In 1993 the leadership of SECUSSA identified four distinct job categories in the field: (1) on-campus adviser; (2) on-campus program administrator; (3) university or agency program representative; and (4) overseas program director. It was further noted that many SECUSSA members begin in one type of position, then move to another, and, especially at smaller institutions, are often asked to wear more than one professional hat simultaneously. (We should note that this book covers mainly the first two job categories named above.)

No matter what their original motivation and entry-level training, education abroad professionals remain in the field because the work is diverse and engaging and the field is dedicated to what they see as important principles and needs in U.S. higher education. The leaders in this field are extraordinarily willing, and able, to act as role models and mentors to newcomers. Indeed, most of the veteran professionals in the field regard mentoring as an extremely important responsibility. As an example, SECUSSA's Lily Von Klemperer Award, bestowed each year on an exemplary education abroad professional, honors an esteemed colleague who devoted much of her career to encouraging newcomers to the field.

The fundamental skills required to be an effective education abroad professional include imagination, empathy, sensitivity, enthusiasm, and patience. Equally important is the ability to create, develop, present, and manage a budget, and to communicate with your institution's managers on their own terms and in language they understand. The real challenge for every practitioner—at all levels of experience—is to build a professional knowledge base on the foundation of this personal conviction and integrity, so as to serve the interests and personal needs of students and institutions. Some of the professional roles you will be asked to perform are described below.

- *Advocate/Facilitator.* You are likely to be the primary promoter of study, work, and travel abroad on your campus, actively pursuing and publicizing overseas opportunities and maintaining as high a profile as possible within the institution. You must create a campus environment where opportunities for international experience are viewed as feasible, desirable, and relevant in the context of undergraduate education. If you are not a leader in these areas, you are not doing your job fully.

- *Liaison/Broker.* You will regularly and frequently be called upon to be an information link among students, faculty, the administration, the admissions and records office, and other campus entities working to initiate and maintain orderly academic and institutional procedures. Unless your campus is unusually coherent and well organized (and your students extraordinarily conscientious), you will have to do an enormous amount of informed and politic coordination. An array of diplomatic skills will be required.

- *Educator/Consultant.* Your primary work is to help each student become better informed and to determine personal priorities, consider all options, make choices, develop a set of realistic expectations, and proceed through the steps and obstacles of your institutional structures. You need a global outlook and pedagogical expertise, and you must share these with your colleagues on the faculty and in the administration. You are likely to know more about the particular educational benefits of living and learning abroad than anyone else on campus. Because these are hard-won insights, you are thrust into the role of educating the faculty and administration—in some instances against their will. This role requires the courage to act in support of your convictions and the experience and determination to work with others to increase high-quality opportunities for students.

- *Economic Manager.* Most education abroad programs are expected to be at least financially self-supporting if not revenue producing. The organizations or institutions that "own" such programs often feel entitled to monetary compensation for the considerable risks they take in facilitating their operation. Sometimes they seek to recover tuition income that flows from regular channels to education abroad. You will be required to know about budget development, fiscal reporting, and financial management.

- *Legal Issues Adviser.* U.S. and foreign laws and a variety of national and local practices concerning banking and currency exchange, taxes, employment practices, leases and purchases (of everything from services to real estate), and risk management apply in differing ways to the activities of professionals in this field. To be an effective manager and a responsible adviser to your employer, you must learn at least which questions to ask about the programs with which you work and how to interpret the answers you receive (see Chapter 19, "Legal Issues").

A great deal of skill and knowledge is required to play all these roles successfully. Generous doses of tact and judgment also help. Being in this field is seldom dull, and the variety of tasks and challenges can be truly exhilarating.

▌ Standards of Professional Practice

As mentioned, the field of international education has developed (and continues to evolve) its own distinct professionalism, including the creation of codes of behavior for individuals and institutions. NAFSA remains at work on this formalizing process. NAFSA's Board of Directors adopted an associationwide Code of Ethics in 1989 after extensive discussions within the membership. As part of this process, SECUSSA discussed the ideal conduct of individuals working as education abroad advisers and program administrators. In 1988 the following standards of professional practice were adopted by SECUSSA. The standards presented below are quoted verbatim.

In general, in terms of *professional conduct,* professionals in the field are expected to:

1. Recognize the boundaries of their expertise, expand their expertise through consultation with colleagues, and make referrals where situations are outside their area of competence.

2. Maintain and increase their skills and knowledge through participation in professional activities, reading, research, and

training programs, as well as through consultation with experts in allied fields and with others in their own field.

3. Assist less-experienced members in developing their own knowledge, understanding, and skills.

4. Refrain from unjustified or unseemly criticism of fellow members, other programs, and organizations.

5. Be alert to and resist outside pressures (personal, social, organizational, financial, and political) to use their influence inappropriately, and to refuse to allow considerations of self-aggrandizement or personal gain to influence their professional judgments.

6. Communicate with honesty and fairness in representing their own services and programs, as well as those of others.

7. Demonstrate cross-cultural sensitivity and respect the ambiguity and complexity inherent in cross-cultural relationships, treating differences between educational systems, value systems, and cultures nonjudgmentally.

8. Conduct themselves in a manner that is not exploitative, coercive, or sexually harassing. Sexual harassment includes sexual advances, requests for sexual favors, or any verbal or physical conduct of a sexual nature that has the effect of creating an intimidating, hostile, or offensive environment.

In *advising*, professionals in the field are expected to:

1. Provide complete, accurate, and current information to those seeking their assistance.

2. Advise with great care to enable students to select overseas experiences (including work and travel as well as academic study) that will meet that student's academic, financial, and personal needs, including specific curricular requirements.

3. Provide ample information on choices to enable individual students to make intelligent and rational decisions.

4. Follow clearly defined criteria in selecting students for programs so as to match students appropriately with such factors as location, language level, demands on academic and personal maturity, and available curricula.

5. Strive to assure appropriate educational guidance of students bound abroad through the development of orientation and reentry programs.

6. Maintain the confidentiality of student records and communications with students.

7. Be committed to equality of opportunity in education, and thus seek to provide information on resources for the physically handicapped, the economically disadvantaged, and other groups that are traditionally underrepresented in study abroad programs.

In *program administration,* professionals in the field are expected to:

1. Make available complete, accurate, and current information on their programs that clearly states institutional affiliations, all costs to participants, coursework available, and arrangements for lodging, meals, and transportation.

2. Develop programs with academic rigor at least comparable to that of the home institution, with credit awarded according to standards used for coursework on the home campus. They do not award credit for travel alone, and they clearly state to prospective participants the academic standards and expectations of their programs.

3. When administering programs abroad, work with the home and host institutions to assist in the proper transfer of credits for overseas study, responding rapidly to the needs of students, but with regard for the academic integrity of the institutions.

4. Develop offerings that immerse students in the cultural richness and diversity available in the locale abroad.

5. Establish budgets to permit participation by students from various economic situations, and in setting program fees, avoid seeking institutional profit.

6. Maintain academic standards of selection when screening applicants.

7. Arrange for and make available the results of carefully designed, unbiased evaluations of their programs.

8. Select faculty and staff on the basis of educational and cultural criteria and attention to the goals of the program, with fairness and objectivity.

9. Provide adequate counseling or referral services for incoming exchange students for whom they have administrative responsibility.

As with any code of behavior, conflicts and tensions may arise as practitioners struggle to meet these goals. Few have the time, energy, expertise, or absolute virtue to live up to these laudable standards on every occasion and in every circumstance. The expectations of your own institution may only compound the challenge by asking you to act in a way that conflicts with the broader vision of this professional standard. It may be difficult to find a path between perfect loyalty to the institution that pays your salary and an unflinching allegiance to a loftily defined (but abstract) code of conduct. Nevertheless, these standards represent the collective wisdom of your fellow professionals in the field, and they are meant to encourage you as you grow in your profession.

▮ Opportunities for Professional Development

Until every education abroad professional is required to be formally trained and certified, a good portion of the knowledge required in the field will inevitably come from experience, not formal training. But, as mentioned above, formal professional development opportunities in education abroad now exist both for newcomers and for those already in the field. What follows is an overview of these opportunities.

Structured Academic Training

More and more undergraduate, graduate, and certificate programs are available to prepare serious full- and part-time students to be education abroad advisers or program administrators. Individuals seriously interested in the profession should seek information from guidance sources and from mentors in the field. In addition to these formal programs, there are a number of short-term, formal learning experiences that can contribute to your knowledge and skills. Among these are SIETAR Summer Institutes, the Summer Institute for Intercultural Communication, the International Leadership Development Institute, East-West Center Cross-Cultural Training for Educational Leaders Workshop, and short-term programs offered by the School for International Training. Further information on these programs can be obtained from NAFSA or from announcements in the *Chronicle of Higher Education*.

It is important to remember that the education abroad field requires a wide range of skills. Nearly everything you learn can be put to good use. In addition to any sort of cross-cultural, intercultural, or travel-specific training, programs focused on developing managerial skills, personnel development, the many issues related to risk management, legal advising, planning and supervision, will be of particular benefit.

In recent years, SECUSSA has sponsored an annual beginner's workshop on study abroad advising. SECUSSA has also sponsored a more advanced workshop on program development and administration, as well as specialized workshops on, for example, programming in Latin America, central and eastern Europe, and Asia. Individual and group opportunities tend to be offered annually and may be regionally based. *National seminars,* for which selection is competitive, are sponsored less regularly, but provide intensive training on specific, current topics of national and professional interest (for example, managing financial aid for study abroad).

In addition to short-term (generally one week) programs, training workshops are conducted by individual universities, NAFSA regions, local NAFSA subgroups, and so on. Information can be found in the "Professional Development" section of the *NAFSA Newsletter,* in NAFSA's online *NAFSA.news,* in the *Chronicle of Higher Education,* in *Transitions Abroad* magazine, and elsewhere.

Those interested in this type of program should also obtain a copy of NAFSA's fact sheet, "Structured In-Service Training Grants." These modest grants are available to individuals currently working in some aspect of educational exchange at a U.S. college or university and may be applied to a training program sponsored by an accredited institution of higher education, provided the training is specifically designed for international educators. NAFSA produces an annual list of many of the training programs to which the grants may be applied.

NAFSA'S Professional Development Program

NAFSA has recently undertaken a major reorganization in order to strengthen the professional development opportunities it could offer its membership. Indeed, professional development (formerly overseen by NAFSA's Field Service Steering Committee) is now one of the three major priorities of the association. The Professional Development Program (PDP) has the goal of helping NAFSA members achieve needed skills, increased expertise, and practical experience in international education through a carefully coordinated series of program activities. NAFSA members now have access to a professional-development program that offers high-quality training at the local, regional, and national levels.

PDP has four components:

1. *The Foundations of International Education Workshops.* The foundation workshops will provide an introduction to the major professions represented within NAFSA. The target audience is both

newcomers and experienced professionals who are assuming new responsibilities. Each workshop will work from a core curriculum and materials and will be offered at both national and regional NAFSA conferences.

2. *Specialized Workshops in Key Areas of Professional Practice.* The specialized workshops will be defined and implemented by the professional sections, with topics shifting from year to year.

3. *The Trainer Corps.* To achieve high quality and uniformity of training, NAFSA will build a corps of skilled trainers and workshop. The Corps will consist of senior professionals who have undertaken a specialized training program on key principles of adult learning, teaching techniques, and matching presentation style and content.

4. *The Certificate of Professional Achievement.* This certification is designed to recognize individual effort and participation in a certain number of workshops and programs.

NAFSA provides funding for this training. *Individual grants* are provided to basic-level participants (those relatively new to the field) and to mid- to senior-level participants (those with three or more years of experience) to visit selected institutions to observe programs and procedures and confer with colleagues. *In-service training grants* are also provided for group seminars. Although eligibility requirements and funding vary for each seminar, successful applicants receive in-depth training on a specific topic.

Active Membership in Professional Organizations

Several professional organizations, in addition to NAFSA, serve individuals and institutions involved in education abroad. Active membership in such organizations is essential if you are to develop as a professional. Unlike scholarly associations that gather to share the results of research activities, the meetings and publications of these organizations are dedicated to networking, sharing ideas, and acquiring new skills. Most of these organizations offer professional development and leadership opportunities.

In addition to its PDP training, NAFSA publishes the *NAFSA Newsletter, NAFSA.news* (an electronic news bulletin), *International Educator* magazine, the *Government Affairs Bulletin,* and more than a hundred professional books and papers. It also holds an annual conference that regularly draws more than 3,500 participants and provides a consultation service to help institutions evaluate the strengths and weaknesses of their programs. Participation in NAFSA activities also has the benefit of bringing education abroad professionals into contact with the full spectrum of international educational exchange.

SECUSSA (The Section on U.S. Students Abroad). One of NAFSA's five professional divisions, SECUSSA promotes all forms of education abroad—formal study, work, and travel—and sponsors workshops, sessions, discussion groups, and social activities at NAFSA's annual national conference and at all twelve NAFSA regional conferences. The national and regional conferences offer basic training for newcomers. Many NAFSA publications derive from SECUSSA's professional interests and activities. SECUSSA sponsors SECUSS-L, an e-mail discussion list open to anyone (see Chapter 7, "Computerizing Operations").

CIEE (Council on International Educational Exchange). More than 300 colleges and universities (U.S. and foreign), youth-serving agencies, and international educational programs are institutional members of CIEE. Members and nonmembers can benefit from CIEE's information and publication services, advocacy efforts, and evaluation and consultation services. CIEE publishes it own newsletter, *Council Update,* and occasionally monographs and books on education abroad. Like NAFSA, it holds an annual conference with sessions, workshops, and discussion groups devoted to a wide array of topics. CIEE administers consortial study abroad programs in many parts of the world and some overseas development seminars for faculty. CIEE also sells the International Student Identity Card, arranges work permits for employment in other countries, and offers a variety of commercial travel services through its subsidiary, Council Travel.

IIE (Institute of International Education). IIE publishes a set of inclusive annual listings of study abroad, *Academic Year Abroad* and *Vacation Study Abroad.* (Peterson's publishes a similar set). IIE also conducts a census of study abroad activity, the results of which appear in *Open Doors,* the institute's survey of international students and scholars on U.S. campuses. IIE's Educational Associates program provides college and university members with complimentary copies of IIE publications and other services, including a newsletter, *Educational Associate.* In 1996 IIE began to provide on-line access to all program information listed in its print guides to study abroad programs, to member institutions that are Educational Associates. IIE Online is a vast Web-based resource.

In addition to these three long-established organizations, education abroad practitioners can affiliate with a number of other national groups. Among them are:

- The Association of International Education Administrators (AIEA): for those with institutionwide positions related to international education.

- The International Exchange Association: an umbrella organization for youth-serving agencies that merged several years ago with the Liaison Group for International Educational Exchange to form the Alliance for International Educational and Cultural Exchange.

- Phi Beta Delta: a national honor society that recognizes programs for campus staff, faculty, and students involved in international education activities.

Many education abroad professionals have also found that they benefit from membership in groups that reflect their background, interest, or avocation. These include the Fulbright Alumni Association, the International Society for Intercultural Training and Research (SIETAR), and those associations related to the teaching of foreign language, area studies, student personnel administration, and specific academic disciplines, among other categories. Many of these groups are listed and annotated in the *International Exchange Locator* published by the Alliance for International Educational and Cultural Exchange, and in the *Directory of Resources for International Cultural Exchanges* published by USIA.

Education abroad staff working on college and university campuses have access to the higher-education groups to which their institutions belong. These groups include the American Council on Education, American Association of State Colleges and Universities, Association of American Colleges, National Association of State Universities and Land Grant Colleges, and so on. All of these include in their research, publications, and conference activities a component on international education that in most cases explicitly encompasses education abroad.

Almost every organization involved in international education has a regular schedule of regional meetings and conferences. Attendance at these meetings is important for the new professional, and participation on the program is essential for those who are more experienced. Meetings and conferences present opportunities to share ideas and points of view, to discuss approaches and practices, to learn about new developments and proposals, and when appropriate, to raise questions about and voice concerns for standards and practices. The forums presented by professional organizations are the best, most consistently available, and most visible means for exploring new ideas, meeting innovators and experts in the field, and sharing one's own expertise and successes with others.

Professional Development Abroad

Overseas travel for the education abroad professional is essential. To advise and inform students, and to design and implement useful, high-quality experiences abroad, one must be as familiar as possible with the foreign countries and cultures in which those programs operate. Many professionals have lived overseas or have traveled extensively in other parts of the world. Most have participated in a foreign-study experience or have become knowledgeable about systems of higher education in other countries. All support the value of participatory learning in another culture—not merely learning about the people and the culture, but learning how people in other cultures learn.

The opportunities described below are by no means inclusive, but they do suggest the variety of ways one can continue to learn from an overseas experience, even if that opportunity is not provided within the context of one's job. To take advantage of some of these, however, a fairly liberal (four-week) annual leave may be required.

Group Seminars and Workshops Abroad

- *Baden-Württemberg Seminar.* The Baden-Württemberg Ministry of Science and Art, in cooperation with NAFSA and AACRAO, sponsors this seminar. It is held at University of Freiburg, Germany, for two weeks in November. On-site costs are covered by the seminar. Participants are elected competitively for an intensive program on the German educational system.

- *Program for Administrators in International Education—Japan and Korea.* Two programs, one in Japan and the other in Korea, are sponsored by the host country's Fulbright Commission and the Council for the International Exchange of Scholars (CIES). Locations vary, as do the lengths of the programs, which take place in the summer. Program costs are covered by the sponsor. This program selects those with at least three years of professional international education experience with a U.S. college, university, or non-profit international educational exchange organization.

- *Program for U.S. Administrators in International Education–Germany.* This annual program (one month in spring) is sponsored by the German Fulbright Commission and CIES. Locations vary. Program costs, including airfare, are covered by the sponsor. This program selects up to twenty participants, including administrators of undergraduate programs abroad, to attend seminars on the German educational, cultural, and political issues.

- *Fulbright-Hays Summer Seminars Abroad.* These seminars are sponsored by the U.S. Office of Education. The locations vary, and the length is from four to eight weeks during the summer. Costs are covered by the sponsor. Applicants must be employed full-time as teachers or administrators in the humanities, social sciences, or social studies at a U.S. secondary or higher-education institution. Language requirements exist for some locations.

In any given year, other overseas seminars and workshops are offered on an occasional basis or for slightly longer periods (three to four months). Announcements of these, as well as current application information about the above programs, are usually published in the *NAFSA Newsletter, Council Update,* IIE's *Educational Associate,* and other professional organizations' newsletters and journals.

Overseas Opportunities Related to Study Abroad Programs

A number of activities abroad are sponsored by other institutions. The sponsors and organizers of some overseas programs that enroll students on a national basis have independent boards of advisers that are occasionally invited to visit overseas program sites. Beaver College, Butler University, the Institute for European/Asian Study, AIFS, DiS, and the Australian Education Office are among the groups that organize these visits. Other study abroad sponsors periodically organize on-site visits to acquaint U.S. advisers with their programs.

Sometimes it is possible to find summer employment leading short-term programs abroad or serving as a resident director of summer study programs, particularly at the secondary school level.

Individual Travel Abroad

There are several interesting alternatives to being a tourist abroad, even within limited time constraints. Literally hundreds of affordable options are available for special interest or adult education travel. Some focus on specific interests (archaeology, bird-watching, women's issues), others on methods of travel (trekking, caravans, river boats), and still others on exotic areas of the world. No single source of information describes all these opportunities, but a good guide—which focuses on educational work, study, and travel abroad with particular reference to adult participation—is published annually in the summer issue of *Transitions Abroad.*

If you are interested in a short-term course in a foreign language, as a refresher or otherwise, there are numerous courses for foreigners. If you want to combine study in a particular subject area with a short-term experience abroad, there are good suggestions in IIE's *Vacation Travel Abroad* and Peterson's *Learning Vacations.* Literally hundreds of voluntary service projects are conducted annually in all parts of the world. Many of the sponsoring organizations recruit individuals for assignments lasting one month or less, for which room and board and sometimes a small stipend is often provided. Again, *Transitions Abroad* magazine is a good resource to use to track down such opportunities.

Publishing Opportunities

Publishing is one of the best ways to share good ideas—and garner some professional recognition in the process. The number of publishing opportunities in the education abroad field is growing. In 1995, *Frontiers: The Interdisciplinary Journal of Study Abroad,* a periodical concerned with the academic and theoretical aspects of education abroad, began publication. In late 1995, NAFSA's *International Educator* magazine became a quarterly; it welcomes articles on education abroad. In 1996, CIEE and the European Association for International Education launched a new semi-annual *Journal of Studies in International Education.*

The major organizations mentioned above publish newsletters, as well as other literature, with a variety of emphases and audiences. There is a constant need for good writers with fresh ideas. Most national conferences provide opportunities to submit juried papers, acceptance of which may include publication as well as presentation. These papers require careful research, considerable planning, and thoughtful writing and rewriting. Newsletters, on the other hand, will accept briefer, timely articles or reports on current developments; very often unsolicited submissions are more than welcome.

In addition, the rapid development of electronic publishing—whether through World Wide Web documents, NAFSA's own Web page, or other electronic journals—is opening up new opportunities for the education abroad professional to gain publishing experience.

Building Specific Skills

Education abroad work calls on a wide variety of skills. These range from good accounting and fiscal management practices to publication layout and design, personnel administration, international travel and tour planning, academic and student counseling, and computer literacy. Because most education abroad professionals work on college or university campuses, classes and training programs—tuition-free in many cases—are available to them in relevant skills (for example, management, computer technology, accounting and finance, graphic design, professional writing). Classes can be taken to fill self-identified gaps or to complement or supplement work already completed. This course work may become part of an advanced degree or certificate program that could lead to additional credentials, increased professional recognition, and promotion.

Whether you are employed by an academic institution or not, there is also ample access—in most parts of the country—to training opportunities. Community groups and service clubs frequently organize training seminars and management courses, as do various industries, management consulting and training firms, and groups with a specific training focus such as Toastmasters International. If you live in an area where there are large industrial employers, you might investigate their in-service seminars and workshops. It is often possible to exchange a professional service for participation in in-house employee training programs.

Skill building can be self-taught as well. The opportunity to research and write grant proposals and to administer a grant award on behalf of a sponsoring institution or community group is a professional development activity. NAFSA makes awards each year to support local and national program proposals that contribute to the educational exchange process, including, for example, the orientation and reentry of U.S. students studying abroad.

A final area in which ongoing training, either formal or self-taught, is absolutely essential is computer applications. Beyond basic data manipulation, word processing, and spreadsheet skills, professionals must understand the uses and implications of e-mail, Web sites, and other rapidly emerging technologies.

Internships

Internships can take a number of different forms: some are institutionalized, and others are developed individually to meet personal and professional needs. Internships frequently take the form of staff exchanges between an overseas study site and the home institution. An idea growing in popularity in recent years is interprogram exchange or internship. In this type of internship, an individual works in a study abroad office or overseas program to perform a specific job for a limited period of time. The individual is expected to contribute his or her professional skills and, at the same time, to learn about the new situation and to carry that information back to the home institution. Although presenting occasional ethical problems in the form of industrial espionage, these job swaps or internship possibilities present rich opportunities for learning for all of the parties involved.

Recent moves to increase the level of professionalism within the ranks of international education, and especially education abroad, are resulting in opportunities for administrative staff sabbaticals, leave programs, and other accommodations. These new opportunities will provide time for employees to pursue studies or experiences that will equip them with the knowledge and experience necessary for professional growth. During the coming years professionals should make an effort to share information about the benefits of these programs and to encourage institutions to support interprogram internships as an activity that will attract and retain qualified employees.

The Education Abroad Office In Its Campus Context

Contributors: Paul DeYoung and Paul Primak

The context for the education abroad office—within your college or university as well as in the broader arena of international education—must be clearly understood and continually reviewed. Regardless of your professional experience or the level of your institution's involvement in education abroad, you need a clear and up-to-date understanding of how your work relates to the college or university's educational mission. You also need to know how your position interacts with structures and priorities established by your institution's mission. You need to understand fully the broad national field of international educational exchange. Without this functional context—the microscheme of internal institutional dynamics, politics, and finances, and the macroscheme of national precedents, professional standards, and accumulated wisdom—your labors will be more difficult.

Imagine sitting in a conference room with your registrar, bursar, admissions officer, academic vice president, financial aid officer, and several faculty members, and announcing that you wanted to initiate a new academic program that would

- require the registrar to recognize courses taught off-campus by faculty unknown to your university or college (and, in the case of some institutions, list them as courses taken in residence)
- deal with coursework, grades, and so forth coming from outside institutions that did not meet regular on-campus deadlines for inclusion in automated record processes
- provide tuition waivers for incoming international students, or send tuition dollars to an overseas institution
- send students away from campus and out of the watchful eye of the faculty for varying periods

21

- send faculty members away for extended periods of time during the academic year or summer session
- have financial aid taken away from the campus and add to the paperwork burden of the financial aid office by requiring consideration of special fees, budgets, and students who are not on the campus
- ask academic departments to accept as equivalent, and therefore applicable to the degree requirements of the institution, coursework taken at an institution that is probably unknown to the department head or curriculum committee.

In effect, education abroad advisers and administrators ask every major functional area of the academic institution to bend its rules and vary its procedures for the benefit of a relatively small percentage of students. Although this illustration may exaggerate the case, it does so for a very important purpose. That purpose is to demonstrate that without institutional commitment and administrative support at all levels, from the president down to the individuals in the registrar's office, it is unlikely that a strong international program can be developed and maintained.

Education abroad, as a component of U.S. *higher* education, represents a diversification of the undergraduate curriculum and a broadening of liberal education. Education abroad's major goals—academic and/or experiential—are largely pedagogical. These goals stem from a seasoned conviction that students who have experienced living and learning on the social and educational terms of a foreign culture will be broadened in ways impossible to achieve on the home campus, will benefit academically and culturally, and will be better prepared to face the challenges of the globalized future than students who do not have these experiences.

We know (or at least we like to assume strongly) education abroad generally improves returned-student classroom performance, assists student development in positive ways, and makes students more likely to become contributing and empathetic citizens of the world. The value of these educational goals, in the context of the often narrowing and isolationist strains of traditional American culture, cannot be overestimated. Having said that, we also need to accept that institutions in the United States are rightly concerned with the academic nature of education abroad. If the education abroad office and the academic offices of the institution have different views of the goals of an overseas experience, there will most certainly be conflict!

Whatever education abroad means for U.S. students and however profound its potential impact, it is, in essence, an institutional activity. For better or worse, it lives within the pedagogical, political, and economic realities of the individual colleges and universities. While reports from national organizations are useful to education abroad offices in providing evidence and support, they do not, in most cases, affect what goes on at individual campuses. More to the point, education abroad cannot and should not be owned exclusively by those who labor professionally in the fields of international education. Rather, education abroad belongs to all members of the academic community.

Education abroad advisers and program administrators who forget or ignore this contextual truth are likely to be frustrated and ineffective. The perennial challenge is to maximize, by conscious and enlightened on-campus planning, what and how students learn outside the campus environs, and to ensure that this educational opportunity is understood and valued—formally or informally—as part of the academic process. "Think globally, act locally" should be emblazoned over the desk of every education abroad professional.

The administration of education abroad programs, however, occurs in a truly remarkable variety of organizational contexts. Some colleges are entirely new to the field and are just tentatively finding their way. Others have in recent years made an initial institutional commitment, establishing a few programs and priorities, yet know that they should be doing more. Still others exhibit a long record history of program development and activity and have reached what may be a real plateau of commitment and activity, or, conversely, a period of stultification.

Institutional settings for education abroad activities range from an individual faculty member's office, to the single-purpose education abroad office—be it for advising only or program administration only—to offices that advise and administer programs, to the comprehensive international education offices that serve the needs of short- and long-term foreign students and scholars, as well as U.S. students and scholars seeking overseas opportunities. Even within the latter category there is no common ground as to staffing levels, reporting lines within an institution, or even objectives and mission statements. A wise education abroad adviser not only knows her own field but is also willing to understand campus politics.

This chapter will examine institutional variables commonly faced by education abroad professionals. It will also review the institutional and national contexts in which education abroad operates.

▌ Institutional Structures and Values

The services offered by the education abroad office are usually suggested by its location on campus. The office's larger role on campus is usually defined by its placement within the institution's organizational structure. Most offices are located in one of two divisions: academic affairs or student affairs. Within academic affairs, the office may be an autonomous unit, part of academic advising, part of one or more academic departments (usually languages) or area studies programs, or part of the college of liberal arts.

Within student affairs, the office might again be an autonomous unit; part of a unit overseeing all international programs (and thus aligned with services for foreign students and scholars); within the campus international center; part of the student union; or part of an office in charge of career counseling, placement, and other off-campus studies.

In small institutions, there may be no office per se; in such cases oversight resides with a designated person in academic affairs or student affairs. In some cases, the person in charge of education abroad advising and/or programming may not even work full-time. This individual may have a split appointment as a faculty member or staff member of a student-services unit. The demands on such a person and the need to interact effectively with all other dimensions of the campus, however, are just as great as they would be at a larger institution.

Certain fortunate education abroad offices—usually at larger universities with well-defined international missions and expertise—are located within a free-standing international programs office whose director reports to a senior administrator, a vice president, or provost. Should the education abroad office be under academic affairs, the office will sometimes have more prestige within the institution and more support from faculty and members of the administration. It is tempting to suggest that an office dealing with the academic aspects of a student's collegiate experience, no matter that they take place overseas, should report to an academic office.

If the office is under student affairs, the personal needs of the student may be better served as he or she prepares to enter a foreign culture, live and learn abroad, and then return to campus. However, the office within student affairs may be more restricted and more student-oriented at the expense of providing essential academic advising and assurances concerning academic credit.

Excellent education abroad offices are found under both the academic affairs' and student affairs' administrative umbrellas, both having

inherent strengths and drawbacks. Keep in mind that the range of services differs from one office to another, and that no single office or individual will be able to offer everything to everybody. Offices located within student affairs may be limited to general advising and travel services,
seldom becoming involved with program development, recruitment and
selection, or academic credit. Offices located within Academic Affairs are
often cut off from the delivery of student services so important in predeparture advising and orientation. The academic education abroad adviser may have responsibilities only for language and other academic programs, with financial resources, time, and institutional pursuits precluding functioning in other areas.

Whatever services offered by your office, they must be clearly defined
relative to your position in the organization and the needs of your constituency. Once these services are defined, you can actively seek the
administration's understanding and approval, which are the foundation
for the office's support and funding. Once you clearly understand the
administrative position of your office and its relationship with and to
other campus offices, you begin to build a political support structure that
can affirm and sustain your role.

Recognizing the characteristics, dynamics, and structures of your institution is the first step in the development—as well as the continuing viability—of your office. Understanding your function within the educational framework of your institution is crucial to success. Such contextual
awareness allows your office to develop and maintain its own character and
also contributes directly to the office's ability to fulfill the institution's international goals. Since all colleges and universities evolve over time, it is
essential that experienced education abroad advisers and program administrators remain in tune with shifting institutional priorities and realities.

Another way of looking at the institutional context issue is to pose a
series of leading questions, given below. The answers to these questions
will help you not only to formulate an action plan (by identifying the
offices you need to work closely with), but also to determine the most
appropriate location on campus for the education abroad office.

- What drives study abroad at the institution? Is it an overall mission
statement, student interest, or the existence of a minimal resource
allocation to allow a basic level of advising?
- Who supports study abroad on the campus? Is it just a few faculty
and administrators, or are there some broad bases of support
among faculty, staff, and students?

- Who, on campus, has trouble with education abroad? What is the reason for their opposition?

▌ Institutional Policy

Education Abroad Advisory Committee

Your best ally is likely to be an informed and supportive advisory committee. It is essential that the committee be broadly based and credible. Ideally, members should represent constituencies at the institution that are invested in international education. Of primary importance are key members of the faculty who support education abroad. It is also wise to have a senior member of the faculty (ideally with current or recent membership on the curriculum committee) as the chair. Members of the administration might include the financial aid director, a business officer, the registrar, an admissions officer, and a foreign-student adviser.

On many campuses, administrative officers are ex officio members of the committee. They should not dominate the committee structure and their role should be confined to an advisory function. Unless it is politically untenable on your campus, try to have a number of recently returned students on your committee. These students can often speak with authority and conviction and offer perspectives that faculty, by their nature, will not have. Finally, consider reserving a seat on the committee for someone who has voiced negative views about the efficacy of international education.

The committee must also have a clear charge detailing its primary responsibilities and its relationship to your job and to other governance committees. This charge should be articulated and presented by a high academic officer at the institution. Clear guidelines as to how the decisions of the committee will be implemented are also necessary. These roles and relationships should be detailed in institutional by-laws. The governing document of one institution states:

> The committee shall formulate policy regarding off-campus study programs; shall review proposals for such programs from departments or divisions and shall report its findings and recommendations to the faculty. In addition, the committee shall review student proposals for participation on college approved study abroad programs and approve or deny their applications. (By-laws, Reed College, 1988)

The roles of advisory committees at different institutions will vary considerably. Not all committees will wish to be involved in reviewing student proposals, especially on campuses where the number of student applications is large. The committee can be responsible for overseeing the application process and setting approval standards. In addition, the committee can provide guidelines for the desired numbers of students participating in programs, which will assist in institutional planning for housing and admissions. Another essential role for the study abroad committee is to assist in evaluating your programs. This should be done on a regular basis and the criteria should be clearly delineated. Curricular input must naturally be solicited from faculty associated with each program, and evaluation of past student participants should be included. The committee's role will be to review each program to see that the broader institutional objectives are being met (see Chapter 18, "Program Evaluation").

Depending on institutional size and the scope of the study abroad operation, more than one committee may be either necessary or useful. Some institutions have a central committee that oversees the work of smaller subcommittees based on country/region or academic disciplines. It is essential that the activities of each committee be clearly spelled out and that different committees intersect though "interlocking memberships."

In an era of competition for funding within institutions, it may be advantageous to have the committee play an advocacy role for study abroad. Much of the advocacy desired will naturally take place on an informal basis such as through conversations with students and colleagues. Should the committee have an official advocacy role, for example representing study abroad in institutional budgetary deliberations, it will be necessary to have that role fully codified so as to minimize potential conflict with other institutionally mandated functions of the committee. Keeping institutional politics in mind, you may need to assign formal advocacy roles to a subcommittee or to form a committee for this role exclusively.

Beyond its formal duties, the committee is your sounding board, your collective ombudsman, and your inner counsel. As such, the committee gives you direction, information, and the authority to act. Your voice and the committee's together can speak to and for the campus.

Setting Institutional Goals

The education abroad advisory committee should guide the process of establishing and maintaining education abroad programming in a manner that contributes to the institution's educational goals. Many institutions do not mention international education in their mission statement.

Others mention international education, but say nothing specifically about education abroad. The committee, in order to establish its legitimacy and to guide its decision-making process, must make sure that institutional policy statements on international education are in place and, further, that education abroad is specifically named as an important component of undergraduate studies.

If this is not the case, the first order of business is to draft policy statements and ensure their acceptance by the administration (working in conjunction with the international students and scholars office, if one exists on your campus). In formulating a statement, all elements of international education on campus must be taken into account: international students, international curriculum development, faculty exchange, on-campus international programming, and education abroad. It is in the institution's best interest that these components work together toward common educational goals. Certainly, the impact of education abroad programming will be influenced by the integration of that experience into the students' overall education. By addressing the question of institutional policy at the outset, the committee can assist individual faculty members, as well as the institution, in placing study abroad in its proper curricular perspective.

Divisions of Labor

With institutional policy as a guide, the education abroad administrator, working with the advisory committee and other staff, must establish working goals and priorities for the office. The primary division of labor is likely to be between student advising and programming (see Chapters 3, 10, 15, 16). In larger offices, these two functions may be done by different persons; in small offices, they both fall in the lap of a single person and must somehow be balanced.

If your institution sponsors programs of its own—or wishes to do so—a heavy portion of your workload will be taken up with program development, administration, financing, promotion, staffing, and assessment. If your institution sponsors no programs of its own, most of your time will be spent trying to become familiar with the programs most suitable for your students and most acceptable to your faculty. In the latter case, with approximately 4,000 academic-year and summer programs offered by U.S. institutions and increasing opportunities for direct enrollment overseas, the task of becoming familiar with all the education abroad options is a formidable one. More often than not, education abroad administrators must shoulder both responsibilities.

It is always worth remembering that no education abroad adviser or administrator starts completely from scratch, either at the beginning of a new job or the start of the academic year. Precedents are in place and activities are ongoing; administrative, faculty, and student attitudes have formed; structures and lines of authority have been established; resources and budgets have been authorized—even if by default. These are the given, and they define the current place of education abroad within the institution.

Ideals and reality rarely coincide in institutional settings. Conflicts may exist between institutional rhetoric and reality; between what some members of the academic community want and what seems to be immediately possible; and between national calls for increased participation in study abroad (or at the very least an individual adviser's commitment to education abroad) and real or imagined institutional fears, hesitations, and limits (see Chapter 1, "Being an Education Abroad Professional"). These divisions are where the study abroad administrator necessarily resides. The question is how to resolve conflicts and move the institution in new directions.

▌ Working Within Your Institution

Whether you are new to the field, new to your campus, or an experienced administrator feeling the pressures to expand and diversify, it will be essential to define the academic, administrative, and financial contexts in which study abroad can best flourish at your institution. The impact of education abroad programming on all other sectors of the university must be anticipated. Key players in each area must be consulted and reconsulted to determine how education abroad affects existing institutional priorities and programs. Fiscal pressures on U.S. institutions is a fact of life, priority setting is evident everywhere, and it necessitates a healthy view of reality from educational abroad advocates.

The education abroad administrator's ongoing agenda should be to initiate, to understand, and to cultivate and maintain relationships among the campus's academic, administrative, and service areas. The many people who have their primary responsibilities in each sphere must be continuously informed, cultivated, and sought for their opinions and perspectives. Where the faculty and academic administrators stand on issues such as credit validation or transfer, and residence and degree requirements will form the foundation that education abroad offices use to administer their programs.

The registrar's office, the financial aid office, the academic advising office, and the bursar's office are also necessarily involved—as are student life (especially if it oversees such services as orientation and housing), admissions, career services, and even auxiliary service departments such as printing, student-activity centers, and the bookstore. The office or persons involved in providing services for foreign students and scholars must always be seen as an ally in the cause of internationalism. It is difficult to think of any college administrative area that is not potentially important to education abroad programming.

However, it is also important that the education abroad office is the initiator of contacts. Perhaps the word "proactive" should be stenciled alongside the inscription mentioned earlier. It is important that your first interaction with other offices on campus should not be because they have a problem or concern about your program.

As noted above, study abroad programs must be thoroughly integrated into the academic mission of the institution. If absent at your institution, this integration should be regarded as the primary personal and professional responsibility of the education abroad adviser. The task cannot be done by one person alone, and it certainly cannot be imposed on the institution. Collaboration is crucial.

Academic Departments and Programs

It is often very helpful to consult with peer institutions on specific study abroad program options, but you can also get good guidance at your own institution by maintaining regular and meaningful communication with academic units, including those, such as engineering, not typically involved with education abroad. Even though your advisory committee should contain faculty members, the committee should not have to rely on just those faculty and the departments they represent. Specific academic departments will support the programs and activities of the study abroad office very effectively, once they see that their interests are not threatened by study abroad. Effective use of electronic communication can foster regular and efficient communication with faculty across the campus.

Many faculty have studied or conducted research abroad and are likely to have strong interests in seeing their students' educations enhanced by an overseas academic experience.

Study abroad will be given more credibility by students and the administration if you develop and utilize faculty interest. Working with key members of the faculty can also be critical for addressing academic policy (for example, program structure or credit transfer). Faculty with expertise in area studies or languages can be especially helpful in addressing issues ranging from program development to student orientation. In addition to their presence on the advisory committee, faculty can be tapped for resident directorships, overseas-study scholarship committees, and other duties (see Chapter 3, "Faculty Roles").

The Registrar and Academic Affairs

If your institution has one or more academic advising offices, they can often complement faculty support. Sometimes faculty members cannot answer questions students have about studying abroad, for example, about credit transfer. The academic advising or registrar's office can help educate students and faculty about the programs and the curriculum offered through your institution. Advising offices may be willing to offer a periodic information series to inform students about study abroad opportunities (see Chapter 4, "Academic Credit").

Financial Aid

Higher-education institutions are legally required to permit students receiving federal and institutional financial aid packages to utilize their funds to help pay for the costs of overseas study. Because of this requirement, it is important to maintain a strong communication link with key persons in the financial aid office. Financial aid regulations are complex and constantly changing. The assistance of key members in the financial aid office is crucial to staying up-to-date on developments and new regulations that have implications for students on study abroad programs (see Chapter 5, "Financial Aid").

Student Affairs

Many education abroad offices rely heavily on student affairs offices to help publicize study abroad programs to newly admitted students and their parents. Involvement in the orientation program can provide early and effective publicity—a key element in successful planning for study abroad. More important is learning to work with Student Affairs deans and advisers who work with students on financial aid, housing, extracurricular activities, diversity, health, and a host of questions of great personal concern to students and parents (see discussion of student development theory, Chapter 10, "Advising Principles and Strategies," and Chapter 11, "Promoting Student Diversity").

Foreign-Student Office

On many university and college campuses, the institutional study abroad program developed in conjunction with, or as an offshoot of, the foreign-student office. Resources available through this office include access to international students and scholars for study abroad program orientations, cross-cultural expertise, overseas contacts, and, occasionally, shared fiscal and personnel resources. Foreign-student offices and study abroad programs have many of the same academic aims and counseling goals. Cooperation between these two primary international units can forge a very strong and productive alliance.

Admissions

The admissions office is usually very experienced in marketing the institution to prospective students. Admissions officers are knowledgeable about curriculum issues, extracurricular programs, and activities offered at the institution. Admissions officers are always seeking incentives to offer to prospective students. With good contacts and a set of good descriptive materials, the admissions office can offer a great deal of assistance in publicizing the education abroad program, while serving its own needs of attracting students to campus. Because admissions officers are generally experienced in producing information about the institution, they are excellent resources to assist in assembling materials and developing a marketing plan for education abroad programs. Working with the admissions office can help integrate the concept of study abroad and international programs into the larger image of the institution (see Chapter 8, "Promotion and Publicity").

Career Advising

Students who have participated in study abroad often aspire to careers in international fields. Given the focus of students and their families on career outcomes of higher education and efforts to measure investment by outcome, career offices have gained a more significant place in institutional priorities. Thus the career office can be a strong ally in developing institutional support for international education if a collaborative relationship in supporting students' career aspirations can be developed. The education abroad office should therefore work closely with career advising personnel to clarify ways in which study abroad can enhance a student's career preparations. Career services offices can assist students in preparing resumes that highlight their overseas learning to potential employers (see Chapter 17, "Work Abroad and International Careers").

▌ Getting Help from External Resources: Institutional Outreach

Even with the support of the various offices and individuals across campus, your institution may still require additional advice, counsel, support, and perspective. There is no reason to reinvent the wheel. Your campus is not the first to wrestle with its current questions and concerns on education abroad. Others have been there and are usually willing to share their observations, solutions, and conclusions. The education abroad advisory committee, and your campus administration, should be aware that national professional associations and organizations involved in international education can help with institutional consultations, services, resources, and programming. They can offer invaluable (and inexpensive) assistance to colleges and universities at any stage of their education abroad program development. Primary among these are the following.

NAFSA: Association of International Educators

NAFSA is the primary professional association for all professionals working in the field of international educational exchange. Membership in NAFSA is essential for individuals and institutions seriously involved in international education. With membership comes reduced rates for conferences, a newsletter, discounted publications, (access to electronic bulletin boards that keep members abreast of developments in the field, a job placement service, and so forth) and a variety of other benefits. NAFSA assists member institutions in identifying consultants, who are chosen for their expertise in specific areas in the field of international educational exchange. These consultants will visit your campus, meet with all relevant administrators, faculty, and students, and prepare a report containing specific recommendations.

Council on International Educational Exchange

Unlike NAFSA, CIEE offers only institutional memberships. Membership in CIEE provides helpful networking opportunities with other institutions, a monthly newsletter and other publications, reduced rates on many services, guidance in establishing study abroad programs, and access to limited scholarship aid for students traveling to developing countries and for minority students. CIEE's work-abroad programs provide short-term paid jobs for students. CIEE also offers an array of travel services though its subsidiary Council Travel offices across the country. In addition to its New York headquarters, CIEE has a number of overseas offices that members can use in program planning.

Institute of International Education

IIE oversees a variety of government-to-government international exchange agreements (for example, the Fulbright program and the International Visitor program) and can be very helpful in program implementation, particularly in the developing world. IIE has regional offices in the United States as well in key locations overseas. Institutional membership in IIE brings with it a monthly associates' newsletter and all its major publications.

American Association of Collegiate Registrars and Admissions Officers

AACRAO's main focus involves admissions and academic transcripting for U.S. colleges and universities. However, the association has several committees concerned with international education as it affects colleges and universities. One of these committees is concerned exclusively with credit transfer questions that arise out of education abroad programming. AACRAO holds an annual conference, which offers discussion sessions on education abroad. AACRAO and NAFSA together have published *Transcripts from Study Abroad: A Workbook* (1986). AACRAO, NAFSA, and the British Universities Transatlantic Exchange Committee (BUTEC) have published *Recording the Performance of U.S. Undergraduates at British Institutions: Guidelines Toward Standardized Reporting for Study Abroad* (1988).

Other Professional Organizations

Although NAFSA, CIEE, IIE, and AACRAO are the primary membership organizations that serve the interests of institutions and education abroad professionals, several other organizations are also noteworthy. These organizations include the International Society for Intercultural Training and Research (SIETAR), which is concerned with intercultural theory and epistemology; the National Society for Internships and Experiential Education (NSIEE), which promotes hands-on learning in nonacademic environments in the United States and abroad; and the Association of International Education Administrators (AIEA). In addition, many persons involved in education abroad are active in various scholarly associations concerned with language and area studies.

Regional and National Consortia

Many consortia of like-minded and/or geographically related colleges and universities have developed study programs around the world—

often in developing countries. Some of the more prominent consortia are the Associated Colleges of the Midwest, the College Consortium for International Studies, CIEE's various Cooperative Study Centers, Denmark's International Study Program, the Great Lakes Colleges Association, the Higher Education Consortium for Urban Affairs, and the International Student Exchange Program. Joining forces makes great sense; institutional strengths often complement each other, and shared costs mean more affordable programs. It is possible to join one or more of these consortia, depending on your institutional interests and qualifications. At the very least, you can learn a great deal from them just from how their programs were established and how they operate.

3 Faculty Roles

Contributors: Bill Barnhart, Tom Ricks, and Paula Spier

Overall, faculty members play a central and critical role in all international education projects, on campus and off. Any college or university that contemplates "globalization" does so at risk without the involvement of its faculty. It is equally the case, that faculty usually come to these responsibilities without much training or background in international education programming. They thus often require the seasoned and pragmatic counsel of campus advisers and administrators. The challenge is not to supplant what faculty are trained to know and to do, but to supplement it with the evolving professional pedagogy, principles, and pragmatism of NAFSA's "international educator."

Developing Faculty Support

As colleges and universities work toward "internationalizing the campus," faculty involvement remains increasingly important. The establishment of new study abroad opportunities and exchanges, special degree programs in international or area studies, the design of special language courses, the establishment of language houses, dormitories, and classrooms, the hosting of international conferences, the creation of distance-learning technology, and collaborative teaching and research, all demand at least some degree of faculty participation, often a great deal. Indeed, significant "internationalization" of undergraduate education can be concretely implemented only with proactive and committed faculty as eager participants in the overall institutional process.

Faculty have important roles to play as

- members of international education policy, advisory and overseas scholarship committees
- general advocates of education abroad and promoters of campus-sponsored, affiliated, and other overseas programs

- advisers and preapproval and transfer academic credit evaluators, in conjunction with your office and/or the registrar
- resources in program development and administration, including cost analysis and budget preparation
- area-studies resources in predeparture orientation and postreturn reentry programming
- international consultants to other campus committees
- campus-based or overseas program directors
- overseas teachers in institutional study abroad programs and exchanges

Collaborative partnerships between academic departments and the education abroad office are critical to campus internationalization. At many institutions the origins of international educational exchange can be traced to faculty who had the courage to take on the challenge of program development and management, often without much institutional support. At others, it is a single education administrator's knowledge, conscientiousness, persistence, and enthusiasm that is responsible for the evolution of faculty participation. Cooperation and the identification of common interests are essential components of the internationalizing process. Looked at from the other direction, the lack of enthusiastic and committed faculty always hinders the development of an international mission and invariably limits student opportunities. Yet saying so does not make it so, and there are many ways in which faculty support is often either withheld or grudgingly given.

As the National Task Force Report pointed out in 1990:

> Even with institutional commitment, attitudes of individual faculty and those prevailing in some departments can be a problem, sometimes even a severe obstacle to forming new programs or encouraging student participation. The explanation for lack of faculty support includes such inglorious reasons as inertia and the egocentric "What's in it for me?". Less crass but equally parochial—and more prevalent—is the attitude among some faculty, even those who ought to be among the strongest proponents of study abroad, that study abroad deprives them of their best students, actually taking them out of their classrooms and reducing their full-time equivalent statistics. But, by far the most frequent cause of lack of faculty interest in or [faculty] opposition to study abroad programs is that they are not perceived to be relevant to or supportive of what faculty do.

These attitudes, even if stated strongly, can amount to an implicit faculty "case" against study abroad. If such reluctance exists on a campus, one of the leading reasons may be that education abroad involvement is not taken into account as a part of the administrative/faculty "rewards system"—meaning that it plays little or no role in tenure and promotion decisions, or is viewed negatively. Department chairs and deans sometimes give little tangible indication that they respect active participation in education abroad. With the exception of overtly international subjects—for example, language and international relations—even dedicated and committed teachers may feel that their international activities are neither recognized nor rewarded.

There can thus be ample suspicion on the part of faculty that it may be detrimental to their advancement within the institution (and the profession) to spend time away from more traditional academic functions, which remain on-campus teaching and research and scholarship—and unfortunately their reading of the situation is not inaccurate. Leading an overseas program, sitting on an advisory committee, or redesigning a course so that it will have an international component may be well down the institutional value scale for promotion and tenure, in the minds of some or many members of the faculty and the administration.

On most campuses, advisers find that those faculty who have themselves studied or otherwise traveled abroad, or are active in overseas research projects, are generally the most supportive of students being given such opportunities. But often those who most need to be included in international affairs are those who are most reluctant. Senior faculty can be unwilling to be perceived as novices in a strange place or try out new ways of teaching and learning. Young faculty, who often make the most natural and energetic program leaders, are frequently afraid to be away while tenure is being decided, or have spouses and school age children who cannot travel easily.

At the other end of the spectrum are those individuals and departments with what amounts to built-in program ownership. Overseas leadership positions may be treated as if they are part of a tenure benefit. At best, students get the experience of a leader who knows and loves the country for which the group is headed. At worst, it is possible for a student group to be neglected by a leader who chooses to devote full-time to personal research interests. Program leadership has also been known to rotate around a department more because "someone needs to go" than because the selected individual is either competent or interested in the program.

One of your jobs as an international educator is, therefore, to work with the president, deans, provosts, department heads, and others, whenever the opportunity presents itself, to encourage, expand, and reward high-quality faculty participation. The 1995 American Council on Education report, "Educating Americans for a World in Flux: Ten Ground Rules for Internationalizing Higher Education," written by a commission of college and university presidents and chancellors, suggests that top-administrative support for campus internationalization is increasing:

> Among the key actions that an institution can take are the following: Encourage faculty to develop expertise in the global dimensions of their disciplines. Encourage interdisciplinary study. Give weight to international experience, skill, and foreign language competence as criteria in hiring new faculty. Provide faculty and staff with opportunities to develop their own international and language skills. Include international service or study among the criteria for tenure or promotion. Institutions have many ways to send a signal to faculty members about what is important. (ACE Report, "Ground Rule Six")

In short, unless campus faculty feel involved in the excitement of what students do and learn when they are overseas, they are not likely to support it for the next generation of students. Some form of institutionally supported international exposure, needs to be an essential part of a school's faculty development policy. This can mean such diverse activities as:

- developing faculty teaching or research exchanges as part of institution-to-institution agreements
- support for independent foreign travel and research
- developing faculty-led programs, from short-term, discipline-specific study tours to semester or year duration
- providing teaching opportunities in host-national managed foreign study programs
- visiting campus-sponsored or -affiliated programs as part of the program evaluation process

As an international educator, you can help further by facilitating a two-way dialogue and information flow between your office and individual faculty or departments. Using NAFSA and other networks of international discourse, an education abroad professional can disseminate information on overseas developments that bear on education abroad programming, and also encourage faculty to provide your office with what they learn from their networks and overseas contacts.

You should also make sure to generate faculty recognition articles regularly, distributing them where they do the most good, citing contributions to the international arena by campus faculty. Your "reward system" should certainly include thank-you letters to returned leaders, listing student satisfaction, host institution comments, quality of course evaluations, the extent to which the course took advantage of the site and the responsible handling of nonteaching responsibilities. Letters of appreciation should be signed by the chair of the international education committee or by a high academic officer. Rewarding praiseworthy faculty behavior can only help in the recruitment of competent faculty leaders.

▌ On-Campus Roles

General Advocacy

Faculty play a crucial and pivotal role in the way your institution envisions and supports a commitment to international education. At best, faculty function as part of the informed and committed international "conscience," in and out of the classroom, on committees, in departmental meetings and budget hearings, and as academic advisers. There is a direct correlation between active faculty support for study abroad and the likelihood that students will see (and seize upon) it as a realistic academic option.

If you work with an International Education Committee, this is the obvious place to initiate and nurture such essential commitment. But it is not the only place. Supportive, internationalized faculty are needed on educational policy committees, in the Faculty Senate, on dean's councils, at department meetings, and on all other formal administrative bodies where undergraduate, and even graduate, pedagogy, and policy issues are considered.

Although faculty can advocate educational policy from a theoretical and intellectual level, students themselves are not likely to think about going overseas unless they get faculty support in course content, in academic advising, and in affirmative views of the worth of overseas study. Students are pretty good at picking up whether or not a respected adviser really thinks studying abroad is a good idea. They are most likely to get this kind of confirmation from faculty who have themselves had cross-cultural experience, or who have had information provided to them by the education abroad office that contains information on overseas opportunities.

Program Development and Administration

Faculty are obvious partners with the international education office in the design and development of study abroad programs, as well as the supervision and evaluation of the courses and credits offered, budgeting, selection of students, and general logistics. However, faculty are also important in evaluating programs offered by other institutions and in advising the education abroad office of the kinds of academic issues that should be considered when reviewing noninstitutional programs.

As noted in Chapter 2, institutions differ widely when it comes to the locus of control for study abroad. Often the international education office does only general overseas advising, or provides logistical support. In this situation, individual faculty members or departments plan and carry out programs in a more-or-less entrepreneurial fashion. In other institutions the study abroad office is the administrator for all credit-bearing study outside the United States, bringing in faculty resource people as appropriate.

The actual management of international programs varies a great deal from institution to institution. It is possible to have several styles of program administration within a single institution, depending on the program. In some cases it is the education abroad office that handles all or many of these activities. In other circumstances the faculty leader is expected to do them all. In the best of all possible worlds there is a natural and comfortable flow of information between the education abroad office, faculty, students, and, if relevant, on-site program leaders. Faculty on overseas program committees may very well be program directors themselves, whose experience and advice provides a resource for shaping college or university policy.

Faculty-led Programs

At many institutions study abroad is synonymous with faculty-led programs—the range being from leading short-term (summer or interim) course-related or discipline-specific study tours to teaching in established overseas U.S.-styled branch campuses to being academic or residential director. Although this approach militates against U.S. students living and learning on foreign, rather than U.S., terms, in point of fact, many students are not temperamentally, academically, or linguistically ready for such integrated experiences. Further, faculty involvement provides assurances to other faculty, to the administration, and to parents that the program will be of comparable quality to campus programs.

Short-term, faculty-led programming has been the major growth area in study abroad programming over the past decade—as noted in Chapter 9, "Demographics." Whatever the impact of such programs on students (and it can be enormous or minimal), it is quite clear that faculty who lead such programs usually return to the campus with deepened convictions about the value of foreign study and are much more likely to become allies of campus advisers and administrators. In effect, leading programs or teaching in them, can be seen as a form of faculty development. Campuses that rely almost exclusively on such programming, however, also report that faculty burnout is high, especially as faculty members learn how much work is involved and how little research time they might have.

New programs that require faculty participation, and a few with no mechanism for carryover, may start from scratch each time. In any case, a pretrip site visit is very helpful. It can make the difference between a faculty leader who feels in control of the situation and one who is not very much ahead of the students. In areas of the world where personal relationships are more important than signed contracts, a pretrip visit may be essential even if all resources are technically in place. The extent to which proposed program sites, structure, and content meet desired criteria is usually considered at the committee level; it may also be appropriate to consider at the departmental level.

Planning for new program content or reviewing current courses and activities comes naturally to most teaching faculty, whether or not they are involved in the program itself. Difficulties are more likely to arise if the faculty being asked to lead programs are expected to move into a pre-existing framework, following someone else's syllabus. Planning for academic and cultural resources usually demands prior experience at the site. Some schools provide a host national who contributes continuity and local expertise so that each new program leader has a base from which to operate. Others use the foreign student services at the host university. Some rely only on the reports of past program directors.

Budgets

Fiscal planning ability is not necessarily part of standard academic training. But faculty with experience directing an overseas program can become obvious partners in planning budgets for overseas centers, or in evaluating existing budget and cost sheets. They can also be excellent consultants in periodic budget audits of both international offices and overseas centers. They can provide an international perspective that most campus auditors do not possess. Such things as planning for currency fluctuation and for contingencies and emergencies, understanding the probable relationship between tuition, financial aid, and cash flow and even dealing with the stomach-wrenching prospect of being responsible for what may seem like enormous amounts of money may seem to be even more of a burden than is managing an established budget in the field.

Affiliations

Colleges and universities are increasingly involved in establishing overseas affiliation and linkage agreements with institutions worldwide. Faculty should be essential members of affiliation committees as well as affiliation advisers. Academic administrators should draw upon faculty experience and expertise in designing and developing agreements. As campus-operated summer and semester programs are necessarily course-driven and campus relevant, so too should overseas affiliations and linkages have faculty involvement in their design, implementation and assessment. (For a fuller treatment of this topic, see Chapter 15, "Program Planning, Budgeting, and Implementation.")

Program Evaluation

As stressed throughout this book, an institution's policy toward education abroad derives from its educational mission, which should indicate support for internationalism. Defining the curricular goals and academic standards that will result in implementation of this mission are clear and mandated faculty responsibilities. All overseas programs—whether operated directly by your college or university, represent linkages with overseas institutions, or are consortially administered—need constant and consistent evaluation.

Faculty members invariably must play an integral part in determining if student participation and performance in a study abroad program meets your institution's academic standards. This means in most cases setting up processes to preapprove programs (as well as anticipated course work) so that students and their parents are assured that credit will be forthcoming if performance merits it. It also means establishing review procedures to examine student performance, based on overseas grades, transcripts, or other records from the program, in order to award credit (see Chapter 4, "Academic Credit").

If your budget allows it, there is every reason to ask selected faculty members to visit overseas host institutions and sites, old as well as new, yours as well as those run by other institutions and organizations. They are the ones charged with making judgments about program quality. If they are pleased with what they see, they are of course more likely to take a vested interest in the programs they have visited and encourage students to participate in them. Faculty can sometimes be encouraged to visit sites in areas where they are otherwise doing sabbatical research or vacation travel. A small travel fund can go a long way when used in this manner. Ideally, faculty visits to programs can also have the effect of building a helpful and personalized support network between overseas sites and your campus.

International educators understand that the total intellectual and personal value of study abroad to students is often based on criteria different from what faculty members may primarily be concerned with and value (for example, course content, teaching style, institutional prestige, library facilities, etc.). The challenge is to convey to faculty before they visit programs an understanding of the importance of looking at the intercultural and extracurricular aspects of students' experience.

As suggested in Chapter 2, it is sometimes helpful to have a known study abroad adversary serving on the Education Abroad Committee. The committee will most likely benefit from the his or her skepticism, and what would have been anonymous grumbling will be aired in a larger, more helpful context. Moreover, such faculty opponents are often won over in the process.

When the committee or international office has concerns about the way in which a member of the teaching faculty is functioning in relation to educational exchange, it is helpful to be able to relate those concerns to institutional policy. If it seems clear that practice is not following policy, then, again, there is no substitute for knowing one's institution. A tactful hint to a dean or department chair will almost always be more effective than a committee discussion or direct confrontation.

Transfer Credit Evaluation

As custodians of institutional academic policy and quality, faculty have a vested interest in the ways in which overseas programs complement the curriculum. Faculty participation in the evaluation of outside programs should be viewed as part of their departmental obligation. Some institutions require that every course taken away from the home campus be approved by a faculty member. Others leave judgments about elective and general education credits to admissions and the registrar in cooperation with the education abroad office. Credit for institutionally or consortially sponsored programs is usually approved by appropriate departments during the planning process, and the courses themselves often appear in the catalog. The allocation of course credit toward a particular student's major is nearly always a departmental decision (see Chapter 4, "Academic Credit," and Chapter 18, "Program Evaluation").

Individual instructors will be more supportive of work done away from campus if they feel they have an evaluative role. There is, at the same time, a natural tendency to think one's own teaching style and course content are superior. Judgments about credit are often made on the basis of equivalency: "Does this course cover what I would teach?" Sometimes the question is the extent to which course content matches an already-approved catalog title. As faculty members become more comfortable with the work done overseas, they are more likely to look for and recommend courses that enrich or supplement the campus curriculum, and for work that could not be covered at home. There is obviously more flexibility in some of the humanities and social sciences, but opportunities exist even in disciplines with tight requirements mandated by graduate schools or professional accrediting boards. Even science students can be encouraged to study abroad when their own advisers and departments really believe in the benefits.

Some of the ways faculty can assist in the evaluation process include

- site inspections of intensive language centers by language faculty during term break
- professional school faculty from engineering, medicine, nursing and business interview students who have completed a similar program abroad
- faculty with region-specific experience counsel both students and faculty intending to study at overseas centers
- follow-up language training for students who studied abroad in less commonly taught languages
- evaluation of all types of educational experiences abroad, including academic, internship and service-learning, for transfer credit
- hosting international faculty delegations from overseas study centers to assess academic credentials

All of this is easier to manage when faculty lead their own students overseas. It is much more difficult when students are placed directly into host institutions.

Program Recruitment and Promotion

Faculty should take the lead on campus in promoting their own programs as well as offer support for others. An economist, or biologist, or art historian who tells a class, "When you go to _____, you will want to _____," is recruiting. So is the one who draws on the experiences of class members who have been abroad, or invites international students and faculty or campus visitors to speak in a class.

Active promotion of faculty-led programs occurs naturally in the classroom and advising context. Every program leader wants students; the problem is more likely to be too much, rather than too little pressure. The challenge lies in the fact that faculty are less vested in opportunities offered by their colleagues, and even less for those run by other institutions. They tend to support programs that they have led themselves in the past, or that they would like to be able to lead in the future. They tend to support those for which they serve on advisory committees and, as noted above, they usually harbor warm feelings for places they have visited. Faculty are equally important in providing an overall atmosphere that can foster interest in study abroad, and education abroad offices should of course encourage such broad-based support.

Admissions

It is natural and usual for faculty leaders to be involved in the selection of the students they will take abroad, if an institution's programs tend to be faculty-generated and led. However faculty can also be important in the selection process for institutional wide programs, working closely with the education abroad office. It can be helpful to have a standard policy with criteria for selection for all overseas program to protect against accepting students in order to fill needful programs. Clear policies and consistent adherence to them can alleviate tensions. Shared authority for selection has many institutional advantages.

Logistics

The ability to provide support and encouragement for international education is not the same thing as the ability to be a good travel agent. Faculty program leaders may, indeed, hire a travel agent to arrange transportation and housing. Some travel agents will offer to set up an educational program as well—this may, or may not, meet institutional standards. Most leaders are blissfully willing to turn over the logistical arrangements to the study abroad office. A few old hands bargain competently for the lowest air rates and best housing.

Predeparture Orientation

Faculty members are often happy to come to information, planning, and orientation meetings set up by the study abroad office, whether for programs they themselves will lead or for other programs, offered by their institution or, indeed, other institutions. Given that study abroad is an academic experience the involvement of faculty in orientation programs and discussions on academic goals and systems of education and styles of learning overseas can underline the academic nature of the experience. American and international faculty can also provide enormously helpful insights on history, social patterns, and tips for survival and daily living. Many are willing to participate in group-building activities and cross-cultural simulations. Students and faculty can benefit from the exchange of values and information, as well as the opportunity to see each other in different settings and roles. (See Chapter 14 for a fuller discussion of orientation topics and procedures.)

Reentry

Faculty members who have lived and studied overseas and continue to maintain family and collegial ties with overseas cultures are excellent resources for reentry programs. They are very empathetic to students returning to their old campus friends and hangouts, an adjustment process that is often difficult. They most likely have undergone a similar experience. Faculty should be routinely informed as to which of their students have recently returned from study abroad. If there is any way the overseas experience can be used in class discussions or in writing assignments, most—though not all—students appreciate this sensitivity and recognition of what they have recently learned, as it impacts on their ongoing studies.

∎ Overseas Roles

If an institution runs stand-alone programs or works with overseas institutions or agencies to put on programs for your students, faculty may be called upon to assume a range of important overseas roles. Such roles can range from having full administrative and academic responsibility for the integrity of the program, as well as personal responsibility for the well-being of your students, to, on the other extreme, carefully monitoring the academic credibility of a host institution's curricular offerings. What faculty do overseas obviously depends largely upon the nature and purpose of the program, along with its design and structure. A six-week study tour for an institution's own students alone clearly dictates a much different set of responsibilities for the faculty leader than, for instance, a full-year residential program, in which one or more of faculty members may teach a course or provide academic counseling to students from a variety of institutions.

In his article, "It's Like Wearing All the Hats" (*Academe*, September–October 1995), John C. O'Neal, professor of French and director of the Hamilton College Junior Year in France, provides an insightful account of the demands of directing a full-year program. Serving a fourth year as director of the Hamilton program, Professor O'Neal likens the overseas experience to being college president and dean and academic adviser and lecturer and psychological counselor and accountant and even, in some cases, repairman. This perceptive article describes these multiple roles as a series of constantly shifting responsibilities for which adequate prior training is likely to be minimal and on the spot problem-solving ability critical. In contrast, a U.S. faculty member accompanying student groups to, for instance, the University of Cambridge's International Summer School, where personal and administrative services are assumed by the host institution, can limit her responsibilities to course evaluation and the academic mentoring of students. Between these two poles, a variety of intermediary roles exist.

What is crucial to each and every instance is that whatever your institution demands of faculty is made absolutely clear to them before they are asked to accept these responsibilities—and that these duties are reviewed and understood by all concerned, well in advance of departure. Except in the rarest of circumstances, the pursuit of scholarly research on the part of faculty working with programs overseas must usually be subordinated to their prescribed teaching, advising, and administrative duties. Since in most instances faculty will have little or no time for doing independent scholarship, it is wise to make this point from the start, clearly and emphatically.

The most successful faculty leaders are those with the physical stamina to endure long hours and a high level of interaction with students and local contacts; the patience and good humor to deal with frequent frustrations; and the knowledge and independence to function well in a culture not their own. If they have pedagogical duties, they need to be eager and committed teachers who know how what they are teaching relates both to the home campus and to the culture of the host country.

They also need to be true leaders, skilled in diplomacy, logistics, and group dynamics. They will invariably be asked to be cultural interpreters and analysts, helping students understand what is going on and how it relates to things back home (or doesn't!). Unless there is someone else on the local scene who really knows its social, cultural, and academic fabric, faculty must be prepared to take on the role of explaining it to them.

Above all, faculty must be prepared to be cheerful and supportive friends-in-need to their students, not simply authority figures.

As noted, what faculty actually do abroad depends on institutional, and therefore program, goals, as well as the structures and resources available. In some instances, only one of the duties discussed below may be relevant. In others, more than one, if not all, make up the job overseas description. Further, whatever is prescribed and expected, chance and circumstance often rise up to demand yet additional imperatives and responsibilities.

Academic Director

The academic director is responsible for the academic quality of the program and must be willing to assure those who need to know that the expectations of both participant and home institution are being met. In some cases, institutions develop the desired curricula and then seek faculty at the study site to teach it, a model that provides the most home institution control. In other cases, existing programs will be reviewed to identify a curriculum that offers the closest possible match. Familiarity with the curriculum and the credentials of the teaching staff, domestic or foreign, prior to the beginning of the program is critical.

Institutions exporting curricula to be taught by faculty they have hired abroad place an additional academic oversight burden on the academic director. Rather than solely functioning as liaison with the faculty hired and managed by the host institution, s/he will also be responsible for continuous faculty review and supervision to assure quality comparable to home institution standards. Needless to say, this is a case where care in selecting faculty prior to the program is very important and can greatly reduce the possibility of having to replace unsatisfactory instructors in mid-stream. The more manageable role of academic liaison generally requires regular class visits and periodic contact with the host institution's academic supervisor, but lessens faculty oversight responsibilities.

Both roles, when done effectively, require extensive and structured student contact. Successful academic directors schedule frequent one-on-one sessions with students and offer additional times for consultation. Some programs require students to keep a daily journal and may also evaluate student assignments, even though host institution faculty are responsible for assessing academic performance. In some programs, the academic director also teaches courses. If this is the case, the daily schedule of teaching, class visits, student tutorials and liaison work with the host institution is likely to be more rigorous and demanding than what U.S. faculty are used to in their U.S. campus responsibilities. They should of course be forewarned and supported in all ways that are institutionally possible.

Administrative/Resident Director

Faculty members can also be called to serve in largely administrative, as opposed to classroom, capacities, with no teaching duties—though being an academic adviser of course is a highly pedagogical role. As administrators, they are responsible for the overall direction of on-site program, which can be both burdensome and something for which nothing in their background has prepared them. Spelling out this authority and the responsibilities that go with it in a contractual agreement between the institution and the faculty member is very important. It also needs to be communicated to local contacts abroad, to students, and to parents.

On site administrative responsibilities necessarily begin well prior to the arrival of students. In the case of long-term resident director assignments, the on-site administrator will likely have been at the study site for several months or more. Housing assignments, course selection and registration confirmation, special dietary arrangements, health issues, special needs accommodation—all must be dealt with before the participants arrive.

The first responsibility of the administrative director usually is to meet with his counterpart at the host institution to review jointly the expectations of each regarding program goals, structures, and resources. Ideally, these matters will have been detailed in a written contract agreed upon when the decision was made to begin or renew the program. Such a contract review and discussion of expectations minimizes conflicts and reduces the possibility of misunderstandings once the program begins.

On-site Orientation

The arrival of the students at the study site brings a whole new set of responsibilities. No matter how explicit and detailed the predeparture orientation program is, each participant perceives the role of the director differently. Some will see the director as their lifeline to familiar security networks back home, while others will see her or him as a potential deterrent to their free and open taste of a new cultural smorgasbord. Defining a middle ground between these extremes should be the objective of the first on-site orientation for the group. It is here that boundaries need to be defined, limitations discussed, risks reviewed and, most significantly, information given regarding when and where the director will be available and for what. In addition, the director must emphasize what is expected of each participant and how important their behavior and cooperation is to the overall success of the program.

The director is responsible for providing reasonable access to opportunities for successful academic and personal experiences. However, caution should be taken not to mislead students or to over-promise things. Experienced directors say that the more directors agree to do for participants, the more students will come to rely on them, rather than learning to take advantage of their new opportunities. On the other hand, students do need seasoned guidance and prudent counsel. No matter how well the program goes, it is inevitable that some postprogram evaluations will reveal unexpected dissatisfaction with the very issues the director was careful to discuss and review in the beginning. For example, the Louvre really cannot be seen in one day and the train to Edinburgh does make eight stops instead of six, and why didn't you know the best route to Cannes?

Budget and Money Management

Depending on the parameters of a particular program, the administrative director will be responsible for varying degrees of budget management and control. In an academic year assignment, this responsibility can easily include attending to monthly payment of program costs such as housing and classroom rent, staff and faculty payroll and expenses for group excursions. Short-term programs of less than ten weeks generally have such payments taken care of through institutional bank drafts sent to service providers in advance, but the director will still need to be prepared to handle unexpected expenses.

Tips to bus drivers and museum guides, last-minute changes in the itinerary, and fluctuations in the currency exchange rate are examples of financial needs that may or may not be foreseeable. The director is faced with the difficult task of managing program finances according to the fiscal guidelines of the home institution. She will be expected to track currency exchange rates, log daily expenses, document contingency expenditures and possibly disburse monies to students all in such a way that the accountant in the travel office—who just possibly has never been abroad—can understand and approve. Needless to say, some familiarity with banking and currency regulations in the host country is imperative.

Responsible budget management of course begins prior to departure. Either the person responsible for institutional accounting or the budget officer in the study abroad office should meet with the director and review institutional policy as it applies to expenditures abroad and how their specific program budget responsibilities fit within that policy. Topics to be discussed include allowable personal expenses, daily per diem rates that often are different for each city, expenses for accompanying family members, acceptance of personal gifts or services from service providers, use of on-site bank accounts and expense documentation requirements.

The director should also be aware that, under some circumstances, the Internal Revenue Service views funds provided to a program director for group expenses abroad as personal income subject to withholding tax unless final budget reports are submitted within 60 days of completion of the program. Understanding the fiscal role of both the institution and the program director is vital. Close collaboration between the director and the home institution accounting office from the beginning of the program to its conclusion is essential to its long-term viability.

Advising Students

Directing a study abroad program for participants who most likely have limited experience in a new culture provides a range of advising challenges that go far beyond what might be required on the home campus. Whoever is in charge of the program will be seen by participants as resource persons who can alleviate the initial confusion and disorientation that confronts them, then guide them along the paths of new knowledge and cultural integration. It is very important to understand the variety of motivations that encourage students to study overseas; not all will be as purely academic as faculty would prefer. Indeed, the desire to get away from the academic pressures of the home campus may be as fundamental as the desire to test themselves in a new and foreign environment. Successful advising therefore must acknowledge this complex of student hopes and desires, providing counsel that balances the twin academic and experiential bases of international education.

Responding to the emotional and mental adjustment problems that some students develop is of course a major challenge. It is also one that the average faculty leader is seldom prepared to deal with. Dr. Brian Riedesel, staff psychologist at the University of Utah Counseling Center, with years of experience in providing cross-cultural adjustment counseling to military personnel, suggests that the occurrence of mental health casualties can be reduced by following some basic guidelines designed to minimize the anxiety that comes with an unfamiliar setting. These include frequent communication with all members of the group, building group cohesion, establishing a sensible pacing of program activities to reduce fatigue, and sensitive leadership.

What is important is that faculty understand that the overseas academic advising they do takes place in a cultural setting that, because it is by definition foreign, can be both liberating and threatening to students. Further, the counsel they are asked by students to provide is considerably more likely than on the home campus to have to address the "whole person" of the student, rather than the more limited version that students share with faculty domestically.

Although most issues faculty directors confront may be fairly routine and can be satisfied with accurate information and foresight, deeper and broader questions are also very likely to arise. Faculty who themselves have not been abroad before or perhaps not for some time should certainly take part in predeparture orientation that addresses such matters as culture shock. It is wise also to bring them into contact with campus faculty who have previously accompanied groups abroad.

As familiarity with their new surroundings increases, it is not surprising for directors to be asked by the very same students who earlier had adjustment problems to recommend the best way, for example, to travel independently. Maintaining a resource library of books on travel, local and regional culture and available community services is a good way to respond to their seemingly endless questions. Here the key is to challenge students to try to integrate what they experience outside the classroom into their primary educational goals for being abroad, not to see it as something extraneous to what "the program" per se asks or offers.

The Role of the Faculty Spouse

Frequently spouses accompany faculty on programs abroad. If s/he is appointed by the home institution to act in some formal paid capacity—as teacher, adviser/counselor, even resident director—then it should be clear from the beginning just what that role is, spelled out in a contractual agreement with the home institution. Often, however, spouses have no such defined role; they are just socially there, accompanying their partner and the group. When this happens, depending on a host of factors, the effect of their presence on the program can be alternatively minimal or major.

Spouses can be enormously helpful to the group, taking on all sorts of informal but essential functions in support of their spouse, the program, and its participants. They can function as a second set of ears and hands for the group leader, can provide counsel and communications to and for students, and can do a host of things that a busy group leader just doesn't have the time to attend to—even to the point of being exploited (sometimes unwillingly, sometimes not) by the program and home institution. Spouses can also be intrusive and, because of their undefined capacity and function, confusing to participants and to others involved with the program, and this can have a negative impact on its success.

As a campus adviser or administrator, you should make sure that what an accompanying spouse is willing and able to contribute to the program (including contributing nothing) is clearly understood by all parties well in advance of departure, so as to avoid any subsequent misunderstandings. If in fact the spouse's abilities are essential to the program, this should be formalized and considered paid work, unless such remuneration is economically impossible. At the very least, this secondary role should be openly and clearly conveyed to the participants during orientation, and to the host institution.

Health Care Coordinator

Travel abroad can bring out a variety of minor illnesses and ailments, and medical catastrophes are of course always possible. The administrative/resident director should not of course be expected to function as the group nurse or medic. However, s/he should be prepared to give health care advice appropriate to the setting and be familiar with the local health care delivery system, as well as how participants can obtain simple health remedies. Under no circumstances should the director serve as "in-house pharmacist" by dispensing any kind of over-the-counter medicines or medical counsel. Proper predeparture orientation on health issues should have informed participants about bringing their own supply of whatever they might need (see Chapter 13, "Health and Safety Issues"). Postarrival orientation can provide an overview of how to treat minor health problems locally and what to do in the case of emergencies.

Emergency Response Coordinator

As the institutional representative, it is the responsibility of the resident director to coordinate the on-site response to any natural, political, or social emergency that may arise. A determination must immediately be made as to the level of risk confronting participants and what course of action is most prudent. A first step would be to contact the home institution and provide complete and accurate information about the nature of the emergency and how it has impacted the participants. An emergency involving the physical well-being of participants would dictate a more rapid response than say, a strike by faculty at the host institution, where damage assessment can take a more measured pace.

The continuing role in emergency response situations is that of liaison with the home institution, which, if prudent, will have assembled a team of administrators who can evaluate institutional response to the emergency based on the recommendation of the on-site director. Once the situation on-site is stabilized, much of the decision-making responsibility will be assumed by the home institution. Of most importance is the establishment in advance of a step-by-step set of procedures that can be referenced by the home institution and the on-site director.

4 Academic Credit

Contributors: Kathleen Sideli and Stephen Cooper

When established campus practices concerning academic credit are fully integrated into education abroad advising and programming, students are less likely to experience problems that can lead to loss of time, credit, or money. There are a variety of ways to set up and approve program credit. Some may be designed for students attending programs your school administers or sponsors through other institutions and agencies, while others may address the situation when students select programs sponsored by an outside institution, or enroll directly abroad. The key is for you to become thoroughly familiar with the policies and procedures of your own institution; to work closely with appropriate academic and administrative personnel to formulate the fairest and most efficient means of assessing student performance; and to counsel students so that they are aware of what they need to do before, during, and following their education abroad experience in order to maximize their chances of applying the credits they earn toward their degree studies.

When determining whether to invest in a study abroad program, parents and students rightly view obtaining credit as a major factor. Those who promote study abroad would agree that it should be considered integral to a student's overall college education. Consequently, issues relating to academic credit are among the most critical facing professionals in the field. The academic importance of credit transfer, in the context of the value of an overseas educational experience, needs to be articulated carefully and consistently. Questions regarding kinds of credit available, who determines the acceptability of courses taken abroad, the academic level and merit of the classes, grades, and whether degree requirements can be satisfied abroad merit consideration before study abroad can be said to be an acceptable academic option for students.

❚ Faculty, Administrative, and Institutional Commitment

Before attempting to help your institution establish mechanisms for evaluating and granting credit for courses taken abroad, it is essential for education abroad professionals to ascertain the institution's stance on study abroad. Colleges or universities that, for fiscal or academic reasons, are reluctant to send students abroad may discourage the practice by imposing limits or denying credit. Other institutions, which may encourage students to spend time overseas as part of their degree programs, need to establish user-friendly policies and procedures to avoid unintentional barriers. Ultimately, if students can incorporate courses taken abroad into their requirements with minimal obstacles, they will be more likely to participate in programs overseas.

Put another way, it is important to determine whether an institution is imposing deliberate hurdles to study abroad (for example, a very strict policy on transfer credit that in fact discourages study abroad) or whether the obstacles are merely bureaucratic (for example, a number of documents to fill out, committee evaluations, time delays in obtaining credit, etc.). You will need to understand which, if either, might be the case at your institution before you can develop strategies for dealing with the obstacles. Finally, the awarding of transfer credit for overseas study needs to be seen in the general context of transfer credit. If it is not, are you able to articulate reasons for treating it differently?

Overcoming Institutional Barriers

Who ultimately decides what coursework taken abroad is creditworthy? If on the one hand the responsibility falls to only one individual or one office on campus, study abroad may never reap the full support and understanding of faculty and advisers and, consequently, will not appear as an integral part of the academic curriculum. On the other hand, if the responsibility is so diffuse that students find themselves being referred from one office to another, they may decide that study abroad is not worth the hassle. Ideally, an institution should have clear policies involving the input of a wide range of faculty and staff; this enables students to easily earn credit for their studies abroad.

Even if an institution is committed to education abroad, negative faculty or administrative attitudes can still create barriers. For example, some faculty members may fear that study abroad will take away some of their best students, especially in certain fields or during junior year, when students typically focus on their majors. These are legitimate concerns and need to be approached with a confident sense of the overall value of a study abroad experience for both the students and the institution. Further, some programs may not appear as academically rigorous, in an American sense, as home-campus studies, thus perpetuating the myth that education abroad programs are lax. Other programs may be challenging and stimulating in ways that actually impinge on traditional academic studies. If upon return students report that they had fewer contact hours in class, spent less time in the libraries, wrote fewer papers, or took no tests or only one exam (perhaps an oral one) per course, faculty doubts may increase even though the students performed at the same level as their classmates abroad. It is important to clear away faculty misperceptions and to face authentic concerns about educational quality early on. It is critical to engage the support of faculty on your campus who are familiar with different higher-education systems around the world so they can inform their colleagues and administrators that education abroad, while different, is not necessarily inferior to education in the United States.

Apart from ensuring that students are advised away from programs that are academically weak, the *National Task Force Report* suggests that the key to working with faculty is to "forge curricular connections" (see Appendix).

> Faculty should participate in program planning, course design, and site selection, and then help to fit the program into the curriculum; they should also sit on an advisory committee to the program. Faculty can be similarly involved in programs calling for direct enrollment in foreign institutions or the design of appropriate internships. Quite naturally, they may become advocates for such study abroad experiences, potential future resident directors, as well as academic advisers to students returning from abroad. Most important, they will become the legitimizers of the program on campus to their more parochial colleagues, to hesitant administrators, and to doubting parents . (See Chapter 3, "Faculty Roles".)

Kinds of Credit

Study abroad staff need to become familiar with the various types of credit U.S. students can earn through overseas study. Some are explained later in the chapter, but some common categories are given below:

Home Institution Credit

Students often enroll in actual home university course catalog or special study abroad courses, sometimes used only temporarily until credit transfer takes place after completion of a student's program abroad. Regular course catalog offerings can be used in those situations where the home university provides the instruction as well as a means for enrolling students who are actually taking parallel courses taught by the faculty of the host school, depending on institutional policy.

Credit by Transfer

When students do not enroll in the sending school's courses, they usually gain credit after evaluation of the host institution's transcript. That document may come from a sponsoring U.S. school, an agency, or a foreign university. Specialists in the home school registrar's or admissions office ordinarily have final responsibility for determining what can be transferred, although they consult with academic departments and use materials supplied by the student to document the coursework done overseas.

Experiential Credit

Some U.S. universities grant credit for various overseas experiences, although rarely for travel alone, including work, service, and internships. Sometimes this occurs through registration in special home school courses for the term abroad, credit and grades for which may result from journals, projects or reports, and postprogram assignments and interviews.

Credit by Examination

Many U.S. colleges will grant credit to students after they return by administering oral or written examinations to determine what they have learned abroad, especially, for example, to measure gains in foreign language proficiency. Some colleges or departments use this device to verify learning in required home campus courses, so it can be an effective tool when the coursework taken abroad does not appear to match that of the home university or when the home school will not recognize or accept courses taken at a foreign school. This approach has helped some colleges satisfy their sense of obligation to meet requirements and limitations imposed by accrediting agencies, for example in engineering and business.

▌ Evaluating Courses and Academic Work from Abroad

Setting Up Procedures

In addition to gaining faculty backing for education abroad, education abroad must be administratively feasible. This means working closely with the various offices and individuals on your campus who are responsible for awarding credit. It also means advising students, registering them and recording academic credit on their transcripts. Whether you work alone or in an education abroad office, you need to determine whether study abroad courses and programs will be evaluated in a similar fashion as other off-campus academic activities (for example, temporary transfer to another institution, internships, independent study) or whether special procedures need to be devised or modified.

Students need clear instructions about who is responsible for informing them how their courses abroad will be treated by their home institution. Whether you administer your own programs abroad, encourage participation in a range of other programs approved by your institution or have students directly enroll themselves overseas, individuals on your campus should be able to articulate the various steps students will need to take in order to receive credit for these various educational experiences outside the United States. Depending on your campus hierarchy, these policy decisions should involve personnel from offices and divisions that may include the registrar, the admissions office, academic advisers, faculty, academic deans, and others.

A key decision is whether courses taken abroad will be held to the same standards as home-campus courses (i.e., similar expectations with regards to contact hours, assignments, papers, exams) or whether the academic traditions of each country will be held as the standard to be met by the courses in question. Different variables may affect the final shape of institutional policies. For instance, universities that use the branch-campus model might indeed expect the courses abroad to parallel those offered on the home campus, while courses on programs that mainstream students would be judged by the host institution's standards. Such policies should clearly treat the applicability of courses, credits, and grades toward degree requirements, including whether the grades are included in the home-campus grade point average (GPA) (see Chapter 16, "Program Designs and Strategies").

Even when the academic chain of command for transfer credits has been established, you may need to devise registration and recording procedures to account for the students' period abroad. These procedures are especially critical for funded students because academic credit and financial aid for them are intertwined. If students are to receive academic credit and financial aid to study abroad, then institutions encouraging education abroad must have failsafe procedures for verifying overseas study. Such procedures guarantee to the administration and faculty, as well as to parents and, when necessary, federal authorities, that students are indeed engaged in an approved course of study even though they are not present on the home campus. Such procedures not only make students' overall experiences more positive, they also help to establish study abroad as an important and integral part of undergraduate education.

In establishing such procedures, the education abroad professional should work within the normal administrative structure of the home institution. This facilitates the processing of paperwork for all involved, especially the students. *It also shows that education abroad can be administered without any major deviations from established practices.* However, at a university where registration and recording procedures tend to be formal and rigid, careful negotiating may be required with key administrators to determine how the system can accommodate study abroad. Registration and recording for education abroad also requires enormous flexibility because of the uniqueness of sending students off campus, while still treating them, in other ways, as on-campus students. Since their time abroad is a legitimate academic endeavor, they should be accommodated as much as possible within the existing framework.

Although various registration and recording systems exist, two approaches distinguish between enrollment in home-campus credit and transfer credit. Home-campus credit is, at times, earned by students participating in programs that an institution administers directly or sponsors through outside consortia or agencies. Transfer credit is earned by students who participate in campus-approved programs offered by a range of other institutions and organizations, domestic or foreign. With home-campus credit, courses and grades are treated like those taken on the home campus. This makes it easier to apply them to degree requirements. Students who earn transfer credit from abroad sometimes have only the courses apply to their overall accumulation of credits; but they should also be able to satisfy degree requirements.

Certain institutions cannot count either the grades from the home-campus-credit model or the transfer-credit model into the cumulative GPA, while others do. Regulations on federal financial aid require that students enroll in, and will gain credit for, courses satisfactorily completed in any approved study abroad program. (Students may also have to be enrolled in some fashion at the home school.) However, the home university disbursing the federal financial assistance does not have to incorporate grades earned from overseas institutions into students' GPAs. If your institution allows students to study abroad under various program models, different procedures may have to be established for each. It is therefore vital for you as an education abroad adviser to understand the details that apply to transfer credit at your institution and to understand any limitations that might apply to transfer credit.

Credit and Enrollment for Programs Administered or Sponsored by the Home Institution

What follows are some concrete suggestions about credit approval and recording procedures under both models; they share many similarities. Please bear in mind, however, that there may be as many procedures as there are institutions, so these models should be considered in the context of your own campus environment and should be used only as a guide to action.

Predeparture Advising

Students should know, even as early as the application process, how their coursework abroad can be incorporated into their overall academic program (see Chapter 10, "Advising Principles and Strategies"). Once accepted into a program administered or sponsored by your institution, students should be required to go through a course approval process according to the policies established by your campus. Course approval forms should be established by a unit such as the registrar, the admissions office, the academic dean or the education abroad office.

Faculty, advisers, and others responsible for curriculum issues need to tell students what course and credit requirements, if any, they can fulfill abroad. Students should also be advised about the materials they need to submit before, during, or after the program if they wish to incorporate their coursework overseas into their degree program. Limitations regarding minimum courseloads, acceptable grades, range of disciplines permitted, and so forth should be established well before the departure date. Unfortunately, syllabi from abroad or firm schedules of courses available may be unavailable during predeparture advising, which will complicate advising.

Registration

Your institution should have a systematic way to enroll or account for the academic period that your students will be off campus. Some institutions have created one or more course numbers to serve as registration mechanisms for programs abroad. These can serve to demonstrate to the institution that a student is engaged in academic study during the absence from campus. Using existing campus courses or special course numbers may involve obtaining a course designation for the program and having the registrar assign a section number each term. This enrollment should allow students to maintain full-time status on your campus during the time abroad and to have their financial aid routinely disbursed.

If the institution has this type of registration procedure, which parallels on-campus enrollment, the education abroad office will have to decide whether its staff or the students themselves process the registration for the period abroad. Your office may be able to better monitor its programs by processing the enrollment itself. If your office takes on this responsibility, you may need to inform other university offices (for example, the student's school, college, or major department, financial aid office, etc.) of the status of the study abroad participant, ensuring that the student has academically viable reasons to be off campus.

You may also want to accommodate students from other institutions who participate in your programs. Some colleges and universities officially register guest participants at their institution under a category of special visiting students and as nondegree candidates. These designations avoid some of the formalities of admitting guest participants to the sponsoring institution. (Other institutions, however, may insist that temporary students be fully admitted before they can study abroad with a program your campus administers.)

Billing

Various fee mechanisms exist for credits earned abroad. Institutions may continue to assess on-campus tuition, establish a special fee based solely on program expenses including an off-campus surcharge or an education abroad office fee or charge a nominal home-campus fee if students pay the bulk of their program fees to a sponsoring or consortium institution. Your campus may link study abroad payments to registration on the home campus or separate the two issues completely.

On-Site Finalized Enrollment

Each study abroad program should have guidelines regarding the reporting to the home campus of actual on-site enrollment. A standard-ized enrollment form may help; many consortia and agency programs have such reporting forms. Once the students have completed their enrollment overseas, the international office at the host institution abroad, the program agency, the resident director, or the student should send the enrollment schedule to the home campus. Some institutions require at this time course syllabi and/or proposed home-institution course equivalents and credit hours for the work being completed abroad. Others prefer that such documentation be provided at the con-clusion of the program.

Some universities have set up equivalencies that have been granted over the years by home-campus departments for specific courses and programs so that students can be fairly confident of receiving similar credit while abroad. Such equivalencies may be established in various ways: by a faculty committee designated to evaluate course materials, by the admissions officer or the registrar who may assess all courses taken abroad with the input of faculty recommendation or by resident direc-tors who suggest course equivalencies to the home campus based on their familiarity with the home and host school courses.

Each student should submit evidence of the course content and work completed to their adviser(s). What is expected from abroad will depend on the policies established of the home campus. Typically, if the pro-gram is one with which the entire campus is familiar and which offers a limited, consistent range of courses, the approval process for credit should be quite straightforward. The staff in the education abroad office should serve as a liaison with on-campus offices, staff and faculty dur-ing this process.

For full-year programs especially, a midyear consultation between the education abroad office and the program overseas allows for the adjust-ment of students' schedules in the second semester, thus precluding sur-prises upon students' return. Moreover, careful monitoring of course-loads at the midpoint of the program, whatever its duration, allows for a smoother processing of coursework and credits once the program is completed.

Registering for the Postprogram Term

Another challenge facing institutions that encourage study abroad is pro-viding their students with the opportunity to register in absentia for home campus courses for their returning semester. This requires work-ing with various campus offices to develop policies, forms, procedures, and timetables. All this can be complicated, given that students study abroad for different lengths of time. However, the development of such procedures means that students are not adversely affected by studying overseas. Conversely, if students are not allowed to register from abroad—especially for courses necessary for their degree—it becomes difficult to convince others that studying abroad does not lengthen the time required to complete a degree.

Postprogram Transcripts

Education abroad professionals, in consultation with various campus offices and administrators, should have procedures and policies for reporting to the home campus the courses, grades, and credits earned abroad. Sometimes, official transcripts, as we know them in the United States, are unavailable abroad. For such cases, each institution needs a policy regarding the type of documentation it considers valid. At the termination of the program, the responsible officer at each program site should send to a designated point—the education abroad office, the registrar, or the admissions office—a transcript or official report that lists all coursework taken by students with the host institution grades and/or the acceptable U.S. grade equivalents agreed on beforehand.

In some cases, home-campus course equivalencies may be provided as well. Some campuses prefer to use foreign course titles on the home campus transcript while others try to match courses with comparable ones on the home campus. Others may do a mixture of both. Where the education abroad office has a central role, it should monitor the submission of appropriate supporting materials to campus faculty who participate in the transfer process.

Transcript Delays

Students, in addition to many program administrators and advisers, are especially concerned about, first, the long delay between the end of classes overseas and the arrival of performance evaluations or foreign transcripts to the home campus, and, second, the delay between the arrival of grade reports from abroad and the posting of credits or release of transcripts from the registrar. Fortunately, the advent of fax and e-mail telecommunications have speeded up the delivery of required information, often saving weeks. However, each campus needs guidelines regarding the authentication of information received through these various technological means.

These delays cause a great deal of student frustration and anxiety. If the interval is too protracted, students will not know what courses to take or if they will graduate on time. Financial aid could be held up. You should do everything possible to help speed up the process. Home campuses should strive to grant exceptions when delays beyond students' control occur.

Typically, it will be necessary to send a standardized course and grade reporting form to appropriate campus offices as well as the student. In this age of electronic record-keeping, paper copies may not be required as long as pertinent offices know that they have on-line access to the course information from abroad. Whether or not overseas grades count in the GPA, or even appear on the transcript, are policy questions that should be determined well in advance and should be made clear to students during the advising process.

The registrar or admissions office may keep on file the original transcript or form submitted from abroad in the event that a student needs to substantiate the time spent abroad to a graduate school or a future employer. Students receiving transcripts from another U.S. school, an agency, or a foreign university should be advised to get several original copies if they plan to apply for graduate or professional schools. This is because some U.S. institutions do not fully document study abroad on their transcripts, because some graduate and professional schools require official transcripts for all coursework taken, and because some U.S. schools will not provide photocopies of the original foreign university transcript to other schools. Where institutions accept guest students, it should be determined who will send official transcripts to their home institutions. Supplementing the transcript with other relevant information available at the education abroad office may prove valuable.

Wherever possible, it may be useful to keep all course information in a database for future reference since various lists of courses taken abroad can be useful to future students. It might also serve to allow you, the registrar, and your advisory committee to gauge how foreign coursework relates to home-campus courses, thus facilitating the annual interpretive process. Of course, the education abroad office will then need to develop its own guidelines as to how much data it will keep and for how long it will keep them.

For more general information on issues relating to transcripts, consult *Transcripts from Study Abroad Programs: A Workbook*, edited by Eleanor Krawutschke and Thomas Roberts and available from NAFSA.

Transfer Credit for Students Not Enrolled in Home-School Courses While Abroad

From the student's vantage point, being enrolled on the home campus while studying abroad is almost always preferable because it simplifies getting academic credit and financial aid. From an institutional point of view, however, this arrangement necessitates a considerable amount of administrative knowledge, effort, and, consequently, expense. Institutionally, a simpler method of addressing credit questions is to handle them routinely as transfer credit—although this puts a greater burden on students. Many U.S. colleges thus choose not to implement on-campus course enrollment procedures unless they are working with students participating in the institution's own education abroad programs. This is especially true for campuses where the education abroad office has only an advising function and does not administer programs.

A more difficult problem arises if an institution has a laissez-faire approach to students dropping out and does not require prior registration in a course or even notification to any institutional office that a student will be leaving to study abroad. In such cases, it is very important that the education abroad office have detailed advising materials explaining to students precisely what they must do in order to receive transfer credit. This information should be written in cooperation with the office granting transfer credit.

Since a student's enrollment at another institution, domestic or foreign, is not evident until transfer credit appears on their transcript, the policy of not registering them in campus courses while they are abroad can be cumbersome (and irritating) for students because they may appear to have withdrawn from the home institution. Moreover, students who are away from the home campus for an extensive period (typically, an academic year) may be required to apply for readmission. Most important, to avoid the appearance of having formally withdrawn from their degree program, students on federal, state, and institutional financial aid need to have a host institution (either U.S. or overseas) complete a written agreement. Further, to receive federal aid from their home university, eligible students may have to be enrolled concurrently at home while in the study abroad program. U.S. colleges have devised a variety of mechanisms for such, in effect, dual enrollment (see Chapter 5, "Financial Aid," for details).

The home institution can reduce transfer problems by

- providing the student with a means to gain prior approval of courses

- having a way to monitor where they are and what they are doing
- assuring students that coursework taken in preapproved programs will be seriously considered for transfer credit
- helping with home financial aid office procedures, for example, by working with the sponsoring institution to draw up a written agreement. This collaboration also obligates the home institution to verify that transfer credit will be forthcoming, provided student performance meets institutional standards.

If your institution wishes to encourage study abroad, it needs to establish a supportive administrative framework to assist degree-seeking students while they are abroad. This can be harder if students enroll directly in foreign universities, even more so if they plan coursework in nonuniversity settings, such as language institutes or art schools not recognized by the host country's ministry of education. Students considering such study should check with their home school's credit-transfer authorities to see if such study would lead to credit by transfer.

The key to a smooth credit transfer is adequate predeparture preparation. Some U.S. colleges take an extremely conservative approach, informing students that there is no way of determining whether or not they will earn transfer credit until the evaluation is undertaken after they return. Obviously, this leaves the student in a risky situation. Many students, and their parents, will not be willing to take the gamble. In this case, the best practical, short-range option for reducing uncertainty about transfer credit is to make available a list of programs for which other students have earned transfer credit. You can also develop written guidelines to advise students about the issues and how to confront them before they depart and after they return. Making the successes of previous students known can go a long way toward assuring uncertain students.

Predeparture Advising

Predeparture advising helps students both to select an appropriate program and to complete the necessary paperwork to ensure that credit will be earned (provided the students do all that is required). Predeparture advising for students not enrolled in the home institution should have in place a prior approval system for study abroad, with a special advising agreement form (see the NAFSA publication, *Forms of Travel*, by Judith W. Carr and Ellen Summerfield, for examples).

Students, with your counsel, should seek as much signed course-by-course preapproval as possible from their academic advisers and relevant departments for the entire period they will study overseas. At this time students should also be informed about any additional requirements they must meet, such as the need to bring back copies of course syllabi, reading lists, written work, and so on. The signed preapproval document should be reviewed by you and kept on file, and the student should take a copy abroad as a reminder of what was agreed upon. The preapproval form, as a sort of contract, gives the institution and students reasonable transfer estimates and commits each to certain responsibilities.

Grading Practices

Students who will earn credits and grades at a foreign university must understand the host school's grading practices, preferably before applying for overseas study. Some countries' grading systems vary considerably from those in the United States. For example, in some universities abroad students rarely receive a grade of A (or its equivalent) in courses. This factor can deter participation by U.S. students planning on applying to competitive graduate or professional programs in the United States. An interesting discussion of one country's grading system and how it might apply to study abroad can be found in the 1991 PIER Workshop Report on the United Kingdom.

Although some foreign universities convert their own grades to U.S. "equivalents," others do not. Further, many U.S. universities take the position that a *C* is a C no matter where it was earned. Therefore, many U.S. schools allow their students to take some or all of their work abroad on a pass/fail or credit/noncredit basis so concerned students can protect their averages.

Reentry Preparation and Postprogram Registration

You may wish to maintain contact with students while they are abroad, concerning at least reentry preparation and postprogram registration for courses. Should students wish to alter their study plans while abroad, they should contact the home school for approval, which entails consultation with relevant departments. Proposed changes may be the result of changes in curricular offerings available abroad, and may occur beyond the student's control. Also, students' interests develop and change during the foreign experience. Enlightened advisers and institutions will accommodate all reasonable changes, but students must bear responsibility for obtaining approvals.

Postprogram Transcripts

To reduce problems and delays with credit transfer, students should bring home copies of course descriptions, syllabi, term papers, and exams, so that this information may be presented to a campus department for review. The most important item the home campus must receive is official proof that the foreign coursework has been completed. In most cases, the student is responsible for seeing that the official host school transcript or similar documentation reaches the appropriate campus office in a timely fashion. It is useful if a copy of this or of the completed transfer of credit is made available to the education abroad office so it stays informed about the nature of the credit students are earning abroad.

Students need to know that an official transcript is one directly issued to the home institution by a recognized institution and bears a seal or stamp. Many institutions reject informal documents reporting completed courses. The American Association of Collegiate Registrars and Admissions Officers (AACRAO) has guidelines on what constitutes acceptable documentation. The person in your registrar's or admissions office responsible for credit transfer should know about AACRAO's guidelines and resources. Other institutions may only accept credit from institutions that are themselves accredited and not from nonacademic organizations that facilitate study abroad.

Awarding transfer credit for foreign study may follow the lines of granting transfer credit for work completed at other U.S. schools. This means that there should be a department at the home college that offers similar or related coursework, although matching identical courses may often not be possible and should not be required. More flexibility may be required for courses taken abroad since the systems and courses are recognizably different from our own. Students usually must earn grades that meet the home school's minimal standards (generally, this is a grade equivalent to a C or, in some cases, a D).

A controversy has arisen about whether federal financial aid can be granted when institutions refuse to transfer credits for courses with a grade lower than a C, since that is tantamount to treating the transferred course differently from a course taken on the home campus. You should check with your office of financial aid for its interpretation of the federal guidelines governing this area.

The home-institution transcript should note the dates and location of the program, the institution issuing the original credit, the number of credits earned, and the courses taken. Grades are not always computed into the student's home-college grade-point average, although some institutions do this. Students who have not received institutional preapproval or any assurances concerning credit nevertheless may still seek credit for bona fide overseas studies, especially if they directly enrolled abroad. Your institution may have a policy that forbids a retroactive request. But under some circumstances your institution may be willing to review all relevant documentation.

■ Other Credit Situations

Nonrecognized Institutions

A question that sometimes arises concerns whether your institution will accept study abroad course credit from an institution whose transcript it otherwise does not recognize. One solution used by some U.S. schools is to have a special testing policy when students attend programs that appear to be academically sound but whose sponsor cannot produce a transcript that your institution will accept (for example, language institutes). It may charge fees for such credit, or fees connected with testing or a special credit review by faculty.

Independent Research

Most U.S. colleges have departmental special topics, field study, independent study, or readings courses. These may prove valuable to students who must complete required home school coursework during their period abroad or who cannot find courses they need at the host school. A combination of such coursework with the host university's offerings can solve various curricular needs of individual students. For example, honors students could do research for their senior thesis. But students in almost any major wishing to carry out a special project could benefit if their home institutions will allow such enrollment.

Ideally, students negotiate with a sponsoring professor at home to establish a plan of study with due dates, enroll officially at the home school for such courses, and complete substantial work abroad. Using e-mail or faxes, U.S. students can stay in touch with their home faculty to discuss progress during the period abroad. The home university should allow flexibility to provide time, when necessary, for the home faculty to evaluate the work done and submit grades after the usual cycle on campus.

In addition, students concerned about graduating on schedule and unable to find needed courses abroad sometimes take advantage of correspondence courses or other forms of distance learning given or allowed by their home institutions.

Internships

Student interest in internships abroad increases annually. Each U.S. university, usually at the departmental level, sets policies on allowing credit for such work. As demand arises, for example in colleges of business administration, even more students will seek internship opportunities. They also often want credit for those experiences, which may or may not be possible.

It is thus very important for you to know your own school's attitudes and policies on internship credit. Commonly, students arrange for internships through other U.S. institutions or agencies, so the questions of transfer credit discussed above apply. Above all, students need to know if they can expect any credit and whether they can use their financial assistance in such programs, and they need to know this early on. By learning more about internships abroad, you can assist your students as well as interested academic units on our own campus on how best to foster this valuable opportunity for education abroad (see Chapter 17, "Work Abroad and International Careers").

Graduate Credit

Most students in U.S. graduate programs are permitted to study abroad only for research purposes, not for course credits, though exceptions exist in certain areas and the decision is often left to the graduate adviser. Thesis or dissertation credit might be available or even required during an overseas stay—which of course necessitates a minimum degree of registration. Some students may be able to enroll in foreign university courses that might not apply to their degrees but nevertheless provide valuable background and training, for instance in a language that, once mastered, allows them to do further research. Finally, some graduate students are required by the conditions of their loans, fellowships, or grants to establish some sort of overseas base and sometimes even to take courses.

Education abroad offices can assist graduate students and home campus graduate schools in various ways. At the very least, we must be aware of our institution's policies on graduate study abroad and stand ready to help when enrollment procedures and credit issues need development or refinement. What you have learned to do for undergraduates can sometimes find applications for graduate study abroad.

5 Financial Aid

Contributor: Nancy Stubbs

The lack of adequate funding for education abroad ought not to be a problem—apart from the national problem about how to guarantee equal access for all students to all of U.S. higher education. The most important duty of the education abroad administrator is to make study abroad a viable alternative. Through knowledge, communication, and networking, regular and alternate sources of financial aid can be found. The time involved may seem daunting, but the rewards to students make the effort worthwhile.

Prohibitive costs—real or imagined—are one reason students do not consider education abroad when planning their undergraduate careers. The bad news is that study abroad can be much more expensive than initial interest might suggest. The good news is that more and more students can use campus financial aid programs to help pay for the experience. Also, the proliferation of education abroad opportunities over the past ten years makes it easier for students to shop around and find programs that fit their budgets.

Some students may not realize that financial aid resources can be used to make an overseas experience affordable. Others may think there are endless scholarships out there waiting to be tapped for that experience in England. The education abroad adviser is increasingly called upon both to provide access to affordable programs and to be an expert on how students can obtain financial assistance.

At a minimum you need to be able to answer the following questions:

- What is financial aid? How do students qualify for it?
- Can financial aid be used for study abroad? For other forms of education abroad?
- What must my campus do to help students use aid for education abroad?

- Are there funds specifically for education abroad? Can I raise money for this purpose?
- How can I help my students find inexpensive programs?
- Am I willing to assist students in investigating scholarship opportunities for study and research overseas?

This chapter will provide ideas about how to learn about financial aid, make it available to students, develop aid specifically for education abroad, and help students shop for the best education abroad bargains.

∎ What Is Financial Aid?

Sources of Financial Aid

Financial aid can be broadly defined as any help that does not originate with the student or his or her family. Financial aid comes from federal and state governments; institutions of higher education; foundations; ethnic groups, clubs, religious groups, and associations; and private and public corporations.

Federal and state government aid is

- funded by taxpayer dollars, or sometimes by revenue-raising devices like lotteries
- most often need-based (i.e., the student must demonstrate financial need to qualify), but can also be merit-based (the student must show some special quality such as superior academic ability or exceptional skill in art or athletics)
- might be targeted to special groups (underrepresented or other nontraditional students, or students entering certain professions such as teaching)
- in the form of grants, scholarships, loans, and/or work-study

Federal financial aid is governed by Chapter IV of the Higher Education Act of 1965, which is reviewed and reauthorized every five years by Congress. In the 1992 reauthorization, language was inserted stating that it is legal to use federal aid for study abroad if the credit earned by the student is approved by the home institution.

Institutional aid is

- any aid funded by the student's educational institution
- based either on need or merit, or both
- most often awarded as a scholarship or as reduced tuition
- sometimes targeted at special groups (ethnic minorities, students

from other areas of the country, certain majors, first-time college students, etc.)

- awarded only to students enrolled at the institution, which often creates a barrier for study abroad students
- sometimes restricted for use only on the home campus or in the home state

Because of the latter two requirements, students who are heavily subsidized by institutional scholarships often cannot afford to study abroad, even if the program costs less than a year at the home campus. This unfortunate fact sometimes clashes with an institution's stated goal of providing international experiences to all students. On more enlightened campuses, all financial aid is usable for education abroad as an entitlement of enrollment in good standing.

Private aid is

- aid whose source is neither governmental nor institutional
- usually available as scholarships or loans
- most often awarded directly to the student, who then uses it to attend the institution of his or her choice
- sometimes includes requirements that it be used in specific colleges or geographic regions, making it difficult to use while overseas

Private aid has the most diverse eligibility requirements and sources of funding.

Types of Aid

There are several types of aid: grants and scholarships; loans; and work/study or subsidized work. Grants and scholarships are most desirable because they do not have to be repaid. Grants are need-based; scholarships are generally merit-based and are often awarded to people who demonstrate a special ability or belong to a specific group. Most students receiving grants must meet some minimum standard of academic progress (for example, enrolling at least half-time during the term the grant is used, maintaining a minimum grade point average). Scholarship awardees must sometimes undertake specific activities (for example, competing in a sport or making presentations or appearances for the scholarship sponsor).

Loans generally have low or fixed interest rates with long repayment periods. Often repayment does not commence until after graduation. Interest on some loans is paid by the government while the student is in school. The student may not need an established credit rating; many government student loan programs do not require a credit check or a cosigner. Many loan funds are self-renewing, meaning that the money repaid by former students is lent to new students. Loans are also routinely made available to students' parents or guardians, though at less favorable terms and with a required credit check.

Loans have become a major part of the standard financial aid package. This trend worries financial aid administrators because of concern that students are borrowing too heavily and will graduate with insupportable debts. Education abroad advisers must consider whether borrowing heavily to study abroad is in the student's best interest. At the very least, advisers must help students understand the implications of borrowing large sums of money.

Work-study, or subsidized work, is based on the premise that subsidizing student salaries allows an employer to hire more students. Most work-study programs are government-funded and require a student to show financial need.

Work-study can be used while studying abroad if program administrators develop an appropriate process for employing and supervising overseas work. Students may work for the study abroad program or may be placed with nonprofit or governmental agencies. Since the extra effort and paperwork required to comply with federal or state regulations for hiring, supervising, and paying work/study students can be formidable, these opportunities are usually quite limited.

▌ Where Can I Learn More About the Aid Available on My Campus?

Most students receive a combination of governmental and institutional aid, and no two students are likely to receive the same package. You should become familiar with the kinds and sources of aid available at your institution. If you need a basic primer on federal government programs, ask your financial aid office for a copy of *The Student Guide* (published by the U.S. Department of Education). This booklet, which is updated every year, defines federal aid programs and provides information on eligibility requirements, responsibilities of the student and the institution, and more.

Your financial aid office is also the best source of information about institutional aid and the bewildering variety of private aid available to college students. The office probably publishes a brochure or booklet that outlines the types of institutional aid available to students. Funds available through academic departments may be listed; if they are not, see if there is a central source of listings, perhaps on a Web page.

Many universities now provide a search service for students who want to see if they can qualify for private aid. This is usually a low-cost alternative to the many commercial scholarship search services. If your institution does this, find out how it works so you can share the information with education abroad students.

▌ What Financial Aid Can Be Used for Study Abroad?

The ideal answer is everything the student would normally receive, plus any special study abroad scholarships that can be found. Using all types of federal financial aid for study abroad is perfectly legal as long as the student is eligible and your institution has approved the courses taken abroad for credit (more about that later). Many states pattern their financial aid rules and regulations on federal statutes and regulations, so that aid can also be used for study abroad.

Institutional and private aid may or may not be available for study abroad, depending on the restrictions placed on the award. This is a problem for students attending private schools where large scholarships are awarded from endowment funds. All institutional and private aid should be made equally available for overseas study as long as students are participating in legitimate approved programs and receiving credit toward their degrees. Denying this support to needy students sacrifices the principle of equal access to all academic opportunities.

▌ What About Other Kinds of Education Abroad?

Most undergraduate aid is geared toward helping students make progress toward their degrees—for example, earning credit. If the overseas activity involves work, internships, field experience, or volunteer activities, most federal, state, or institutional aid cannot be used.

One exception is if the activity does generate credit. If internships or field experiences are allowed for credit on your campus, find out how that credit is arranged and see if international experiences can be added to the list. The other exception is private aid designed to encourage an international experience even if it does not include formal study. A check of one of the funding books for international scholarships includes grants for travel, social work, undergraduate research, the exploration of architectural trends in major world cities, and unpaid work at various ecological or biological research stations.

■ Common Excuses for Not Allowing Aid to Be Used Abroad

"Federal and state regulations allow aid to be used only on this campus." Federal law says that students cannot be denied aid just because they study abroad as long as coursework is approved for academic credit by the home institution. Federal regulations provide for the use of agreements to contract out a portion of the student's education, thus allowing students to study abroad or even to study at a different U.S. institution.

"Our campus is tuition-driven, so aid must be used to support this university, not some campus in another country." This argument is contrary to regulations when it is used for federal aid. Congress makes federal aid available to help individual students pay for their educations, not to support colleges and universities.

"We don't have enough aid for students who are on campus, let alone for those who study abroad." An important principle of federal and most state aid is that all eligible students must have equal access to that aid. To deny aid to students engaged in a preapproved educational activity would violate the principle of equal access.

"It's too hard to track students who leave campus. Giving them aid would cause problems during an audit." U.S. Department of Education audits are conducted at all institutions that award federal aid. If too many errors are found, the government can restrict or even refuse further aid appropriations. Denying aid for study abroad is against federal law, but it is true that special arrangements must be made to properly track students and their aid.

"It takes too much extra work to handle study abroad students." A lot of extra work is often involved, especially in systems where the student is expected to take care of his or her own aid problems. But extra work is often required for other groups of students. This is not a valid reason to deny access to aid.

It is not in your institution's financial or academic interests to deny aid for study abroad. Students and parents are increasingly aware that federal aid can be used to study abroad and are far less likely to accept excuses. As the study abroad administrator, you are responsible for helping your institution see this. You need to educate financial aid administrators and help develop proper standards and controls to ensure that aid is properly awarded, disbursed, and tracked. Education abroad administrators can and must be involved in this process, both to help students and to help financial aid officers fulfill their legal obligations.

▌ How Is Awarding Aid for Study Abroad More Difficult?

Three financial aid processes become more complicated when students study abroad—qualifying for financial aid, having it disbursed, and applying for it overseas.

Qualifying

- Students must be enrolled in a degree program to receive federal and most state aid.
- Students must beenrolled for a certain number of credit hours during the semesters they receive aid.
- Study abroad credit has to be approved for credit by the home institution before the student leaves. This must be defined on each campus, and an appropriate process devised.
- The 1992 reauthorization of the Higher Education Act allows the "reasonable costs of study abroad" to be used to determine how much aid a student should receive. Students attending low-cost institutions can qualify for more aid if the cost of study abroad is higher.
- Study abroad budgets must be devised, and the cost of each study abroad program must be documented.
- Data the student submits on aid applications or other forms must be verified, sometimes with source documents like tax records and sometimes by verification from the study abroad office. This may occur after the student has left for the study abroad site.

Having Aid Disbursed

- Students must sign award notices, loan promissory notes, and other official forms.
- Federal and most state aid cannot be disbursed more than ten days before the beginning of the term.
- Federal and state grants and some kinds of loans (Direct Loans, Perkins Loans, etc.) are applied to the student's account at the home institution.
- Some other loans (Federal Family Loans) and private scholarships are disbursed in check form. It is possible to designate a power of attorney to pick up checks and to sign them, including federal loan checks.
- Refunds must be disbursed after home campus fees are paid. Some institutions electronically deposit refunds in students' accounts.

- There are federal rules governing whether aid must be repaid if students withdraw in a certain period of time.

Applying for Aid for the Next Semester or Year

- Students have to reapply for federal/state aid each year.
- Satisfactory academic credit must be shown each term, normally by getting passing grades for a full-time load of credit.
- Award notices and other documents must be sent to students for their signatures, or must go to a person with a valid power-of-attorney.
- It may be necessary to allow forms and other documents to arrive after normal deadlines to allow for international mail delays.

■ How Can You Help to Make Financial Aid Available?

Three words come to mind—knowledge, communication, and cooperation: Knowledge of what's available and how it is awarded is necessary to understand how aid might be used by education abroad students. Communication with several offices, including financial aid, the registrar, the bursar, and academic departments, is needed to coordinate special policies and procedures for awarding aid to education abroad students. Cooperation is required to properly award aid, to verify its use, and to avoid violating federal and state law. You must also be a determined and resourceful activist, lobbyist, and proponent for using current funds and for finding new funds. Without your active leadership, nothing new is likely to happen.

Where do you begin? First, accept the fact that financial aid for study abroad will probably involve more work for you and your office, as well as for several other administrative offices on the campus. The extra work is generated by the need to create new procedures. The following questions will help you define where new processes or procedures are needed on your campus:

- Who decides if the study abroad program provides credit acceptable to the home institution? What procedures and forms must be developed?
- How are study abroad students identified and rostered on the aid-giving campus? (Many state loan agencies that monitor the use of student loans now have direct access to campus computer records.)
- Who determines the budget for a study abroad program?
- What if the study abroad program begins earlier or later than the date federal aid can be legally disbursed?

- How are refunds disbursed to students? Should refunds be paid to another institution if it administers the program?
- Who shows students how to get powers-of-attorney and how to use them for loan checks and refunds?
- Who notifies the financial aid office if the student withdraws?
- Who monitors academic progress and records grades and hours once the program is finished?
- What should be done if the grades are not received from abroad before the beginning of the next academic term?
- Who communicates with the student and/or parents if there are financial aid problems while the student is away?
- How does the student get aid applications for the next academic period? Should application deadlines be extended for study abroad students?
- How will study abroad payment schedules be altered to allow students to receive their financial aid before paying?
- How must computer systems be altered to allow for the special needs of study abroad students ?
- Who is going to pay for all of this and do the extra work?

Answering these questions will take time, concentration, and good communication with the appropriate departments. An invaluable discussion of these and other problems can be found in NAFSA's *Financial Aid for Study Abroad: A Manual for Advisers and Administrators* (1989). This book covers strategies for meeting the special needs of study abroad students, models for working with faculty and administrators, and a more detailed explanation of financial aid.

The questions outlined above can be even more complex when the student wishes to go on a program sponsored by another institution. There is a way to contract out part of a student's education and still give that student federal aid. Consortial or contractual agreements allow students studying for a limited time at another college or university to use federal aid. While a contractual agreement will solve some of the problems mentioned above, the agreement will also require another layer of procedure.

One of the best resources for establishing these new procedures is networking. Contact other institutions and see how they have solved similar problems. Call nearby institutions that run study abroad programs. Contact NAFSA or CIEE for a list of institutions with large education abroad programs, or go to regional or national NAFSA or CIEE conferences and meet colleagues. Remember: each campus has individualized systems, so there is never one perfect way to award aid. Even the best advice will have to be molded around your institution's policies, which will require knowledge, communication, cooperation, and skill on your part.

▌ Outside Funding and Scholarships

There is very little in the way of private funding for undergraduate education abroad. The financial aid discussed above can be applied to the costs of studying abroad, as part of Federal support for undergraduate study, but does not specifically represent a Federal commitment to support overseas study. Indeed the faltering beginnings of the National Security Education Program (NSEP) represents the only such Federal commitment of this sort, and its future is not guaranteed. This lack of broad-based funding often limits participation in education abroad to those who can afford it through parental and/or institutional support. Even with greater access to federal and state aid, there are numerous examples of students who do not qualify for need-based financial aid and cannot find an extra $1,000 to $4,000 to participate in a study abroad program.

Because sources for extra funding are limited, the education abroad office must consider three primary strategies: (1) identifying those funding sources which do exist and assisting students to secure them; (2) developing additional funding sources for your campus; and (3) finding and utilizing study abroad programs whose costs are approximately the same as costs at the home campus.

Identifying Funding Sources

Build a modest library of funding books that include scholarships for undergraduate study abroad. Many of the basic international funding books include a few entries for undergraduates. Listings of these books can be found in "Resources for Education Abroad: A Bibliography" (see Appendix). Make these available to students in the study abroad office, or perhaps ask the campus library to stock them in the reference section.

Have you been surfing the web? A good general resource for financial aid is The Financial Aid Information Page (http://www.finaid.org). This free resource on financial aid for higher education lists information about aid, advice about finding aid, and even has a special section for financial aid for study abroad. A different resource is the University of

Minnesota's Online Study Abroad Directory, with over 200 entries (http://www.istc.umn.edu/osad/scholarship-search.html). These new resources are a good supplement to the printed information that has been available for many years.

Other sources of funding are the general grants, loans, or fellowships awarded by private organizations, businesses, churches, and others. Scholarships that can often be used for study abroad may be awarded on the basis of personal attributes (ethnic or religious background, parents' field of employment, children of veterans, descendants of immigrants from specific countries), or on academic focus, major, or career path. The challenge for you and for your students is to locate appropriate and relevant funding.

To find this type of aid, students do not necessarily have to pay the sometimes high fees charged by commercial search services. Most financial aid offices or campus libraries have resource books that list these types of scholarships. Many financial aid offices offer their own search service, which costs less than commercial companies. Students can do their own free search using a web site called fastWeb (Financial Aid Search Through the Web). This site, provided by the Financial Aid Information page and Student Services Inc., allows students to search a database with more than 180,000 scholarships and loans (http://www.studentservices.com/fastweb).

Many cities have branches of international friendship organizations, such as Alliance Française, Goethe Clubs, the Dante Alighieri Society, or the League of United Latin American Citizens. Many such organizations have modest programs that aid students who study or do research in their country of interest. Check your area to identify these organizations and to see if they have scholarship programs (or would like to begin a program).

Rotary International has a yearly competition for students engaged in study or research abroad. The Rotary International Scholarship is a well-known example of support for undergraduates and graduates going abroad. Contact your local Rotary Club to see how students can apply for the scholarships. Ask those local branches if they would consider creating a special award for local high school graduates who study abroad.

The Council on International Educational Exchange (CIEE) offers a limited number of travel grants funded out of its sale of the International Student Identity Card. These awards are specifically for students engaged in study or research in third world countries, where the cost of round-trip transportation is often very high. Students can qualify for these travel grants by (a) participating in a CIEE program, or (b) being enrolled in program sponsored by a CIEE member institution, or (c) being from a CIEE member institution. CIEE also offers small scholarships for minority students from the Robert Bailey Fund. Certain other universities (for example, Syracuse) and agencies (for example, AIFS) offer need- and merit-based scholarships for students participating in programs they themselves sponsor.

However, assisting your students in locating viable sources is perhaps the easier half of the challenge. What remains is the need to work with them to make effective and potentially successful applications, knowing that they will be competing with similar students from other institutions. Competing for scholarship support can be very time-consuming, and even plenty of hard work does not guarantee success. Thus, before your office becomes involved in advising students about scholarship opportunities or administering such scholarship competitions, it is worth spending some time thinking through what is involved.

Administering scholarships for study and research abroad can be rewarding to an office, can bring it into contact with students and faculty who might otherwise not come within its scope, and can bring a certain degree of prestige to the office, if the institution takes seriously the benefits of having scholarship winners from its campus.

Although there are indeed students who can, with almost minimal help, turn in applications that have "winner" stamped on them, experienced scholarship advisers know that most scholarship applicants, successful and otherwise, need advising—some to a surprising extent. Does your office have the resources to provide this kind of support? If not, you will need to try to convince your institution that additional resources are required.

It is no less true for scholarship administration than it is for study abroad in general that faculty support and involvement is often very necessary in order to produce a successful process. This can take a number of possible forms:

- forwarding names of students they regard as strong applicants for particular scholarships—something your office may have to elicit.
- advising students on award-selection criteria and helping them prepare their applications. For example, referring students to faculty who might know which physics departments in France are the most appropriate in certain fields.
- serving on or chairing interview panels, since many scholarships

require an on-campus review process. It is very important to decide on the intent of any campus interview and make this purpose clear both to the applicants and to those on the committee. Accordingly, ask faculty to serve who can best meet the objective of the interview.

- writing strong letters of recommendation and support, which is often the sine qua non for student success.

Equally important is securing an unequivocal institutional commitment to having students win prestigious awards—an honor that not only assists them economically but also augments their academic reputation. Such proactive commitment encourages the campus community to provide students with the guidance they need at various stages of the application process.

As noted in Chapter 8, "Promotion and Publicity," most institutions engage in significant outreach and publicity on behalf of education abroad. Information about scholarships could naturally accompany education abroad promotion. But most offices find they need to develop a whole new strategy to encourage students to pursue scholarships. This strategy needs to take into account the following challenges for the adviser:

Are your students realistically strong candidates for national scholarship competitions? This, of course involves both knowing which scholarships are suitable and feasible for your students, the selection processes, and knowing your students well enough to be able to advise them individually. Your office strategy must also take into account how much effort you can put into getting more applicants, as opposed to working more closely with fewer applicants. Some scholarships may not be administered by the education abroad office itself, which can nevertheless act as an advocate.

Fundraising

Consider raising funds to create an education abroad scholarship fund. Begin by contacting your campus development office to see if an appeal can be worked into an annual fund drive—perhaps targeting alumni who have studied abroad. Working with the development office allows you to get expert advice about raising money plus access to mailing lists, postage, the alumni magazine or newsletter, and the local community. Your pitch should be that academically qualified and interested students should not be denied the educational and career advantages of an overseas experience because they lack money.

Some education abroad offices set up program budgets that generate some funding for students on financial aid. Others charge an administrative fee or surcharge to all students studying abroad, some or all of which is put into scholarship funds. If your office administers programs of its own, or charges students who study abroad a fee for services, consider collecting a small sum per student to fund scholarships.

At the University of Texas at Austin, the education abroad office worked with the student government to add a nominal amount to normal student fees, thereby generating a large pool of money to support overseas study. Other institutions have tried this, and some now have successful study abroad scholarship programs funded by student fees.

Finally, examine your institution's policies for charging study abroad students tuition or other fees. Does your campus make money on study abroad because students are charged normal tuition for the privilege of being enrolled while abroad or for having credit transferred back? Is that tuition then used to pay for the students' program costs and perhaps to fund the education abroad office, or is there a portion that reverts to the university's general fund?

If the latter is the case, build a coalition of students, faculty, and perhaps alumni who are interested in seeing some of that money used to fund scholarships for education abroad. This would be an equitable way to, for instance, help offset the loss of other institutional funds that cannot be used for study abroad. If your institution encourages students to study abroad, this is another way for your administration to put its money where its mouth is.

Finding Low-Cost Programs

The first thing one must do is define "low cost." What is inexpensive for a student at a major private university could be prohibitive for a student at a community college. Ask the following questions:

- What is the total cost for a year's education on your campus? Is there differential tuition for residents and nonresidents? Higher cost for living in town than in dorms?
- What is the actual cost of study abroad programs you administer? Don't forget roundtrip airfare, visa costs, the cost of communicating with people at home, shipping costs, housing, mandatory field trips, and so on.
- What is the actual cost of other study abroad programs that your students may use?

It never works to compare apples with oranges, but many students do just that. They fail to think of the total cost of a study abroad program. Of course, most students probably don't have any idea what they actually spend for a year on your campus, either. As the education abroad administrator, it is your job to help students assess the realistic cost of study abroad and to compare that to the realistic cost of study on your campus.

It is impossible to assess costs for all possible programs—the 1996–97 IIE's *Academic Year Abroad*, for instance, has 4,200 entries. It is possible to target programs used most often by your students and to ask their administrators to provide a breakdown based on your cost categories. This will allow you and your students to compare program costs intelligently.

When you can compare the cost of study abroad to the cost of your students' education, you can search for low-cost programs. Where to look? Start with the list of Rock-Bottom Study Abroad programs, conceived by Jon Heise and Linda McGowan at East Carolina University. This list, which defines what low-cost means and is updated on a regular basis, is available through many study abroad web sites.

You should also put your networking skills together to find low-cost programs for your students. Ask colleagues at similar institutions which programs they use. Watch the study abroad e-mail networks for discussions of inexpensive programs, or ask the networks for feedback on this topic.

You can also ask your faculty for ideas about low-cost programs, but you might find them more interested in issues of academic quality than in cost. Some feel there is a strict correlation between level of quality and cost, so inexpensive programs, they reason, must be academically suspect. Others have had positive experiences with low-cost programs and know that they provide an excellent education for students. If you don't know how your faculty feel about this issue, begin to talk about it, or you may find that you are helping students find programs that are deemed uncreditworthy by academic departments.

Why should you care how much programs cost? If you believe that education abroad is a vital part of an undergraduate's education, you must ensure that students not only have access to quality programs, but that they are programs the average student on your campus can afford. No amount of access to financial aid will convince some students that study abroad is affordable. You must do it for them.

The Office Library And Resources

Contributors: Margaret Warpeha, Larry Laffrey, Catherine Gamon, Heidi Soneson, and Richard Warzecha

An adviser who has been employed for even a minimum amount of time becomes aware of just how much material is available, in various formats, that might be of interest to their students. The development of electronic communications has only made this challenge greater, although we are nowhere near to approaching a paper-free resource office. Advisers, however, do have to be ready to assist their institution in formulating questions as to the kinds of programs that are appropriate for that institution and then maintain a comprehensive resource library on such programs. This could result in a highly selective library of materials or it could be that almost any program is acceptable to the institution. In other words, an adviser needs not only to provide information to students but to engage with the institution on broader questions of suitable education abroad opportunities.

An important question for all education abroad advisers and administrators is how to design, organize, and maintain the office library with resources that are essential for its particular mission. Building a useful library of resources will require that an office carefully evaluate the variables within the following major areas:

- the mission of the office and the institution's commitment to education abroad,
- the academic interests and needs of your students, and
- the availability of resources (monetary, personnel, office space, etc.)

This evaluation should provide some direction through the process of designing, organizing, and maintaining an office library that is both useful and appropriate for the needs of the students and the institution.

▎ Office Mission and the Library

By definition, a good resource library is defined by whether it contains the materials needed for the determined range of advising and programming supported by your institution. Consider at the outset (and review annually) the function and scope of your advising services and/or program administration: this will influence the resources you make available to students and the resources you need to perform your job effectively.

Try to answer the following questions. Your answers will help you determine the amount and type of resources you will need.

- What types of information and services does your office currently provide?
- Does the office provide information and advising on your institution's own programs only? Other institutions' programs only? Or both?
- Is the office responsible for setting up and administering your institution's own programs or consortia programs? Are these programs run exclusively by your office or in conjunction with other academic departments or area studies programs?
- Is the office responsible for awarding academic credit? If so, for your institution's programs only, or for any programs?
- Does the office provide information on credit-bearing academic programs only?
- Is the office responsible for providing predeparture orientations, contact with students while abroad, and reentry programming?
- Does the office also provide information on short-term work opportunities and other experiential programs overseas? Does it offer advice on scholarships for study and research overseas? Travel opportunities?
- Which of these services, if any, are you required by your institution to provide? Which of these services do you voluntarily provide?
- Who are your clients and what are their needs?
- Does the office serve primarily undergraduates or graduate students?
- Is the mission of the office to incorporate an education abroad experience into students' degree programs?
- How are the demographics of your institution (for example, a large nontraditional or commuter population) likely to affect program choice of your students?

- Does the office aspire to serve all constituents of the campus community, including faculty, staff, and alumni? (Is it reasonable to expect that it can do so?)
- What other offices on campus complement your work? Is your office the only office on campus involved in international education, or is it part of an inclusive international programs office? If it is independent, does it share resources and work closely with the office that provides services to foreign students and scholars?
- What is your office's relationship to the academic dean's office? To the registrar's office? To the financial aid or scholarship office? To the office of transfer credit?

▮ Professional Goals versus Institutional Policies

Advisers are often caught between their loyalties to the institution and its stated goals at any given period of time, education abroad "standards of professional practice," and their desire to serve the expressed interests of individual students. This conflict has implications that impinge on the availability of library resources and related counseling. When institutional policy limits students to a few approved programs, the library materials may be limited to these programs as well. As an adviser, what do you do when these programs increasingly do not serve the needs and interests of certain students? Will you make information on other programs available?

Some advisers express a strong desire to provide complete and accurate information about all education abroad opportunities, regardless of institutional policy. If you are one these advisers, you will need to be a strong advocate of expanding overseas opportunities on your campus. Advisers have a professional obligation to work with the faculty and administration to broaden the institution's vision of education abroad, especially by recognizing that traditional models of study abroad do not serve all interests or needs. The 1990 National Task Force on Undergraduate Education Abroad made the following still-valid comment:

> For students who are older, of minority background, employed (46% of full-time students under 25 are employed at least part-time), disabled, or have limited funds, study abroad often is not perceived to be an option. The needs of such students are mostly ignored by the more typical study abroad models and structures. Undergraduate interest in work experiences abroad is increasing

rapidly and certainly at a faster rate than study abroad program participation. Internships, various types of cooperative education arrangements, voluntary service, and independent study/research projects are among the approaches that could generate academic credit or be academically or professionally relevant to degree programs at the home institution. Serving the needs of such students requires an inclusive vision of education abroad, and the policies and resources needed to support it.

Making Resource Choices

No education abroad office is obliged to provide information on all programs available to students. Even advisers with ample budgets, time, and space will make conscious choices about materials, rather than ordering everything and then considering how to use it all. In smaller offices, the issues are even more pointed.

The supermarket approach makes sense only if every program option is open to all students. For instance, compiling a large library on an array of programs may be a fruitless exercise if the institutional policies limit student choice by

- curtailing student access to information about programs;
- allowing students to participate only in approved programs;
- permitting institutional funds, including financial aid, to be applied only to home-institution programs, or a selective number of other programs; and
- denying academic credit to students attending other programs.

If this is the case, it may be more prudent to provide critical information in depth while limiting the breadth of general resources. Nonetheless, an adviser may still choose to provide extensive materials on travel, culture, experiential programs, and scholarships that complement and support the approved programs.

As a further example, if your office has a very narrow scope (for example, you advise only for your own three programs in England, France, and Spain; your institution does not allow financial aid to travel; your office has no role in the awarding of credit; or does not assist students who want to work abroad) obviously your resources can be limited in breadth (but not necessarily in depth).

On the other hand, if the office advises students on all of the institution's own programs, on affiliated programs, and on a variety of programs offered by other institutions and agencies; if it has a voice in matters of credit; if students come seeking information about work, scholarships, and travel abroad; if the adviser works closely with the financial aid office; if the office is responsible for orientation and reentry; or if the office has adequate space and budget, then it may be necessary to have an extensive range of materials on hand. However, even at institutions that actively encourage participation in a large variety of programs, there are still good reasons for limiting materials (for example, to focus student attention, to conserve space, and after consultation with faculty in appropriate disciplines concerning programs that might attract their students).

Most offices fall between these extremes and need to make conscious choices about resources. An adviser may wish to be all things to all people, but neither available space, budget, nor time will allow this. The following are four issues that an office may want to consider when making key resource decisions. But remember, a good resource library should concentrate on materials that best serve the general needs of students from the institution, featuring programs, locations, and opportunities carefully chosen through work with an advisory committee, returned student evaluations, and advice from colleagues in similar settings.

Academic versus Experiential

Often, institutions distinguish between the value of academic and experiential programs. It is important to stress that academic and experiential are not—however precisely defined—mutually exclusive. These terms vary with time and from institution to institution. Even carefully controlled branch-campus programs abroad have an important experiential dimension by virtue of taking place in a foreign culture. Conversely, an internship or a teaching project is often as intellectually and interculturally stimulating as any classroom experience on the campus of a major foreign university. Still, a fundamental question remains as to the degree of emphasis an institution is willing to place on education abroad programs that are not strictly academic in the traditional sense.

The degree of institutional support that now exists for domestic work programs, internships, fieldwork, public service, and independent study is usually a good guide to whether the institution may support nontraditional educational activities abroad. It is worth noting that although many institutions have not taken a proactive stance on experiential education, students at all campuses are beginning to express an interest in such activities, often with the belief that such experiences will prepare them for careers and for life—at least as well as, if not better than, a classroom experience. Unless there is another office on campus that provides such counseling and information, your office or library may need to be ready for requests of this nature (see Chapter 17 for more complete information on work abroad).

Expanding Destinations

Increasingly, advisers are assuming responsibility for diversifying educational opportunities. A very significant percent of the U.S. undergraduates who study abroad still go to western Europe. Current faculty strengths and institutional interests may only reinforce these traditional patterns. Complicating the matter further is the fact that programs in developing countries are more difficult to establish and maintain. However, student interest in studying or working in other regions is growing in spite of the established preferences.

Through the efforts of education abroad professionals, some institutions have dramatically increased the numbers of students choosing sites outside of Western Europe. NAFSA and CIEE have encouraged more programming in Asia, Africa, and Latin America. Several scholarship programs (ISIC, NSEP, IIE Regional Awards, Department of Education Doctoral Dissertation Research Abroad in Non-Western European Area Studies grant, etc.) either specify or give preference to students studying in nontraditional sites. Information on programs in western Europe is more abundant than information on opportunities in the developing world, but such information is available (see Chapter 12, "Promoting Whole World Study Abroad").

A dramatic and effective way to challenge students to consider nontraditional locations is to provide ample and attractive materials on these locations. The following are a few tips to augment existing resources and to generate interest in specific geographical areas:

- Work with language departments and/or area studies programs. Good relationships with departments can lead to faculty referring individual students and possibly even bringing a class to your library. Certain areas, whether emphasized in the home-campus curriculum or not, capture students' interest and imagination because of current political or social developments.

- Obtain useful written resources focusing on nontraditional sites, such as articles from *Transitions Abroad* magazine.

- Identify students who have returned from study, work, or travel to nontraditional destinations. Students who have had recent, positive experiences abroad are often eager to share their experiences and to get involved in international activities on the home campus. Returnees can help promote interest in nontraditional education abroad sites by sharing their personal experiences with prospective students through roundtable talks, presentations, and poster sessions.

Financial and Access Issues

Should an education abroad library only contain information on programs within the economic reach of the average student? This is an important and troubling question. Most students finance education abroad from the same resources that pay for their domestic studies. Sensitivity to program costs is important when collecting and displaying information.

A sensible solution is to balance your library with information on appealing programs at a range of costs, perhaps concentrating on programs that most students can best afford. You should also be taking a proactive stance in lobbying for the fullest possible use of financial aid funds for study abroad, as well as collecting information on scholarships, fellowships, and grants available to students (see Chapter 5, "Financial Aid").

Coordinate Efforts with Other Campus Offices

Not having exactly the right book or pamphlet on hand for every single student is not as much of a problem if your campus has other resources. You may choose not to duplicate materials that are available in other campus units or in the community (for example, a career office, internship office, college or local library, travel agency, International Center). Being knowledgeable of the resources in these units so that you can direct the search is a valuable service to students. For education abroad advisers, this knowledge will be useful when hoping to coordinate resources and efforts with similar or related offices on campus.

For example, if you are severely lacking in office space, you may want to consider working with the college library to house copies of the frequently used books (IIE, Peterson's, etc.) or an entire education abroad section. This has several advantages. The main library will have more extensive hours, and more space for materials and for students who are doing research. In addition, the increased accessibility will broaden the base of students who are exposed to and become interested in international activities.

On the other hand, if your campus is very large and students are just as likely to seek help in one office as another, it may be reasonable to have as much information available in as many locations as possible or have the many offices specialize in a certain area. With the rapid growth of the Internet and electronic communication, offices are finding that it is no longer necessary to house all information in one physical location.

Linking the information provided by the various locations on campus via the World Wide Web, creates, in essence, a 24-hour office that allows students to research their overseas options by "visiting" all of the campus Web sites related to education abroad. Technology is affecting both the amount of information that can be found and the means to both access and disseminate this information. The use, by advising offices, of electronic communications and information storage on Web pages fosters this sense of an ever open office and also allows students to research their overseas options without having to come into the office. In the next few years there will be tremendous challenges to advising offices in determining just how they will make use of this new means of communication (see Chapter 7, "Computerizing Operations").

■ Setting Up a Resource Library

The Basic Library

The space available for the education abroad library is of paramount concern. A full-scale, multimedia resource library requires extensive space, not only for the bibliographical materials, but also for computers, copy machines, typewriters, printers, fax machines, and the furniture and equipment for performing a range of various administrative and clerical functions. Space is necessary for students to sit down and pore over materials; a presentation area for small meetings is very important; and some private space for advising students is essential.

Ideally, all libraries would have enough space to meet all these needs—and be located conveniently in the middle of campus. However, this ideal set-up is rarely the norm, and most advisers have less space than they need. Although it is possible to operate in a room that serves as your office and as a repository of materials, the minimum standard is two rooms: one for materials and one for individual counseling. If a third is available, this room can function as a general reception area staffed by an assistant, secretary, or peer counselor who also helps direct students to the information. The following is a generic grouping of the types of materials a well-stocked education abroad library is likely to contain.

Institutional Policy Information

Offices might want to produce their own materials to give an overview of the office resources; to explain institutional policies on program selection and approval, credit, financial aid, and other essential concerns; and to clarify the advising process and application procedures for your and/or other programs. This can be done on single information sheets or can be summarized in a handbook. Other information sheets can be developed to summarize opportunities in certain geographical areas, for students in particular academic disciplines, for minority students, for students with disabilities, or for certain categories of pursuits (for example, summer work abroad). Many of your colleagues will have extensive collections of such materials and will be glad to share copies.

Reference Books

IIE's *Academic Year Abroad* and *Vacation Study Abroad,* and Peterson's *Study Abroad Guide* give an overview of the full range of study abroad programs now available to undergraduates, though the IIE volumes list many programs open only to sponsoring institution students. CIEE's *Whole World Handbook*—no longer in print, though recent editions are available—had the advantage of listing study, work, and travel abroad programs, but the disadvantage of listing only those programs sponsored by CIEE member institutions. What still is lacking is a comprehensive reference book listing overseas institutions that accept direct enrollment inquiries from U.S. students and that also have support offices in place.

Program Brochures and Catalogs

Your office will most likely be flooded with promotional brochures. Many will be well-designed, with seductive prose, sophisticated graphics, and photographs. The best will detail with candor what the program is and what it is not, what it offers and what it does not. What you keep for your library and what you throw away will depend on considerations enumerated above. For most students, seeing a range of opportunities and program pitches is a useful exercise that aids in making a final selection. Consider taking advantage of the many materials that are now available on-line (see Resources for the Virtual Library below)

Foreign University Catalogs

If students are interested in directly enrolling at foreign universities—for undergraduate or graduate study—it is worthwhile to house foreign university catalogs. The *International Handbook of Universities* (Stockton Press), *Commonwealth Universities Yearbook* (Association of

99

Commonwealth Universities), and *The World of Learning* (Europa Publications) are good references on foreign universities, listing addresses, phone numbers, departments, and faculty. Many foreign university catalogs are now being mailed to U.S. education abroad offices; some are also available on microfiche, which saves file space but requires a special reader. In addition, many foreign universities have Web sites and include their catalogs along with other materials. Some catalogs provide extensive information on the curriculum that can assist students get preapproval for courses.

Program Evaluations/Peer Advising

Many advisers place copies of evaluations completed by recent participants alongside program brochures. An alternative is to arrange evaluations or peer advising forms by country (and often, within this, by city or region). Peer advising forms are completed by study abroad returnees to help prospective students select study programs and thus include information not always asked on evaluation forms. It is useful to give students a way to learn from past participants either through a system of peer advising or another way of encouraging student-to-student contact. Evaluations are an invaluable resource as long as students respect the confidentiality of past participants and are aware that every student is likely to have a different experience (see Chapter 18, "Program Evaluation").

Scholarship, Fellowship, and Grant Information

This information comes in many forms: pamphlets, fliers, chapters of books, complete reference volumes and databases with search capabilities (one is currently available on-line). Screening can help identify false leads and blind alleys, as well as those support schemes not available to undergraduates. However, an office has to come to some decision as to what it means to provide information on scholarships. Does it then provide advice to students applying for these awards; will the adviser read over proposals, give advice on interview technique, and perhaps even involve faculty in working with students on their applications? While it can be argued that involvement in scholarship advising and administration can bring prestige to the office and credibility in the eyes of faculty and the administration, it can mean a considerable investment of time (see Chapter 5, "Financial Aid").

Magazines

From time to time, interesting magazine articles appear that support education abroad or highlight the culture or politics of a particular country. It is helpful to place such features in the files with program brochures and country information. *Transitions Abroad* magazine, which appears six times a year, is a unique compendium of information and perspectives on study, work, travel, and living abroad. Many articles are written by students or other program participants, and each issue contains new ideas and solid leads on how to obtain more information; there is also a resource guide series. This is a magazine students actually read, so it is worth subscribing to it, as well as excerpting and filing some of the articles separately. NAFSA's quarterly magazine, *International Educator*, while not devoted exclusively to education abroad, also contains valuable features. More recently, a more theoretical and academically oriented journal, *Frontiers: The Interdisciplinary Journal of Study Abroad*, promises to provide a forum for the discussion of issues that face study abroad.

Videos, Films, CD-ROMs, and Slides

Your library may include a set of slides, photos, or films taken by past program participants. More and more programs are also making brief videos available. Videos or CD-ROMs made by your own office (an excellent student project) can be used to cover the basics of study abroad before a student sees an adviser. IIE also has a good general video called "Planning for Study Abroad." Not all such products are equally appealing or effective, but at their best, images of living and learning abroad, coupled with honest responses (given on site) from program participants, can have a great impact on students.

Interactive Self-Advising Programs

Some attempts have been made to produce interactive computer programs to take students through the process of how to choose an education abroad experience. At the time of writing, however, there has not been one that has been successful enough to become a model for the field, although AIFS's Web page is one indication of what will be possible in the next few years.

Classifying Library Materials

How you classify materials is as important as having the materials. Even a small collection of books and brochures needs to be carefully organized. If a brochure is in the library, but cannot be found when it is needed, it becomes useless. Therefore, it is very important to design a system that is orderly, user-friendly for students, and relatively easy for staff to maintain. Remember, it should be as easy to retrieve materials from the library as it is to file them away. The following are two examples of how some education abroad offices have organized their library materials.

Files

Some libraries divide program materials into files that are either country- or region-specific. Each of these files is then subdivided into categories such as study, work, travel, funding, and general (dealing with more than one category). These files can be housed in a file cabinet or in "magazine boxes" placed on a shelf. One drawback to this option is that materials within each folder are difficult to organize and will get out of order.

Binders and Boxes

Some libraries place education abroad materials in three-ring binders and magazine boxes. All materials are first divided into sections such as study, work, travel, and scholarships abroad. Within each section, materials are then subdivided by region, country, or other designated category. Materials that are hole-punchable are properly labeled and placed in the appropriate binders. Thicker materials (books, videotapes, etc.) are similarly labeled, but placed in the corresponding box next to the binder. Materials stay in order if stored in binders, but binders make filing and copying more awkward.

There is not one perfect solution that works for every office or even all types of materials. Taking into consideration the space available, education advisers should experiment and design a system that keeps things in order, is accessible to students, can handle heavy usage, and is easy to maintain. Try a variety of clerical supplies (for example, color-coded files and labels, plastic covers, clip binders, etc.) and see what works. Tip: Visit education abroad offices in the area to get an idea of how others have organized their libraries.

Once the library has an established system, advisers will need a way of explaining it; if the adviser is the only one who understands its logic, it is of no use. An important part of an advising appointment is instructing the student on how to use the resources. An ideal advising office would have a self-help introductory guide to the office and its resources. Not only does this help the student, but it also reduces time spent on answering very basic questions.

Collecting Library Materials

The bulk of program brochures is likely to arrive unsolicited and free, but many valuable items will not. You will need to place your name on certain mailing lists and research and order new materials. You will need to decide how to spend your budget wisely, since you probably cannot buy everything. Also, take the time to weed out superseded materials; if you don't, the library will no longer be useful. It is essential to consider the time, staffing, and procedures involved in periodically editing and updating library resources. The positive side to this chore is that it is a useful training tool for the beginning adviser or peer counselor.

The Virtual Library

With the advent of the use of the Internet on campuses, many of the resources traditionally stored on other media have migrated to this new technology. Although the size of an office's staff and budget will often determine how much it makes use of the Internet, choosing to have part of your resources in a "virtual" library has some advantages. By creating a Web site, even an office with a small physical space may be able to provide a great deal of valuable information via the Internet. Certain resources, for instance databases, can be made more accessible than before. By linking your Web site to other on-line resources, you can easily add resources with little cost and time.

On the other hand, creating a Web site can have drawbacks. Setting a site up can be both expensive and time-consuming. It might also require computer skills that your current staff lacks. To save money, you may want to consider using student talent in developing a Web site. Often computer-savvy students can provide both the technical understanding of how to create a Web site as well as some ideas of how students might best be reached using this new medium. The key is to communicate exactly what you want and need. When starting a Web site or planning to incorporate Internet access in your office, the first stop should be your institution's office of computer services. They will be helpful for both training on how to use the Internet as well as how to create your own Web pages.

During your planning stages, advisers should also take the time to consider other issues involved with "going digital." First of all, consider how providing information via the Internet might influence how the office makes contact with students. Could students choose not to come into the office because they feel they have received all the information they need on-line? Or is this risk worth taking considering the larger audience you can reach?

103

Second, how much information should an office put on-line? Most successful sites started with humble beginnings and grew over time, so it might be good to plan a slow, thoughtful growth of the Web site. Keep in mind, it is not feasible to put every resource on-line and keep it up to date, so it may be wise to decide which are most important to have on the Web site.

Once these larger issues are resolved, offices will then need to decide whether they would like to set up their own Web sites, offer Internet access within their library, or simply list useful Internet resources within their resources in other media. The question of how offices, which link to many other sites, can assure credibility of such information is an issue that will need to be faced by any advising office that encourages students to use that office's Web page to investigate overseas opportunities

Below are some resources that offices might consider including in a "virtual" resource library. This list is not meant to be comprehensive, but should give an idea of what is becoming available on the Internet.

Searchable On-line Databases

The Institute of International Education (http://www.iie.org) recently established on-line access to all program information in its printed guides, but such access is limited to IIE's Educational Associates. Peterson's Guides (http://www.petersons.com), Studyabroad.com (http://www. studyabroad.com), and The International Study and Travel Center at the University of Minnesota–Twin Cities (http://www.istc.umn.edu/osad/) have established on-line directories for selecting study abroad programs. Currently, the only on-line database for study abroad scholarships is provided by The International Study and Travel Center's Online Study Abroad Directory (http://www.istc.umn.edu/osad/). This site emphasizes scholarships open to undergraduates. These resources vary widely with the services they provide, and advisers should experiment to find which are most helpful.

Useful Education Abroad Web Sites

For general information concerning work, study, and travel abroad, check out the Council on International Educational Exchange's site (http://www.ciee.org) or The International Opportunities Program (IOP) at UCI'S Center for International Education (http://www.cie. uci.edu/~cie/iop/), and "Resources for Colleges and Universities in International Exchange" (http://www.usc.edu/dept/overseas/links.html) created by the University of Southern California. To find information concerning visa applications, check the U.S. State Department's Bureau of Consular Affairs Home Page (http://travel.state.gov) or The Embassy Page (http://www.embpage.org/).

Overseas University Web Sites

Many universities abroad have their own Web sites. The information provided often includes course descriptions, staff and student directories, and general descriptions of the institution. This can be useful for students planning to directly enroll at a university abroad, as well as those planning to go on an exchange or other study abroad program hosted by a foreign school. Useful resources for finding foreign university home pages include Yahoo! (http://www.yahoo.com/Education/Universities/) and Christina DeMello's list of universities abroad (http://www.mit.edu:8001/people/cdemello/univ.html).

NAFSA's Web Site

Finally, NAFSA's Web site (http://www.nafsa.org) provides additional resources for international educators, and is linked with other sites of interest to NAFSA members. Please keep in mind that the URLs given may change over time. Part of the responsibilities of maintaining a resource library with Internet information is insuring that the these addresses are current. To find sites whose URLs may have changed, use search engines (InfoSeek, Yahoo!, etc.).

▌ Keeping Yourself and Your Library Up to Date

Although the bulk of the resources will be available to everyone, advisers will need to determine what resources they require—as a professional—in order to have the background information to assist others. Beyond basic NAFSA, IIE, and CIEE reference guides and training manuals, advisers may want to keep abreast of new developments in the field through subscriptions to professional newsletters and magazines, such as the *NAFSA Newsletter* and the IIE *Associates Newsletter*. Many organizations now have Web sites and through list servs and e-mail, communication with study abroad colleagues is faster and easier than before.

You will probably need to have annual copies of IIE's *Academic Year Abroad* and *Vacation Study Abroad*, and updated catalogs of the most popular study abroad programs with your students. It is also wise to keep up with new publications on the history, development, and professional practice of international educational exchange. Your should make sure you know what publications are currently made available from NAFSA,

CIEE, IIE, AACRAO, SIETAR, Intercultural Press, and AIFS. In addition, advisers may wish to have a variety of reference materials on cross-cultural theory and training.

The bibliography found in the Appendix is recent and inclusive. It includes hard-copy and Internet resources on study, work, and travel abroad and consists of three major sections:

- A selection of basic reference materials for the education abroad adviser, divided into various subcategories.
- Items considered to be essential to advisers or to a basic resource library (marked with an asterisk).
- A list of organizations and publishers that can furnish advisers with the publications listed in the bibliography as well as publication lists and/or free information on study-, work-, and travel-abroad.

Computerizing Education Abroad Operations

Contributors: Ruth M. Sylte and James L. Buschman

Computer technology can help the education abroad office operate more efficiently and more professionally, enabling overworked staff to devote more time to advising and program developmen, and less to mundane paperwork and record keeping. An initial investment of resources and patience (while the office adapts to new systems and resources) will be amply repaid by innumerable long-range benefits.

W hen the SECUSSA Sourcebook was published in 1975, computers were far from the thoughts of most education abroad advisers and administrators. That they existed was known; that they were able to store information was accepted; but that they might transform the operation of education abroad offices was inconceivable. Yet two decades later computers have become as much a part of the day-to-day life of the education abroad office as advising students and implementing programs.

But the rapid technological advances in computers, software, and their uses mean that computer advice quickly becomes outdated. For example, in the early 1990s the U.S. Department of Education awarded NAFSA a grant to consider the uses of technology, especially as a means of electronic communication, and how developments might affect the conduct of international educational exchange. Those involved in the project were encouraged to brainstorm about possibilities without necessarily considering what was practical or whether the technology existed.

One idea they discussed concerned a futuristic means of obtaining information. Wouldn't it be great, the project participants wondered, if one could find study abroad opportunities, by accessing a remote site and finding all the program brochures, including graphics, already loaded? One would be able to move from this site to many other sites. In other words, there would no longer be a single site where all information would be stored, but rather many individual sites, each connected to the others. This seemed little more than a pipe dream at the time, so the project participants moved to more realistic goals.

Within a year of the close of the project, international educators were talking about the World Wide Web and beginning to use it. What had been a fanciful hope is now a practical reality for many campuses.

This rapid development in computer technology shows no sign of slowing down. This chapter should therefore be seen as containing not only sound counsel in general computer matters, whatever the technological changes, but also technical counsel that, in due course, will become dated. Therefore, for further and ongoing guidance, education abroad advisers and administrators are encouraged to consult members of MicroSIG (NAFSA's Microcomputer Special Interest Group), as well as their own on-campus or local computer professionals, to keep abreast of developments in computer technology and software applications.

The purpose of this chapter is (1) to guide advisers and administrators as to the hardware they need; (2) to discuss the different types of software now available and how each can be used in support of an education abroad office; and (3) to offer some advice on the value of new means of electronic communication.

■ An Overview

As most observers would readily admit, computer technology has revolutionized the using, storing, and sharing of information. In so doing it has transformed huge areas of social, professional, and organizational life, including just about all aspects of the professional field of education abroad. Today, even the smallest college office can benefit from (and, equally important, afford) what computers and related communications systems offer. Such technical assistance has ceased to be the exclusive preserve of the large universities with graduate programs in science, engineering, and technology.

In effect, no education abroad office can accomplish its many tasks efficiently without the assistance of computers—especially as it struggles to maintain contact with its many constituencies with limited staff, space, time, and budgets. Moreover, the effective use of computers no longer requires the education abroad professional to possess highly technical knowledge. You can now take advantage of the various ways in which computers help you record, collect, analyze, disseminate, and share information—activities that are at the center of any education abroad office.

In addition, computer and software costs (relative to scope, speed, and performance) have declined. Even offices with modest budgets can avail themselves of this indispensable technology. In order to get the most out of your investment, however, it is still necessary to train staff in the most efficient use of the technology.

Following is an overview of the basic components of a fully computerized office, along with some considerations you should keep in mind in relation to assessing your own office needs, whether you are in a start-up or a review situation.

The Basic PC Unit

The basic desktop PC (an IBM/IBM-clone personal computer using a DOS or Windows platform or a Macintosh or Macintosh clone running Mac OS) has become increasingly powerful, with more applications (software) and accessories available than even dreamed of a decade ago. Personal computers are, as noted, becoming simultaneously less expensive and more powerful. Experts once predicted that the capacity of the mainframe would be the capacity of the personal computer six years later. They were right. This redounds to the benefit of all users on limited budgets.

The world of microcomputing remains divided on which of the two principal PC platforms is better for the office. The divide is, however, rapidly becoming moot. Files may now be shared easily among a number of Windows/Mac platforms and software applications. Sharing files among Windows, DOS, and Mac platforms is often a simple matter of using conversion programs that are easily available and are now built into many software packages as a standard feature.

The world of computing has now defaulted to color monitors. Modern, high-resolution color screens are easier to read than older screens. For staff members who will be on a computer for the majority of their workday, it may be wise to consider getting larger monitors that help avoid eye strain and other computer-related injuries.

Laptops

Today's laptops can now perform all the tasks previously limited to desktops—with the added advantage of mobility. Amazingly versatile and powerful notebook and even pocket (for example, Newton) computers are now sold with built-in modems, CD-ROM players, fax capability, sound cards and much more.

This is the age of laptop and notebook computers. People who travel often find laptops very useful, as do people who take their work home. As noted above, laptops and notebooks and their software should be compatible with the software used in the office. By "telecommuting" via a modem and laptop it is possible to access the office computer and/or the Internet from home or while on the road. But remember that laptops still are, by definition, portable, meaning that screens are small and the risk of eye-strain with extended usage is real. Ideally, an office laptop *supplements* other office systems and equipment.

LANs

Local area networks (LANs) are more and more the rule, providing much flexibility through the sharing of resources and files between offices and coworkers. It is now standard for organizations to have an internal network that links individual offices to a larger central computer that acts as a file server. On a LAN, computers and printers work through phone lines or Ethernet connections. PCs and Macs can be integrated onto the same network.

Any move toward a LAN should be thoroughly investigated with the campus systems administrator, university computer center, and telecommunications office to answer some of the following questions: Is current equipment adequate? What will be the complete cost of a LAN? What is expected from a LAN? How much trouble is involved in maintaining a LAN? LANs do take time to maintain, but they offer the opportunity to share files without using disks; maintain officewide calendars; store and retrieve archival information; and communicate easily from office to office.

Disk Space and Expanded Memory

Software programs are becoming larger, which means they occupy more memory and space on a computer's hard disk. It is important to consult the systems administrator or the computer center on campus to ensure that computers have sufficient hard-disk space (to store software applications) and RAM (random-access memory, used to open and operate the applications) to accommodate future developments. When purchasing any new computer equipment, the possibility of future upgrades in memory should always be considered. Study abroad offices tend to have little money allocated to the replacement of computers, so it pays to think ahead and get advice.

Printers

There are choices galore! Important considerations are the per-page cost, the quality of printing (impact, laser, or even color printing), print style, speed of printing, ability to print complicated graphics, and the amount of noise the printer produces. Printing multicopy forms may require an impact printer, while many other tasks are often easily handled by laser printers. Printer speed is an important consideration. A slow printer bought to save money may in fact cost more in the wait time required to complete the document.

Internet Access via Modem

Internet access is growing exponentially—both on and off college campuses—presenting the education abroad office with new opportunities to promote services to students through World Wide Web sites, newsgroups, listserv and mailing lists, with students having access to the information 24 hours a day, even without entering the office. Most sophisticated modern computers have an internal modem, a unit that allows your PC to "talk with" any other computer with Internet access. The Internet can be accessed via an Ethernet connection through a LAN or by a direct link to the university mainframe computer. It can also be accessed through a dial-in connection using a computer with a modem. The speed and sophistication of modems have increased dramatically in recent years, paralleling their decline in price. Such modems make it possible to connect at very high speeds over ordinary phone lines to other computers and servers around the world.

Modems (including wireless remote modems) may also provide the ability to send and receive faxes and offer voice-mail capability, reducing or eliminating the need for separate stand-alone fax machines or telephone answering machines in a modern education abroad office.

Scanners

Scanners, also coming down in price, can copy almost any text or graphics directly into your PC files, saving hours of laborious data-entry and formatting time. If your office cannot afford one, your campus may have units you can borrow for specific tasks.

Computer Furniture

Unless your office's existing furniture accommodates your new computer equipment perfectly, be prepared to invest in desks and chairs made specifically for computers. The new equipment must be comfortable to use and ergonomically correct. If it is not, it may go unused or contribute to serious health problems, such as repetitive stress injuries (RSIs) or carpal tunnel syndrome. Check with your computer center and health center to get advice.

▌ Assessing Goals, Needs, Support, and Resources

In this rapidly developing technological environment, making decisions regarding equipment can be a complex matter that will require using campus resources as much as possible. Here's how to get the most for your money—buying only what you need and can best use.

Step back a little and assess what it is your education abroad office does that computerization can help it to accomplish. Which of the following is key to your needs? Is your aim to store information in a more efficient and retrievable manner? To develop better means of communication through electronic mail? To encourage desktop publishing within the office? To benefit from the World Wide Web to publicize programs and services? All of the above? Something more? It is likely that you will have selected more than one of the above, perhaps even all.

Whatever your answer, the main point is that it is vitally important for an office to establish clear goals and priorities before purchasing or upgrading any equipment. Sufficient time should be allowed for all staff to have a say in the process of determining office needs. Before looking through computer catalogs and visiting showrooms, it is important to examine the office, determine its needs, talk to knowledgeable colleagues and professionals both on campus and off, and gain some understanding of the larger issues involved in purchasing computer hardware and software.

Budgets and Real Costs

The real cost of computerization is always more than the price tag on the hardware. You will require software programs and ergonomically comfortable and safe computer furniture. Staff must be trained, which will take both time and money. Computer equipment will occasionally need servicing, and, eventually, upgrades in power, storage space and memory will be needed to keep up with advancing technology. Building an office's computing capacity by increments over a period of years, rather than investing in a complete system all at once, may be the best approach. It is important not to begin by buying older systems that are already outdated and perhaps cannot be serviced. The convenience factor should be considered in addition to an item's price.

The more expensive versions of some equipment and some software programs may cut labor costs significantly because they are quicker, can accomplish more with a single command, and may not have to be replaced as often. A rule of thumb is to replace hardware every four years to remain somewhat up-to-date with the technology. One way to do this is by replacing 25 percent of the office computer hardware each year. This strategy spreads the expense over a manageable period and is a much better option than replacing all equipment and software at the same time. This complete overhaul can be an unfortunate event that can cost tens of thousands of dollars in one budget cycle!

Upgrading

Obsolescence is an unfortunate but standard fact of owning and using computers. Sadly, machines bought only two or three years ago will seem to be out-of-date if your needs increase or better technology has appeared on the market. On the other hand, changing should not be a matter of fashion, but rather of genuine utility. Thus, if word processing, basic record-keeping, and Internet access are sufficient for your office, older computers will still function adequately, though all equipment will sooner or later wear out. Whether or not to upgrade might depend on your answers to two basic questions:

First, how much can your office afford to spend? Is there an annual capital budget that will allow you to purchase some new equipment every year, or will this need to be lobbied for at longer intervals in competition with other campus offices? Compare the costs of upgrading parts of an old machine to purchasing a new one. Long-term budget planning is usually essential when dealing with computer needs, so that you need to give some forethought not only to how long it might be before a whole system might need replaced, but how funds will be established for such major purchases.

Second, what truly needs to be upgraded? If one major upgrade to the system (memory or hard drive) has already been made, it may be worthwhile to upgrade the microprocessor. If nothing has been upgraded for two or three years, a new machine may be a better option. If upgrading one component means having to upgrade others, it is easy to spend a considerable amount of money that could be better used to purchase a new machine. Microprocessors, the brains of a computer, have consistently doubled in speed and halved in price about every 18 months. It is probably not cost-effective to invest in upgrades that will only temporarily extend the life of an old computer—a lifetime that grows shorter with each passing day.

The bottom line is that it may be better to think of a computer the way many people think of automobile, by becoming prepared to invest in a new one every three to four years. Cars can take people from here to there, but a computer has the ability to bring the world to your doorstep.

Training

Every upgrade in equipment or software will impose a learning curve on the people who are going to use the new technology. It is important, therefore, to be cautious about technology and associated "bells and whistles"—but not so cautious that your systems become outdated as soon as they are installed. Although no one wants recent innovations to pass them by, one should avoid investing in technology that exceeds staff skills (potential, as well as current) or overall office needs. Concentrate on what is necessary to do business, and then choose equipment and software that meets those needs while allowing for growth. Once the system and software have been decided upon, staff should immediately begin preparing for their use.

Courses taken before the equipment arrives can instill enthusiasm and set appropriate expectations, but it is essential to be realistic about the time required to completely install an effective computer system or application. It can take anywhere from one week to a month to "computerize" an office, and the first six months with the new system may seem very labor intensive as the staff gets used to the technology. To get a good return on any investment, a significant commitment must be made on the front end; serious discussions should take place among all staff who will be using the new equipment.

A common concern about computers is that they do not seem to make work any easier because it can take so long to learn to exploit their (and their operators') full potential. Although there will always be an intensive learning period when dealing with new and innovative technology, an extra investment in training will save much time and frustration when the technology is finally in use. For most new users, any available computer (or applications) class will be advantageous. If time, money, and ambition are limited, then choosing simple, user-friendly technology is the best.

Maintenance and Service

It is good to be familiar with what can go wrong with computers and to be prepared to deal with problems. The more sophisticated the equipment, the more technical expertise will be required to operate and maintain it. Safety nets should be built into administrative budgets. Offices are increasingly realizing the necessity of having at least one staff member with some degree of technological expertise. If possible, someone within the office should be designated as a technology troubleshooter, with a job description reflecting this additional duty. Without such a person, outside resources will need to be called in. If they exist on campus, the costs may be minimal. The cost of this service from outside contractors, however, can be very high.

Campus Coordination

Assessing the existing systems on your campus, especially if there is a campuswide standard that has been determined, is of course essential. Most institutions find it advantageous to sign contracts with software and hardware vendors. The systems administrator, campus computing center, or the equivalent can help determine what brands and models are available at special prices—and which are specifically excluded. It may also be necessary to consider what, if any, computer equipment will be shared with other offices, since their requirements and priorities may also need to be taken into account.

You should research what equipment or software your institution actively supports through knowledgeable staff or service contracts. Many software packages are free to educators or are available at a minimal cost. Bargain computers and software programs for which no local service is available, or that are incompatible to existing programs, are very poor investments.

Data Security

Protection from accidental loss and theft are important concerns. Most software can be set to produce automatic backups every time an original file is changed. In addition, it is wise to have some form of complete backup run on each hard disk, preferably every day. Peripherals and software can do this or, for computers on a LAN, a nightly backup can be done of all files on the servers. The systems administrator will have more information.

Data can also be protected from unauthorized eyes. While some computers actually have locks and keys that prevent unapproved use, it is more common for software to require a series of security passwords before allowing access. It is especially wise to keep a password lock on initial access to a computer, to e-mail, and to any databases where confidential information may be found. Most computer security experts agree that the most secure passwords are six to eight characters in length, contain no recognizable words (from any language), and comprise a mixture of letters (both upper and lower case) and numerals. Personal passwords should never be given out to anyone.

Software Programs and Applications Compatibility

As with hardware, software programs should be capable of "talking" with each other. There will be many occasions when you will want to be able to send a personalized form letter to a list generated from a database, or to pull a financial table from a spreadsheet to use in a newsletter. These tasks can be easily accomplished when software programs are compatible. Office software needs should be assessed and software purchases standardized. Early discussions with staff will pay off in the end when everyone is comfortable with the software choice(s). Colleagues' preferences may be taken into account but it is essential to find out which software programs are supported by the systems administrator or computer center, especially if the campus has a multiple-user license that makes certain packages affordable for on-campus users. Once it is decided what software is most appropriate all staff should be encouraged to learn and adapt to this software.

Applications

Of the many computer applications currently in use in advanced and well-equipped study abroad offices, many are useful to any office. The systems administrator or campus computer center will have information on campuswide standards or suggested applications. Where these exist, software may be available for prices far below retail. Anyone with a computer and some design sense can produce surprisingly attractive documents with word processing, spreadsheet, relational databases, and desktop publishing software.

After the initial outlay for the program and the appropriate printer, publications can be produced on desktop computers and with laser printers for a fraction of the cost of traditional typesetting and design. Current software programs are versatile and permit frequent editing and design changes. There are also graphics programs specially designed to produce large banners, attractive announcements, and flyers. These programs offer a variety of styles, producing simple images or eye-catching displays. The combination of hardware and software needed is now affordable for almost any office, and many basic software applications for the office use now come bundled as "office suites." The compatibility between the applications helps make their use more efficient.

Word Processing

Word processing applications are used for correspondence, brochures and information sheets, newsletters, mailing labels, and mass mailings that use address databases. Word-processing software will be most effective if it can use information from spreadsheet, database, e-mail, calendar, and presentation programs.

Desktop Publishing

Desktop publishing programs are used to "lay out" documents in a way that makes them visually appealing and easy to read. Making the most of such programs requires at least some design sense, but nearly anyone can get good results after a little basic training. Available programs range from very basic applications that are often found in software bundles to much more sophisticated and expensive programs. The user of the layout program can create text and art work within the program or "import" it from word-processing and illustration programs. When choosing a desktop publishing program it is important to consider the form in which your finished documents will be published and to consult printers or Web masters about the types of files they can accept.

Spreadsheets

The flow of information in and out of a study abroad office is constant, and the need to take stock often vital. A spreadsheet program can make organizing and tracking this information easy. Common spreadsheet functions include line budgets and graphic representations. In each case, a number of variables (for example, enrollments, exchange rates, GPAs, fees, or program expenditures) can be automatically recalculated using a computerized spreadsheet.

In budgeting, for instance, some spreadsheet programs can automatically update costs expressed in dollars against the latest exchange rates of foreign currencies. The effect of increases or decreases in enrollment on budget can be instantly revealed. Any office that uses roughly similar budget categories year after year will quickly discover the benefits of using spreadsheets. Year-to-year comparisons of budgets are easy to grasp when information is presented in pie charts, line graphs, or other graphic devices supported by all popular spreadsheet programs. It is crucial that users of spreadsheets for financial purposes fully understand the spreadsheet application since small design flaws can result in wildly erroneous calculations.

Databases

Relational database programs can organize, manipulate, and retrieve data in a variety of ways. This means that new data need be entered only once, creating a resource that can be accessed repeatedly for multiple purposes. Relevant data usually include personal and academic information on applicants. Entering the information requires basic computer skills. For the database to be most effective, information needs to be entered in a consistent fashion (for example, students' majors should always be abbreviated the same way) and kept up to date.

Many databases use modifiable lists for ease and accuracy of entry. A good software package will prompt at every step and display an alert if there has been an error. It may be possible to download student information (permanent addresses, GPAs, majors, etc.) directly from the registrar's database to the education abroad office. At least one education abroad office encourages students to apply for programs over the World Wide Web, freeing staff altogether from the need to enter the most basic data. Once information is in the database, retrieving it is no more complicated than typing.

Most database programs allow a request to include an unlimited number of fields in a single report. Information can be sorted by year, last name, major, GPA, home address, zip code, birthday, e-mail address, and so on. So, for example, participant names and addresses can also be extracted and merged with a standard letter on a word-processing system. Some systems permit standard letters produced in this way to be further customized by staff, permitting individualized written correspondence at a fraction of the normal effort. It is also possible for word-processing documents generated in this way to be stored in the regular files of the database. The first step involved in setting up a database is to decide what categories or "fields" of information will be important, as well as the maximum number of characters each field can hold.

Database uses for study abroad include the following:

- lists of participants (local and permanent addresses, telephone numbers), resident directors (social security numbers, majors, birthdates, passport numbers, etc.), registrar/bursar information (names, social security numbers, program, number of credits), selection committee, news bureaus (name, program, year, hometown—sortable by zip code);
- form letters such as those announcing an applicant's acceptance to a program, personalized according to the fields (for example, name of student, address, specific program, dates of program, etc.);
- mailing labels or file labels that can be printed with either local, permanent, and abroad addresses in a variety of formats;
- printouts to be given to interview committees with standard infor-

mation (for example, interview date and time, name, class standing, major, GPA, current language course, and past language courses); and, most importantly,

- statistical information that can be used for targeted marketing, applicant follow-up, advocacy, etc.
- statistics on how students found out about the programs they chose;
- student majors (to be used in recruiting efforts by helping an office decide where to target advertising); and
- student GPAs before and after overseas studies.

Course and grade databases, when related to each other, can report the final results of each student and create course equivalency lists for the resident director and students at each program site, so they can see how coursework has been accepted at the home university in the past.

Presentations

Presentation software helps you to design and prepare slide, overhead, and computer presentations. These can be particularly helpful for professionalizing and standardizing the look of orientations, information sessions, and workshops. Many presentation programs are easy to use and affordable, allowing even a beginner to quickly create professional presentations.

▌Internet Access

No office today should be without basic access to the Internet. The Internet is the network of networks, not owned or governed by any one entity, that provides a common way for individual networks to offer services. Many software packages are available that will provide connection to the parts of the Internet detailed in the following paragraphs. It is important to check with the campus computer center before purchasing software to determine how Internet access is provided on campus and what applications are recommended and supported. Any campus may have a special arrangement to provide technical support for "bundled" software (a series of applications packaged together) at a considerable cost savings, since a number of major software companies provide free or discounted software to educational institutions and nonprofit organizations. Careful investigation may save many dollars.

E-mail and Newsgroups

E-mail is the most basic and widely used Internet service. The term is used both for the overall process and for the messages carried electronically from computer to computer. Even those who do not have the capabilities to use a web browser can access gopher, newsgroups, the World Wide Web, and other information by e-mail. E-mail is an effective way to communicate with colleagues, faculty, and students through the use of distribution lists, electronic newsletters, and individual messages. Since it is worldwide and often free to users once an institution has made the commitment to participate, it is an excellent way to manage routine communications with staff, faculty, and students at many locations abroad, especially those linked to universities.

E-mail availability at an overseas program site is increasingly attractive to students. E-mail can be used for certain types of advising through the development of a Frequently Asked Questions file and an e-mail account to which preliminary questions can be addressed. Past participant profiles, along with evaluations, can be accessed. Electronic newsletters can be developed to keep in contact with students and faculty and used to announce deadlines, visits by program representatives, new programs, and so on.

Newsgroups (also known as Usenet) are a system of worldwide bulletin boards that allow people to exchange comments, ideas, programs, and more. The system consists of over ten thousand newsgroups on virtually every topic.

Gopher

Gopher is an information retrieval method that uses menus to allow the user to easily browse text-based resources at the home institution and on other servers around the world. Gopher originated at the University of Minnesota (home of the "Golden Gophers"). Gopher programs (clients) are available for UNIX, DOS, Windows, Mac, and more. Gopher technology is text-based; it does not support graphics.

World Wide Web

The World Wide Web (WWW) is the universe of Internet-accessible information. It is currently the most advanced, relational information system on the Internet and embraces within its data model most information in previous networked information systems (e-mail, gopher, telnet, newsgroups, FTP, and IRC). The Web consists of documents and links. The documents are created with HTML (hypertext markup language), which allows "links" to be embedded in these documents. The links can point to other documents, images, video, and sound files located locally or elsewhere on the Internet. Using a Web page makes an office's information and brochures, complete with pictures, accessible instantaneously across the campus and the country.

Links are underlined words or icons. Several Web browsers (programs), such as Netscape and Internet Explorer, allow users to easily traverse this global information superhighway.

The World Wide Web is used by a large and increasing number of students who are accustomed to navigating through a series of well-crafted "home pages." It is presently possible, using available technology, to set up a web site with program information and documentation that can also be accessed by location, GPA eligibility, calendar, language, curriculum, accommodations, costs, and so on, controlled by student preferences and open 24 hours a day.

Telnet and File Transfer Protocol

Telnet is a simple network utility designed to connect to machines across the Internet. When users access telnet, they are actually logging into another computer from a distance.

File Transfer Protocol (FTP) is an application and method designed to transfer data and text files between different systems, such as Unix, Macintosh, or PC computers on the Internet. Using one of the FTP softwares available, it is possible to transfer files between an individual computer and any remote computer. This can be an easy way to exchange files with colleagues or to build a web site.

▌ NAFSA's MicroSIG and Advising Resources

General advice and specific, practical assistance with computer concerns are available from MicroSIG, NAFSA's "Microcomputer Special-Interest Group." MicroSIG members can help education abroad professionals learn what others have found to be successful in their offices and to develop new electronic solutions to everyday problems. MicroSIG can also advise in selecting, purchasing, or setting up equipment and in using Internet access (e-mail, WWW, gopher, etc.), desktop publishing, databases, and other common computer applications. Since 1985, MicroSIG has provided a diverse menu of computer literacy training for the NAFSA membership.

The bulk of MicroSIG activity has been in five areas: (1) assisting those who administer the SECUSS-L and INTER-L listservs as a communications medium and training vehicle for international educators; (2) sponsoring sessions at NAFSA national conferences; (3) presenting sessions and distributing resource materials at NAFSA regional, state, and district conferences; (4) publishing the MicroSIG Newsletter; and (5) designing technology and internet training to be used in local, regional, or sectional NAFSA computer training workshops.

Information on MicroSIG may be obtained from the authors, from the NAFSA Central Office, or directly from NAFSA's World Wide Web site (http://www.nafsa.org).

The SECUSSA Discussion List

The electronic resource with which advisers are perhaps most familiar is SECUSS-L (secuss-l@listserv.acsu.buffalo.edu), the listserv for members of SECUSSA run by volunteer members of MicroSIG and operated at SUNY-Buffalo. More than 800 advisers on almost every continent subscribe to the list. The SECUSS-L archives are available on the Web at http://listserv.acsu.buffalo.edu/archives/secuss-l.html.

SECUSS-L is a mechanism for sharing knowledge, information, and perspectives about overseas educational opportunities with other professionals in the field. It is primarily intended to be of use to advisers, program administrators, and other international educators involved in study and work abroad programming supported by U.S. college and university campuses or coordinated in conjunction with overseas educational institutions. SECUSS-L is the only U.S.-based electronic forum dedicated solely to the discussion of the issues of education abroad for U.S. students.

The goals of SECUSS-L are to:

- provide notices of all local, regional, and national meetings and conferences of interest to study abroad advisers and program administrators;
- offer succinct summaries of new articles, books, essays, and other writings on education;
- carry out brief surveys of trends, opinions, and perspectives when a national sample is needed quickly;
- give brief announcements—so that interested parties can seek further information on their own—of new programs or of significant new developments in established programs;

- function as an essential link in the Emergency Communications Network in times of global crises, and to provide current and accurate information from overseas and across the country;
- raise and discuss broad, national issues and problems concerning education abroad, internationalizing the campus, gaining cross-cultural competence, and so on;
- provide a forum for asking questions and receiving counsel and perspe___ ___m more experienced and/or informed colleagues;
- revi___ ___ information on the educational systems in c___ ___ndergraduates wish to study—changes that ___ abroad opportunities; and
- ___ the field.

___ listserv forum run by MicroSIG at inter-___du. More than 3,000 international educators at hundreds ___s and programs around the world currently subscribe. ___t study abroad issues are discussed on SECUSS-L rather than ___, professionals whose duties include other aspects of international ___ education beyond study abroad, or who simply want to stay broad-___ to date, subscribe. INTER-L provides a variety of information ser-___es to international educators. At its basic level, it is an instant forum for soliciting help with obscure questions of credentials equivalence, visa issues, or the myriad other questions that daily confront international educators. It is also a rapid and cost-effective vehicle for distributing general information. Further, it is an on-line library, with materials available instantly, 24 hours a day through the INTER-L archives.

SECUSS-L and INTER-L are only a few of more than 10,000 listservs, each serving a different specialized audience, and almost all freely available on the Internet. The news and reference resources available through these other listservs are often invaluable to international educators, even though they may be directed to another primary audience.

Lingering Doubts

Although it is no longer possible to deny the multiform opportunities offered by computerization, there remain various concerns over its ultimate impact on not only the education abroad office, but on the overseas experience of students. Some of these concerns are addressed below.

Impersonality

Communication with "machines" is thought by some to be taking the place of personal interaction and advising. It can be argued that this is the most misleading concern of all. Electronic communications used well fosters access to more students, quick dissemination of initial information, and, ideally, more productive interaction once the adviser and the student do meet. Computer-assisted advising should never replace personal counseling. At best, Web sites and e-mail can help students through some early questions, give them some basic guidelines and information, and prepare them and their advisers for further discussions. On a national level, electronic communication via SECUSS-L and other listservs has increased professional discourse between and among international-education professionals and allowed us to follow national debates on issues of concern to the field.

Haves and Have-Nots

Computerization, from campus to campus, is clearly uneven. Some colleges and universities are simply behind in making a serious institutional commitment to these new communications technologies. They will, in due course, catch up. Others are held back because they lack economic resources. This has clearly created, at least for the moment, a society of haves and have-nots. At present, most of the traditional means of communication (print, telephone, fax, etc.) remain in place and should certainly be used by anyone wanting to make sure that whatever needs to be said and heard is put in forms that are received by all. But, the cultural and technical imperatives that drive computerization are not likely to abate, and indeed are likely to increase in the future.

Overload

Doesn't the burgeoning of access to e-mail mean more office time spent on-line, answering questions, taking time away from other tasks? Certainly students are using e-mail for all sorts of communications, and this can indeed have an impact on the workload of office personnel. But since one of the goals of an education abroad office is to increase communications with students (and not only on-campus students) and faculty about (and within) programs, this is a "good problem." One very effective way of dealing with an increased number of questions is to develop on-line Frequently Asked Questions files and standard response notes, and to make effective use of e-mail applications such as Pegasus, Eudora Pro, Microsoft Exchange and others that allow advanced functions.

Using the Web Effectively

Searching the Web is often thought to take too long, and there is no guarantee that anything out there will be useful. In other words, is browsing these new systems of information storage a productive use of time? It is true that, in some cases, it is possible to get carried away browsing the Web, but responsible use is no more time-consuming than reading the many journals that arrive in education abroad offices and are often read with little regard to the relevancy of their content. The key here is to teach students and ourselves Web use that is efficient and effective. Appropriate and efficient use of Internet search engines is fast becoming as important a professional competency as library research skills have always been.

Overseas Overuse

No one doubts the utility of having e-mail linkages between the home campus and overseas program sites. These are clearly of immense help in facilitating quick and inexpensive routine (as well as emergency) communications on the part of staff and students. Many advisers are concerned, however, that the growing access to cyberspace by students who are studying abroad prevents them from cultural integration and adaptation. There are certainly many instances in which students do maintain a lifeline to their American friends, family, and domestic computer habits, and in some cases this can seem to work against the purposes of education abroad. It is helpful (and appropriate) to remember, however, that there will always be students who overdo some part of their experience abroad, whether it be telephones, e-mail, or cappuccino cafés. Seasoned advisers suggest that student overdependence on maintaining contact with "home" is likely to decline the longer students are overseas, and that good counseling on the drawbacks of overuse can be effective in convincing students that they should be focusing on adaptation, not escape.

Promotion And Publicity

Contributors: My Yarabinec and Harlan Henson

*Most likely, you will be responsible for bringing good pro-
grams into being, advising students about the plethora of
opportunities that exist abroad, and for using your imagination and persuasion to publicize and promote these
opportunities to your students, faculty, administration,
and local community. Appropriating some of the methods
of sound marketing and advertising can work to your
advantage. This is not a matter of employing public relations hype or slick promotional gimmicks. Good and effective promotion involves knowing your market and knowing the best range of programs for your market, then
using a variety of convincing strategies to sell your programs and services.*

Convincing more students, faculty, administrators, parents, legislators, foundations, corporations, and the American public to support increased overseas opportunities is both a political and rhetorical
task in the best senses of these two words. That is to say, it requires education abroad advisers and administrators to attract attention to the
value of education abroad through sound promotion and effective publicity so that students will be persuaded to participate and to select programs wisely. The value of overseas programs must be sold to many
potential constituencies through persuasive and compelling arguments.
Such efforts can be assisted by some basic marketing principles. There are
three simple rules to successful promotion: variety, repetition, and
appropriateness.

Repetition and variety go hand in hand. The first ad or brochure a student sees may not be effective, and a repetitious message will be dull and
useless. A repeated message in a variety of formats is more likely to get a
student's attention and help bring the message to a conscious realization.
The student who passes your poster, then reads an article in the campus

newspaper, then picks up a free bookmark promoting your office; or the student who sees a well-designed flier, then receives a brochure at student orientation, and then hears a classroom presentation is more apt to realize the possibilities of overseas education and the potential that such programs offer.

Before defining what is appropriate publicity, you must clearly identify your audience. Advertising a study abroad program to students who do not qualify, cannot afford the cost, or are not free to go when the program is offered does little good. Focus your advertising on various groups of students (for example, science majors, minority students, classics students, students with a 3.0 GPA, fraternity or sorority members, etc.) and tailor your message accordingly, if possible. You also need to ensure that your message reaches the faculty and parents who support the students. If your advertising is not geared to a particular audience, you could be engaged in a frustrating and wasteful exercise.

▮ Promoting Your Office and Work

Few professionals in education abroad have a business background; consequently, commercial sales techniques are often alien concepts. Also, other aspects of your job—counseling students, developing programs, working with the faculty—may seem more important and enjoyable. You may also possess the lingering suspicion that "selling" educational experiences is inappropriate. However, as a relatively new, often misunderstood, and still somewhat invisible part of undergraduate education, the field of education abroad needs to build support in every way possible, on and off campus.

Most people are aware of the publicity required to ensure that a campus event is well attended or a worthwhile social cause is supported. Kiosks and bulletin boards crammed with fliers and posters and ample ads and notices in the school newspapers are common sights on every campus. Making the campus community aware of your office and services may represent a huge challenge, but you need to devise a conscious strategy to advertise your programs and to promote your services.

Although it can be counterproductive to promote education abroad to students before securing the broad support of the faculty and administration, gaining such support can be facilitated by demonstrating student interest. If you already have the support, but education abroad has low visibility and participation levels, your challenge is to reach students with the message that education abroad exists and is possible for them. If your campus has many programs and a long history of involvement in international education, then you may need to broaden and diversify programming into new academic and geographical areas, and to attract students from a wider spectrum of the student body.

If your office is part of a larger entity—academic advising, student affairs, career services, or international programs—you may need to differentiate your services from those around you. A higher profile will increase awareness of your services, remove misunderstandings about your purpose, and also make it easier for supporters, volunteers, money, and contributions to find you. A higher profile will also draw the attention of campus administrators. If the education abroad office receives positive and regular media coverage, the office will be noticed by the administrators who weigh allocations of budget, personnel, space, and other resources.

Important Marketing Tools

You cannot begin to advise students until they have demonstrated an interest in studying or working abroad, and then come into your office to look at materials and seek your counsel. Your challenge is to get students to this exploratory point.

College Promotional Materials

Increasingly, high-school students are looking for education abroad opportunities as part of their college education. It is imperative that your institution's opportunities be a prominent part of any promotional materials sent to potential students. You should work with the admissions office to ensure that education abroad is promoted in an engaging fashion in print, photos, and graphics, and that admissions counselors stress these opportunities at college fairs and in interviews with students. You will want to meet regularly with the admissions' office recruitment staff to let them know about new and/or continuing programs abroad. If you have developed a general flier or poster (see p. 130), they should be on display in the admissions office. Campus tours for interested students and parents should pass your office or building. Campus tour guides can, perhaps, identify your office as the "gateway to the world" or "gateway to X number of foreign countries" as represented by your campus-sponsored programs.

Freshman Orientation

Working with students and academic affairs, you should prepare a presentation that will urge students to begin thinking about how to include a study or work program in their undergraduate education. This is a good chance to distribute materials and to invite students to your office. Using some enthusiastic and articulate returned students as part of your office's presentation can be especially effective.

The College Catalog

The education abroad opportunities and the services of your office should be prominently featured in any academic/student services catalog your campus publishes. This information should explain how to include overseas studies in a degree program and feature your own programs, as well as the range of other programs available. Policies and procedures also need to be spelled out. If your institution offers special financial aid for study abroad, or even if it only allows the application of normal aid packages, this should be made clear. In addition, departmental entries might indicate study abroad opportunities for majors, and the index should be cross-referenced to facilitate locating opportunities by country and language.

Fliers and Posters

Promoting education abroad will be much easier if your office can produce a general information flier. This flier needs to be attractive (though not necessarily expensive); the language needs to be straightforward; and good graphics are essential. Developing an eye-catching poster for general use on campus is also a good way to call attention to your office and its services; the poster should highlight the excitement of studying or working overseas. Such a poster can also be used to advertise general meetings and meetings about particular programs, if blank space is left at the bottom. It might also mention related products or services offered by your office (for example, international student ID cards, rail passes, youth hostel cards, books, etc.). Several campuses utilize "school colors" on posters to emphasize the connection of the study abroad program to the home campus.

General Information Meetings

Most experienced advisers and administrators agree that there is a great value to hosting general information sessions or open houses for students exploring overseas opportunities. How you set up and publicize this meeting depends on the size of your campus, the facilities available, what help you can get from others, and a number of other variables. Most meetings are held at the beginning of each semester or quarter. On some campuses meetings occur monthly; on others, weekly. Having supportive faculty, key administrators, recently returned students, and peer-counselors participate will help create interest and enthusiasm. Although your own remarks will stress the academic and personal values of education abroad, as well as institutional policies, your goal might be to encourage students to come to your office and begin exploring their options (see Chapter 10, "Advising Principles and Strategies").

Education Abroad Fairs

In recent years, many campuses have begun annual education abroad fairs as a very effective way of publicizing education abroad to large numbers of students. The basic idea is to bring together in one large space—during an afternoon, evening, or for an entire day—representatives and/or past participants of many different study and work programs, so interested students can ask questions and get further information. Although such an event serves the interests of promoting particular programs to students, it also boosts the idea of overseas study and highlights the varieties of options. Though fairs are aimed at students, they also provide opportunities for faculty and administrators to get to know programs and to realize the diversity and quality of current national programming. Some of the bigger fairs include information on international work and travel. Others are conducted in conjunction with international student organizations and celebrate global diversity.

Organizing and operating a successful fair is a major undertaking. It requires careful long-term planning, good timing and publicity, and the need to oversee a multitude of logistical details. You will need a great deal of help from your staff and from other offices. Just deciding whom to invite and how to arrange for their practical needs is a major chore. But the cumulative impact of a well-attended fair can be powerful and long lasting. A fair—compared with most other means—can bring an extensive amount of information to a large number of students economically and efficiently. It will certainly boost the profile of your office. Very useful advice on how to put on a successful fair can be found in the pamphlet, "Organizing Successful Study Abroad Fairs" (AIFS Advisers' Guide #3). You should also develop strategies for dealing with post-study abroad fair questions. Students often are confused by seemingly similar, yet clearly competing options.

Promoting Education Abroad Through the Internet

Internet services, which include e-mail and the World Wide Web, have added some exciting new tools for publicizing study abroad and disseminating useful information (see Chapter 7, "Computerizing Operations").

E-mail

Electronic mail is the most widely used service on the "Internet." It is a very basic text-based communication that allows its users to communicate very rapidly with each other. One of the useful functions of e-mail is that files can be attached to a message and accessed on the recipient's computer. This can be used to advantage in sending copies of press releases or any additional supplemental information to your targeted audience.

E-mail also allows users to create "address books," and a single message can be sent to everyone, or selected individuals, listed in an address book directory. Some address books that could be useful in publicizing study abroad opportunities could include faculty and administrators, academic advisers, students who have contacted your office with a particular country or academic major interest, study abroad alumni, campus media, student clubs on campus, etc. This provides an easy method to notify a large number of people of your activities, information meetings, new programs, your study abroad fair, the visit of a program representative to your campus, and the like.

Yet another useful function of e-mail is that it allows a copy of sent messages to be saved. This is particularly useful in that it allows a "form letter" to be sent in answer to common questions and requests.

E-mail also provides an excellent way to keep in touch with students overseas and to pass their comments on to other interested parties. For example, journalism majors who you have encouraged to serve as "foreign correspondents" for your campus newspaper can file their copy in this manner. If the university or program overseas does not have e-mail accounts available to students (many do), the students should be encouraged to find a local service provider.

Finally, remember that most universities allow one or more e-mail accounts for an office. If you wish to use e-mail to disseminate information about your office or receive inquiries from the general public, it is highly advisable to establish an office account separate from your personal account. Also remember that, because an inquiry comes to you through e-mail, you are not required to respond to the question in full detail. Some issues are too complex to resolve by an e-mail message. Instead, for example, you might simply respond by suggesting that the student come in to pick up some of the printed material, or make an appointment, or attend one of your information meetings and "tag" this message with a schedule of the office hours and advising availability.

The World Wide Web

The Web is an exciting new Internet service, and its uses and application for universities and study abroad programs are virtually unlimited. The Web is user-friendly because it supports documents with a mixture of text and graphics. Its great versatility comes from the fact that it allows documents to be linked to one another, regardless of geographic location.

Universities and study abroad offices can provide a wide array of information on the Web. A "home page," typically the first page accessed, identifies the university or office and provides a table of contents. Each item in the table of contents is a link to an appropriate page. In this manner, the Web provides an informational hierarchy of sorts that allows the browser to go from the general to the specific, for example, from the university to the study abroad office to a specific program or supporting document.

Some of the specific applications of the World Wide Web for publicizing your program and services, and encouraging students to study abroad, include

- links to and from other universities and programs
- images of the places your study abroad programs go
- links to information sources on the Web
- "clickable" image maps
- links to an FTP (file transfer protocol) site

It should also be noted that interactive forms on the Web are becoming increasingly easy to make. This can contribute to the move toward a "paperless" office. Some universities already have on-line application forms for study abroad programs. This is something that will facilitate a student's application process and become increasingly common.

Mobilizing Returned Students

One of the most important resources for publicizing the study abroad experience is the number of study abroad alumni at your campus. These students can talk to classes and provide information to interested students. To best utilize this population, they must be mobilized in some structured manner. Several colleges and universities have made "STARS" out of students who return from abroad. STARS is an acronym for study abroad returnees and short-term work abroad returnees. They can contact faculty and make brief classroom presentations. They gain practice with public speaking, enhance their resumes, and have a captive audience for their photo albums. At some institutions, a modest honorarium is provided. Other institutions have organized Alumni Councils or International Education Assemblies (bringing both study abroad alumni and students interested in studying overseas together). Having these groups officially recognized by the Associated Students (or equivalent) on your campus can also often provide funds for activities from the Associated Students budget.

The marketing strategies of variety, repetition, and appropriateness are covered by STARS or similar programs. Returned students represent a variety of majors who have studied in different countries around the world. Their presentations complement and supplement other forms of publicity, and the "word of mouth" message from experienced persons seems ideal in terms of appropriateness and credibility.

Other Publicity Ideas

Piggybacking

If you have kept abreast of other events on campus, you may be able to piggyback your education abroad message to other international activities. For example, if international students give presentations in courses that focus on their home country, they could be encouraged to end with an invitation to study overseas. Similarly, if there is a foreign film series on campus, general brochures about your office could be left at the entrance to the auditorium.

Class Assignment

You might contact faculty in marketing, advertising, and public relations to ask whether publicity projects can be assigned by your office. One institution gained a Web page, a study abroad logo, a new poster, and sample press release formats from such a project. The class assignment became a useful way of piggybacking on an existing activity.

All of the promotional opportunities listed above can greatly bolster the image of education abroad on your campus. Ideally, these opportunities will prepare students to begin the advising process. Promoting particular program opportunities requires another set of strategies.

▌ Publicizing Particular Programs

Getting the right students interested in the right programs is one of the major challenges facing education abroad advisers. But it is perhaps even more difficult to get the attention of a particular group of students once you have identified an overseas program that might interest them. In order to reach these students, a targeted promotion needs to be defined and carried out.

A targeted approach involves identifying a group of students who you think are appropriate for a specific overseas program and then devising a publicity campaign aimed at the group. Some examples are a campaign devised to attract English literature and history majors to an exchange program with an Irish university; a campaign directed at Latin American studies, public policy, or social work students (and those with African-American or Hispanic backgrounds) to interest them in an established program in the Dominican Republic that has good coursework in urban studies and economic development and offers a social service agency internship; and a campaign directed at architecture and art history students to attract them to a program in Denmark that focuses on contemporary Scandinavian design. Each of these programs must be marketed in a way that will attract the desired audience. Your promotional tools include

- program posters, brochures, and other such objects distributed in areas frequented by the targeted students, including departmental libraries and hallways
- outreach to academic advisers and faculty in relevant subjects (visits, mailings, e-mail communications, and program materials)
- articles in department newsletters
- advertisements in periodicals such as *Transitions Abroad* and the *NAFSA Newsletter*
- classroom presentations
- special mailings, e-mail communications, and meetings for students who have declared relevant majors.

In addition to promotional efforts to students with particular academic interests, you can design campaigns directed at students seeking (1) programs in particular geographic regions (for example, Africa, eastern Europe, or the developing world); (2) programs that are highly experiential or service-oriented or require a lot of independent research, rather than spending time in the classroom; (3) programs that are not in English-speaking countries but offer a curriculum in English and the opportunity to learn the language and live with families; (4) programs that are equipped to accept students with physical or learning disabilities; and (5) perhaps even good programs with moderate admission requirements that do not require a very high GPA for admission.

Inasmuch as the profile of students who have traditionally studied abroad is so narrow, it is very important to promote overseas opportunities to the nontraditional study abroad student. Publicize low-cost programs and announce all scholarship opportunities. Your publicity should make this vast majority of students reconsider education abroad and make them aware that your office is ready and eager to talk with them (see Chapter 11, "Promoting Student Diversity").

Using the Media

Every campus has its own forms of communication, such as the campus newspaper, radio station, and video channel. Although the campus-centered focus of these media seems to exclude concerns with faraway places, there are many ways to get the media's attention, and ultimately the attention of students. Since student media often have a commercial base, paying for ads in the newspaper to boost your office or programs is one option. Make your press releases appealing to student editors and encourage follow-up features. You might also host a reception for reporters from the paper.

As advantageous as these tactics are, most education abroad offices do not have large discretionary budgets for advertising and hospitality. Another approach involves increasing personal contacts with editors, writers, and media managers. Why not meet with the faculty adviser and editors of the campus newspaper, go over articles, make follow-up calls, or encourage students to submit articles about their experiences? When you begin to see announcements and features appearing, always remember to thank the newspaper. It is also surprising how often a specially invited reporter actually comes to events and programs. Always remember that outreach from you and your office should always be cooperative and collegial.

The Campus Newspaper

The campus newspaper may appear daily, several times a week, or weekly, so knowing deadlines and timing your message for optimum impact is often tricky. In addition, you should be familiar with the various columns and announcements that appear regularly.

Feature Articles

Features are desirable because they usually provide an implicit pitch for the value of education abroad, in addition to adding a human-interest element, whether through participant interviews or personal accounts. Such articles also remind all readers, including faculty and administrators, of the benefits of your office. You can often be proactive in suggesting tie-ins between planned feature topics and your programs. For example, most campus newspapers perennially run articles about love and dating for their edition on or near Valentine's Day. A possible tie-in could be how a student feels about the differences in dating practices in his or her host country while overseas on one of your programs. Tie-ins and suggested story topics should always promote education abroad in general and your office in particular. Consider also encouraging any of your students departing for an overseas experience to serve as "international correspondents" to the campus newspaper. This opportunity is of particular interest to journalism majors and is usually of interest to the campus newspaper as well.

The Calendar Section

Most campus newspapers provide a regular opportunity for disseminating information in a calendar section. Find out the requirements and deadlines and submit as many announcements as possible. Take advantage of this free service to announce meetings to discuss your programs, deadlines for applications, visits by representatives from other programs, fairs, and other international events. The calendar section can also help your office identify events that attract students who might be interested in an overseas experience. For example, you might consider distributing pamphlets or fliers at a Japanese art exhibition or a guest lecture on international business.

Letters to the Editor

Letters can be written by you, your office, or returned students in response to some related matter. Make sure that students identify themselves as alumni of your programs. A letter need not be explicitly about overseas study or a particular foreign country. For example, an article about the business school could inspire a follow-up letter suggesting that study abroad will help make Americans culturally and linguistically more successful in pursuing careers in international business.

Personal Columns

Since students often read these, an occasional, cleverly worded message in the "personals" section of your campus newspaper may attract more curiosity and attendance than a more expensive advertisement. For example, "Darling, he suspects! Meet me at the Study Abroad Information Meeting, Next Wednesday, 7:30 p.m., in McLaren Hall. Turtledove."

Other Campus Publications and Media

Do not overlook opportunities to get out your message in all campus publications. Do not be shy. Internationalism is hot, and your office can be a pivotal rallying point. These publications might include

- faculty and staff newsletters
- department newsletters
- alumni magazines and newsletters
- any publications put out by your campus international center
- all admissions brochures
- college home pages on the Web.

The campus radio station may run public service announcements. Student-accessed electronic bulletin boards are becoming increasingly common and can provide a very receptive audience. Advertising in periodicals that reach students likely to be receptive to education abroad should also be considered if your budget permits.

Points to Keep in Mind When Using Campus Media

Avoid confusing and blank terms as well as abbreviations, acronyms, and jargon. What may seem clear to you may be confusing to others. Make it as easy as possible for the writer or media contact to understand your point. You should be readily available, responding quickly with additional material and offering to identify students for the article. Be understanding when your articles do not get published. Always be certain that announcements and articles include details about where to get more information.

Your chances of having your article published and published accurately will improve if you use the following tools:

The Press Release

Press releases should be provided for every suggested story to ensure that key information is included in the final version. Always remember to include who, what, where, when, why, and where to turn for more information. Try to limit the release to one page and always be sure to include a contact name and phone number of a person who will actually be available; reporters will not call back again and again.

A Press Kit

This should include a cover letter (highlighting the essential elements of the story), the press release, an information brochure (if any), all pertinent information, and your business card.

Photos

These can be submitted with the press kit or sent separately along with a caption. Photos with captions will provide further interaction with the writers and editors. If you need the picture, make sure you arrange to have it returned.

Follow-up

Give feedback to the media. Thank them for covering your meeting or printing your story.

Other Methods

The campus media may be one of the best ways to launch your message, but a number of other means serve the same purpose. Examples include

- display cases
- fliers on campus bulletin boards
- banners
- information booths
- classroom presentations
- videos on loan at the library
- representation at campus festivals and activities
- photography exhibits
- bookmarks, printed with your message.

Community Media

Members of a campus community do not live in a vacuum. They watch, listen, read, and notice what is conveyed to them by the local media. Utilizing the local media can be especially effective in smaller communities, and should not be overlooked as a worthwhile promotional tool in urban environments. One advantage of dealing with community media is that, as professionals, these media representatives are more stable than their student counterparts. This stability allows you to develop personal relationships with the hope of seeing more return for your publicity efforts.

Initially, you should approach the local media with basic news stories, such as an article honoring students chosen for a particular study abroad program. When approaching the community media, it is even more important to use the standard tools of press releases, press kits, and so on. All earlier suggestions made regarding the campus media also apply to the community media. In addition, do not be afraid of sending your news often; the local media are always looking for filler. The return is that your message is presented to a larger audience.

On occasion, the media will seek you out, as when there is civil unrest in a country where students from your campus are studying. These occasions cannot be anticipated, but given the number of students now studying and working overseas, you should be prepared for such situations and the ensuing media inquiries. Remember that anything you say to the media will be taken as an official statement representing your institution. Therefore, be prudent and work in cooperation with your campus public information office and other appropriate authorities. Remain pleasant and fair at all times in your dealings with the media. Do not promise more than you can give and consider carefully the confidentiality of your information. Staying calm in times of overseas crises and responding professionally to campus and media requests for information can do wonders for the reputation of your office.

D chat
with
me

Talked about
10/6

|

SPECIAL
I S O
EVENTS
for Parents Weekend
October 10-11-12

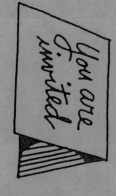

...e letter home to your parents (telling them what they mean to you in ...s Weekend), stick it in an addressed envelope, and give it to Carla **by** ...**r 10, 1997**. ISO will then send your letter via airmail *free* to your folks ...if they are presently in the U.S.)! It would be nice to say that we are ...n this way since they can't be with us!

...ents Weekend Banquet in the Dining Commons on Saturday, October 11. ...ery tasty) meal! However, you **must sign up ahead of time** outside the ...s and *pick up* a ticket from the Advancement Office people there. They ...n October 1, 2 and 3 from 11:30 - 12:30 or you can pick up a ticket ...inda in the Advancement Office. You cannot come without a ticket!

II

Part Two
Advising

The Current Demographics Of Education Abroad
Contributors: Beatrice Beach Szekely and Maria Krane

Advising Principles And Strategies
Contributors: Cynthia Felback Chalou, Barbara Lantz, Janeen Felsing, and Kathy Lutfi

Promoting Student Diversity
Contributors: Margery A. Ganz and Valerie M. Eastman

Advising For Whole World Study
Contributors: Joan A. Raducha and Michael D. Monahan

Health And Safety Issues
Contributors: Mickey Hanzel Slind, Deborah C. Herrin, and Joan Gore

Predeparture Orientation And Reentry Programming
Contributors: Ellen Summerfield, Rebecca Sibley, and Helen Stellmaker

The Current Demographics Of Education Abroad

Contributors: Beatrice Beach Szekely and Maria Krane

Increased attention to the goal of internationalizing the American campus has led to a greater need to keep track of who participates in international education activities. Campus administration and faculty increasingly value accurate information on their own students and programs and on how they compare with those of other institutions, as well as with national norms. Education abroad advisers and program administrators, for their part, require accurate information about why U.S. students go overseas, how they make choices, where they go, and what they study.

Your office may need to generate its own operational budget and/or compete with other administrative units for limited institutional resources. Accurate record keeping is therefore crucial for benchmarking and for sound budgetary decision making. Facts and figures substantiate program development and funding requests. The information in this chapter is intended to help put your own institutional activity within the national context.

Although much is positive about recent developments to collect and collate information on students who study overseas (or indeed who go overseas for work or internships), we should not be too satisfied with the current state of data collection, or even interpretations of any data that are available. There is much that we do not know about U.S. students and their overseas experiences, at both the national and institutional level. Most professionals openly admit that we have incomplete information, to a lesser or greater degree, on

- how many students participate in an overseas experience each year
- what motivates them
- where they study and why

- what they study
- how long they spend studying overseas
- gender and ethnic diversity
- academic disciplines at their home institution
- short and long-term effects of an education abroad experience.

Although this is not to demean the numerous surveys presented and discussed in this chapter, we need to be aware of what we don't know.

It is important for all education abroad advisers and administrators to consider what data are needed, how they can be collected, and what conditions might prevent the collection of this information. It is instructive and necessary to understand what is occurring at a national level, but any meaningful national data necessarily depend on data collected by individual colleges and universities on the activity of their own students. Again, "Think globally, act locally."

Most institutions in the United States know, to a fairly accurate degree, just how many foreign students are on their campus. But if you ask these same institutions how many students from that campus spend some time overseas, reliable data are frequently scarce. There might indeed be good reasons for this—after all, study abroad is a fairly recent phenomenon on many campuses, and accurate record-keeping may be slow in forming. This should not prevent your office from doing its best to identify these reasons and work on improving data collection in cooperation with such offices as the registrar, institutional research, and academic departments. The information provided in this chapter can be used to develop institutional surveys; questions concerning an overseas experience could be included in senior surveys, etc.

For ten years (though only every other year until this year) the best data available on institutional study abroad activity have been systematically compiled by the Institute of International Education (IIE), complementing its long-standing compilation of data regarding foreign students in the United States. The results of this work, plus other data collection, enable international education professionals to begin to understand the profile of the study abroad population and to build programs that meet student interests and needs.

Most education abroad professionals agree, however, that much more research on students abroad and their impact on U.S. higher education at the individual, institutional, and national levels is needed. The validity and inclusiveness of the data that the IIE survey collects are dependent on the active participation of every institution with students now earning credit for overseas study. At present, many such institutions do not report figures to IIE, and thus the national picture is quantitatively incomplete.

In addition, experienced observers contend that underreporting and overreporting continue to exist, and many would like to see national figures on a host of matters not now covered. Finally, little information has been gathered on students who engage in education abroad that goes beyond participation in formal, credit-bearing overseas academic programs. This experiential activity includes short-term work abroad, paid and unpaid internships, service learning, volunteer work projects, and some forms of organized educational travel (see Chapter 17, "Work Abroad and International Careers").

The NAFSA/IIE Interassociational Data Collection Committee has encouraged colleges and universities to improve their records of international activities in which their students participate, and improvements have occurred. As education abroad campus adviser and/or program administrator, it is your responsibility to encourage your campus to develop systematic ways of collecting data on the activity of students and programs, and then to ensure that these data are regularly summarized and sent to IIE in response to its biannual survey.

■ Recent Studies

Taken together, the following sources represent the state of the field in providing a national understanding of who is venturing abroad on academic programs, where they come from, what they seek, and how they fare.

Open Doors (1995–96)

As noted above, IIE has for many years conducted an annual census on international students and scholars studying and doing research on U.S. campuses. These data—covering overall numbers, national origins, sources of financial support, fields of study, enrollments, and rates of growth at virtually all accredited colleges and universities—are published in *Open Doors*. Over the years, IIE has sought similar kinds of data on U.S. students abroad. Various methods have been used to gather this information.

Initially, surveys were conducted by contacting foreign institutions of higher education and requesting data on the numbers of U.S. students enrolled. Over the past ten years, concluding that many U.S. students were enrolled in branch-campus or free-standing study abroad programs and not at foreign institutions, IIE surveyed the directors of U.S. university-sponsored programs. Neither approach proved wholly satisfactory, so IIE research staff, working with the leaders of NAFSA's Section on U.S. Students Abroad (SECUSSA), redesigned its questionnaire and process.

IIE now seeks to gather information directly from U.S. campuses, using education abroad professionals as key contacts. The survey used for the most recently published *Open Doors* volume reports data for the 1994–95 academic year.[1] Campuses are asked to provide information only about their *own* students, not about students from other institutions who might be enrolled in *their* programs (who would be counted by their home institution). The measure is credit earned and counted toward home-institution degree studies, whatever and wherever its origin.

The IIE questionnaire is thus to be filled out by the office best able to furnish accurate data on each campus—usually, this is the office administering study abroad, though sometimes institutions have two offices, one that administers programs for that institution and one that advises on other programs.[2] By giving ownership to the stakeholders within the international education professions, the response rate for the survey has increased to 84 percent of the 1,206 campuses surveyed.

It should be noted, however, that this number (1,206) represents only about a third of *all* U.S. two-year and four-year degree-granting institutions of higher education. Recommended categories of data currently collected include personal, academic, and study abroad program categories.[3] Armed with this information, advisers and administrators can analyze and present their work effectively. Through *Open Doors,* IIE research staff provide the most comprehensive information available on U.S. study abroad. These findings represent the basis of much of what is presented in the second half of this chapter.[4]

Single-State Surveys of International Education

There is much to be gained from data gathering and analysis of demographics at the level of the single state. Information on study abroad, student work abroad, and educational travel can then be surveyed and analyzed in comparison with the national profile. Practitioners at particular colleges and universities will learn how their state is doing relative to others, and the degree to which their international education efforts are typical of work at similar institutions.

To date, the only such survey is the New York State Task Force on International Education, which summarizes data provided in response to the same questions asked in *Open Doors* for academic year 1993–94.[5] All the baccalaureate institutions of New York were surveyed in 1995, and data for two-year institutions are being reported in 1996. New York State study abroad students represent over 10 percent of the national undergraduate study abroad enrollment, a relatively large proportion, which enhances the value of this data set well beyond its single state representation.

In other states, various councils or commissions on international education are active, but have not yet undertaken systematic data collection. Now that IIE has established a firm methodology and strong institutional participation rate, it may be time to break the national data down into replicable regional, state, urban/rural, and other subsets, which would make possible comparative studies and analysis. Such work will yield the information needed to relate the study abroad offering to its various constituencies.

In the International Interest (1992)

Although focused in its institutional sample, this study is of enduring interest for its scope and implications. *In the International Interest* examines the international activities of 52 "small, selective, independent colleges that are dedicated to liberal education"—referred to as the "International 50." Results show conclusively that there is a great national divide between what is possible at affluent private institutions and what is possible at larger, more academically complex institutions—especially those supported by public funding and enrolling students from more diverse socioeconomic backgrounds. The more recent New York State Task Force report came to the same conclusions. *In the International Interest* found that a significant exposure to internationalism at the undergraduate level produces strong postgraduate results in international commerce, service, and scholarship.[6] Graduates of these few colleges, plus a few others like them (which accounted for just 1.8 percent of all baccalaureate degrees awarded nationwide in 1988)

- make up 10.4 percent of the enrollment at graduate schools of international affairs;
- have received 9.1 percent of the Ph.D.s awarded in all international fields, and 11.4 percent of the Ph.D.s in European history, 15.5 percent of those in Russian, and 120.4 percent of those in Japanese;
- represent more than 10 percent of the United States' ambassadors and 9 percent of the nation's foreign service officers;

- are three times more likely to have majored in foreign languages or area studies than their peers at the national major research universities and 5.3 times more likely than are all college graduates nationally;
- enter into the Peace Corps in proportions 2.5 times greater than their peers at all colleges and universities; and
- are four times more likely than lawyers to specialize in international law than might be expected by their numbers.

The report argues that these impressive contributions to international studies, diplomacy, and other fields stem from the common values and attitudes of liberal education, which challenge parochialism and encourage students to be open to change, acquire effective communication skills, learn foreign languages, and see ideas in their full complexity. It also illustrates, albeit indirectly, two other important points: first, the majority of other small, private colleges have not made this commitment to internationalization or achieved these results; and, second, the resources required to bring these results about are far beyond those now available to many private and most public universities.

In sum, much, but not everything, can be learned from the statistics and studies at hand. The following profiles, however, represent the best available information on overall numbers of study abroad students and the schools they come from, program types, destinations, fields of study, academic rank, length of stay, and gender. Other points of reference come from data on foreign students in the United States and patterns of practice that have long been evident.

▮ Basic Characteristics of U.S. Students Abroad

Overall Numbers

Although a few U.S. colleges have had study abroad programs since the early twentieth century, it was not until the 1950s and 1960s that students began going abroad in significant numbers.[7] In its earliest years, study abroad was largely limited to students from private colleges and universities. This has changed over the last three decades, with a notable increase in college students interested in study, travel, internships, and work abroad. Within standard Carnegie categories, research institutions send the most students abroad, followed by those focused on baccalaureate, master's, and doctoral degrees, with significant growth in the small associate degree sector.[8]

TABLE 9.1

Total Number of U.S. Study Abroad Students, 1985/86–1994/95

	1985–86	'87–88	'89–90	'91–92	'93–94	'94–95
Students Reported	48,483	62,341	70,727	71,154	76,302	84,400
Institutions Reporting	709	804	715	754	836	1,019

Source: IIE

As Table 9.1 indicates, during the nine years for which data have been collected, U.S. study abroad participation has grown from 48,000 to 84,400, an increase of 75 percent, with the greatest growth in the decade of the 1980s. The number of reporting institutions has increased by close to 43 percent, which may account, in part, for the overall enrollment increase. The rate of increase has slowed in the 1990s to only 2 percent per year, but growth between 1993–94 and 1994–95 was more than 10 percent. The sample of 1,019 reporting institutions included in the *Open Doors 1994–95* survey represents only one-third of all U.S. colleges and universities (two- and four-year).

As a percentage of total enrollments in the broad spectrum of U.S. undergraduate education, in comparison with the 10 percent targeted by the National Task Force in 1990, study abroad remains a rather marginal activity quantitatively speaking, something undertaken by about only 1 or 2 percent of all students prior to graduation. A 1992 survey conducted by the American Council on Education of 510 two- and four-year institutions yields the same conclusion.[9]

There is great variation within the overall pattern, however. Well-endowed private, liberal arts colleges are frequently sending abroad 20–40 percent of each graduating class, and some send even more. Close to half of all liberal arts colleges classified as Baccalaureate I Carnegie institutions reported that 6.4 percent of their students had studied abroad in 1993–94. Major private universities may not achieve the numbers of some of their smaller counterparts, but many are in the 6–10 percent range. At the other extreme, many U.S. institutions send negligible numbers of students abroad. Interesting and noteworthy campus-to-campus exceptions exist at all levels.

Discussion of the barriers to increased participation that have prevented attainment of the National Task Force goals lies beyond the scope

of a chapter devoted to the presentation of demographic patterns. Apart
from external factors that are strongly related to economic forces, internal factors inhibiting growth within individual educational institutions
are identified and analyzed in the New York State Task Force report.

The New York State data show participation rates similar to those in
the national profile. Principal internal factors limiting increase in the
growth of study abroad participation that are identified therein include
limited institutional commitments to international education, funding
issues, inadequate language preparation, inadequate campus-based support services, and incomplete access to information about available
opportunities.[10]

The failure of Congress to fund fully the National Security Education
Program (NSEP) of 1992, ongoing problems related to the defense and
intelligence service obligations assumed by NSEP grant recipients, and
current reductions in funding to the United States Information Agency,
the Fulbright Program, and other source agencies, does not suggest that
in the near future government funds will spur a hefty resurgence in the
rate of enrollment increase.

As noted, these figures are for participants in credit-bearing study
and internship programs. Estimates from experienced NAFSA and CIEE
colleagues suggest that at least another fifteen to twenty thousand U.S.
undergraduates work abroad each year or engage in some other form of
experiential education (for example, teaching, volunteering, field
research, independent study). If one adds these students to the IIE figures for 1994–95 and factors in a presumably large number that have
simply not been counted, a liberal extrapolation places the total number
of U.S. undergraduates engaged in some form of education abroad
annually, excluding independent travel, at well over 100,000.[11]

Duration of Stay

From the 1940s through the 1960s, "junior year abroad" was the widely
accepted term for what we now call education abroad. Then the dominant pattern was to study overseas during one's entire junior year—usually language and literature, culture, history, art, and politics. Because this
was done almost exclusively by students (most of whom were female)
majoring in one of these areas, all courses counted toward the major and
a full year's worth of credit was guaranteed. Over the past two decades,
the pronounced trend has been away from year-long programs and
toward programs of a semester or less with much course work taken outside major fields.

As the IIE 1994–95 data show (see table 9.2), fewer than 15 percent of U.S. students studying abroad now do so for a full academic year— though the absolute numbers of students may have remained constant. Roughly equal percentages (around 37 percent) of students now participate in academic semester (13–15 weeks) programs and in programs of shorter duration (academic quarter, summer, January term, or at other intervals in the academic year). Students who go abroad for language immersion are more likely to spend a year; students with minimal or no language skills typically spend a semester or less.[12]

Short-term programs represent the fastest-growing sector; they often enroll nontraditional students with more diverse social, economic, and ethnic backgrounds, and often offer innovative models of study abroad programming, such as field seminars or independent research. On the other extreme, many short-term programs are discipline-specific, faculty-led, study tours, while others offer short-term intermediate language immersion experiences.

Many observers view this pervasive shift toward shorter and shorter stays abroad as regrettable. They point out that the education impact of a year-long program (ideally a full-immersion, language-based program involving traditional course work at a foreign university), where the student has the time to develop interests and make friends, is much greater than that gained from a shorter program. There is also some evidence that U.S. students shy away from the longer programs because they may feel threatened socially or academically by a whole year abroad, worry about the separation from friends and loved ones, or be reluctant to put aside other campus pursuits for this long. Short programs have also grown in appeal for financial reasons and because of the flexibility they provide to students who are intent on completing degree requirements as quickly as possible.

United States institutions now offer close to 2,000 programs during the academic year; they are listed annually, along with another 500 programs that are not accredited by U.S. institutions, in IIE's *Academic Year Abroad 1996–97*. An additional 1,800 programs are listed in IIE's annual volumes of *Vacation Study Abroad* (also for 1996–97), 60 percent of which are sponsored by accredited colleges and universities.[13]

There is no doubt, in sum, that more and more students are having an educational experience abroad prior to graduation because of an abundance of short programs. Moreover, many students who study abroad as undergraduates have already participated in short-term or even year-long study abroad, volunteer, or educational travel programs during high school. For them, study abroad is but one international experience among several short- and long-term sojourns that may stretch into their professional careers in the global workplace.

TABLE 9.2
Duration of Study Abroad, 1994–95

Duration of Stay	Students (%)
Calendar Year	1
Academic Year	14
Summer	30
Semester	39
Quarter	5
Other	11

Source: IIE

Data are scarce on the numbers of U.S. undergraduates studying for degrees at foreign institutions of higher education. Indeed, foreign-degree studies are not normally seen as a species of study abroad, which is usually intended as part of the U.S. baccalaureate degree. Again, it should be noted that all but 2–3 percent of the 454,000 foreign students studying in the United States during 1995–96 were seeking U.S. under-graduate or graduate degrees. This sharp contrast is due in part to the less specialized nature of the U.S. baccalaureate and the greater liberali-ty of U.S. institutions in accepting transfer credit compared with their foreign counterparts.

In recent years, the student mobility schemes of the European Union—first ERASMUS and now SOCRATES—have moved European universities closer to adopting many American practices with regard to short-term study programs in other countries. An attendant European Credit Transfer Scheme supports the increased rate of student participa-tion. Reforms in Britain and elsewhere, promoting the 'semesterization' of the academic year and a parallel 'modularization' of course offerings, facilitate mobility, not only for European students but for American and other international students as well who wish to study abroad for a semester in Europe.

Gender

Open Doors data show what study abroad professionals who gather good data at their home campuses know already, that nationally most students studying abroad—nearly two out of three—are women (again, the figures for incoming foreign students are just the reverse).[14] There are several explanations for this imbalance, though few valid justifications.

First, study abroad has traditionally been associated with foreign language study and the liberal arts, and women have tended to dominate enrollments in those fields, particularly in the European languages. Although the pattern is changing, study abroad programs are not nearly as numerous in engineering, business, agriculture, and the technical sciences—traditionally male-dominated fields. Female enrollment in science and technology fields is increasing; as more women study engineering and more men major in French, things will presumably change.

Second, but much more conjectural, the imbalance reflects U.S. cultural values. Societal and parental expectations in the United States have traditionally encouraged young men to pursue "serious," career-oriented degrees, while young women are encouraged to "cultivate" themselves and/or prepare for marriage.

Additionally, women are usually expected to excel in social relations, and crossing cultures for successful study abroad requires social interaction skills that are commonly associated with femininity. Given the prevalence of such sexism, and the notion that a study abroad experience is somehow frivolous, we can see why more women than men have traditionally studied abroad. But because these assumptions are changing, this gender imbalance may soon even out. It would be interesting to know what the gender breakdowns are for study abroad in particular host countries and for types of programs, whether traditional classroom learning, experiential and field learning, or internships.

Program Sponsorship

IIE defines a program as either a group of students studying in a foreign setting or just one or two students participating in a bilateral exchange. Accordingly, 71 percent of students covered in the 1994–95 IIE survey enrolled in programs identified as sponsored by their own institution, either acting individually or as part of a consortium of institutions; 29 percent enrolled in programs run by other institutions or organizations.[15]

Although it is clear that most U.S. students study abroad through programs or arrangements made by their own schools, the distinction between these two types of sponsorships is murky. A college or university may have an arrangement whereby its students enroll directly in a foreign university but without representation of the sending institution abroad through a formal on-site program office. Are such students study-ing on one of their institution's "own" programs or something else? As is known, a myriad set of administrative structures supports study abroad from the United States; indeed, one of the hallmarks of the enterprise is the rich set of networks that each sending institution can create to serve the needs of its students best.

There are academic and economic reasons for this pattern. First, U.S. institutions want to maintain as much control as they can over academ-ic quality and, by extension, the integrity of their degree. Such ownership ensures faculty and administrative support and builds student interest and momentum from year to year. In addition, owning one's own pro-grams (even though they entail capital expenses) helps to control costs directly and avoid what is known as "tuition flow" to other institutions. Such programs can also be used as recruiting devices for on-campus study. Institutional study abroad linkages may provide opportunities for faculty research, the recruitment of foreign students and scholars, and joint projects. Ground breaking U.S. study abroad programs work col-laboratively with universities in both developed and developing countries to promote mutual institutional growth while amplifying the undergrad-uate experience.

Two other reasons merit consideration: earning credit and using financial aid. At many institutions, students are more likely to realize full-credit transfer for study abroad and can more easily obtain and use their financial-aid packages when they participate in study abroad programs through their home institutions. Direct enrollment abroad and study through other programs have tended to make both more difficult although this situation has changed since the reauthorization of the Higher Education Act in 1992 made it mandatory to offer federal finan-cial aid funds, which are almost exclusively loans, for study abroad.

Academic Level

U.S. students go overseas for study mainly as undergraduates.[16] IIE data on study abroad show only about 7 percent of U.S. students abroad are graduate students. That percentage is suspect because many doctoral candidates complete unreported research sojourns abroad for varying lengths of time, supported by a wide variety of funding mech-anisms. Of the undergraduates, most are juniors, with only a few fresh-men, sophomores, or seniors; 15 percent of students now studying abroad do so before their third year, and another 16 percent do so after it. Only about 2 percent of the national total reported by IIE is enrolled in two-year degree programs, but this is a portion of the study abroad population that may be expected to increase. An unreported number of U.S. students enter college or university having studied abroad in between their secondary and tertiary education. The establishment of joint international degrees and year-long master's degree programs in universities overseas may cause the proportion of study abroad within the graduate sector to increase.

Destinations

IIE data show that about two-thirds (65.5 percent) of all U.S. students continue to choose to study in Europe (see table 9.3), with 23 percent going to the United Kingdom alone. Of the 12 most popular countries, six are in western Europe. Mexico, Australia, Israel, Japan, Costa Rica, China, and Russia are modestly popular. Overall, the two-thirds figures going to Europe marks a decrease from three-quarters four years ago, indicating increased interest in the non-Western world. Interestingly, the countries popular among U.S. students stand in almost diametrical opposition to the countries that send students to the United States. Relatively few western European students, for instance, come to the United States for study, while relatively few U.S. students choose Asia (7 percent), although that percentage is increasing.

The popularity of western Europe, including the United Kingdom, can be explained in several ways. There is a history and longstanding precedent. Since U.S. students began academic sojourns abroad, beginning in the 19th century, they have mainly gone to western Europe—at first for theological training, then for medical education and graduate research, and more recently for undergraduate study. This is an American tradition reflecting our country's European origins.[17]

Second, language study remains a mainstay of study abroad, and the languages of western Europe—Spanish, French, Italian, and German— remain the most commonly taught in U.S. high schools and colleges. These preferences are still not seriously threatened by instruction in Arabic, Chinese, Japanese, and Russian, despite the huge percentages of the world's population who speak those and other languages less commonly taught in the United States.

The exception to this correlation of European language dominance with the popularity of Europe as a study abroad site is the increased popularity of Latin America, chosen by 14 percent of study abroad students. Taken altogether, the Spanish-speaking countries of the world attract over one-fifth (22 percent) of study abroad students, including 7,500 students, or 9 percent of the total who study in Spain.[18]

Students without foreign-language proficiency, or who do not wish to pursue language study (and this is, alas, the case with most U.S. undergraduates), have been increasingly welcomed over the past decade in Australia and New Zealand, as well as Britain and Ireland. In addition, numerous programs that include at least some courses taught in English have appeared elsewhere in Europe. Studying in English has opened up curricular possibilities, allowing students of business, engineering, science, and many other fields to take courses of high academic quality and receive credit toward their major.

The power of the English-language worldwide is reflected in the fact that 28 percent of U.S. students abroad study in countries where English has official status. This includes some countries—principally in Africa and Asia—where English is not the native language of sizable percentages of the population but where English speakers need not learn the native languages to get by. [19]

TABLE 9.3
Regions Hosting U.S. Study Abroad Students, 1987/88–1995/96

| | Study Abroad Students | | | | |
| | 1987–88 | '89–90 | '91–92 | '93–94 | '95–96 |
Host Region	%	%	%	%	%
Africa	1.2	1.3	1.8	1.9	2.1
Asia	6.1	5.0	5.9	6.5	6.5
Europe	75.4	76.7	71.1	67.4	65.5
Latin America	9.2	9.4	12.3	13.4	13.7
Middle East	4.7	2.7	2.7	2.8	3.2
North America	1.4	0.8	0.9	0.7	0.7
Oceania	1.2	1.9	3.1	3.4	4.2
Multiple Regions	0.8	2.2	2.1	3.8	3.8

Source: IIE

Ethnicity seems to continue to affect student choices, and this appeal has continued to work in favor of European destinations, given that most Americans are of European descent. Small but significant increases in the numbers of students studying abroad in non-Western countries are often attributable to students seeking to connect with their cultural heritages in other world regions. Some students choose to study abroad because of their religious beliefs.

Media attention, as well as tourism, may also make Europe an attractive study destination. Conversely, newspaper and television coverage of political unrest, violence and terrorism, poverty, or other forms of social instability in parts of Africa, Asia, Latin America, and the Middle East, as well as eastern and western Europe, periodically inhibits student flow. Given the quick pace of changes that take place in our world today and the instant reportage afforded by telecommunications, study program professionals often find themselves scrambling to keep up with the pace of world events. Environmental pollution in some of the world's major cities can pose health factors that also influence students in choosing study abroad sites. The stability and reputation of well-regarded educational infrastructures are often the deciding factors for students and their parents.

Finally, we should not ignore the impact of peer pressure and campus precedent. U.S. students frequently go abroad with their friends or in groups, having been persuaded to do so by friends who are past program participants. In short, whatever the adviser or faculty member says, groups of individuals, however socially bound, influence each other's decisions. Truly adventurous souls going overseas on their own, on a program nobody from their college has chosen before, are in a minority. Students seem greatly swayed by the prospect of studying abroad with a professor from their own campus on a program run by their own institution.

Field of Study

U.S. students pursuing overseas study report (intended or declared) academic majors in the humanities or social sciences more than in any other fields of study (see table 9.4). These particular fields have traditionally supported cultural inquiry and are often tied to foreign language requirements. Language majors make up an additional 10 percent of the total. Notably, the 48 percent subtotal for these two groups represents a significant decrease from only four years ago, when 47 percent alone were humanities and social sciences majors, and 12.5 percent more majored in languages.

TABLE 9.4

Major Fields of U.S.Study Abroad Students, 1985/86–1994/95

Field of Study	1985–86	1987–88	1989–90	1991–92	1993–94	1994–95
Social Sciences & Humanities	39.7	45.9	48.4	38.4	37.1	37
Business & Management	10.9	11.1	10.9	12	13.6	14
Foreign Languages	16.7	14.8	12.5	14	11.3	10
Other	8.2	6.8	6.8	7.6	7.7	6
Fine/Applied Arts	6.9	6.4	6.1	9.9	7.7	9
Physical Sciences	3.8	2.5	3.7	3.8	5.3	7
Education	4.1	4.0	4.6	5.7	4.0	4
Dual Major	–	–	–	–	3.6	4
Undeclared	4.2	3.8	3.4	4.1	3.6	3
Engineering	1.6	1.4	1.3	1.6	2.3	2
Health Sciences	1.7	1.4	1.1	1.1	1.7	2
Math & Computer Sciences	1.3	1.2	0.8	1.1	1.1	1
Agriculture	1	0.7	0.4	0.7	0.9	1
Totals	100%	100%	100%	100%	100%	100%

Source: IIE

Students often expect to receive credit in their major fields, while others certainly in the minority use study abroad as a time for exploration in other areas. IIE data are limited to revealing the on-campus major fields of study abroad students, not what is actually studied overseas. That research requires analysis of transcripts received. Nor can the IIE data measure the degree to which students actually study in the languages of the host countries, when those languages are not English, nor the degree to which students are immersed in the indigenous academic life of the host country or if they take courses given in a familiar, U.S. teaching style and format. These questions and others that could tell us, for example, how many students are pursuing internships abroad and what those programs look like in the aggregate are important to profile the learning experience.

Close to 14 percent of the students surveyed in the 1994–95 IIE survey were business and management majors, a proportion that has registered modest but consistent increase over time and that reflects the growing number of U.S. students choosing this major. Like internships, academic study abroad in the fields of business and management may be viewed by some students as possible preparation for a return overseas, once their undergraduate studies are completed, to work in international business.

Other students, who seek employment closer to home after graduation, will likely value their international education as training for productive association with coworkers of diverse backgrounds within the multicultural American workplace. A recent Rand study has identified cross-cultural competence as an important qualification in the profile of successful job candidates for employment in the global workforce of the next century.[20] It is usually argued that students who study abroad in a foreign language, often among that minority who are away for a full year, equip themselves with a greater measure of cross-cultural competence.

The aggregated 12 percent of study abroad students majoring in engineering, science, and agriculture needs to be recognized because of a pattern of small but consistent increase in recent years, echoing that identified for students studying business and management. Remarkably, this percentage of students majoring in engineering, scientific, and agricultural fields now equals that of foreign language majors studying abroad. Curricular restraints and requirements are traditionally the factors inhibiting study abroad in science and technology. Persistent efforts to establish study abroad opportunities, despite the confines of rigid course prerequisites and sequencing, are likely responsible for the recent growth. Often these students can do elective work overseas in courses dealing with world issues, history, language and culture. The challenge is to provide curricular options sufficient in range and specificity that such students do not fall behind in progress toward degree completion.

Further, because the United States is thought to excel in science and engineering, teaching and resources, students and departmental advisers alike may need to be convinced of the value of gaining a comparative perspective on one of these fields through study abroad. International students, on the other hand, continue to head for the United States expressly to study business, engineering, and science, a curricular emphasis of almost completely the opposite pattern.

Student Attitudes and Backgrounds

Beyond the basic characteristics of the U.S. student abroad, revealed principally in the national IIE surveys, information is available on the attitudes and background of U.S. students who have studied and worked abroad from the Study Abroad Evaluation Project (SAEP).[21] Although the data are somewhat out of date and limited in the number of U.S. students studied, the SAEP remains an important resource for cross-national comparison of study abroad in Europe and the United States. The Council on International Educational Exchange, working with the Darden School of Business Administration at the University of Virginia plans a comprehensive survey of the entire U.S. academic community, beginning this year, that should provide a more current picture, from the viewpoint of study abroad sending institutions. SAEP data were based on participant interviews and surveys.

Family Background

Participants in study abroad programs, especially those of a full academic year in duration, have been largely the sons and daughters of college-educated parents who are also well traveled, often speak other languages than English and may have lived overseas. Parental influence is often decisive in the study abroad decision. As one would expect, study abroad students from the International 50 colleges typically come from families in which both parents have college degrees, have traveled abroad, and speak foreign languages.[22]

Study abroad students bring to the experience a broad spectrum of previous international experience, about which we lack solid information. We do not have current data to measure the numbers of students studying abroad as undergraduates who have not lived, traveled, or been abroad before; neither do we know the numbers of those who have done so, sometimes with multiple sojourns overseas while growing up. Nor do we know the number of international students earning degrees at U.S. universities who are studying abroad as part of that experience. In an increasingly global world and with increasing numbers of students from multicultural and international backgrounds enriching U.S. campus populations, it would be useful to know these parameters.

Race and Ethnicity

In response to urging from NAFSA colleagues, *Open Doors 1994–95* included information for the first time on the race and ethnicity of study abroad participants, at least for the 43 percent of the total sample who could be so identified. Not surprisingly, given the privileged background that the study abroad population has traditionally reflected, 86 percent of the 1994–95 total reporting was recorded as white.[23] This correlates with the traditional popularity of European countries as study abroad destinations, but not entirely.

Students of all races study in all regions of the world. Five percent of the study abroad population is recorded as Asian-American, but a higher percentage of students study in Asia; five percent is also recorded as Hispanic-American, but 13 percent study in Latin America, and more than 20 percent in all the Spanish-speaking countries.

As a nation with an almost entirely immigrant population, it is a delicate, but undeniably interesting issue to consider the relative degrees to which students from the United States cross cultures when they study abroad. Do they choose a country or region of the world that closely reflects an ethnic heritage? Only 3 percent of the study abroad population is recorded as African American. The pursuit of student diversity to reflect home campus populations and the offering of optimal choice among destinations worldwide remain top priorities (see Chapter 11, "Promoting Student Diversity").

Financial Resources

A good deal of misery and myth surrounds the question of how students fund their programs abroad. It is typically thought (outside our field) that those who go on programs abroad represent only the affluent. Although the picture is incomplete, evidence suggests that study abroad students draw from a variety of sources, including personal savings, scholarships and loans, and family support. The key variable, as all study abroad professionals know very well, is less family background than the availability of financial aid.

The 1994–95 data reported in the current *Open Doors* survey show institutional financial support for study abroad. The good news is that 62.3 percent, or 357 of the 573 institutions responding to this question, offer aid for all study abroad programs approved for the transfer of credit, which amounts to a comprehensive, needs blind financial aid provision.[24]

Particularly since federal financial aid funds must be extended to study abroad, in light of the last reauthorization of the Higher Education Act, it behooves everyone in the field to be on top of the administration of financial aid within their own institution and to support efforts of NAFSA colleagues working hard to lobby for fair application and extension of government supported aid provisions. (See Chapter 5, "Financial Aid.")

Academic Ability

Study abroad students exhibit above-average scholastic performance and, as a result, usually are confident about their academic qualifications. For admission, most programs, whether administered by a student's home institution or sponsored externally, require a grade average of B, or a 3.0 cumulative grade point average. The needs of academically average students, who might flourish overseas and come back to the home campus prepared to improve their performance, are of interest. Correlation studies of grades achieved before and after the experience, in comparison with students who have not studied abroad, would be valuable, as would studies measuring the effect of study abroad on language learning.

▮ Summary

The emergent profile of the study abroad population shows a plateau in participation rates achieved at the middle of the present decade. In the wake of rapid growth in the 1980s, the 1990s seems to have settled down to a much more gradual increase, with a current upswing. It is beyond the purview of the present chapter, whose purpose has been to profile current study abroad participants, to ponder the reasons for the slowdown.

There are discernible patterns within the slowed rate of increase; non-Western countries show growing popularity, as do fields of study in such nontraditional fields as business and management, science, engineering and technology. Shorter study abroad sojourns with less emphasis on language learning continue to gain in popularity; women students continue to outnumber men. We are a long way from achieving diversity among study abroad students to match home-campus populations.

As noted above, despite much improvement, much work remains to be done in collecting data and studying participation, at both national and institutional levels. This is essential in order to support the goal of making international education available to greater numbers and types of students who wish to study in different fields and countries.

International educators agree on the need to work actively with IIE research staff and other colleagues on data collection.[25] It is a complex task to measure U.S. student mobility worldwide. Arguably many more students than those included in the data at hand have traveled abroad, but not as part of their formal study. On the other hand, most U.S. students stay home, from a lack of inclination or interest, though many are simply unable to go abroad, discouraged by circumstances or insufficient financial and other support.

It is in our shared interest to provide the data that truly demonstrate how we are doing and allow us to plan and extend the international education provision. Data collection by individual institutions provides micro-level material that feeds into macro-level, national, or other types of research. Many hypotheses, if tested, would likely yield valuable results from the data at hand. It is hoped that this review of current demographics will contribute heuristically to further work.

Notes

1. The 13-member NAFSA group that worked with IIE on revisions in the survey was led by Jane D. Cary, SECUSSA chair 1993–94, whose correspondence and conversation during April 1996 are much appreciated.

2. We are grateful to Todd M. Davis, IIE Research Division, for conversation (March 22, 1995) and for permission to cite the data and use the tables included in this chapter.

3. Elizabeth Sutton, IIE Research Division, "Essential Information for Study Abroad Data Systems," unpublished.

4. *Open Doors 1995/96: Report on International Educational Exchange,* ed. Todd M. Davis (New York: IIE, 1996); see the appendix for student participation totals for each reporting institution, grouped by state.

5. "Overcoming Barriers to Study Abroad: the Case of New York State," A Report of the New York State Task Force on International Education. Cornell University, December 1955.

6. David C. Engerman and Parker G. Marden, *In the International Interest: The Contributions and Needs of America's International Liberal Arts Colleges* (Beloit, Wisc.: Beloit College, June 1991).

7. Richard D. Lambert, "Study Abroad: Where We Are, Where We Should Be." Paper delivered at the 41st Annual Conference on International Educational Exchange, New York, 1989, p. 13.

8. *Open Doors 1995/96,* table 10.3, 131.

9. E. El-Khawas, "Campus Trends," American Council on Education, Higher Education Panel Report, no. 82 (Washington, D.C.: ACE, July 1992).

10. Urbain J. DeWinter, "Study Abroad in New York State: A Status Report," *Open Doors 1994/95,* 180.

11. Compare with the earlier estimate of under 100,000 by John Bowman, "Educating American Undergraduates Abroad: The Development of Study Abroad Programs by American Colleges and Universities," CIEE

Occasional Paper, no. 24 (New York: CIEE, November 1987) 13-16, as cited in the original version of this chapter.

12. For discussion, see Bill Hoffa, "An Expanded Rationale for Education Abroad in the 1990's and Beyond," *Transitions Abroad* (September/October 1994), 28–29.

13. IIE, *Academic Year Abroad,* 1996–97, and *Vacation Study Abroad,* 1996–97 (New York: IIE, 1996).

14. *Open Doors 1995/96,* table 10.9, 137.

15. Ibid., 131.

16. Ibid., 137.

17. Bowman, "Educating Americans Abroad," 13–16.

18. Aggregated from *Open Doors 1995/96,* table 10.1, 120.

19. Ibid., and see "Overcoming Barriers to Study Abroad," New York State Task Force on International Education, appendix D, "The Language Aspect of Study Abroad," 5, citing data from *Cambridge Encyclopedia of Languages,* 1987.

20. T. K. Bikson and S. A. Law, "Global Preparedness and Human Resources, College and Corporate Perspectives" (Santa Monica, Calif.: RAND, 1994), 28, 69.

21. Barbara B. Burn, Ladislav Cerych, and Alan Smith, eds., *Study Abroad Programmes,* and Susan Opper, Ulrich Teichler and Jerry Carlson, *Impacts of Study Abroad Programmes on Students and Graduates,* Higher Education Policy Series 11, vols. 1 and 2 (London: Jessica Kingsley, 1990).

22. Opper, Teichler and Carlson, *Impact of Study Abroad Programmes on Students and Graduates,* chap. 2, "The Participants," 23–40.

23. *Open Doors 1995/96,* table 10.9, 137.

24. Ibid., table 10.3, 131.

25. "International Education in the '90s, Study Abroad Advisers Reflect on the National Task Force Report," ed. Bill Hoffa, *Transitions Abroad* (September/October 1995), 89.

10 Advising Principles And Strategies

Contributors: Cynthia Felback Chalou, Barbara Lantz, Janeen Felsing, and Kathy Lutfi

There are many types of successful advising. What works for one person may not work for another; what worked this year may not work next year. What is clear is that advising is a very complex and dynamic interpersonal process that cannot be reduced to easy formulas or universal answers. Nevertheless, the relations between you and your students will be enriched and deepened the more you know about your institution, program options, student maturation, and cross-cultural training. Carrying out your strategies and putting your knowledge to work will benefit both your institution and your students.

E very college and university has its own philosophy, policies, and approaches to education abroad; these factors greatly influence the commitment, style, and level of advising available to its students. Whether your institution has generally restrictive or very open policies with regard to education abroad, it is important to know that you don't need to know everything in order to do your job well.

As discussed in Part One of this book, advisers often have few formal means of learning all they might be asked to know in order to counsel students on education abroad opportunities. Nevertheless, to be a successful adviser of students considering study abroad, you should work toward gaining the following skills, knowledge, and experience:

- a complete and objective knowledge of the range of classroom-based and experiential programs available to U.S. undergraduates—and not just programs sponsored by your own institution
- a knowledge of institutional policies related to program approval, admissions standards, graduation requirements, credit transfer, and financial aid, and a strong working relationship with academic units, so that education abroad can be integrated into degree studies.

- strong interpersonal counseling skills and advising techniques, based on familiarity with undergraduate student needs and development theory.

- an understanding of the cross-cultural learning process and an ability to prepare students and others for the challenges of living and learning abroad and for reentering U.S. society and reintegrating their experience abroad into their academic studies.

■ Basic Knowledge and Skills

Knowledge of Education Abroad Programs

It is important for education abroad advisers to be knowledgeable about the range of credit-bearing education abroad programs—those sponsored by their own institution and those sponsored by other institutions and agencies, both classroom-based and experiential. There are hundreds of diverse programs all over the world, and nearly 4,000 academic-year, summer, and short-term programs. Owing to this massive number of offerings, advisers cannot be familiar with all aspects of these programs; rather, you should familiarize yourself with the resources available and instruct students on how to obtain the information directly.

IIE's *Academic Year Abroad* and *Vacation Study Abroad* and Peterson's *Study Abroad* and *Summer Study Abroad* are probably the most useful resources to many study abroad offices, especially those in which students are referred to outside programs. Instructions are available in the front of the IIE and Peterson's guides on how to use these comprehensive listings of education abroad opportunities.

Some of the programs listed in the IIE and Peterson's guides are open only to students from sponsoring institutions; some are open to others only on an occasional basis, when spaces remain; many are not available every semester or year. A careful reading of the eligibility requirements in each listing of the IIE and Peterson's volumes will elicit this information. Students may contact the host institution even if the reference indicates *"For own students only."* Additional programs may also be discovered via the brochures, catalogs, fliers, and posters mailed out by sponsoring organizations and agencies.

You can help your students interpret the information by developing a critical eye for details in the guides and literature. Lily von Klemperer's "How to Read Study Abroad Literature" (1976) offers sound advice on reading program literature. This guide has been reprinted in annual editions of IIE's *Academic Year Abroad* and appeared as Appendix 5 in the first edition of this volume.

Unless your institution has a policy that prevents your students from participating in outside programs, program representatives may visit you during the year. These visits represent an opportunity for you, your faculty, and students to learn about new programs or to update information on ongoing programs. From these visits and from the program materials, you should be able to answer the questions listed below.

Similarly, this list is helpful as a guide to students when perusing the resources and it may help narrow down the seemingly unlimited options to a more manageable number. A helpful technique in advising students is to recommend consideration of the most limiting factor such as low GPA, limited resources, or elementary language ability. With this in mind, students can immediately refer to that section of the program description to determine its appropriateness to their needs. Questions to consider when reviewing programs include:

- Is it operated by an accredited degree-granting institution or an agency from which my institution has agreed to accept transfer credit? Does it satisfy all the criteria my institution has established for study abroad programs? Will it accept students who may not receive credit from my institution? Will students be interested even if credit is not possible?

- What are the program's entrance requirements and course offerings? Which students are most suitable? What GPA, coursework, and foreign-language proficiency are required? Are courses taken directly at a foreign university or are students taught separately? Are internships available?

- To what extent do students interact with the host culture? Are the classes with mainly U.S., international, or host-country students? Are the courses offered by a host institution? Are the instructors American or host nationals? How are students housed? In apartments with other U.S. participants? In residence halls with other foreign students? In residence halls with native students? With families in a homestay or in a boarding arrangement?

- What administrative support is provided in the United States and abroad? Is there an office in the United States that facilitates admission and provides predeparture information? Or should students be prepared to complete applications in the foreign language and send them directly abroad? Is a resident director on site, or are students expected to be mature and experienced enough to cope on their own?

- What are the inclusive costs? What is *not* included in the program fee? Does the program offer scholarships or work-study options for eligible students? Can student loans or tuition scholarship be applied to program costs?

If key information about these programs is vague, misleading, or missing, you or the student should request that it be supplied or clarified. It is appropriate to ask for course descriptions and syllabi, program evaluations, and names and addresses of previous participants. Contacting education abroad advisers at other institutions is also a good way to learn about an unfamiliar program. The point of these actions is not to find the "perfect" program (be suspicious of evaluation reports that fail to report problems), but, rather, to ensure that a particular program meets your institutional standards and is appropriate for a particular student.

Additionally, you should present students with the option of alternative programs—internships, work, service learning, or teaching. Students are increasingly drawn to such opportunities as they grow to understand their educational relevance and value. Such programs often make education abroad possible for students who cannot afford it. Students who see traditional study abroad as cloistered and limiting may be open to a more indigenous experience, one lived in closer contact with the native language and culture (see Chapter 15, "Work Abroad and International Careers").

Knowledge of Institutional Policies

Colleges and universities with a tradition of education abroad have evolved a philosophy of education for study both on campus and abroad. They also have implemented policies and criteria for program selection, student participation, and the awarding of degree credit. Most institutional policies are restrictive in some ways and open in others. It is important to understand the rationale and philosophy of education that underlie study abroad policies and to be in touch with the range of faculty and administration opinion regarding study abroad. On many campuses, study abroad remains controversial even with clear and well-established policies and criteria, while it is enthusiastically endorsed on others. In either case, you become the interpreter of policy to both students and faculty and often have the opportunity to shape policy to meet institutional as well as student objectives.

When education abroad policy is restrictive, participation is limited to programs sponsored and/or approved by the home institution. All unapproved programs are thus deemed off-limits. It becomes your task to know well those programs and foreign institutions that receive home institutional approval and to utilize policies and procedures to facilitate student participation. It is also important to remain informed about developments in the education abroad field that may recommend programs for inclusion or exclusion by the home institution. Changes in scheduling, curricula, staffing, cost, and accreditation are some factors that may alter the suitability of programs for participation by students from your institution.

Maintaining an up-to-date library of brochures and catalogs of those programs students have used in the past, consulting World Wide Web home pages for those programs that have them, and participating in e-mail lists to learn about new program options are good ways to keep abreast of program developments. Interviewing students when they return and reflect back on their experiences can provide critical insight into the functioning of programs and their suitability for future students (see Chapter 7, "Computerizing Operations").

Finally, you may well have students whose interests may be served best by "unapproved" programs. When there is a petition process to handle such instances, your ability to help students receive permission to participate depends on your intimate knowledge of program strengths, experience with prior petition outcomes, and willingness to coach students in crafting persuasive petitions.

Institutions with more open policies permit their students to select from a wide array of study abroad program offerings. This approach rests on one or all of the following assumptions: (1) all accredited U.S. and foreign institutions sponsoring programs can be counted on to ensure quality; (2) the most important task of the education abroad adviser is to help students choose the program best suited to their particular goals, needs, interests, academic preparation, and financial circumstances; or (3) there is no such thing as a perfect program, only a perfect match between the right student and the right program.

Proponents of this approach argue that, ultimately, it is the student who must take responsibility for making a success of his or her international experience. They point to instances in which students have had excellent learning experiences on mediocre programs—and vice versa— to prove their point. If this is the approach of your institution, then obviously it is in the students' best interest to become familiar with as many resources and programs as possible.

Education abroad advisers are also called upon to explain institutional procedures and criteria for transferring credit from programs abroad

169

to the home transcript (see Chapter 4, "Academic Credit"). Important issues include:

- Who must approve a student's plan for study abroad? The student's academic adviser? A faculty committee? A dean? Your office? You?
- What documentation is required to transfer credit? A transcript? A grade report? Tutor or instructor written evaluation? Copies of course syllabi? Reading lists? Written work, including essays? Class notes? Exams?
- Who evaluates and/or transfers credit from study abroad? The home campus registrar? A faculty committee? The major adviser? Academic departmental representatives? A dean? Your office? You?
- What degree requirements are students free to pursue abroad? Requirements for the major? General education requirements? Language requirements? Elective credit only?
- How are grades reported on the degree transcript? As U.S.-style letter grades? As grades awarded in the system of the foreign institution? As pass/fail? Are they included in the degree program GPA?
- Can students earn credit for out-of-classroom work, such as independent study projects, internships, volunteer work, or fieldwork?
- Is there a procedure for students to appeal credit awards? What is your role in the process?

Students, parents, faculty, and even fellow administrators from time to time turn to advisers for answers to these questions. In explaining these procedures, it helps to have a solid understanding of the philosophy of education that underlies them so that the rationale for decisions, especially those that spark controversy, can be made clear.

Education Abroad Advisers Do Not Stand Alone

At institutions of higher education, whether they be small colleges or large research universities, education abroad advisers belong to a staff of academic or student-support personnel, and each student services specialist has his or her area of expertise. It can be useful to know well the division of labor at your institution in order to guide students to the appropriate office for information about matters relevant to education abroad, such as financial aid, leaves of absence and readmission, codes of conduct and disciplinary procedures, health and travel insurance, billing, inoculations and visa requirements, storage and shipping, travel arrangements, and for information about housing contracts and preregistration procedures upon return to campus.

Some of this information may be available to you, or it may be your job to provide it. Indeed, it is a rare education abroad adviser who does not feel overextended in the range of expertise expected to do the job well. So it can be helpful to advisers as well as to students to make use of other offices and personnel when they are available. Again, you do not need to know everything in order to do your job well. Rather, you simply need to direct students to resources that will tell them what they need to know, a skill they will require when they study abroad.

▌ Student Development and Cultural Learning

Professionals in the education abroad field know well the potential for learning about the world, another country and its people, our own country, and ourselves through study abroad. It is the cultural learning—including language, values, politics, economics, patterns of daily life, and even the awareness of culture itself as an organizing principal—that differentiates study abroad from study on campus. Academic coursework is an important vehicle for this learning, but cultural learning occurs in less systematic ways as well.

Education abroad programs vary in their mechanisms for introducing and integrating students to the host culture. Program models are differentiated in Chapter 16. When advising students, it is important to help them identify not only the country, city, and optimal timing of study abroad, but also the program model most appropriate to their individual background preparation and learning styles. Students with sufficient foreign language skills, prior area studies coursework, or prior experiences abroad may be ready for direct enrollment in a foreign university or other "immersion" program. Students without much prior study of the language and culture may need a program patterned after the more traditional campus-based model. But prior preparation and background are not the only important variables in determining the program model appropriate for an individual student.

Students also vary in their ways of engaging the world and taking in information. David Hunt (1979), David Kolb (1984), and others have offered some paradigms for identifying learning styles. David Hunt's approach is to look at a student's need for structure. He identifies three stages of development:

- *Unsocialized (high structure):* This type of person requires much structure and guidance and has little tolerance for ambiguity.

171

- *Dependent (moderate structure):* This type of person can handle some ambiguity but is still very much dependent on the teacher for providing the framework for the learning process.
- *Independent (minimal structure):* This type of person likes having input into her own learning process; she is open to choices and is self-directed.

When working with students making choices among program models, it is useful to reflect on their education thus far and select some important learning experiences in or outside the classroom, listing the key characteristics of the learning process and environment. Are they more inclined to learn through relating to people and being involved in experiences, by looking for meaning and being open to different perspectives, by logically analyzing ideas and planning systematically, or by taking risks and influencing people and events through action? To get started on this process, you can review with students their academic records with an eye for courses in which they did very well and/or very poorly, and then analyze why they did or didn't do well.

A useful tool in the process is the learning-style inventory put together by David Kolb and available from McBer and Company. This inventory includes a short questionnaire, charting an individual's learning stage and identifying the preferred learning style.

Chapter 16 describes the program models and designs from which students can choose, based on their learning styles. Three pedagogical models of study abroad are traditional, direct enrollment, and experiential. These are discussed below.

Traditional Models

In traditional study abroad programs the primary "academic" learning takes place in a classroom, where the instructor gives lectures and readings. Student learning is assessed through examinations, which may include essay questions as well as short answer and multiple choice. In this type of learning environment, the instructor sets the learning goals, imparts knowledge to the student, and evaluates the student learning.

Variations in the traditional model include course components, which take students into the host community through field trips, internships, and service learning projects. Others provide seminars, including faculty or student-led group discussions, which serve to synthesize information presented in the course (for example, lectures, reading, field trips). Students who feel most comfortable with a highly structured learning environment should consider this more traditional branch campus model.

Direct Enrollment

As in traditional study abroad programs, the primary "academic" learning takes place in a classroom, where the instructor gives lectures and readings. In European institutions, faculty give lectures and assign readings as in the United States; however, students are responsible for how much work they do and when they complete it. Faculty give minimal direction and most of the learning requires self direction. Rather than being evaluated on class participation, quizzes, and tests through the term, students are graded on a final exam at the end of the term or the year.

Variations on the direct enrollment model include, among others, evaluation based on rote memory, seminar-type learning as described under the traditional program model, and internships. Students who apply to a foreign university through a U.S. institution or other outside organization receive some additional academic support. Some also provide courses only for U.S. students, which are taken alongside courses in the university itself. Students who are self-disciplined enough to structure their study time appropriately (i.e., not try to cram all the studying in during the last few weeks) and are fairly independent should consider direct enrollment where the classroom environment is fairly structured with faculty set up as the primary director of learning.

Experiential Programs

These study abroad programs, which take an experiential approach to teaching and learning, involve the students and teacher intellectually in the learning process. In addition to the "academic" learning, some experiential programs incorporate personal and spiritual learning into the course experience. Rather than learning in a traditional classroom, the host community and/or the environment becomes the classroom. There is a wide range of experiential programs and some traditional programs offer experiential components such as field trips or internships.

A common component of experiential programs is that students become involved in the learning process by defining learning goals for themselves within individual courses and/or for the program as a whole. Learning is often assessed by students and faculty through class participation, journals, individual or group projects, and research papers. Most programs have a specific academic focus (for example, sustainable development, women's studies, environmental studies) and others focus more generally on language and culture. Most involve language study and homestays and/or community living. Some offer internships or service learning opportunities. Students who work well on their own and are self-directed would do well on these programs.

The most obvious objective of foreign study is learning about another culture. But learning to learn *in* another culture is an equally valid objective. Students must also be prepared for living and learning in cultures that are different, often dramatically so, from the one in which they were raised. Certain predictable phenomena are encountered by everyone who enters a new culture. A period of disorientation and discomfort lasts until the signals and clues of living in that culture become understood.

The adjustment cycle often follows predictable patterns—typically, initial elation and excitement, followed by confusion and discomfort, which often leads to depression, anger, and even hostility. As surroundings become more familiar and communication skills improve, firmer social relationships develop. The cycle is complete when the new culture is accepted and appreciated. It is important to remind students that education abroad is not just an adventure, but involves stresses of adjustment integral to the growth and development they will gain from the experience.

Chapter 14, "Predeparture Orientation and Reentry," provides suggestions for preparing students for the challenges of the specific cultural settings they will encounter. Wherever they are headed, and however long their stay, all students can benefit from a discussion of cultural learning while they are planning for education abroad. Encourage students to monitor their own strategies for coping with stress, disenchantment, and loneliness on campus. This will help them to assess their readiness for the extra psychological challenges of study abroad.

Each person enters a new cultural setting with particular identifying characteristics or social markers. Most societies recognize "student" as a special status and/or stage of life. U.S. students of all ethnic, racial, or religious backgrounds will bring new interpretations of their own identity abroad, different from those that students encounter on their home campus. The role expectations for college-age women abroad may be particularly out of keeping with college women's expectations for themselves.

The yearning for independence, which often preoccupies college-age Americans and may motivate them to study abroad, can backfire in a cultural setting that downplays the importance of the individual and independent action. Helping students understand that cultural differences can sometimes be uncomfortable, that they may face stereotyping, and that they may receive very different treatment abroad is an important part of preparing students for cross-cultural learning.

Chickering and Havighurst (1981), Perry (1970, 1981), Bennett (1986), and Paige (1993) offer theories of developmental processes applicable to persons making the transition from adolescence to adulthood. Perry's, Bennett's and Paige's theories are particularly useful in identifying the potential for intellectual and moral development through cross-cultural experience. The cultural learning that comes with study abroad has the potential to encourage students to assess and evaluate positions of knowledge, to become comfortable with ambiguity, tolerant of cultural differences, and to be aware of cultural paradigms.

Learning to appreciate cultural and social relativism without giving in to nihilism and to question assumptions and understand their place in a particular frame of reference allows students to empathize with others who are different and to formulate judgments that transcend narrow attitudes. While some programs make cultural learning an explicit part of their curricula, others provide the medium for cross-cultural experience but leave analysis and insight to the student.

When students return to campus, they are likely to experience another period of adjustment, with sometimes unexpected difficulties. It is not unusual for students to feel themselves to be very different from their peers precisely because of their study abroad experiences. Advisers can be a good audience for students reflecting back on their experiences abroad.

Organizing meetings and social gatherings for returning students can help them forge new friendships based on their common experience of study abroad. For those students who leave their off-campus study sites early due to illness or other unhappy circumstances, advisers can be the most important link to the home campus, collaborating with appropriate university offices and representatives to provide the student with an appropriate path back to campus.

▌ Advising Procedures and Strategies

The following section will discuss advising strategies successfully used on many campuses, based on the principles outlined above. These include one-on-one advising as well as suggestions for alternative strategies.

One-on-One Counseling

The advising process begins at the front door, with a welcoming staff and an appropriate environment. An up-to-date education abroad library and orientation to its use, as previously suggested, are essential if students are to understand that selecting a program is an interactive process and that they will ultimately be asked to make their own informed decisions.

Whether students are greeted by a study abroad adviser, a secretary, a student assistant, an informational video, a World Wide Web home page, or an interactive computer program, these initial exchanges should explain basic procedures and produce some introductory information on both sides. Encourage students to read through the introductory materials, begin to explore the range of possibilities open to them, and schedule an appointment for the next stage.

Initial Advising Session

In the initial contacts, it is important to establish an open and honest relationship. Find out a little about the student: year in school, major and minor discipline, academic background, previous travel, language competency, occupational interest, time of year planned for going abroad, possible length of stay, tentative thoughts on study versus travel or other experience abroad, preferred amount of program structure and guidance, financial resources, and parental attitude.

Try to determine the student's preferred learning style as previously discussed in this chapter. This information is fundamental to helping a student to define his personal abilities, goals, and perceptions.

This background lays the foundation for the most important question of all: "What are your reasons for wanting to go abroad?" At this initial stage, some students will have a clear idea of what they hope to accomplish, while others will not—they simply want to experience another culture and are open to a variety of possibilities.

The general principle is that it is best to go abroad primarily for a unique learning experience. It is never wise to go only to escape from problems existing in the home situation. Inform students that, while a change of location may at first seem to relieve some personal pressures, the problems may be considerably increased by anxieties. These are often caused by the loss of security of a familiar setting and the need for adjustment to a foreign culture, educational system, and social environment.

Some students may seek to go abroad to be closer to friends or family. If this is the case, recommend an experience that fulfills that need. Instead of exploring expensive study abroad opportunities, work or volunteer abroad may be an option, enabling the student to be close to loved ones without the expense.

In most cases, a student has already discussed studying abroad with their parents or friends. If there is hesitancy or reluctance concerning their reasons for wanting to go abroad, delicately probe the issue. If parental support appears to be a barrier, suggest to the student that you are willing to contact the parents directly. By providing basic information and reassurance, you can ease the minds of both the parents and student.

The student should be reminded that a study abroad experience requires careful planning. Most advisers recommend four to twelve months for planning. Longer lead time is needed for longer programs. Time is needed to initiate discussion with the student's academic department to learn the policy for granting study abroad credit. The adviser and student should determine what effect study abroad might have on degree credit, time of graduation, and advantage in the job market after graduation.

Following this discussion and the clarification of the student's goals, provide information on a wide range of opportunities abroad. Introduce and discuss these options to acquaint the student with the various choices available. Encourage the student to spend time in the education abroad library reviewing information on study possibilities, beginning with those administered by the home campus or consortia in which it participates. Recommend appropriate programs and indicate apprehensions concerning less sound choices when the student requests such information. Encourage certain students to consider nontraditional study sites.

Directed Research

To further assist the student in independent predeparture research, recommend specific reference books where information about the foreign institutions and educational systems from program sponsors can be gathered. Resources in the main campus library, foreign government information services in New York City, cultural offices of embassies in Washington, D.C., and consulates in other major cities also may have useful information about the educational systems, institutions, and programs, and also about the life and culture of different countries. The more the student knows about the foreign country, culture, and the educational system and its expectations, the better she can cope with it once there.

Refer students to persons whose knowledge about a particular area of the world is more current and extensive than your own. These resources include students, faculty, and community members returned from abroad; international students, scholars, and community members; and returned Peace Corps volunteers. Students who have returned from the same program or institution abroad will be able to answer the specific questions that are often pressing for the outgoing student; and other resource persons may provide supplementary information and insight.

This informational exchange fulfills several critical needs: (1) the returnees share their experiences with a hungry audience, helping to validate and continue their international experience; (2) genuine interest in the host country is expressed to international visitors; (3) the outgoing student recognizes the institutional and community interest in international education; and (4) the local international network expands as support is provided before, during, and after the experience. Referral to one returned student can often lead to contact with this wider community network.

Follow-up Advising Sessions

Encourage students to consider program costs and available ways of meeting them by talking early with parents and the financial aid office. Costs of programs should be checked, making sure that all items of expense are included. Some program literature may indicate what the program charge covers but omit such essentials as lunches or weekend meals, health and accident insurance, and transportation. Note that almost all study abroad students spend substantially more on elective travel than they expect.

Most students need encouragement. If their language proficiency is inadequate, they should undertake intensive study. Or, if the student cannot afford a study abroad program but is skilled in a language and reasonably self-sufficient, you might encourage the student to undertake independent study or consider working abroad. In this way, the student will be able to pursue options most suited to his capabilities and financial resources.

After a student has carefully reviewed the options, help her choose the best programs and submit the applications in a proper and timely manner. Encourage the student to apply to more than one program unless there is reasonable certainty of acceptance by the first choice.

From the student's point of view, the initial challenge of study abroad is to choose an appropriate program or foreign institution and to prepare a successful application. The study abroad application process can provide the student and the adviser an opportunity to plan thoroughly the undergraduate degree program and the place of study abroad in it. With a good match of study abroad with academic program and student interest, study abroad can expand and enrich the home campus curriculum.

If your job entails academic advising, an understanding of on-campus curricula and degree programs is just as crucial in this endeavor as a sound and wide-ranging knowledge of study abroad options. If your role is more strictly administrative, it is still helpful to students to encourage this careful work with their faculty advisers.

This collaboration with students in the process of choosing and applying to study abroad also provides the opportunity to help students develop effective strategies for shaping their future careers. The skills required to write an effective essay of intent, a component of nearly every study abroad application, are applicable to job applications and to applications for graduate or professional study.

The language and cultural learning that occur through study abroad are more effective with good preparatory training, and they can be valuable credentials for some future career paths. The advising and application process thus provides an opportunity to encourage students to make mature assessments of the relevance of study abroad to their future goals and to make their study abroad not only a productive learning experience but a significant episode in their professional development.

To supplement the application process, provide advice on institutional policies and procedures pertaining to

- the payment of tuition and/or program fees;
- refunds if the student does not go or withdraws before the program is completed;
- prior approval for courses taken abroad, if required at your institution
- submitting records of study completed abroad for evaluation and credit;
- registration, housing, and on-campus parking upon return; and
- independent study or direct enrollment.

Throughout the entire advising process, supply suggestions and guidelines to assist the student in further defining personal goals, in addition to supplying the information previously discussed. When you do not know an answer, either find the information requested or recommend a person or address to contact for information.

Keeping records of the students' names, addresses, qualifications, and interests enables you to call or write a them when new information comes in, to keep in touch through a newsletter while abroad, or to contact them upon return. Copies of applications, prior credit-approval forms, letters of recommendation, and transcripts should be kept in some cases, but be aware of regulations concerning confidentiality of student records.

Alternative and Supplemental Strategies

One-on-one counseling is the best way to share your knowledge and experience with students and to help them reach responsible decisions. But the time demands on both advisers and students often make it difficult to devote the energy and concentration these discussions deserve. The time with the study abroad adviser is only part of the process. Students should also be examining your library's written materials— essential information on such topics as institutional policies and procedures, credit transfer, program evaluations, required travel documents, using the library, low-cost airfares, predeparture readings, summer jobs abroad, and so forth.

If you do not have such materials, refer to NAFSA's publication, *Forms of Travel*, a collection of useful model forms. Advisers can use other resources as well to make more efficient use of limited time and to add to the effectiveness of the advising process. Some of these are:

- *General Meetings.* Many education abroad offices either begin each semester with a large general-information meeting for students who are considering education abroad, or hold such meetings periodically. Such meetings need to be fully promoted to everyone, and it is sometimes helpful to have key deans and faculty present, as well as returned students. If attendance is good and you have prepared a lively overview of institutional policies, the options that exist abroad, and how to approach and use your office, meetings can result in increased enthusiasm and the prospect of beginning personal advising at a higher level.

- *Small Group Advising.* It is also useful to arrange meetings for smaller groups of students interested in: (1) your own programs; (2) program types (for example, language-immersion programs or programs with internships); (3) particular countries or regions; or (4) programs geared to specific majors (for example, engineering, business, music, nutrition, etc.). A group session may take a little longer than talking with one individual, but it will take much less time than successive individual interviews. These sessions can also include returned students, visiting exchange students, faculty who have interests in these areas, or visiting program representatives.

- *Referral to Colleagues.* You may not need to answer all questions—especially the most technical ones—when others on campus either know more than you do or have the authority to make decisions in certain areas such as credit transfer, financial aid, billing procedures, and the like. In short, take advantage of your campus network; remember that others are also there to assist students. Referring students to others not only saves time but also lets students know that support for education abroad is institutionwide. It also helps to strengthen relationships between your office and other key ones on campus. Referrals to faculty members involved with particular programs should also be common.

- *Peer Advising.* With proper training, returned education abroad students can serve as the best recruiters and as effective advisers. The training might include discussions on what they considered important in their experience, what information and counseling they had (or did not have but needed), how to reach more students, and especially on how everybody's experience abroad is unique, yet has common elements. It is critical to provide complete training so the peer advisers are thoroughly informed of programs and procedures.

Be judicious in your selection of peer advisers because some students have difficulty generalizing about their experience to make it relevant to others. Distinguish students who simply "had a good time" from those who seem to have grown and matured. Interesting and committed students who made the most of their opportunities abroad and who have a real desire to use what they have learned to assist others can be very effective adjuncts in the advisory process.

References

Bennett, Milton. "A Developmental Approach to Training for Intercultural Sensitivity." *International Journal of Intercultural Relations* 10, 2: 176–96.

Bibliography of Research on Experiential Learning and the Learning-Style Inventory (Boston: McBer, 1992).

Chickering, Arthur W. and Robert J. Havighurst. "The Life Cycle." In *Modern American College: Responding to the New Realities of Diverse Students and a Changing Society,* ed. Arthur W. Chickering and Associates (San Francisco: Jossey-Bass, 1981).

Hunt, David. "Learning Style and Student Needs: An Introduction to

Conceptual Level." In *Student Learning Styles: Diagnosing and Prescribing Programs* (Reston, VA: National Association of Secondary School Principals, 1979).

Kolb, David. *Experiential Learning: Experience as the Source of Learning and Development* (Englewood Cliffs, N.J.: Prentice-Hall, 1984).

Paige, R. Michael, ed. *Education for the Intercultural Experience*, 2d ed. (Yarmouth, Maine: Intercultural Press, 1993).

Perry, William G., Jr. *Forms of Intellectual and Ethical Development in the College Years* (New York: Holt, Rinehart and Winston, 1970).

Perry, William G., Jr. "Cognitive and Ethical Growth: The Making of Meaning." In *The Modern American College: Responding to the New Realities of Diverse Students and a Changing Society,* ed. Arthur W. Chickering and Associates (San Francisco: Jossey-Bass, 1981).

Smith, Donna and David Kolb, *User Guide for the Learning Style Inventory.* (Boston: McBer, 1985).

11
Promoting Student Diversity

Contributors: Margery A. Ganz and Valerie M. Eastman

As an education abroad professional, you work hard to extend the benefits of the international education experience to all students. With only 2–4 percent of all U.S. undergraduates now studying or working abroad as part of their degree studies, and with these students representing a very narrow slice of the social, racial, ethnic, academic, and preprofessional pie that is U.S. higher education, getting on with the task of international education represents an immense challenge that can be ignored only at our national peril. Put differently, because nontraditional students represent the "majority" of students, not to give more priority to their interests and needs is a formula for irrelevance and defeat.

In Chapter 9 the authors profiled U.S. students now studying abroad. They found that students outside the affluent mainstream have not participated significantly in education abroad. Indeed, this paucity of nontraditional students (at least in proportion to their numbers in U.S. colleges and universities) is conspicuous. As CIEE's Advisory Council for International Educational Exchange observed in "Educating for Global Competence":

> Students who study abroad are from a narrow spectrum of the total population. They are predominantly white females from highly educated professional families, majoring in the social sciences or humanities. They are high achievers and risk-takers. Many have had earlier overseas travel or international experience. Whether by their own choice or lack of encouragement to do so, there are fewer men, members of minority groups, students from nonprofessional and less-educated families, and fewer students from science, education, or business among undergraduates who study abroad.

The Report of the National Task Force on Undergraduate Education Abroad: Getting On with the Task (1990) (see Appendix) describes the challenge as follows: "Efforts to expand the number of undergraduates who study abroad must address the lack of diversity among them.... Even though minority enrollments in U.S. colleges and universities increased overall to 8 percent of all four-year college students, minority participation in study abroad has increased little, representing only a tiny fraction of all undergraduate study abroad students."

"Getting on with the task" means that proactive efforts are required of every adviser and program administrator. Although real obstacles do exist, especially curricular and economic ones, part of the problem is the perpetuation of individual and institutional assumptions. Such assumptions clearly limit what does and does not happen. One important barrier to study abroad is the widespread misconception of families, students, and their institutions that study abroad is not an achievable goal. Making such an experience for such students "an achievable goal" therefore remains your primary challenge. How you address these misconceptions, however, depends less on available resources and precedents than on the amount of imagination, energy, and sense of priorities you can bring to the task.

What you can accomplish obviously has something to do with the level of commitment to international educational exchange that exists on your campus. But it has even more to do with your institution's policies on equal access. The convenient and traditional commitment may inspire advisers to promote opportunities only to students with sufficient resources and backgrounds to take advantage of what is available. After all, one of the strengths of education abroad is that it continues to attract self-motivated and adventurous students who usually do not need to be told that international living and learning is worthwhile, but just require some assistance to work out their programs. Because most international educators agree on the need to expand numbers overall, and because only a fraction of undergraduates who could be participating in overseas programs actually do so, there is plenty to be said for concentrating efforts on this large group of traditional students who are more likely to actually go overseas.

But beyond the national goal of encouraging more students to have a significant international experience abroad prior to graduation, there are moral obligations to push beyond traditional norms, to include a wider cross-section of the undergraduate student population—including, but not limited to, those from more diverse racial and ethnic backgrounds, older students, male students, students with physical disabilities or learning disabilities, gay students, and those majoring in business, science, technology, education, and the arts. What, in short, is your answer to the entitlement question from either an institutional or individual perspective? If education abroad is as important as we believe and say it is, how can we possibly defend making it available only to certain categories of students?

▌ Deciding and Implementing Priorities

As noted above, the typical student who studies abroad is not difficult to categorize. On a national scale, only about 1–2 percent of the approximately 13 million U.S. undergraduates participate in some sort of education abroad program—3–4 percent if only four-year institutions are considered. Often, at small, private, liberal arts colleges, the percentages are substantially higher. For instance at the Claremont Colleges, Middlebury, Bowdoin, and other affluent institutions approximately 50 percent of the students study abroad, and at Kalamazoo the numbers are even higher. But, given national averages, it would be logical to infer that those who remain on campus represent by far the dominant U.S. tradition.

But because our goals in the field of education abroad are to increase numbers *and* diversity nationally, our focus must be on identifying types of students who do not traditionally participate in education abroad—at least in proportion to their numbers in the U.S. undergraduate population. Once identified, these students must be given viable opportunities. Some subgroupings of nontraditional students (that is, in relation to the tradition of study abroad) include:

- those majoring in subject areas other than the humanities and social sciences, such as business, science, technology, nursing, engineering, architecture, music, art, education, agriculture, and so forth;
- those attending community colleges, technical colleges, and other two-year degree-granting institutions, which now account for more than half the total undergraduate population;
- male students, who still make up less than 40 percent of all enrollments;
- part-time and older students (over twenty-five years old), now constituting a third of all U.S. undergraduates;
- those with minority backgrounds, as defined by their racial or ethnic heritage (African, Hispanic, Asian, native American, and so forth) or by sexual orientation;

- those with physical or learning disabilities; and
- students from economically disadvantaged backgrounds.

Students in most of these categories—especially part-time, older, minority, and community college students—are not likely to have the funds even to consider education abroad as an available option, much less an "achievable academic and personal goal." During the first two years, GPA, language and major prerequisites must be addressed. Students need to know, and meet, these curricular expectations, and they must avoid spreading themselves in too many different directions with student government, athletics, overloads, etc.

As the National Task Force on Undergraduate Education Abroad pointed out in 1990, different types of programs are needed to suit different types of students. Diversifying programs is one means of appealing to more diverse participants. To expand study abroad to encompass 10 percent of all undergraduates and diversify both participants and destinations, merely replicating and multiplying current program models is unrealistic and inappropriate. As the Task Force's report says, "The needs of nontraditional students are mostly ignored by the more typical study abroad models and structures." New models and structures must be developed pragmatically by individual institutions, consortia, or other appropriate organizations. Features to consider include more short-terms stays, flexible language requirements, "no-fee swapping" of students between U.S. and foreign institutions, and built-in work or service components that reduce costs.

As an example, Spelman and the Claremont Colleges, including Scripps, have a domestic exchange program where students pay their own fees and get like treatment at the exchange school. The institutions have agreed that Spelman women may also use the study abroad programs of Scripps, Pitzer, and Claremont McKenna for the same costs, while students from the Claremont Colleges come to stay on campus at Spelman. This flexibility has enabled more Spelman students to go to Zimbabwe, Ecuador, and France than might otherwise have been able to go, simultaneously enabling African-American students to have a "majority education" semester in the United States.

Such variations on expanding program models as a means of opening up education abroad opportunities to a new range of undergraduates are discussed in Part Three of this book. Expanding the curricular relevance of study abroad and experiential programs will also be discussed in these chapters, as will reasons why colleges and universities need to do more to promote them as options. On the other hand, many traditional study abroad programs are perfectly suited to meet the needs of many nontraditional students. The question is how to develop an advising emphasis that will capture their attention and meet their particular needs (see Chapter 16, "Program Designs and Strategies").

It is the rare institution that has not made efforts in recent decades to open itself up to new kinds of students. As a consequence, most colleges and universities have achieved a far more diverse student body than was the case a mere quarter-century ago. But whether your institution is a small, private rural college, a midsized public university located in a town, or a large, urban "multiversity," it remains highly likely that the nontraditional students, whether constituting a minority or majority of the total enrollment on your campus, do not participate equally in education abroad programs.

There are a number of exceptions to this general truth—institutions that through good leadership and dedication have overcome many barriers to education abroad. Some large public universities, such as the universities of Colorado, Massachusetts, Minnesota, California, Oregon, Washington, and Kansas, as well as Michigan State University and California State University, have good affirmative action policies and send 5–10 percent of their undergraduates abroad—few from privileged backgrounds—many through direct-exchange arrangements with foreign universities. Some private colleges, such as Kalamazoo, Middlebury, Bates, Bowdoin, and Dartmouth, can show that minority students, with full financial aid, study abroad in percentages proportional to their numbers on campus. Others, such as Spelman and Scripps, have had unusual success in developing superior support services for nontraditional students, which has led to increasing numbers of minority students from those schools studying abroad.

▌ Advising Students with Nontraditional Racial/Ethnic Backgrounds

Spelman College, the oldest African-American women's college in the United States, has been sending its students overseas since 1957. Over the past nine years, under the presidential leadership of Johnnetta Cole, numbers have increased dramatically. In 1996–97 Spelman will send just over 12 percent of the junior class on semester or year programs. Approximately half of those students will go abroad in full academic-year programs; about 25 percent are pre-med majors. Increasingly through institutional exchanges, Spelman women are able to study abroad in Africa, Britain, the Czech Republic, and the West Indies. A small number of Spelman students come from families able to make the financial commitment (which can be as much as double the cost of a year on campus), but most have to work hard to come up with the money. Money is the real barrier for these students, not hesitation about the value of a period overseas.

Scripps College, a member of the Claremont Colleges, is a small, private liberal arts college for women in Southern California. It enrolls 700 students, 28 percent with minority backgrounds—about a quarter of them Hispanic. Often the Hispanic Scripps student comes from a family, most often from the Los Angeles area, that speaks Spanish at home. She may be the first member of her family to attend college and may well be the primary English-language spokesperson for the family. Many such students have to balance their studies with their responsibilities as a resource person for other family members.

In spite of very extensive support services, the attrition among Hispanic students is higher than for white students. Still, out of the 80 Scripps students who studied abroad in 1995–96, 24 percent were non-white and 5 percent were Hispanic. The Spelman example may not be fully applicable to many other historically black colleges and universities, nor may the Scripps example be fully applicable to public institutions with large percentages of Hispanic students. But much of what each school has accomplished merits close inspection. And both authors of this chapter are happy to help other advisers get started in reaching their minority populations.

▮ Advising Students With Physical Disabilities

With special counsel and experience, advisers can learn how to advise students with physical disabilities. A survey conducted in 1984 by Mobility International USA (MIUSA) revealed that only 1 percent of all participants in international educational exchange in 1983 had physical disabilities, while 71 percent of the organizations responding to the survey indicated that they had not enrolled a single disabled student in their programs. That same year the *Statistical Abstract of the United States* showed that 14.4 percent of the U.S. population was disabled. This is a glaring lack of proportional representation and represents a challenge to study abroad advisers.

The MIUSA survey also examined a number of current professional perceptions regarding disabled students and education abroad programs. When asked why they might not be providing opportunities for disabled students in their programs, colleges responded that they (1) could not find host families for disabled students, (2) encountered negative attitudes on the part of staff here and overseas, and (3) felt they could not provide what they saw as extra assistance needed by the disabled participants.

These findings suggest that education abroad advisers need more information and training about disabled students. The first task is for advisers to realize that barriers to participation in programs abroad, for most disabled students are more psychological than physical. These barriers are evident in the skepticism of administrators both at home and abroad and in the publicity we produce for our programs. In other words, limits are imposed on the disabled student before the question, "Can I study abroad?" is even broached.

Perhaps the most significant barrier is the overseas program administrator who assumes that he or she must make the program site completely accessible and provide special services at the expense of activities and materials for other program participants. An MIUSA official illustrates the situation well: An important distinction is in the use of the word accessible. Perhaps some of your hesitation "is in thinking that if you accept a disabled person, your program must be able to meet their needs in every way." Most people with disabilities are very well aware that the world is not "accessible." A problem that might seem insurmountable could be something they cope with regularly.

To meet these needs, Mobility International offers a host of services that colleges and universities are encouraged to utilize. These include:

- information for host families being recruited for disabled participants
- a checklist of individual needs for disabled students
- special training for staff

The 1991 *Americans with Disabilities Act* (ADA) defines what institutions must provide for students with learning or physical limitations. Because it mandates certain actions, ADA may well have legal implications for the education abroad office, just as it does for the institution as a whole. Therefore, advisers and administrators should consult with university counsel and with those responsible for campus services to disabled students, about any liabilities to which the education abroad office may be exposed under the ADA and its still evolving regulations. Fortunately, there is no shortage of published information explicating the act; the office of the university counsel or the university personnel office should be able to direct you to appropriate resources.[1]

∎ Pragmatic and Proactive Strategies

For many minority and physically challenged students, just enrolling in college is a tremendous step, graduating from college is a dream, and going overseas to study is often unimaginable. There is a special urgency today to work toward eliminating racial, ethnic, and other attitudinal barriers to all the riches of higher education. By taking affirming actions, it is possible to show students who have faced discrimination (and are likely to face it again) that the education abroad office and the institution are truly committed to helping them in every way possible.

Having said this, education abroad advisers should be aware that it is absolutely a mistake to assume that all, or even most, minority students will be interested in exploring their cultural roots—in Latin America, Africa, Asia, and so on. The degree to which such students feel the importance of investigating their heritage in education abroad planning is something that advisers and faculty need to explore during the advising process—as discussed in other chapters.

Traditional ways and means used to promote education abroad opportunities often have to be reexamined very thoroughly when advising nontraditional students, whose concerns often require additional time and resources. The remainder of this chapter suggests a variety of pragmatic and proactive strategies that can be used in the advising process itself to increase the numbers and diversity of students who will not only consider but also participate in education abroad programming.

Secure Top Administrative Support

The rhetoric of increasing diversity is the easy part. Doing it is the hard part. Without the president's and the board's genuine commitment to increasing participation in education abroad, the chances of success are minimal. This does not mean doing the impossible, but rather making the fullest and deepest contract with nontraditional students to do everything that is institutionally possible to assist them. Equally important is that this contract be communicated clearly and frequently to other members of the administration, faculty, and student body. Finally, because new resources will probably be necessary, there must be an institutional willingness, at the highest levels, to secure and utilize them.

If there is talk about doing more, but no positive steps are taken, these issues need to be addressed at the highest levels possible. Students are only frustrated and angered, and staff demoralized, if promises are made and then broken. The key is to remember the expertise that has been developed in the education abroad office and to use this to persuade those who have the authority to make a difference to do so. At some level, the argument has to emphasize principles to which your institution is publicly committed: namely, providing all students with equal access to all the fruits of higher education, preparing all students for the international, interdependent world of the next century, and providing a competitive edge vis-a-vis other students in the job market.

Build Faculty Support

The advising process cannot succeed without strong faculty involvement and support. With regard to encouraging nontraditional students into education abroad, this support is even more crucial. The case for studying abroad, when made by a faculty member from a similar background or with like disabilities, will always be doubly persuasive. When they themselves have had international experience and can talk about how this has helped them in their work and life, students are going to be even more persuaded. When such mentors exist, their assistance will prove invaluable (see Chapter 3, "Faculty Roles").

The education abroad adviser should also facilitate connecting the student with other colleagues and faculty via telephone and/or e-mail about studying abroad. For example, if an African-American student is reluctant to study in Japan, refer that student to a colleague at a comparable college known for a strong commitment to study abroad that has a larger pool of student experiences. In addition, CIEE now has a program on the Web to put nontraditional students in touch with similar students who have already studied abroad; the system works in liaison with the study abroad advisers of the returned students.

If, as often is the case, an institution's programs have grown out of language-department interests, then faculty in other departments will have to be contacted to identify other geographic areas and appropriate programs that have a stronger likelihood of appealing to these students. Again, shorter programs, those with work components or in nontraditional study destinations may have an appeal.

It is important, also, to take special note of faculty who teach courses that might appeal to nontraditional students. These might include, but are not limited to, any ethnic studies courses offered at your institution, non-Western history courses, certain philosophy courses or courses that survey non-Western religions, and so forth. Faculty can provide information and assist in outreach to their peers and to students.

The following kinds of faculty should also be cultivated:

- faculty who serve as mentors or advisers to student organizations or clubs whose memberships reflect large numbers of nontraditional students (for example, African-American fraternities and sororities, Asian-American clubs, La Raza)
- faculty who have specialized in fields of research that bring them into frequent contact with the student or ethnic populations who do not participate in education abroad.
- faculty who sit on a campus committee or task force charged with looking at the issue of representation in education abroad. Such a committee will also provide the education abroad office with a core group of allies.

Utilize All Current Financial Aid and Seek Special Funding

Increasing the participation of nontraditional students is, more than anything else, limited by current economic realities. Without adequate family or personal resources, students are dependent on institutional financial aid from both private and public sources. Otherwise, most of these students simply cannot consider most education abroad opportunities, no matter what other inducements and arguments are used. In this regard, federal financial aid legislation and such initiatives as the National Security Education Program will make a major difference because one of the purposes of such legislation is to enfranchise more students (see Chapter 5, "Financial Aid").

Every student has a unique financial picture, but it is important to work with the director of financial aid to establish fundamental policies. The bottom line should be to make sure that what aid now exists for an individual student on campus can "travel" abroad. Institutional policy must be set up in a way to ensure openness and flexibility. Spelman and Scripps, for example, let every dollar of aid money go with students, with the exception of work-study funds. However, federal loans and grants, Perkins Loans, and the college's own "Need-Based Grants" and other types of institutional support can be used to replace college work-study.

Special minority scholarships from foundations can sometimes be used for education abroad. You may have to bring these to the attention of your financial aid office and assist in the extra effort to track them down. However, the Robert Bailey Scholarship for Minority Students through CIEE is a good place to start. The number of programs that offer either special grants for minority students or are willing to make fee waivers abroad is growing slowly. Spelman and Scripps colleges also encourage students to solicit assistance from their churches and from service organizations, hometown newspapers, and even from extended families. Often even rather small amounts of seed money may have surprising multiplier effects.

A new program open to minority students interested in pursuing international careers is the Institute of International Public Policy, sponsored by the Woodrow Wilson Foundation, as well as the Hispanic Association of Colleges and Universities; the United Negro College Fund; the Higher Education Council of Native Americans; and the Asian American Association, funded by the Department of Education. The program seeks to identify sophomores with a least a 3.5 GPA who can make a multiple-year commitment to the program, which includes a public policy institute in the summer after the sophomore year, a scholarship for half the costs of a semester or year abroad, a Woodrow Wilson Summer Institute after the junior year, an internship abroad, or further intensive language training after the senior year and support for graduate school at an institution belonging to the Association of Professional Schools of International Affairs (APSIA). This type of multiple-year commitment is making a real difference in the lives of these students, all of whom during the first two years of the program had never been abroad before.

Cash-flow presents a problem for low-income families. The student may receive full financial aid abroad, but must pay for, for example, passport, visa, vaccinations, airfare charges, and security deposits to hold their places two to three months before the term begins. Without additional financial assistance, these expenses may dissuade students from going overseas. There needs to be a way to help students with these very real needs. Options advisers should explore include (1) getting your institution to guarantee fees to programs so that parents will not have to pay everything in July or December; (2) expediting loan and grant check endorsements in advance; (3) using revenue earned by sale of Eurail and Britrail passes, ID cards, and so on, to create special funds; (4) working with a limited number of specific programs to arrange special scholarship aid; and (5) working with the development office to raise special funds to support nontraditional students.

Work Closely with Student Services

Most institutions have designated at least one person to provide advice and counsel especially for nontraditional students. Large campuses are likely to have formal, specialized offices that provide on- and off-campus assistance for specific groups of students and to promote cultural diversity. One prominent author has observed that the move for greater internationalism and the emphasis on cultural diversity are intimately related but not always correlated effectively with each other because of the persistent social, economic, and political tensions in the United States:

Many in minority communities speculate as to whether internationalism is a more comfortable concept for American society to deal with than its own national cultural diversity. Not until recently, and only in limited circles, has the following notion been entertained as plausible: that understanding international cultures is linked to the understanding and respect for the "international" cultures represented by the many racial and ethnic groups in the United States. Ironically, rather than embodying this concept, the movement to internationalize U.S. campuses is occurring on many of the same campuses where racial tension and violence are becoming increasingly more common.[2]

As this perception suggests, the relationship between the education abroad office and the offices and professionals charged with providing special services and promoting cultural diversity can easily become enmeshed in struggles for recognition and resources on campus, as well as in broader, unresolved social tensions. Moreover, students can receive conflicting messages. It is therefore imperative to take proactive steps to work with these colleagues with the overall benefit of the student in mind.

A broadened and deepened appreciation of cultural diversity is almost always the result of a good education abroad experience, and this benefit ought to be applicable both on campus and in life. A perfect example of working together to provide the best results for the students is when staff from the study abroad office go to events held for minority recruitment, weekend meetings and even minority alumni gatherings to talk about the ways that minority students can benefit from and finance study abroad. In fact, one school has even solicited its minority alumni to help set up scholarships for minority students to study abroad.

Furnish Role Models

Most education abroad professionals have themselves experienced a formative international sojourn. But given the limited substratum of American society that has traditionally furnished students for education abroad, very few professionals in the field of international educational exchange currently come from any of the nontraditional group backgrounds. This vacuum represents a very real perceptual and communications problem and makes it even harder to overcome the perception that education abroad is not for everyone.

In the short run, every opportunity should be used to hire full- or part-time staff with nontraditional backgrounds. Student peer counselors can also serve this function, as can faculty advisers willing to work within the structures of the education abroad office.

Begin Early

The college literature must give the unequivocal message to those considering admission that education abroad is not an incidental activity but integral to the degree and something that can enrich most majors. In addition, the literature must tell minority students and those with special needs that others like them have participated successfully in such activities. Sometimes this can be done simply by making sure that such students are visually represented in institutional promotional brochures, catalogs, fliers, videos, and view-books that mention education abroad activities—and especially in brochures for your own programs.

If such materials quote students, make sure that some quotations come from minority and special students who have studied or worked abroad. In addition, including nontraditional students in publicity materials is an effective way to promote study abroad as an accessible program.

A "class picture" or a photographic display in your office can serve to provide a pictorial image with which an interested nontraditional student can identify. Even if there is only a single representation from any given group, a student will see that students like himself or herself have gone before; such students will ultimately feel affirmed that there is a place for them in international education.

An education abroad office should also be a welcoming and friendly environment to the nontraditional student. Decorations or wall hangings from Africa or Latin America, Chinese calligraphy, brass decorations from the Middle East, and other ethnic or regional decorations will not only make your office, resource library, or general public space more colorful, international, and interesting, but also will signal a particular welcome to the student of color or ethnic minority.

The interest in nontraditional students should also be reflected in the resource materials or library. Material of interest to "students of color," "ethnic minorities," "disabled students" "gay/lesbian students" should be identified. Even if the resources are few, the office commitment to providing relevant information will offer encouragment to students.

By taking part in general campus orientation and promoting education abroad as early in the school year as possible, seeds are planted and interest nurtured. This is also a good time to assure students that services extend to all. Education abroad offices should also be present at orientation sessions for minority students or students with disabilities. One especially effective tack is to stress that studying overseas will give them a competitive edge. How many minority students applying to graduate or medical school will have spent a year overseas? For instance, how many African-American female engineers do you know who speak Shona, Japanese, or French and have spent a year overseas?

Work with Parents

For many nontraditional students, just being away at college is hard enough, so thinking about living outside of the United States is almost unimaginable. For their parents, it is, if anything, even harder to conceive, and indeed may be truly frightening. Early and ongoing interaction with the parents is therefore essential. Advisers should take the initiative and contact the parents as soon as their daughter or son shows serious interest in going abroad. Anticipate their concerns, especially feelings that their family unity appears threatened by this separation.

Whether in person, by letter, or phone, it is important to discuss: (1) how study abroad could be valuable to their child in specific academic, career, and personal terms; (2) how the college chooses particular programs; (3) the support services that will be available (orientation, overseas support services, and services on return to address the possibility of readjustment problems). Participation in parents' weekend to talk the whole process over with them, is also proactive and rewarding. Also talk about money. Sometimes parents call with very basic questions. They need support too.

Students should be encouraged to discuss their plans as early as possible with their parents. After all, this must be a three-way conversation. Doubting parents can be put in touch with parents whose daughters or sons have studied overseas. At Scripps and Spelman this peer counseling tactic has proved very effective in calming fears. The University of Lancaster runs a support service to put parents with questions in touch with similar parents whose children have studied at Lancaster in the past. Sometimes a minority parent talking to another minority parent is reassured by a contact with whom he or she can talk frankly and ask questions he or she might be hesitant to ask a white administrator. It is also helpful to communicate with the parents while students are overseas.

Send the parents copies of all the orientation materials, and continue to send updates to them during the course of the program.

Select the Right Programs and Work with Them

A great deal of attention needs to be paid to the process of helping individual students select the right program. It makes some sense, however, to do a measure of preselection, even before you begin advising students. Choose groups of programs that have worked well in the past—and perhaps a list of countries best avoided. Racism and discrimination exist in just about every country, though the targets are different. Determinations must be made about which programs are able to protect students from the worst of such offenses and which are not. Although it is true that qualified students can handle almost any overseas program, special preference should be given to programs that exhibit a good track record with minority students. Reputable programs will usually be honest in facing their built-in limitations of what they offer and will make adjustments when they can.

A common and well-founded perception among students is that education abroad is a largely Eurocentric undertaking. This can be disappointing for students from more diverse backgrounds who are either seeking something closer to their own cultural heritage or simply are not drawn to Europe. For these students, it is especially important for advisers to go out of their way to promote education abroad programs in Africa, the Caribbean, Latin America, Asia, and other nontraditional destinations. Of course, not all minority students will want to study in such locations, but it is critical to let them know that such opportunities exist in abundance.

Shorter programs need also to be pointed out, as well as programs that might have internships, practical training, volunteer work, or service learning as components. Indeed, anything that challenges or enhances the overall study abroad experience is worth doing.

It is also useful to work closely with programs before the process of application, informing them of students' particular needs, seeking assurances that they can be met, and ascertaining potential problems abroad, in, for instance, housing or social life. Such conversations might also explore ways to offset borderline GPA, class rank, or low SAT scores—perhaps by writing cover letters or suggesting getting particularly good faculty recommendations. Acting as an advocate for minority students, a suggestion can be made that they strengthen the group. Because most minority students don't want to be the only nonwhite student in the program, check with minority institutions to see where they are sending students and with whom so that your minority student might find other peers on the program.

It is often much easier to be admitted to one of the numerous excellent education abroad programs than to get accepted by very selective undergraduate institutions. Nevertheless, these programs need to be convinced that applicants are serious, informed, and qualified, and applicants need to be convinced to finish those applications in a timely way without fear of rejection. Advisers can act as mentors for students when they are communicating with programs and especially in helping them to prepare their applications. Mentoring is never an easy process, and students may need practical advice, assurances, and some prodding.

With regard to assisting students with disabilities, as noted above, many organizations exist to provide information about assistance and resources abroad. Such information can be found in two MIUSA publications: *A World of Options for the 90's: A Guide to International Educational Exchange, Community Service, and Travel for Persons with Disabilities* and *A New Manual for Integrating People with Disabilities into International Educational Programs* (see list of health information resources). Together, these two publications provide not only an introduction to the educational background for administrators and advisers but also a list of resources, both in the United States and abroad, to make international education a reality for disabled students. Using SECUSS-L is another resource to provide information on which programs and universities will be able to accommodate physically challenged students.

Early confirmation of the kinds of support programs and universities have for learning disabled students who will need more time for exams or to offer other courses instead of regular foundation courses, will encourage students to consider an overseas experience. Disabled participants mainly want to know what their options are and what trade-offs they must make in order to study overseas and it will be necessary to inform and educate the student about what conditions will be like at the site. This is the primary responsibility of the education abroad adviser. The final decision to participate or not is up to the qualified applicant with the disability.

Use Returned Students

At almost any college the most active and vocal support for education abroad comes from returning students. Using returning minority students to help recruit others can provide affirmation and assurance that an office cannot provide alone. If students had good experiences, they become the most effective advocates. There is no substitute for this sort of student-to-student contact. For example, two of the most often asked questions at Spelman are about where to get products to do hair and how close U.S. armed forces bases are to the program site. The students always have the answers. Many programs will also be willing and able to put nervous students and their parents in touch with past participants from nearby colleges.

In addition, education abroad offices should consider developing special written materials on minority and disabled student experiences abroad. With the help of a NAFSA grant, Brown University published a booklet quoting students' candid reflections on their choice of country, living situation, expectations, and actual treatment, and the influence of the experience on their outlook and further studies. While most of these reflections gave notes of caution and not all experiences were equally positive, the overall impression is highly affirmative.

Face Racism and Discrimination Squarely

During both individual counseling sessions and especially during orientation programs, it is vital to be open and realistic about the possibility of outright racism abroad, about the likelihood that disabled students may have to contend with insensitive attitudes and inadequate facilities and gay students with the presence of homophobia. These realities do exist and may even be present where an adviser might not anticipate them. If students know about these attitudes and customs up front, they will be better prepared for the worst they might find overseas, and being prepared makes life easier. Again, the seasoned insights of returned students, direct or indirect, provide points of reference and truth that students will respect and appreciate—not the least of which is that, whatever negatives existed for them abroad, the experience was vital and important.

In orienting students for the overseas experience, and in confronting discrimination and intolerance, it should be remembered that gay/lesbian and bisexual students may also suffer prejudice overseas. Fortunately there is a growing body of published work which addresses the needs of these students when overseas. Sessions for such students, as for students of color, disabled students, etc., should also be included in the general orientation program and discussion leaders for gay/lesbian concerns can now be recruited more easily from among faculty, staff or students; however, a discussion group leader need not be an openly identified gay or lesbian to successfully facilitate group discussion concerning intolerance (see Chapter 14, "Predeparture Orientation and Reentry").

Institutions that have already offered this kind of orientation session report that students benefit from the experience, feel affirmed in their identities and less alone, and often are able to contribute pertinent information from among themselves. Such students are usually enthusiastic about becoming facilitators on their return. Information and advice is most useful when it is culture specific—and usually country or even region and place specific. While some generalizations are possible, what is true of Paris will not describe the reality of rural France, much less of Germany or Spain; what is true in cities will not hold for villages; what is true on campus may not be true in the neighborhoods; what is true for parents may not be true for their children.

On the other hand, discussing these issues of racism and intolerance in a broader manner can result in a stimulating and educational discussion for all. It can assist in making these concerns pertinent to a larger number of diverse populations who can learn from each other, rather than marginalize the issue or label it specific to, for example, "students of color." At San Francisco State University the issue of racism is dealt with during general orientation in a special interest workshop entitled "Diversity Issues: Being a Racial Minority in a Racial Majority Society." Similar workshops were "Being a Sexual Orientation Minority in Heterosexual Society Overseas," "Disabled Minorities and Attention to Their Needs Overseas," and " Women's Concerns and Overseas Travel."

Students may also find that their "Americanness" is a more important factor in determining their treatment abroad than their racial or ethnic heritage or physical abilities. They may also find that the United States is not the only country with a complex of minority cultures.

Notes

1. Forest C. Benedict, Kirk D. Beyer, Kathleen E. Donofrio, and John M. Toller, eds., *ADA Compliance Manual for Higher Education: A Guide to Title 1* (Washington, D.C.: College and University Personnel Association, 1992).

2. Holly Carter, "Black Students and Overseas Programs: Broadening the Base of Participation," Council on International Educational Exchange, 1991.

12

Advising For Whole World Study

Contributors: Joan A. Raducha and Michael D. Monahan

As a study abroad professional, you have the opportunity to open the whole world to the students on your campus. Program destinations in Africa, Asia, Latin America, the Middle East, and Oceania offer students opportunities to not only see but to live in a part of the world where the majority of the world's population lives, where decisions that will affect the world's environment are being made, where vital links in the developing global economy reside. Study abroad in these regions can be safe, can provide unique academic and career opportunities, and can offer meaningful personal experiences that students will treasure for the rest of their lives. As one study abroad participant observed, "When people say 'You'll be a different person when you come home,' it may sound melodramatic, but it's true. If you open your eyes and take risks, you'll learn more than you could ever imagine. I dream of Tanzania every day."

For advisers there can certainly be no more interesting and important challenge than to make known these unique opportunities and benefits and thus prepare U.S. students to be productive citizens—not only of their own country but also of the whole world.

Study abroad opportunities for undergraduate students now span the whole world. As the borders of opportunity have opened, students can now live and learn in places they may have dreamed of since childhood or learned about just the previous semester. Countries in Africa, Asia, Latin America, the Middle East, and Oceania, which previously hosted only a handful of U.S. students, now are able to welcome many more.

As a group, these nontraditional destinations provide intellectually challenging, economical, and often markedly different cultural experiences from the more traditional programs of western Europe. Assisting your administration, faculty, students (and their parents) to understand the value and viability of students living and learning in these previously neglected areas is one of the primary challenges facing an education abroad adviser and/or administrator.

It is increasingly evident that more students are looking for study abroad program opportunities beyond those that have existed for many years in western Europe. The Institute of International Education (IIE) publication *Open Doors,* reported that in 1994–95, approximately 35 percent of U.S. students who studied abroad chose destinations in Africa, Asia, Latin America, the Middle East, and Oceania; only 20 percent were doing so a decade earlier. There are good reasons to expect this demand to increase, as more students realize that the whole world is open to them. Advisers and administrators need to become informed about these "nontraditional" destinations, and education abroad professionals must be prepared to make the case for such destinations on their campus.

For decades, scholars and study abroad professionals have championed the cause of whole world learning, but many countries and regions were still considered dangerous or off-limits. But the world has changed and become more open and interconnected. Increasingly, educators and government and business leaders are enjoining students to learn about and study in those parts of the world that are of growing relevance to the U.S. national economy and to U.S. national interests generally. Dated assumptions and groundless fears have given way to a clearer understanding of what is and is not possible in all corners of the earth, while telecommunications readily informs us where and when U.S. students might not be welcome.

The transnational movement of labor, the migration of entire populations for economic or political reasons, environmental sustainability, and interdependent economies—these are just some parts of the overall *global* picture. First-hand exposure to, and study of, the whole world is therefore a critical learning experience as we prepare for the twenty-first century, and campus advisers must strive to bring these opportunities to the attention of well-qualified students.

Study abroad programs in nontraditional destinations include programs in modern cities with rich histories stretching back to antiquity, such as Cairo, Jerusalem, Beijing, and Bangkok. They also take place in far-off regions inhabited by ethnic or linguistic groups considered minorities by a country's dominant culture. Although stereotypical thinking often labels such locations as "Third World" or "developing," many countries—Brazil, Thailand, and Indonesia are prime examples—are highly sophisticated and developed societies in terms of urbanization, industrial output, and technology. In other nontraditional study abroad locations, millennia-old subsistence farming practices continue virtually unchanged. Opportunities thus exist for students to study in rural villages in Kenya to modern, skyscraper-filled Singapore, to countries possessing a range of development.

Study abroad in almost any country challenges students to learn about themselves. In non-Western cultural settings, however, everyday life is likely to be radically different from anything a native-born U.S. student will have experienced. Such differences, small and big, nuanced and dramatic, create a multifaceted learning environment that stimulates intellectual and personal growth of an order different from what is often possible in more culturally congruent surroundings. Academic learning in such sites can be greatly enhanced by these daily recognitions of cultural difference, as well as by unexpected similarities in values and behavior. This is a point made by almost every student returning from such an experience.

For some students, a nontraditional program site provides an opportunity to explore the meaning and relevance of their ethnic roots. Sometimes what they discover adds a totally new dimension to their lives. At other times, they learn that they are far more "American" than they knew, and these students must come to grips with this new knowledge. Whether they are welcomed or shunned, students report that such receptions tend to deepen the impact of the program. Advisers, however, should be wary of assuming that all students with a strong ethnic attachment to a study abroad destination wish to explore their roots—some do and some don't.

For other students, a nontraditional setting provides the opportunity to belong to a minority, whether this outsider status is based on ethnic, racial, linguistic, religious, economic, or some combination of these identifications. Such changes in cultural status, from mainstream to minority, can be disturbing at first but can eventually lead to profound insights. This in turn has the effect of making U.S. students better and more empathetic citizens in their own society, where diversity and stereotyping are conspicuous features.

The attraction to a particular country in Africa or Asia, Latin America or the Middle East, may of course be primarily intellectual and linked to a specific discipline. Whether this interest stems from a long-held fascination with the pyramids and pharaohs of ancient Egypt, a desire to understand the economic miracle of the New Dragons of Southeast Asia, an interest in Zambian music, or an urge to see the impact of deforestation on the rainforests of Brazil, these students may feel compelled to study these phenomena first-hand, to learn about such things in the places that gave them birth and nurture. Again, it is the rare returning student who does not comment on the intellectual and personal rewards of studying in such unique surroundings.

Finally, given that three-quarters of the world population lives in Asia, Africa, Latin America, and the Middle East, the United States needs a generation of citizens who have had first-hand experience of living in and learning about these tremendously important areas, with their myriad cultures and explosive growth potential. Such experience forms a base upon which to build the new global competencies we need if we are to meet the challenges of an increasingly transnational and global future.

▌ The First Step: Educating Yourself

Institutional Strengths and Goals

Given the proliferation of program choices, the expansion of international education, and increasing concern about cost, a critical issue is how nontraditional study destinations fit into institutional goals. One approach is to link, very directly and deliberately, the institutional mission to study abroad in nontraditional destinations.

In practice, this may require a careful review of what your institution aims to accomplish through internationalism. It may mean an emphasis on medical research in developing countries, a stress on understanding the development process, or on teaching students to learn "in the field" about cultures that are radically different from their own. Some institutional missions may focus on foreign language and area studies or stress an intellectual effort to understand and analyze globalization or environmental sustainability in the new millennium.

In any case, institutions interested in study abroad in nontraditional destinations may do well to "build by strength" rather than to encourage student participation or program development in areas where the home campus has no interest or expertise. The rationale for this approach is to strengthen learning in a more cohesive, sustainable, and in-depth way by linking study abroad curricula and learning to on-campus education. Study abroad should build upon rather than provide a hiatus from on-campus learning.

To do this, of course, education abroad professionals must be intimately familiar with the academic and cross-cultural strengths of their institutions. This often involves, in one way or another, compiling an inventory of international expertise and interests, assessing this in light of study abroad needs, and then strategically targeting priority interests. It also involves building incentives for faculty to become more directly involved in study abroad, often through professional development, contacts with counterparts abroad, and opportunities to enhance teaching and research.

Sources of Information

Information about education abroad in nontraditional destinations can be found in many of the same places that you look for traditional programs, for example, IIE's *Academic Year Abroad* and *Vacation Study Abroad* and Peterson's *Study Abroad*. Special attention should be paid to the cross-referencing of countries or regions, programs, and curricular offerings. The magazine *Transitions Abroad* also often publishes useful articles on study abroad in nontraditional locations.

Increasingly, information is available on-line. A quick search of the Web will reveal a plethora of information about programs sponsored by colleges and universities as well as not-for-profit organizations. You may also want to consult your college or university library for suggestions on books that focus on nontraditional study abroad sites and higher education. *African Studies and the Undergraduate Curriculum,* edited by Patricia Alden, David Lloyd, and Ahmed I. Samatar (Boulder: Lynne Rienner, 1994), is one good example. You may also find the Association of Professional Schools of International Affairs (APSIA) publication, *Undergraduate International Studies on the Eve of the 21st Century,* helpful, particularly if your students are exploring cutting-edge curricula and teaching in international studies and you are interested in how higher education is responding to a changing world (see Chapter 6, "The Office Library and Other Resources").

Networking with peers is a valuable approach. Whether in person, at a conference, over the phone, or (increasingly) through e-mail, you can gather relevant information on opportunities from your colleagues. Through SECUSSA, the study abroad section of NAFSA, you may join SECUSS-L to explore issues related to nontraditional study destinations.

There are 119 campus-based Title VI National Resource Centers located around the country. A primary mission of these centers, focusing on a particular region of the world, is to establish, strengthen, and operate undergraduate and/or graduate centers focusing on language and area or international studies. Many have students who have studied in the geographical area covered by the center and international students from the countries in those regions.

Most of these centers also have an outreach mission, so you are encouraged to consult with them for advice on orientation programming or on ways to establish contact with specific faculty experts. Some of these centers are located at universities that operate study abroad programs, open to qualified students from other campuses, in nontraditional study destinations.

As an example, in 1995 the cooperating Title V1 African Studies Centers received a FIPSE grant to bring together education abroad professionals and faculty in that discipline in an effort to initiate discussions on fostering more study abroad in Africa. (A list of these centers can be obtained from the Center for Education, U.S. Department of Education, Washington, D.C. 20202-5331.)

Your own institution may have resources that you have not fully utilized. Individual academic departments, area studies programs, and other thematic or interdisciplinary programs are excellent places to search for information on appropriate study sites and foreign universities for direct enrollment. International studies, foreign language, and area studies faculty are often deeply familiar with universities abroad and can offer both general guidance and specific suggestions on courses of study.

Evaluating Programs and Procedures

Education abroad professionals are responsible for identifying and evaluating procedures for programs organized by others. This is true for any study abroad program, but the level of questioning and the need to have confirmation are perhaps more important for programs to nontraditional destinations. You may want to ask the following questions as you evaluate a program:

- What are the academic and cross-cultural strengths of the program? What unique study, field research, or internship opportunities does the program present?
- What kind of orientation is provided by the program?
- Do programs have the faculty and staff experience and expertise to deal with situations that can change rapidly?
- If classes are canceled at a local university, is the program prepared to organize special classes or develop special project opportunities for students so that the time abroad is not lost academically?

- What is the nature of the health support infrastructure? Is there a plan for evacuating a seriously ill student if necessary?

- Does the program make sure the students are registered at the local U.S. Embassy so that the students will be contacted and advised of State Department policy in the event of a political crisis that may turn dangerous?

In the event of an emergency, the program managers have the primary responsibility to manage the situation. Familiarizing yourself with these aspects of the program profile is helpful, however, inasmuch as you guide a student through the process of selecting a program.

If the student is enrolling directly in a foreign university with your assistance, you should determine what the local support infrastructure for the student will be:

- Does the university have a foreign student office? What services are provided?

- How is the academic station at that university? Has there been, for example, a history of closings?

- Is there a local group that can (usually for a fee) provide a contact for the student on nonacademic areas of the experience? (There are many cultural learning centers around the world staffed by local people or expatriates who have long grappled with cultural learning issues).

▮ The Second Step: Advising Students

Academic Issues

One student participating in a women and development study abroad program in Mexico said: "For the first time in a long time, I finally felt like I was not only being challenged to think but that I was actually thinking. I think this educational process will have a profound effect on the rest of my life." In discussing nontraditional program sites with students, advisers often tend to focus on the problems that may arise. Although potential problems certainly must be addressed (see the section below), advising should also stress educational goals and potential benefits of study abroad in nontraditional destinations.

Program Design

The types of programs in nontraditional destinations vary along the same lines as traditional study abroad programs: direct enrollment in foreign universities, reciprocal exchanges, group programs directed by

U.S. faculty or a local resident director, independent study programs with a heavy emphasis on field learning, and so forth. Programs vary in length from summer or short-term intersession opportunities to semester or full academic year programs.

Fieldwork Projects

Many programs in nontraditional regions now encourage students to take classes alongside their local counterparts, but they also require all students to conduct a fieldwork project on a selected topic. While conducting fieldwork projects, U.S. students often have access to professionals and other human resources much more readily than they would in a Western setting. Contacts with authors, community workers, and government leaders have ignited the imagination of students and taught them a great deal about conducting primary research. The information collected abroad by many students has formed the basis of a senior thesis.

Language Learning

Even if a European language is the language of instruction in the academic setting, students who have an interest in indigenous cultures can often obtain instruction in less commonly taught languages. Such study can open whole worlds of culture and ideas. Needless to say, local inhabitants do not expect that their native language will be mastered by short-term visitors, but they greatly appreciate any efforts to learn some of it, even if only idioms, greetings, and social expressions.

Coursework

The structure of local universities, even in Asia and Africa, is very often modeled on a European rather than American style of education. Students may find the relationships between faculty and students more formal, or classrooms less well-equipped, than on their home campuses. Figuring out how to bridge the formality gap can be a challenging but rewarding cultural experience. A well-run program will supply students with models of how past participants have managed, and students learn that a poorly equipped classroom is not an impediment to learning.

Advising Questions

The question of "Is this the right program for me?" is a vital one. Students from many different backgrounds have enjoyed and benefited from the challenges of nontraditional programs, but finding the right fit is important. Among the many questions that you should encourage your students to consider as they explore study abroad in nontraditional destination are:

- What is it, precisely, that can best be learned in this particular site?
- How well can I adjust to the classes? (For example, classes may meet for longer periods of time, may feature less discussion and more lectures, as is typical in many non-U.S. institutions).
- What if a computer facilities, library systems, books, and other learning resources are inferior to those on the home campus?
- How will a different level of material development affect my learning?
- Will I be able to focus on my academic work while adjusting to different ways of living, different transportation challenges, a perhaps radically different diet and housing situation? (see Chapter 10, "Advising Principles and Strategies".)

Personal Concerns

Learn as much as you can about the program site to which the student will be traveling and of course refer them to faculty members or to other students who have been there. Encourage the prospective student to think about what is important to them and to learn about how well their needs can be met at the site they are considering.

Arrival Adjustment

Many students report years later how the first smell, the din of sound, or the taste of certain foods made a strong impact on their experience, sometimes positive and sometimes negative. When they are negative, it is important for students to know that most situations can be managed and can be enriching if they are prepared to be open-minded and adaptable. Students may need to be encouraged to give themselves time to put these initial experiences into context; what seems like an insurmountable problem on the first day when recovering from jet-lag can soon become a humorous memory.

Pace of Life

A student who studied in Tanzania wrote:

> If you're considering going to Tanzania—*GO*. Being in a non-Western nation has opened my eyes to different ways of approaching life. When trains run 16 hours late, time takes on a new meaning. When you ask a total stranger on the bus where to buy tomatoes, and they change their plans to spend 3 hours

209

with you at the market, human kindness and generosity feel alive and well again. The world, and possibilities for life feel vast, and college seems very small, but not insignificant. I acquired a new energy and vigor, and felt I was finally engaging in something worthwhile.

The insights and joys this student found in the situation are there, but to a student who needs to be on time, the same situations could have given a negative tone to the experience.

Living Arrangements

Programs in nontraditional destinations run the gamut of housing choices similar to study abroad in other parts of the world: home-stays, apartment living, and dormitories. Many students have relished the relationships they developed with other students in dormitory situations or getting to know the local food vendors and market places when they lived independently and had to take care of their everyday needs. Home-stays are often encouraged at least at the start of the program but it is not necessarily the best housing situation in nontraditional destinations.

Accustomed to independence, students may balk at the expectations a host family makes, whether the issue is curfew, neatness, or attendance at meals. In balance, most students who live with a family for at least part of the time abroad find the cultural benefits, the language learning opportunity, and having the necessities of life managed by someone else reasonable trade-offs for any limits on their freedom. Getting to know a family often offers an opportunity to understand the relationship between rural and urban segments of society. Students meet visiting relatives and sometimes household help who have re-located to make a living wage.

Local Expectations and Norms

Gender- and age-specific behaviors are defined differently in various cultures. Some students may be concerned about how they will be treated and in what ways they will be expected to alter their behavior. Experiencing differences in behavioral norms is an important source of learning in the study abroad experience. Before they leave, students should be encouraged to read novels and newspapers and view films about the region to identify local norms they may encounter and find unsettling. Knowledge will help them to adjust themselves so that they can derive maximum benefit from the year.

Advising Questions

Among the more personal rather than educational questions students should ask themselves are these:

- How flexible can I be, and in what aspects of life?
- Do I find new and different types of food interesting or a personal problem? (A student who is a vegetarian may have no problem in India in a Hindu community but may find it difficult to manage in a Muslim setting unless willing to compromise on diet for the duration of the program.)
- What are everyday necessities and what can be forgone? (Students may need to do without creature comforts, from toilet paper to regular electricity to work supplies.).
- What about a need for privacy? (In some cultures, young people who want or need privacy may find themselves ostracized as antisocial.)
- How accepting can I be with regard to different gender role expectations?

(See Chapter 10, "Advising Principles and Strategies.")

Financial Issues

Although many of the financial questions about study abroad in nontraditional destinations are similar to those regarding study abroad elsewhere, there are a few special concerns and opportunities you may wish to highlight during your advising of students interested in less-common study destinations. These include, for example, the fact that immunization and international travel costs may be higher for students heading to nontraditional sites, while daily living expenses (room, board, local commuting, etc.) may be lower. Educational costs vary greatly, depending, among other factors, on whether the selected program's fees are based on local or U.S. tuition and administrative expenses. In the final analysis, like any other study abroad program, a comprehensive budget should be made available to prospective participants.

With regard to special funding opportunities, students' attention should be drawn to scholarships and grants designated for study in "critical" areas or in developing countries. Among the most well-known of these are, for example, the Council on International Educational Exchange (CIEE) grants for study in the Third World and the National Security Education Program (NSEP) scholarships for study in selected critical areas which are currently underrepresented in U.S. study abroad.

It is also important that the international office at your institution work creatively to secure special funding for study in nontraditional destinations. This might include, for example, a strategic focus on direct reciprocal exchanges with selected universities beyond the common destinations, scholarships for the study of less commonly taught languages, or other grants strategically committed to build incentives for study in underrepresented areas of the world. The selection criteria of existing scholarships might also be reevaluated to include a preference for nontraditional destinations. For guidance on financial aid, see the NAFSA publication, *Financial Aid for Study Abroad: A Manual for Advisers and Administrators* (see Chapter 5, "Financial Aid").

▌ The Third Step: Preparing Students to Go

Orientation

Orientation is an important component of *any* study abroad program, but it becomes particularly critical for programs in nontraditional destinations. Some programs provide orientations in the United States prior to departure, some provide orientation upon arrival in the host country, and some do both. When looking at a program profile, draw the student's attention to what kind of orientation will be provided. Some students may not want or need to know much before they get to the site; for many, however, pre-departure orientation is essential.

A good orientation at a minimum will include students or travelers who have spent time in the region, ideally international students from the country/region in question, a discussion of health and safety issues, how to handle emergencies, and basic information on academics and appropriate cultural behavior (see Chapter 14, "Predeparture Orientation and Reentry").

Emergencies: It Probably Won't Happen, But Just in Case

How often do emergencies actually arise? Not often. But this is a real concern for many students and their families when thinking about studying abroad outside familiar areas. Most programs in nontraditional areas are operated by organizations that have expertise in the region and with study abroad. And most students who are independent enough to choose a direct enrollment option are resilient and enterprising.

Prevention is the key concept in discussing health and safety with students. This is as true at home as it is in any study abroad situation. No one has control over all elements in the environment, but students can control how they respond to the general situation and to unusual events.

But the farther away the program, the more remote the site, and the less developed the country, the more likely the situation will take on a more profound sense of urgency. The five issues addressed below are probably among the most frequently cited with regard to study in nontraditional sites abroad:

Natural Disasters

Floods, earthquakes, mudslides are phenomena that know no geographic boundaries. Differences certainly do exist, however, in terms of facility to manage damage after events have occurred. In a sense, each situation will be a unique event and students should be encouraged to use their common sense, but more importantly to seek out local authorities for information about what they might expect and how to respond before anything happens.

Strikes

Labor strikes are a nearly universal phenomenon, but in certain developing countries they are more frequent than in others. With regard to the academic implications of a strike, a successful program will have made plans for students to take special classes or to conduct a fieldwork project until the situation is resolved. Safety can also be a concern in a strike situation when emotions can run high. In this situation, advise students to avoid demonstrations, where events may unfold quickly in unpredictable ways.

Political Turmoil

Political instability can lead to street demonstrations and greater instability. Demonstrations that get out of hand can result in the use of tear gas and crowd control weapons wielded by police. As a guest in a country, it is prudent to avoid these situations. From a distance, it may seem that the whole country is involved; if anxious parents call, it may be that you as an adviser can be helpful by pointing out that demonstrations in a capital city probably have no effect on students studying several hundred miles away in another city or even on other parts of the capital city itself.

Health

Most program managers with experience in programs in the developing world say that students who follow health guidelines provided by the Center for Disease Control (CDC) and the program administration rarely become seriously ill. Simple diarrhea is not uncommon while one adjusts to a new diet and the local water, but it need not lead to anything more than a few days of mild discomfort.

Prevention of illness should start before the students leave home by obtaining immunizations and learning about prophylactic drugs, such as medication for malaria. Once abroad, following guidelines on drinking water, and food as well as using preventive measures like sleeping under a mosquito net and using insect repellent can help students avoid many of the ailments encountered in developing countries. Students can, and do regularly, return from programs in nontraditional locations as healthy as they were when they left. It is absolutely indispensable to have qualified medical personnel provide health orientation to study abroad participants (see Chapter 13, "Health and Safety Issues").

Crime

Petty theft is a problem that students will often encounter, particularly if they are in a relatively poor country. But prevention can go a long way toward avoiding being the victim of a crime: storing valuables in a locked cabinet, not wearing jewelry when traveling, carrying wallets where they are not visible or easily reached in a crowded bus are all easy measures that help to ensure the security of one's belongings. Personal crimes are no more, and often less, common than in many U.S. cities; but since our students are more visibly foreign, particularly soon after arrival, they may be especially vulnerable at that time. Traveling in pairs, and learning about the city or town in which one is living and identifying areas of the city to avoid, are good preventative measures.

■ The Fourth Step: Talking With Parents

As the father of one study abroad participant said, "When our daughter first told her mother and me that she was planning to take her junior year in Egypt, we were not at all pleased. Why would she want to do such a bizarre thing in such a strange place?" Some programs provide an orientation for parents either in person or via mail. This is a good idea, for it establishes a line of communication that may be very helpful in case of a later, perceived crisis ("my child promised to call weekly and he hasn't") or real ("my child phoned yesterday reporting a serious illness, and I need to know if I should fly her home").

Orientation is a way to encourage parental involvement in the study abroad experience of their child. An informed parent will be better able to put into context a letter written in a homesick moment and to support their child's experience. Some of the most enthusiastic supporters of study abroad are parents who have watched through correspondence, or a site visit, the growth and development of their child.

Parental Concerns

The images Americans have of nontraditional destinations are based to some extent on the media coverage of these regions: spectacular natural disasters, major health crises, and political instability. Little news space in the U.S. press is devoted to the broader context and history of these problems, and they are often generalized to whole countries or even continents even when the actual impact is limited to a specific geographical location. It is therefore not surprising that the general public in the United States, including many parents of prospective study abroad participants, have a less than positive reaction to the thought of their child living in a nontraditional study abroad location.

There are, of course, real problems in developing countries, including, for example, shortages (food, water, electricity), and bona-fide concerns about health care. However, well-constructed study abroad programs address these issues and create a healthy working environment for participants.

It is important to have information available for parents who are concerned about their child studying in a part of the world that may seem (and be) so remote from their own experience. There are several ways to address parental concerns, including making yourself available to answer questions comprehensively; organizing an information session on study abroad designed specifically for visiting parents; having accurate and well-written materials available on programs in nontraditional sites; and establishing a bank of parents of former students whose phone numbers ?you can share. Carefully prepared information can address the concerns of many parents. As study abroad professionals, the task is to make such information readily available to them.

13 Health And Safety Issues

Contributors: Mickey Hanzel Slind, Deborah C. Herrin, and Joan Gore

Students have a right to expect a safe and healthy experience during their time abroad, but they sometimes bring poor health habits with them and may act more foolishly overseas than at home. Moreover, the world beyond U.S. borders is sometimes filled with health and crime problems and political instability unlike any found at home. There is no way that all dangers and risks can be eliminated, nor will students always act in their own best interests. Your responsibility to your students is to ensure that they receive all the information and assistance they need and that they understand their own responsibility for maintaining their health and well-being. Your responsibility to your institution is to see that your program complies with relevant statutes and regulations and that institutional liability is minimized through careful planning. As the adage observes: "an ounce of prevention is worth a pound of cure."

Most students who study, work, or travel abroad—indeed perhaps most people who go abroad for any reason—are less prepared than they should be for the possibility of sudden injuries, illness, depression, or other health contingencies. The American folk wisdom of travel has warned travelers minimally to avoid the local water and to be prepared for upset stomachs. There are many health concerns, however, that are less common yet considerably more dangerous and unexpected. Some are of such recent development that travelers may not know how to take the proper precautions or how to locate overseas medical help. The worldwide spread of AIDS, for example, has focused attention on the need for appropriate knowledge of health issues in preparation for overseas living. Moreover, even routine ailments (the flu, toothache, dizziness) or minor accidents (a broken limb), when endured far away from home, can take on a threatening and disorienting aspect.

Students should be encouraged to take responsibility for their own health and wellness. Nevertheless, advisers and program managers are responsible both for informing students of the hazards that may await them and for coordinating an appropriate and effective program of support. Education abroad administrators should be concerned for the health and safety of students not only to protect the student but also to protect their institution from liability, an issue that is becoming increasingly complex on campuses. Health and safety issues must be addressed by institutional policies, sound operating procedures, and responsible programming decisions (see Chapter 19, "Legal Issues").

In addition to health issues, education abroad students often bring with them quite unrealistic social assumptions. For example, they may believe that serious crime exists only on U.S. streets, or, alternatively, that foreigners will rob them blind at every opportunity. Further, although students may be model citizens on campus and believe they will know how to behave abroad, the experience of being in a foreign land can be unsettling, with its tricky combination of new social demands and freedoms. Thus, aberrant or unexpected student behavior patterns, by U.S. or foreign standards, are not unknown in education abroad.

Students may also have to deal with social and political change abroad, which can sometimes come quite suddenly and on occasion become dangerous and even violent. They can, in their naiveté or enthusiasm, easily get caught in the crossfire, perhaps literally. Recent years have given us numerous examples of U.S. students and programs experiencing both imagined and very real threats of international terrorism and war—statistically, London and Paris streets may be safer than those of New York, but not necessarily than those of Cairo or Tel Aviv. Judging the safety of study abroad destinations must be part of overall program planning, part of which must be consultation with university counsel on the question of institutional liabilities.

The issue of appropriate student conduct during times of stress abroad is something that can and should be addressed during advising and orientation. Sound health and safety preparations by students will contribute significantly to their experience abroad. Advisers have a key role to play in raising awareness of the issues, providing resources and information, and motivating students to take charge of their health and well-being while abroad. Advisers should make every effort to create an environment that encourages students to raise health concerns without risk of discrimination and accommodates those with special needs.

▮ Health Issues

Because education abroad professionals are not likely to be health-care experts or to know if an individual student's medical history may contradict standard recommendations, there are limits to the medical counsel you can offer. Your primary role, then, is to **develop partnerships** with those who can do so. Each campus must determine the baseline of information to be provided, and develop approaches and materials that meet the needs of its own programs and students.

You should begin by forming a partnership with the student health service on your own campus. An ongoing dialogue may not only help to obtain their involvement in health orientations or a modification of insurance policies to meet your students' needs but may also keep student health personnel informed of your office's activities. This can be vital for students who return from abroad and subsequently need treatment for an illness contracted abroad (for example, malaria). Public agencies, such as public health services and international travel clinics in the area are also invaluable resources.

Fortunately, with the increase in technology, particularly the Internet, access to information is increasingly easy. The Centers for Disease Control (CDC) has many on-line services; the State Department manages the Consular Affairs Bulletin Board, has information such as foreign country HIV requirements available by fax and provides information through the Department of State's Foreign Affairs Network; and NAFSA's Section on U.S. Students Abroad (SECUSSA) maintains an e-mail discussion list, SECUSS-L, where questions can be asked and good information received. NAFSA also has a variety of printed publications available on health and insurance issues. The American College Health Association (ACHA) has cooperated with NAFSA on student health projects and is also a good resource.

World Health Problems

Some health problems, such as diarrhea, are worldwide; others, such as malaria, are found only in certain regions. The CDC provides detailed information about health conditions in all parts of the world, as well as recommendations for vaccination and prophylaxis, and general tips on staying healthy while abroad.

Almost everyone encounters diarrhea, particularly when traveling in the developing world. Mild forms of diarrhea are readily treated, but severe dysentery can have long-term effects. Malaria continues to be endemic in tropical regions despite an increase in community preventive measures. If students will be in Africa, Asia, Oceania, Central America, or South America, they should be made aware of these problems and given information on how the problems are appropriately prevented, or treated if contracted.

Sexually transmitted diseases (STDs) such as gonorrhea, syphilis, and herpes continue to pose health risks for travelers in virtually any country. The HIV virus, which is responsible for AIDS, is not only transmitted sexually but also through contaminated hypodermic needles, which in some countries are reused, and blood supplies, and thus presents a general health risk abroad. Contracting hepatitis or cholera is also a possibility in countries with untreated drinking water.

Given the grave physical consequences of contracting such diseases, students must be alerted to the transmission routes and appropriate preventive measures and, if necessary, treatments. At the same time, students should understand that their risks are not dramatically greater abroad, even in developing countries, than they are in the United States. Also, they should not be encouraged to regard foreign health care as inferior to that available at home because the opposite is often the case. As with other advice you give, a balanced approach is the best.

Preexisting Physical Problems

Students with known and ongoing medical problems, such as allergies or diabetes, must take special precautions in preparing for and managing their situation overseas. They need to anticipate how their new environment and the stresses of study abroad can impact their health.

For example, a student with allergies needs to ensure that specialized medications will be available, and a diabetic needs to consider the consequences of contracting malaria. Because you cannot specifically address each student's medical needs, you must prompt them to obtain medical advice from someone who knows their medical history and is familiar with conditions in the host country. At the same time, students with common and foreseeable medical problems need to know that they are likely to be among many fellow sufferers and that adequate treatment will more than likely be available.

The situation for students with physical handicaps should of course have been addressed at the earliest stages of the advising process—well before orientation. Students with disabilities must be sure at the outset, even before the application process, that adequate facilities and personnel exist overseas and that they will be welcomed and their needs met.

As noted in Chapter 11, Mobility International is active in encouraging programs and campuses to serve students with physical handicaps and in helping students to identify programs that have the will and ability to assist them with their specialized needs. Such students know what these needs are and only seek assurances that they will be met so that they can participate fully in the program. With the passage of the 1991 Americans with Disabilities Act, which codifies the obligations of institutions to the disabled, program administrators should check with university counsel to ensure that the program is in full compliance with the act and its implementing regulations.

Issues of Substance Abuse

Whatever their behavior on U.S. campuses, students free from U.S. laws and mores regarding the use of alcohol sometimes slip into—or maintain—patterns of alcohol abuse while abroad. Such abuse occurs for a variety of reasons: a mistaken impression of how alcohol is used in their new surroundings, cheaper costs in some countries, a lower drinking age, more lenient laws against drunkenness, or just a desire to experiment or fit in.

Your orientation should address any program requirements regarding alcohol consumption as well as the consequences for abuse. Information should be provided about the use of alcohol in the host country. Students who attend Alcoholics Anonymous meetings in the United States should call AA beforehand for information about meetings, and language of participation, abroad. Students in AA should be encouraged to provide this information as part of their medical background so that the overseas program administrators can take this into consideration when planning social functions.

Although most countries, with the exception of those with religious prohibitions, tolerate social drinking, the use of inebriating or hallucinogenic drugs is seldom allowed under any circumstances. Drug abuse by study abroad participants is less common but more severe than alcohol abuse. It carries with it not only immeasurable health risks but also very serious cultural and legal consequences. Risks are immensely complicated by impure drugs, shady and often criminal contacts, and rigid legal systems that impose severe penalties. In the area of drug abuse, too, the possibility of institutional liability justifies a careful consultation with university counsel to ensure that your program complies with the 1988 Anti–Drug Abuse Act (specifically the provision relating to drug-free workplaces) and other federal legislation.

Nutrition

Living in another culture necessarily entails a change in diet and altered eating routines and assumptions. These changes are usually beyond student control. Sometimes, students find that their diet abroad is considerably healthier than the one they followed at home. In many countries, people eat less processed food than Americans, drink less coffee and sweetened soda, eat more grains, fresh fish, dairy products, vegetables, and fruits, or generally eat less and have a more active life-style.

At the other extreme, people in poorer countries may eat what they can get, prepare foods in unsanitary ways, and suffer from various kinds of vitamin deficiencies. If this is the case, students will, and should, have some reasonable concerns about how either to adjust to such a diet or to supplement it. Whatever the situation, you can be sure that what students eat, do not eat, dream about eating, or hate eating will be a very important part of their thoughts and conversations while they are abroad and for years to come.

It is not feasible, or even advisable, to try to impose American eating habits and foodstuffs on a foreign culture. It is possible to learn in advance what the foreign diet consists of, and then to make some decisions about what nutritional counsel to give students. For your programs, such information should be readily available; otherwise, get it from program representatives or people who have lived there. Because you are probably not a nutritionist and your students may well be going to many different countries, perhaps the most you can do is discuss the situation in each country in the information sheets you keep in the education abroad library, and try to provide some general guidance on sound nutrition during predeparture orientation.

Emotional and Mental Problems

The possibility of known, or new, emotional and mental problems emerging overseas is seen by many experienced education abroad administrators and advisers as a health and safety concern second only to alcohol abuse in its potential negative impact on an education abroad experience. Like substance abuse, its primary impact may be on the well-being of one person, but its side-effects can carry over to others—even to an entire group. What is clear is that preexisting emotional difficulties are often intensified by living in a foreign culture. Contrary to the belief of many students and their parents that an overseas experience might be just the thing to cheer someone up, a stressful experience in foreign surroundings can have the opposite effect. In addition, there may be even fewer resources in foreign settings to help a student deal with such problems.

As will be discussed in the next chapter, culture shock by itself can often have a temporarily shattering and disorienting effect on even the most secure students. It is a real and very normal adjustment phenomenon, with predictable psychological and social dimensions. In almost all cases, it is also something for which students can be prepared through proper predeparture and on-site orientation. But students who carry with them serious, unresolved emotional problems can jeopardize themselves and their program. The challenge to the education abroad adviser and program administrator is to know, first, how to prevent this situation from happening, and, second, what to do if and when it occurs.

As discussed in Chapter 10, you should stress the importance of having a clear and positive motive when discussing the range of challenges facing any student who chooses to study or work abroad. Let your students know that going abroad just to get away from something does not make sense. Additionally, one-on-one counseling should give you an opportunity to judge the emotional stability and maturity of most students. If you have reservations, this is the time to share them openly and directly.

If you see no obvious problems, or if students are determined to hide problems from you or do not recognize or acknowledge them, you can only proceed as if none exists. To search or probe further, for example, by asking your counseling center if a given student is in therapy, probably constitutes a breach of the confidentiality of student records. By involving the counseling center in your advising and orientation, however, you can acquaint them with the risk factors of study abroad, such as culture shock, and also involve them in discussing with students, in a group, issues they may face overseas. Then, when you send them the list of study abroad participants, in the same way you inform the registrar or housing office, the counselors will have the appropriate background and will be able to act on the information.

Students who will not admit problems face-to-face are also likely to disguise them on their applications. Most letters of recommendation ask for comments on a student's emotional, as well as intellectual, maturity. But only the especially astute faculty member may be able to discern such characteristics and then be willing to state them for the record. Thus, it is very hard to know in advance which students may have emotional or mental difficulties overseas. In some instances, your instinct might suggest that a particular student's participation might not be beneficial to the program or the student. In such cases, you may wish to consult university counsel and professionals at the university health service or counseling center about the right approach to take.

Privacy and confidentiality are difficult issues, particularly when decisions about a student's participation in study abroad may be based on instinct or hearsay. An education abroad professional must be ready to work closely with counseling centers to better understand students' emotional concerns and to make sure that those experiencing difficulties are not excluded from an education abroad experience; rather, there should be sufficient opportunities in advising and orientation for students and advisers to discuss the kind of stress and strain that can accompany studying overseas.

Foreign Medical Practice

The manner in which medical help is obtained, the way patients are treated, the conditions of overseas medical facilities, and how health care is afforded often present marked differences from U.S. practice. Students need to be prepared for the reality that U.S. health-care values, assumptions, and methods are not universally practiced. Indeed, even the notions regarding the onset of illness or points at which expert attention is required are to some degree cultural phenomena. Students also need to be advised about any foreign country requirements on health issues that might exclude them.

In some countries, especially in northern Europe, medical standards, judged by U.S. criteria, will turn out to be superior in effectiveness and lower in cost. In other countries, standards are low enough that some medical needs cannot be met. The key is to know in advance, and be prepared for all contingencies. The availability of emergency medical help is a particularly important area of concern. Students need to face the possibility that they may need emergency help. Their orientation materials should offer general principles for finding such help while overseas.

Medical and Accident Insurance

No college or education abroad program should allow a student to travel abroad without sufficient medical insurance coverage for all possible medical needs, including coverage for medical evacuation and repatriation of remains, accident and life insurance. Many institutions can make arrangements to extend the policy that covers students on campus, sometimes for an extra fee. Sometimes this arrangement applies only to home-campus programs, sometimes to all programs. In addition, a number of national agencies now sell medical and accident insurance policies designed especially for education abroad program participation.

It is your job to work with others at your institution to decide what sort of insurance coverage you want for your students, how to acquire it, whether or not to make its costs a part of your own fees, and how to make certain that all students sign up for it and understand how it works. In addition, students must be informed about mandatory vaccinations and other inoculations. Some programs and some visa applications require a physical examination, which you may or may not be able to arrange for students through your campus health services. All such requirements and procedures need to be communicated to students as early in the advising process as possible, perhaps as part of your handbook, and then reviewed carefully during predeparture orientation.

One important issue in dealing with insurance is to convey the importance of verifying any parental coverage that a student might insist is adequate overseas. When students are included on a parent's insurance policy it should be required that verification is obtained that confirms that the coverage meets your programs requirements and is valid overseas for the duration of the program.

▌ Personal Conduct and Safety Issues

Students returning from an education abroad experience invariably observe that they have matured in confidence, direction, and ambition. They talk about learning to think and act for themselves and to make significant decisions for the first time in their lives. These reflections suggest that for most students the experience of living and learning abroad fosters greater independence. One of their freedoms is to make mistakes, and one of the initial mistakes they often make is to assume that local customs, mores, and even laws are not quite real or do not apply to foreigners. In due course, they realize that this is not the case, and sometimes they pay for their transgressions.

It may be nearly impossible to explain to a group of students about to go abroad exactly how they should and should not behave in all places and circumstances; moreover, even assuming that what you have said is accurate, it may or may not be fully taken in or believed while the greater realities of campus and U.S. domestic life surround them. Much of the challenge of preparing students is presumably covered in the on-site orientations. But it is possible, and worthwhile, to remind them, in no uncertain terms, that (1) they are indeed guests in their new country and should always behave with this in mind; (2) each program has its own

225

rules of conduct, always for good reasons; and (3) being "foreign" does not excuse them either from knowing or from obeying the civil and criminal laws of the country.

Crime

As on U.S. campuses (as opposed to U.S. streets), education abroad programs often take place in relatively protected and safe environments. These may be foreign university campuses or isolated facilities with good security. But just as some theft, drunkenness, vandalism, even rape, occurs on U.S. campuses, some of your students may fall victim to crime while abroad.

Again, on-site orientation programs bear the burden of providing detailed information on safeguards against possible crime in the area. As part of your advising and orientation, you can impart a general sense of the situation in each country where your students study and direct their questions to program sponsors for further information. You might also work up a list of general do's and don'ts while abroad.

Threats of Political Violence

In recent years an enormous amount of attention has been given to the threats of political terrorism and violence said to be specifically directed against Americans abroad. Although few such instances have occurred, this does not mean that these threats were hollow or that in the future no Americans abroad, or more specifically, students, will become targets or actual victims. It is important to take precautions against the possibilities of such occurrences. It is equally important not to be intimidated or to add to the misinformation and panic that popular journalism has tended to promote.

Decisions about where to find programs and whether or not to send students to programs judged to be in troubled areas are made at the institutional and program levels. Your role vis-à-vis your institution is to provide solid information about the program's history, its administration, the type of orientations provided, and so on. This information can be obtained via e-mail and the Internet and by remaining in contact with your colleagues on other campuses and in programs abroad. In addition, you need to ensure that your institution has developed a crisis management plan that covers emergencies, such as deciding when and how to cancel programs, or determining who has authority to obtain emergency medical assistance for a student. An institution's risk management office is a useful ally in such discussions.

With regard to students (and their parents), the most you can do is to assure them that your institution is responsible and informed and will act to protect their safety at all times. During orientation, lay out some ways for students to minimize risks and avoid obvious dangers. These might include advice on making travel arrangements, keeping a low profile, dressing conservatively, avoiding large groups of other Americans, and generally keeping out of harm's way and political entanglements.

The question of institutional liability for students' injuries suffered abroad is a murky one. Here, too, a consultation with your university's legal counsel may be warranted, particularly since many insurance policies exclude coverage for acts of terrorism, riots or civil disturbances. (see Chapter 19, "Legal Issues").

∎ Predeparture Orientation

In many ways, predeparture orientation is a culmination of the advising process. Students who have paid attention to orientation sessions before going abroad should find few surprises. The information you review and the materials you distribute on health and safety issues (as outlined above) are not intended to alarm students or parents. Rather, the materials should guide them, once more, toward intelligent, rational preparation. In view of the seriousness of health and safety issues to the success of their overseas experience, predeparture orientation should make up a commensurate portion of your program (see Chapter 14, "Orientation").

The following paragraphs describe the health and safety information you might wish to include in the materials you provide to your students.

Predeparture Medical Examinations

Students need to complete all appointments well in advance of their departure date, including immunizations and assessment of special health problems. They also need to take care of any gynecological and dental check-ups that would fall within the time overseas. It is very important that they obtain copies of important health records, including

- blood type
- eyeglass and contact lens prescriptions
- prescriptions for medications being taken (written in generic terms to obviate the difficulty of obtaining brand-name medications overseas)
- EKGs and X-rays (when these are relevant to a student's medical situation)

- doctor's statement about any special health problems
- dental records, particularly if special procedures or medications are indicated.

The student should take all these records abroad.

What to Pack

Students should take extra prescription drugs in original containers (except where their importation is specifically prohibited), as well as a copy of the prescription for the generic names of these drugs. They should be packed in different places, and not in luggage that might be lost or stolen. Students should also consider bringing syringes or other instruments necessary for self-administration of medications, check to ensure that importation is not prohibited, and bring a doctor's note authorizing their use.

It is strongly recommended that diabetics take a supply of disposable hypodermic syringes and needles, except where prohibited, to protect against the possibility of HIV infection in countries where needles and syringes are reused by medical personnel. In addition, students should pack extra eyeglasses or contact lenses and dentures; a small first-aid kit containing adhesive bandages, antibiotic ointment (such as Neosporin), sunburn ointment, aspirin or other painkiller, antidiarrheal medicine; and, depending on the region visited, water purification tablets, antihistamines for allergy relief, salt tablets, skin moisturizer, insect repellent and sunblock.

Printed Information about Health and Safety

Students should be strongly encouraged to pack all relevant information sheets prepared by the education abroad office, as well as other materials from campus and local health agencies covering some or all of these topics. Printed materials should include

- cautions about alcohol and drug abuse, emphasizing that customs regarding alcohol and drug use are often different in other cultures, that laws controlling drugs and alcohol are likely to be different from those in the United States, and that penalties for abuse may be severe.
- descriptions of persistent and epidemic diseases such as dysentery, hepatitis, malaria, and AIDS, with information on their transmission, prevention, and treatment.

228

- information about the physiological and psychological consequences of jet lag, culture shock, homesickness, loneliness, changes in diet, lack of exercise, and so on.

- general instructions for emergency medical situations—using an emergency telephone system (like the 911 system in the United States), calling an ambulance, a hospital or doctor, an embassy or consular office, or a large hotel and asking for the name of the physician who is called when a guest needs emergency attention. The International Association for Medical Assistance to Travelers (IAMAT) provides a list of English-speaking doctors worldwide.

- general advice on nutrition, including ways to supplement diet deficiencies.

- special advice for handicapped individuals and those with temporary physical disabilities.

- full health and accident insurance policy coverage information and identification, including notice of special limitations or instructions on applicability and instructions for filing claims while overseas.

- region-specific health information.

- a list of prudent advice on how to minimize the possibility of being victimized by crime.

- tips on how to keep a low profile during political emergencies.

▌ Region-Specific Information

For programs sponsored by your institution, you have a responsibility to provide ample information on health and safety issues in each country. This information will be furnished by the program staff, faculty, and past participants, but must be put into final form through your efforts. The question is how to determine what information should be imparted during the predeparture period, and what is more effectively given during the on-site orientation and through the normal counsel of the resident director.

If you do not operate your own programs, or if sizable numbers of your students participate in programs sponsored by other U.S. or foreign institutions or agencies, you may not be specifically responsible for intensive predeparture information for every specific region. Nevertheless, one way to ensure that students are properly informed is to provide the following information:

- special medical requirements for admission and for obtaining visas or other documents from the foreign government, including immunizations, physical examinations, and tests.
- the nature, prevention, and treatment of region-specific diseases. This should include, where appropriate, information on how to handle injections, emergencies, and/or blood transfusions in areas affected by AIDS.
- local diet and eating patterns, including the need for and availability of nutritional supplements.
- laws regulating the import and/or possession of medications, hypodermic needles, condoms, and other contraceptives.
- details on obtaining medications.
- how patients are likely to be treated, what kind of facilities they will find, how payment for services is handled, and students' legal rights to obtain services.
- how to locate routine or emergency professional medical help, including names and telephone numbers of hospitals, clinics, and doctors, emergency-system telephone numbers, and self-help programs like Alcoholics Anonymous.
- medical and accident insurance information for policies connected with the program.
- what to include in a medical kit for travelers.
- facts on local crime and the political situation.

Programs will be happy to provide this information upon request.

▌Selected Health Information Resources

Alcoholics Anonymous World Services. POB 459, Grand Central Station, New York, NY 10163, 212.870.3400. Provides a directory of international AA meetings for members only.

American College Health Association. POB 28937, Baltimore, MD 21240-8937, 410.859.1500

Centers for Disease Control. 1600 Clifton Rd. NE, Atlanta, GA 30333. 404.639.3311 (general information) 404.639.2888 (emergency information) http://www.cdc.gov/travel/travel.html

Department of State. Overseas Citizens Services. 202.647.5225. An automated menu provides information on current epidemics and health conditions worldwide. It also includes information on travel advisories, U.S. passports, the types of assistance provided by Citizens Consular Services and the Citizens Emergency Center, as well as visa information for visitors to the United States. In addition, it allows access to the information contained on the Overseas Security Advisory Council (OSAC) Electronic Bulletin Board. These databases are updated daily.

Foreign Affairs Network (DOSFAN). http://www.state.gov/index.html. Has information such as per diem rate, Background notes, contacts, and phone numbers.

Forms of Travel. By Judith W. Carr and Ellen Summerfield. NAFSA: Association of International Educators. Working Paper #51. 800.836.4994.

Health Check: For Study, Work, and Travel Abroad. By Joan Elias Gore and Judith A. Green. NAFSA: Association of International Educators and CIEE: Council on International Educational Exchange. 212.661.1414.

Health Information for International Travel. Available from the Superintendent of Documents, U.S. Government Printing Office, Washington, DC 20402. 202.512.1800

Health Concerns in International Travel. Shoreland Inc., POB 13795, Milwaukee, WI 53213. 800.433.5256

HIV Listings. 202.647.3000, or send SASE to the Public Affairs staff at the Bureau of Consular Affairs, 2201 C Street, NW, Room 6831, Washington, DC 20520

IAMAT: International Association for Medical Assistance to Travelers. A nonprofit, worldwide organization with excellent information on malaria prevention and other region-specific knowledge. 736 Center St., Lewiston, NY 14092. 716.754.4883. There is no fee for joining, but a donation is welcome. IAMAT may be joined by students or education abroad advisers.

International Travel Health Guide. By Stuart R. Rose, M.D.; updated annually. Travel Medicine Inc., 351 Pleasant St., Ste. 312, Northampton, MA 01060. 413.584.0381.

A Manual for Integrating Persons with Disabilities into International Educational Exchange Programs. Edited by Susan Sygall. Mobility International USA, POB 10767, Eugene, OR 97440. 541.343.1284

National AIDS Clearing House (CDC). 800.458.5231, http://cdcnac. aspensys.com:86

Passport's Health Guide for International Travelers. By Thomas P. Sakmar, M.D.; Pierce Gardner, M.D., FACP; Gene N. Peterson, M.D., Ph.D. 1986. Passport Books. National Textbook Co., Lincolnwood, IL

A World of Options: A Guide to International Educational Exchange, Community Service, and Travel for Persons with Disabilities. Edited by Christa Bucks. Mobility International USA, POB 10767, Eugene, OR 97440. 541.343.1284.

14 Predeparture Orientation And Reentry Programming

Contributors: Ellen Summerfield, Rebecca Sibley, and Helen Stellmaker

The increasing emphasis on developing effective predeparture and reentry programs reflects an understanding that the time abroad must be embedded in an educational continuum. Education abroad advisers and administrators have meaningful pedagogical roles to play in working with faculty and staff to prepare students to make the most of their new learning and living environment, maintain a line of contact during the experience, and finally assist them in the complicated process of reintegration into degree studies, campus life, and career preparation.

P redeparture orientation, participation in a program abroad, and reentry should be seen as parts of a continuous and unified process. The profound learning that leads, at its best, to multiculturalism and ethnorelativism necessarily begins well before departure and continues long after return.[1] Thus, the philosophy of education abroad programming cannot be limited to the actual time spent in another country, but represents a three-phase, inclusive learning process.

This chapter focuses on basic, practical guidelines for designing and running predeparture and reentry programs. Although it touches on the advising process in general, as well as on health and safety issues, these concerns are covered more fully in adjoining chapters.

∎ Predeparture Orientation Programming

Predeparture orientation is intended to help prepare students for a meaningful and successful educational experience abroad. It needs to be very wide-ranging, and include everything from practical concerns with passports and ID cards to profound questions concerning one's personal responsibilities in an interdependent, multicultural world. The major goals are to

- provide essential practical information;
- motivate students to learn more about the host culture as well as about themselves as Americans, prior to departure;
- help students develop cross-cultural sensitivity and become familiar with the process of cross-cultural adaptation;
- help students gain a better comprehension of world issues and examine their roles as global citizens; and
- assist students in investigating their academic objectives overseas and how these goals might fit into long-term academic goals.

To plan an effective orientation is challenging. It is important to show the utmost respect for students, who are generally impressionable and may easily accept misconceptions or oversimplifications. Ethical issues and pedagogical quandaries emerge early: How do you motivate students and create excitement without raising false hopes or expectations? How do you warn them against the dangers they might meet without causing unnecessary apprehension? How do you prepare them without depriving them of the joys of discovery? How do you discuss differences among cultures without introducing or reinforcing stereotypes?

Because these questions have no easy answers, a predeparture orientation can be a stimulating process for the adviser and the students. When done well, the orientation will generate enthusiasm for learning and set a tone of openness and receptivity to new experiences. It should increase student confidence in their ability to meet people and communicate across cultures but also make them see that they are to be involved in a very complex process of two-way communication. It helps them learn to appreciate and enjoy differences and to understand their responsibilities as guests in another country. Finally, it helps to create a network of peer support. As students get to know each other they come to realize that they face many of the same issues regardless of their destination.

Designing the Program

In designing the orientation program, you must decide on the following:

- format: one session, weekly sessions, weekend retreat, or academic course
- content: balances between practical and philosophical, culture-general and culture-specific, and academic and nonacademic
- process: intellectual or experiential; reading, telling, and showing or experiencing
- group dynamic: large, lecture-style or small and interactive

These decisions will depend on your budget, staff, and time limitations as well as on your educational philosophy and the needs of your students. Most advisers believe it is both reasonable and necessary to require attendance at a predeparture orientation program and that students who do not attend demonstrate a lack of seriousness about their impending time abroad. Some schools that run their own programs automatically dismiss such students from study abroad participation. This approach is not possible, however, in large schools and those where students enroll in many different programs. Whatever your policy, students should be informed of expectations when they first apply to study abroad on any program.

Designing an orientation is a creative process.[2] Clearly, even a well-planned orientation cannot answer everyone's needs and achieve every goal. Recognize that you are striving to move toward your goals rather than to achieve them fully and that you will build on your learning and experience with each cycle. Time constraints will shape the design of your orientation.

If only a few hours are available, the adviser must concentrate on the essentials and provide students with the incentive and information to explore many things further on their own. If you can schedule a series of weekly meetings or a weekend retreat, an even more effective orientation can be designed with time for practical details as well as cross-cultural training. The advantage of weekly meetings spread out over an academic quarter or semester is that students have time to absorb new ideas. A weekend retreat, on the other hand, has the advantage of capturing the students for an intensive period. If the retreat can be held off campus, students tend to be more involved and receptive.

A one-day orientation might be structured as follows:

Morning session

8:45   Coffee and donuts

9:00   Welcome and introductions: discuss purpose of orientation

9:15   Presentation on culture (for example, a video, or a speaker, to introduce basic concepts)[3] and large group discussion

10:00   Academic issues: how to benefit from a different educational system

11:00   Small group meetings to review practical details

12:00   Lunch (international foods and group by region, if possible)

Afternoon session

1:00–1:45	Health and safety (large group)
1:45–2:15	Gender/diversity issues (large or special interest groups)
2:15–3:15	Political and historical awareness (by country or region)
3:15–3:30	Break
3:30–4:45	Cross-cultural awareness—"How to Learn" about United States and host country (small or large group, depending on needs)
5:00–6:00	Dinner (international, if possible)
6:15–8:15	Simulation exercise and debriefing[4]
8:15–8:30	Closing (questions, handouts, evaluation)

There are many possible variations on this type of retreat or workshop. The cross-cultural component and simulation exercise can take place on a different day, depending on student needs. Special interest topics that appeal to smaller groups can be offered as a menu from which students or parents choose, for example, being a minority or lesbian or gay student abroad, information for parents, bicycle touring, or women overseas. Again, more time may be needed to be devoted to academic issues.

An excellent form of orientation is undoubtedly an academic course, which allows students to investigate cross-cultural issues in depth and offers the additional bonus of credit. There are many professional-development opportunities available for advisers interested in learning to teach such a course.[5]

Whatever the format, advisers must take care to recruit the most competent resource people available. In a university setting, these might include faculty members, community experts, medical personnel, international scholars and students, returnees, and—if the budget permits—overseas personnel. All resource people should be briefed prior to the orientation to clarify responsibilities and strategies. For example, returnees can lead a session for their peers when they have a thorough list of topics to be covered. It is a good idea to caution returnees against assuming that one's experiences will apply to everyone or getting sidetracked into travelogues.

Since education abroad is academic and experiential, one can argue that experiential techniques are particularly appropriate as a form of preparation for living and learning overseas. Cognitive methods should not be replaced, but you should consider blending and combining the two. The experiential method can include a broad range of activities: simulations, role playing, films, games, and field exercises. Excellent sources on experiential education are *Beyond Experience* (2d ed.), edited by Theodore Gochenour, *Intercultural Sourcebook, Cross-Cultural Training Methods* (vol. 1), edited by Sandra Fowler and Monica G. Mumford, and *Experiential Activities for Intercultural Learning* (vol. 1), edited by H. Ned Seelye (see Appendix 1). The Peace Corps and the School for International Training have developed useful manuals describing experiential techniques and exercises. You and your facilitators should be thoroughly familiar with such activities before attempting them with a group. Be prepared for some learner resistance and for the fact that experiential learning is often more time-consuming and risky than presentations and lectures.

If you decide to incorporate experiential techniques, you should nevertheless begin the session with traditional approaches. This will help to build trust within the group and make it easier for students to make the transition to the emotionally more risky experiential methods. Careful sequencing is also important with regard to content. It is usually better to begin with the culture-general and move on to the culture-specific so as to provide a framework and to hold the students' interest. (They are naturally inclined to want to hear about their own target countries.) Whatever your decisions, you should realize that attention to sequencing, pacing, and differences in learning styles is extremely important to the success of the orientation.

It is a good idea to begin any announcement about the orientation program, and the session itself, with a brief explanation of why it is necessary. Although many students genuinely welcome the opportunity to prepare for study abroad, they naturally resist planning for far-off events, especially if the orientation is held in May and the program participants are not leaving until late August. Thus, it is important to explain what the orientation is all about and what it can and cannot do. Students should be disabused of the idea that an orientation can prepare them for all eventualities and cover all topics. Rather, they should learn that this brief time together is intended to provide a foundation on which they can build.

What you cover in your orientation depends on the profile of your students' programs. Also, your students might be receiving other orientations. All respectable programs are likely to offer some type of on-site postarrival orientation program; the only exceptions might be for students enrolling directly in foreign universities, though many such institutions do offer new-student orientations. Although it never hurts to go over the essential matters more than once, you should know what is awaiting your students, and then design your program to complement this.

If you are working only with your own programs, you can find out what is done on-site by consulting with appropriate faculty or staff. Also, most reputable programs that recruit students nationally will send you literature about their on-site orientation programs. Nevertheless, you may still need to design your own orientation program based on the information at hand and some guesses about what is being done elsewhere.

Practical Details

The nuts-and-bolts portion of orientation provides straightforward, factual, and essential practical and academic information. A thorough handbook that includes basic information is indispensable and will save valuable time in the orientation sessions. It will also allow students to refer to the material later, both before and during their stay abroad. The adviser can help students gain a command of the many practical details. This gives them a sense of security, but at the same time makes clear to them that not everything can be covered. Educators can be driven batty by the "How many towels will I need?" syndrome. These details must be handled thoroughly and professionally but not be allowed to dominate the orientation.

Your checklist will probably contain most if not all of the following:

Logistics

- passports, visas, other essential documents
- international travel arrangements (if any)
- housing, host families, and meals
- packing, luggage, and shipping regulations
- phoning, mail, e-mail, and other communications
- foreign currency, transferring money abroad, credit cards, and money exchange
- postarrival travel information (Eurail passes, international ID cards, youth hostel cards, guidebooks, etc.)

Academic information

- educational philosophy overseas, role of faculty, styles of learning
- preapproval forms for course work (if required)
- credit-approval policies upon return
- preregistration for the next term

- institutional policies and procedures
- addresses (e-mail, fax, and/or mail) of academic advisers

Legal considerations and responsibilities

- waiver forms
- cancellation policies[6]

Health and safety (see Chapter 13). If they are familiar with overseas travel and related issues, medical personnel may lend greater credibility in the presentation of the following topics:

- medical and dental check-ups
- inoculations
- prescription and over-the-counter medicines
- emergency medical needs (diabetes, epilepsy, allergy to penicillin, etc.) and availability of medical care
- jet lag and postarrival illnesses
- depression and eating disorders
- AIDS/sexually transmitted diseases/contraceptives
- alcohol and drug abuse or use
- health insurance coverage

With regard to both health and safety, your institution's written materials should include a list of emergency contacts and telephone numbers. The U.S. Department of State publishes various pamphlets—such as "Your Trip Abroad" and "Tips for Americans Residing Abroad"—that can serve as valuable references for advisers on practical details, including passports, visas, customs regulations, and travel advisories.[7]

Gender/diversity issues. Faculty members who specialize in these areas may be willing to share information and insights. These topics may be incorporated into other sessions, but their importance will be highlighted by having specific sessions:

- male and female roles and relationships abroad
- norms for personal space abroad
- appropriate clothing/body language
- independence, group or individual norms
- lesbian and gay concerns
- minority students abroad

Country or regional context. It is a challenge to convince students that predeparture knowledge of political and economic systems and historical events, and of how these shape culture, is important. Returnees and faculty members can be helpful in doing so. Possible topics include current national or international concerns; political and economic systems; human rights; population distribution; health and welfare; the state of technology; relations with the United States; the role of the military; political unrest and terrorism; crime patterns; and law enforcement.

I Introducing Cross-Cultural Issues

Even though the practical-details portion of your orientation programs is intended to concern itself with straightforward facts and information, cross-cultural issues may emerge almost immediately. If you are prepared to weave in cross-cultural information as appropriate, the presentations will be more useful and interesting. For example, if students are to live with host families, they will probably want to know where and with whom they will live, whether there is a commute to classes, whether meals will be provided, and how they can be reached by mail or phone. But this information—if you are in a position to supply it—is not devoid of a cultural context.

Even the simplest matter, such as providing the names of the family members, raises cross-cultural questions. How should the family members be addressed? Are first names appropriate? Should formal or informal forms of address (for example, *tu* or *vous* in French, *tu* or *usted* in Spanish) be used? Thus, in order to prepare for everyday life with a family—the basics of how to dress, eat, bathe, greet people, show affection—students need to gain insight into how and why family life and relationships in the host culture may differ from the those in the United States.

Do families value privacy or togetherness? Are there clearly defined gender roles? Are restrictions placed on women? Does the extended family play a large role? What is the role of children? What role does religion play? If students understand that family life in the host country tends to be more formal than in the United States, they will not be as inclined to interpret reserve as unfriendliness. If they know that hot water and electricity are expensive, they may be less likely to offend with what are perceived as wasteful North American habits.

Although you cannot even begin to cover all such culture-specific questions that may arise during an orientation program, by being ready to focus in detail on some, you give the message that apparently minor matters will shortly loom very large in their lives while abroad. The more thoroughly students understand underlying cultural values—such as determining why families behave as they do—the better they will be able to define their own roles and interact comfortably.

Just as the details of housing must be placed within a cultural context, so can the discussion you introduce on academics. For example, if students are to be partially or fully integrated into foreign universities, they need to know basics of how and why the foreign system is different from our own. Because they will probably be expected to function more independently than at home, they need to know about the underlying philosophy of education so as not to conclude that the foreign university is unorganized or inefficient simply because there may be less supervision and regulation.

If you feel you need some expert advice on these and related matters, there are many helpful sources mentioned in Appendix 1. Those new to international educational exchange are strongly encouraged to attend regional or national NAFSA conferences to network with colleagues and to participate in preconference workshops that focus on designing orientation and reentry programming.

Culture-Specific Issues

International educators and specialists generally agree that the "how to learn" orientation is more effective than attempting to impart extensive information on host cultures in the limited time available.[8] Moreover, if you have students going to a range of countries, there is no way that all culture-specific questions can be effectively answered, even in a preliminary way. The orientation time is therefore best spent emphasizing why students will have to take considerable initiative in order to gain the culture-specific knowledge they will need once they leave campus and arrive on distant shores.

One late-twentieth-century reality you may want to address in your orientation is that there are few pure cultures left, especially in countries and capital cities that have experienced considerable immigration. To prepare students going to London to expect to meet only the English and only to hear BBC English is to add to the shock they will feel when they have a roommate from Pakistan or Hong Kong and find they cannot understand the accent of the student next door from Derbyshire or Glasgow. Nor will they find only the Chinese in China or the Danes in Copenhagen. Indeed, contemporary society is often as multicultural in composition, especially in the urban areas (and especially on university campuses) as anything U.S. students might think they are leaving behind.

241

For traditional students from white, middle-class backgrounds, this awareness may bring some initial disappointment. For minority students, this news may be a relief in that they may believe such heterogeneity provides more social choices and options. For students trying to immerse themselves in German or Italian, being caught in a milieu where English is a common language may also cause them to have to work harder to speak the target language. Students will have a far less national, yet a much more international, experience than they had planned.

If these realities are neglected in your orientation, your students may feel misled. You should therefore seek to discuss the realities of multiculturalism abroad. As culture-specific knowledge becomes less applicable, culture-general truths become more important than ever, as does the necessity of learning to live with people of widely different backgrounds.

When preparing students for study abroad in non-Western or developing countries, advisers need to give more advanced attention to culture-specific information. Readings, films and slides, experiential techniques, and presentations by experts and returnees can be very effective. Students going to Japan, for example, should have a basic familiarity with everything from how to take a bath and use chopsticks to the philosophy of gift-giving and the nature of a collective society. Orientation for students going to Latin America should range from using public transportation and reacting to expressions of anti-Americanism to sensitizing oneself to the issues facing developing nations. Students going to any non-Western or developing country should also have some concept of gender roles in that country and should reflect on how they will feel as a member of a minority (see Chapter 12, "Promoting Whole World Study").

As these issues suggest, a thorough orientation for non-Western and developing countries is particularly demanding and may well require more time than for countries more similar to the United States. The complexities of world multiculturalism cannot be adequately addressed in a limited time frame, but you would be remiss not to address these matters in some way.

Culture-General Issues

Helping students begin to understand broad cross-cultural perspectives and develop cross-cultural sensitivity may be the most crucial aim of any orientation program. Unless they have lived abroad before for an extended period of time, they will probably not be conscious of the profound ways in which culture affects our lives—our sense of time, our beliefs, our relationships with nature, work, and other people. They may be shocked to find that their assumptions, values, behaviors, and perspectives—which seem perfectly normal and natural to them at home—do not necessarily apply abroad. Although there is no way to forestall the fish-out-of-water sensation experienced by almost all students, especially at first, they can be made aware that at least mild culture shock is normal and to be expected. This will bolster their chances of making the necessary adjustments.

Students who have taken courses in cultural anthropology will have at least an intellectual understanding of these ideas. For others, the concept of culture—what it is, how it affects us, and how to cope—is succinctly and effectively described in Robert Kohls's *Survival Kit for Overseas Living*. You may also wish to assign other interesting readings such as "Body Ritual Among the Nacirema," which can be found in *Toward Internationalism*, or selected chapters in *Intercultural Communication: A Reader*. The videos entitled "World Within Reach," "Cold Water," or "Going International" can also be used effectively in predeparture orientation.[9] Yet reading about culture and culture shock is not the same as experiencing it. Therefore, no orientation program should assure students that to know about another culture is the same thing as being completely comfortable living in it.

Still, it is worth trying to help students build some cross-cultural skills and attitudes prior to departure. Your goals might include exercises and discussions aimed at improving self-reflection, coping with transitions, communicating verbally and nonverbally, and developing sensitivity to and tolerance for differences. In his list of 16 "skills that make a difference" Robert Kohls emphasizes maintaining a sense of humor and living with some failures (*Survival Kit*, 106–107). However one might categorize and define essential coping strategies, you need to emphasize that the process of adjusting to a new culture and learning new intercultural skills is at times difficult and painful. Students must be prepared for the fact that while living abroad is often exhilarating, there are also periods of disappointment, homesickness, and frustration.

Many advisers find it useful to introduce the pertinent concept of culture shock and even to discuss the conjectural U- and W-shaped curves of cultural adjustment charted on a graph.[10] The argument is that if students understand that some form of psychological and social disorientation is a natural part of virtually every sojourner's experience, they will probably not feel as dismayed or worried as they might otherwise be when the symptoms emerge.

Do not overdo this discussion and send unintended negative messages. Stressing survival skills or coping mechanisms alone may suggest to students that the most they can expect is to merely survive or cope in a hostile environment, whereas the key is to prepare them to surmount these possible early frustrations so as to integrate themselves more fully into their new surroundings.[11]

Role-playing, culture-learning games, and simulations, when properly conducted and debriefed, give students courage and help them assess values. If students can watch themselves as participant-observers in an unfamiliar group at home, they can learn how to deal constructively with their feelings abroad.

Americanness: Know Thyself

Although students readily accept the importance of learning about the culture of their host country, they may not at first see the importance of refreshing and expanding their knowledge about the United States. The orientation can help them understand that, as representatives of their country, they will be expected to be knowledgeable about many aspects of U.S. history and current affairs. Also, they should understand that their observations of the host culture will be more meaningful if they have a basis for comparison.

An important aspect of the "how to learn" approach is stressing the need to develop curiosity and ask questions of oneself, and of others when appropriate. The *Trans-Cultural Study Guide* or *The Whole World Guide to Culture Learning* (see Appendix 1) provides an excellent basis for independent learning through questioning. With regard to answering questions about one's own country, *American Ways: A Guide for Foreigners in the United States,* by Gary Althen, provides insights into American behavior as a basis for comparison with other cultures.

As we begin to help students develop the skills they will need to interact effectively with host nationals, we cannot neglect to give some attention to skills needed for interaction with other Americans. Many of our students travel and live abroad as part of a group of other Americans. Their psychological well-being and the success of their experience often seem to depend as much on their relationships with their American peers as with the host nationals. Thus, some time spent talking about group dynamics, peer pressure, and cooperation within groups will be well invested. If possible, the orientation should include some social activities and free time to help create a positive group identity prior to departure.

Global Citizenship

As students leave the United States and step into another culture, they are stepping into new responsibilities. During orientation, it is important for them to explore questions concerning their responsibilities in an interdependent world. The difficulties associated with this type of preparation are immediately apparent because they will be confronting political, social, moral, and even spiritual questions.

But if we avoid the issue of responsibility altogether or regard it as tangential, are we not in danger of doing what Munir Fasheh calls "talking about what to cook for dinner when our house is on fire"? In Fasheh's view, international education should be mainly concerned with the development of a sense of responsibility toward ourselves, toward others, and toward future generations, all of which are threatened by psychological, social, and material structures that education has been at least partially responsible for building.[12] His views concur with the ideas of other educators such as Joan Bodner, Elise Boulding, and Betty Reardon, whose books provide valuable reading for advisers searching to define their own positions.

▌ Reentry Programming

Reentry is an important aspect in the study abroad continuum. A strong reentry program can provide needed perspective and cohesion to the experience abroad. The most commonly expressed goals of such programs include helping students to

- readjust to American culture and campus life after living by the educational and social terms of a foreign culture;
- reflect upon and articulate their experiences to themselves and others
- assimilate and incorporate what they learned abroad into their ongoing degree studies; and
- consider how they might build on what they have learned for postgraduate studies or career opportunities.

Reentry programs may be neglected primarily because of the false assumption that students returning to a familiar environment do not encounter any serious problems. After all, the time spent abroad represents only a small portion of a student's life. Returning home should be easy. The startling truth may be quite the opposite: some researchers now suggest that reentry shock, also referred to as reverse culture shock, can be even more severe and debilitating than culture shock, perhaps for the very reason that the problems are so unexpected.[13] It can also be traumatic for a different reason: life responsibilities (such as getting serious about a career) may have been shunted aside while abroad, and all of a sudden become pressing.

Reverse culture shock can include such symptoms as disorientation, alienation from family and friends, rejection of one's own culture, boredom, and lack of direction. More specifically, students may find that they have little in common with their old friends; that beyond polite inquiries no one seems very interested in listening to them talk about their experiences abroad; that attitudes of family and friends seem parochial; and that there is seemingly no place to go with the knowledge and skills learned abroad.[14] Moreover, life on the home campus often seems restrictive and unexciting.

In designing an approach to reentry programming, it is helpful to consider three phases: what can be done while students are still abroad, what can be done immediately after they return, and long-term support and advising.

What to Do Before Students Return

By keeping in contact with students while they are abroad, you can facilitate a smooth transition home. If students are kept informed and sent necessary information for their return—on-campus housing forms, academic registration materials, financial aid applications—many problems will be avoided and students will be less likely to feel they have been forgotten. Recent catalogs, issues of student newspapers, and other relevant information can help the students stay abreast of changes on campus and thus be better prepared for their return.

One of the sources of ongoing student anxiety involves getting credit. It is important to reassure them that if they take their studies seriously and have followed established procedures for credit approval, they should receive the anticipated amount of credit. If students have e-mail addresses of major advisers on campus, their credit worries can be reduced considerably.

As is the case with predeparture orientation, however, what you can do from this side depends to a great degree on the range of programs your students enter abroad. If you run only your own programs and work closely with your staff overseas, obviously you can do more than if your students are enrolled in a variety of different programs and scattered all over the world.

If your students are scattered and are in many different programs, you may at this stage only be able to send a newsletter containing some advice and counsel. The effectiveness of such correspondence will depend to some degree on whether it is part of a series of letters your office has written to students during their time abroad, or one of the few times they have heard from you. It may also depend on the rapport you established with students during your advising sessions and your predeparture orientation.

If you send a letter, let students know that (1) you look forward to seeing them again and hope the experience has lived up to expectations; (2) you know they might have changed and grown and that many things may now look different; and (3) you are ready to assist them in any readjustments they feel are necessary.

If your students are on your own institution's programs, the reentry program can, and perhaps should, begin in the host country a month or two before departure, depending on the length of the stay overseas. Overseas personnel may meet with students to discuss and prepare for the reentry process. The simple act of alerting students to the potential for stress or dissatisfaction may help to minimize difficulties later on. It is important here, as during orientation, not to predispose students to react negatively upon return.

On-Campus Reentry Programs

Marking the occasion of your students' return to campus by some type of formal welcome-home reception, dinner, or party is almost always worth the effort. This gives students the opportunity to come together, talk about their experiences, and celebrate with faculty and other invited guests, such as recently arrived exchange students and school administrators. Such occasions may be more possible on small campuses than large ones.

Whether or not you host a social event, some sort of formal general meetings or sessions should be attempted. As with the social event, it may be hard to gather in all returned students—much harder than it might have been with predeparture programs. Some study abroad offices have set up e-mail networks for program returnees to facilitate communication. Still, organized meetings will be welcomed by many returnees. They need the opportunity to talk about their experiences and will recognize that others who have had a comparable experience will be more likely to empathize with them than the other students on campus. There will be many issues of interest or concern, from worries about credit to more personal anxieties. Moreover, students who may be going through the same type of reentry malaise can often help each other by voicing the difficulties and discussing possible solutions. This is also a good opportunity for you to be able to identify students who are experiencing severe reentry problems so that you can later recommend personal counseling, as appropriate.

The first key to having a successful group session is to make sure that everyone has a chance to participate. This might mean holding several sessions so that groups are small enough for informal talking. The second key is for you to discover what the students are feeling. They will likely relate that their experience abroad was "special" and "unique" and not easily explained to those who have not had it. But most important of all, the session must balance their understandable desires to celebrate and remember what they have accomplished with your objective of helping them build on this experience during the coming year and thereafter. Dawn Kepets's *Back in the U.S.A.: Reflecting on Your Study Abroad Experience and Putting it to Work* (Washington, DC: NAFSA, 1996) is an excellent booklet to use in reentry workshops. A trainer's guide and manual are included with bulk orders. Craig Storti's *Art of Coming Home* (Yarmouth, ME: Intercultural Press) is a valuable resource as well.

At the California State University, an effective one-day reentry workshop has been designed to address reentry adjustment problems by connecting them with career concerns.[15]

The workshop is structured as follows:

8:00 a.m.   Arrival, coffee

8:30–12:00

- Introductions
- Small and full group discussion of reentry concerns
- Continuing your international experience: full group discussion with handout
- What do you know about the world?: a short quiz with challenging questions

12:00–1:00   Lunch and memory lane, a sharing of souvenirs

1:00–5:00

- "The World Says Hello": a video from the Monterey Institute of Foreign Studies regarding jobs around the world
- Working overseas: presentations by representatives from business, the Peace Corps, and others
- Working in the United States: Jobs with an international dimension: presentation by representatives from education, travel, business, and so forth

248

- Where to find the jobs? Discussion of sources and bibliographies
- Evaluation and closing statements

For those with time constraints, another option for a reentry session is a one- to two-hour meeting facilitated by study abroad staff and purposefully unstructured. Possible discussion questions might include:

- What were your personal highlights?
- What was the balance between classroom and experiential learning? How did the courses compare with your expectations?
- How would you describe your living situation abroad?
- What are your perceptions of the United States now?
- How has returning to friends, families, and campus been for you?

The academic course is a more ambitious and comprehensive reentry model, and it is being used successfully at some colleges and universities.[16] This course is designed and taught by one or more members of the faculty, often in conjunction with the education abroad adviser. Sometimes the course is directly linked with a predeparture course or course component, and it usually combines cross-cultural theory with culture-specific content.

Students draw on their recent experience of entering a foreign culture, living in it, then leaving and returning to their home culture. They are also given opportunities to develop and extend the culture-specific knowledge they gained from living in a particular country or region. In some cases, such a course also enrolls foreign students, as part of their orientation to living and learning in the United States. Although this is not a course for every student, for some it is extremely useful and gratifying.

Program Evaluation

An important part of reentry is the evaluation process. Students should have the opportunity to evaluate the program they experienced and to reflect on their own progress and achievements. The results are invaluable both in making adjustments to your own programs and in advising students about your own and other programs (see Chapter 18, "Program Evaluation").

Counseling Following Return

Once the students have been welcomed home, completed their evaluations, and resumed their normal studies, there is a strong temptation to view the cycle as complete. But very important work still lies ahead. You can play an important role in helping students identify with appropriate professors, courses, and departments. Many advisers routinely inform faculty of which students in their classes have been abroad and may have special expertise or perspectives to share in class. You are in a position to encourage all students who studied foreign languages overseas to continue to do so through coursework, independent study, and other opportunities such as language houses and conversation circles.

Should students find that their experiences abroad have caused them to rethink or modify their majors, you can help them identify new areas of study and refer them to appropriate departments. They may even wish to explore new majors or minors in international studies, international business, or international relations. Even if students make no changes in their major or minor fields of study, you can help them to identify courses with international content. Advisers can also assist students who wish to pursue graduate study in an international field.

In addition to providing academic counseling, you can also facilitate returnees' involvement in local international activities. Many institutions prepare a handout, that lists local and on-campus international activities, graduate fellowships and scholarships, and work-abroad opportunities as a guide to students looking for continuing international involvement. Among the many ways for returnees to act as resource people and at the same time continue their own learning are

- becoming involved with international students (Big Brother/Sister, host family, roommate, ESL tutor, international clubs);
- acting as peer counselors or student workers to help with recruiting and orientation;
- volunteering in local elementary schools;
- leading orientation sessions;
- joining international organizations (Amnesty International, peace groups, etc.); and
- participating in other international activities on campus and in the community (speakers' bureau, international symposia, photo contests).

Career Counseling

There is no question that a large number of students, having returned from a meaningful time overseas, no matter which program or destination they chose, will have decided to (1) go abroad again as soon as is practicable and/or (2) pursue a career that involves travel and work abroad. You should therefore make certain that these returned students visit the school's career center as soon as possible. On the other hand, some career offices, even those with international career resources, have little experience with students who wish to apply what they learned on an education abroad program toward a definite career goal. Thus, it makes sense to work with this office to develop joint programs to assist students in designing strategies to market themselves (see Chapter 17, "Work Abroad and International Careers").

Notes

1. The term *ethnorelativism* is used by Milton Bennett to describe the final stage in the development of intercultural sensitivity ("A Developmental Approach to Training for Intercultural Sensitivity," in *Theories and Methods in Cross-Cultural Orientation*, 179–186).

2. For a stimulating discussion of the multidimensional approach, see Janet Marie Bennett's article, "Modes of Cross-Cultural Training," in *Theories and Methods in Cross-Cultural Orientation*, 117–134.

3. "The Chairy Tale" is an intriguing ten-minute silent film available from the Syracuse University film rental service. For suggestions on using the film, see Pusch's *Multicultural Education*, 201–203. Further information on cross-cultural films can be found in Pusch's book (pp. 270–275) and in Ellen Summerfield's *Crossing Cultures Through Film* (Intercultural Press, 1993).

4. "Bafa Bafa" and other cross-cultural simulations written by Garry Shirts can be ordered from Simile II (POB 910, Del Mar, CA 92014) or the Intercultural Press. A discussion of Bafa Bafa can be found in Pusch's *Multicultural Education*, 175–177. Barnga and Ecotonos are other excellent simulations available through Intercultural Press. Any simulation requires practice before attempting it with students.

5. The Intercultural Communication Institute (8835 SW Canyon, Suite 238, Portland, OR 97225, fax 503-297-4695, e-mail ici@pacificu.edu) offers excellent summer workshops. Similar opportunities are available through NAFSA: Association of International Educators and SIETAR (Society for Intercultural Education, Training, and Research International, 808 17th St., NW, Suite 200, Washington, DC 20006).

6. The waiver form, or student-agreement form, should outline overall program policy and regulations, such as rules of conduct, grounds for dismissal from the program, financial and/or academic penalties for early withdrawal from the program, and a disclaimer for responsibility from

accidents or injuries incurred during periods of travel or resulting from circumstances beyond the university's control.

7. Advisers may wish to subscribe to SECUSS-L, the electronic mail network of study abroad professionals, for useful information and discussion with colleagues. To obtain U.S. Department of State Travel Advisories, consult http://travel.state.gov/travel_warnings.html.

8. "Background Notes on the Countries of the World" are factual pamphlets available from Superintendent of Documents, U.S. Government Printing Office, Washington, DC 20402, or at the following Web site: http://www.state.gov/www/background_notes/index.html. "Culturgrams" are short briefings on one hundred and twenty-five different countries available from Brigham Young University, David M. Kennedy Center for International Studies, Publications Services, POB 24538, Provo, UT 84602-4538, 1-800-528-6279, http://www.byu.edu/culturgrams. Both publications provide brief background information on many world countries and cultures and can serve as points of departure for further research. In addition, a vast amount of useful travel, historical, regional background, and health information is available on the World Wide Web on the Internet. Study abroad offices are increasingly using the World Wide Web as a means to advertise their own programs, as well as to provide background information to those students who seek to help themselves.

9. Cross-cultural films and videos, "Going International," "Valuing Diversity," "Cold Water," and others are available from the Intercultural Press. Even though the first two were made for the business world, the ideas can be applied to student travelers as well. "The World Within Reach, A Pre-Departure Orientation Resource for Canadian Students Planning to Study or Work Abroad" is a 55-minute video, with a user's guide and is easily broken into segments; it is available from Wayne Myles, International Centre, Queen's University, Kingston, Ontario K7L 3N6, tel. 613-545-2604.

10. The term *culture shock* was first used by the anthropologist K. Oberg in *New Cultural Environment Culture Shock and the Problem of Adjustments* (Washington, D.C.: Department of State, Foreign Service Institute, 1958); see also S. Lysgaard, "Adjustment in a Foreign Society: Norwegian Fulbright Grantees Visiting the United States," *International Social Science Bulletin* 7 (1955): 45–51; and J. T. Gullahorn and J. E. Gullahorn, "An Extension of the U-curve Hypothesis," *Journal of Social Issues* 19, no. 3 (1963): 33–47.

11. For an insightful discussion of how language may create negative expectations, see James McCaffery, "Independent Effectiveness," in *Theories and Methods in Cross-Cultural Orientation*, 159B178; see also Peter S. Adler, "The Transitional Experience: An Alternative View of Culture Shock," *Humanistic Psychology* 15, no. 4 (Fall 1975): 13–23.

12. Munir Fasheh, "Talking about What to Cook for Dinner When Our House Is on Fire: The Poverty of Existing Forms of International Education.," *Harvard Educational Review Journal* 55 (February 1985): 123–126.

13. Nan E. Sussman discusses the hypothesis that "reentry stress and shock is more severe than initial entry shock" in her article, "Reentry Research and Training," in *Theories and Methods in Cross-Cultural Orientation*, 241.

14. A two-page "Inventory of Reentry Problems" is found in *Reentry/Transition Seminars. Report of the Wingspread Colloquium* (1976), 4–5.

15. My Yarabinec, San Francisco State University, has contributed this reentry workshop model used by the California State University–Long Beach International Programs. It is given here in somewhat abbreviated form.

16. For more information on such courses send requests with stamped, self-addressed envelope to Dr. Judith Martin (Department of Communication, Arizona State University, Tempe, AZ 85287-1205), or Dr. Bruce La Brack (Department of Sociology, University of the Pacific, Stockton, CA 94211).

Part Three

Program Development And Evaluation

Program Planning, Budgeting, And Implementation
Contributors: Paula Spier, Jack Henderson, Tom Roberts, and Henry Weaver

Program Designs And Strategies
Contributors: Heidi M. Soneson, Cheryl Lochner-Wright, and Joseph Navari

Work Abroad And International Careers
Contributors: William Nolting and Jane Cary

Program Evaluation
Contributors: Ronald Pirog, Michael Laubscher, and Patricia C. Martin

Legal Issues
Contributors: Gary Rhodes and Robert Aalberts

15

Program Planning, Budgeting, And Implementation

Contributors: Jack Henderson, Tom Roberts, Paula Spier, and Henry Weaver

New study abroad programs appear each academic year, often in astonishing numbers. Frequently, these programs disappear within a short period of time. What distinguishes programs that survive from those that do not is largely a matter of proper planning and implementation. The purpose of this chapter, therefore, is to demonstrate how much thought and effort it takes both to set up an academic program abroad and to sustain it over the years.

With so many established programs in place, the first question is, does your institution need another? Many colleges believe it makes economic sense to have their own programs. This may or may not, in fact, be true. As demonstrated below, starting up a new program means a major investment of human and financial resources. Depending on how it is budgeted and supported, however, it might lose money, break even, or create a small surplus.

Even if the new program makes ultimate academic and economic sense for your institution, it also represents a commitment that has to be sustained, perhaps over a long period of time, often in changing circumstances. The willingness to make this commitment is therefore essential. If there is little commitment or scanty start-up resources, it might be more prudent to consider working jointly with another institution, a consortium, or an agency—or simply utilizing extant programs.

For colleges currently offering no programs, setting up the first program overseas is likely to be a major administrative undertaking—more so than at institutions with a number of other programs already in place. On the other hand, even if you have gone through the domestic process before on your own campus, campus politics and economics have probably changed. Certainly circumstances overseas will differ from one country to the next. What worked in France may not work in Germany or China; what was possible in 1973, may now be impossible to repeat.

Given the welter of institutional contexts, below are provided three case studies on the creation of three successful programs. The first, Dickinson College's French-language junior-year program in Toulouse, focuses on how a small, liberal arts college established a department-based program for its own students. The second gives an overview of how a public state university system, the University of California, through its Education Abroad Program, set up a multifaceted exchange program in a developing country, Indonesia. The third concentrates on how the Institute for European Studies, acting on behalf of its constituent member colleges and universities, began a semester program in the social sciences in London.

▌ Preliminary Issues and Questions

Each program has its own history and represents a sequence of specialized responses coming out of the needs and interests of particular institutions, both here and overseas, at a given point in time. Nevertheless, as is evident, numerous issues addressed in each of the following accounts are common to all three. Further, the planning and implementation stage questions and considerations are similar in all three cases. Perhaps the most critical stages occur at the outset, in the planning and exploration phases. These stages are listed below with brief commentary. They emphasize the critical questions that must be addressed by anyone undertaking the difficult task of starting a new program.

Admittedly, new programs being considered by your campus may not resemble fully any of the academic semester and year programs described below. Indeed, since short-term programs now enroll almost half of all U.S. students studying abroad, it could be argued that this chapter should include examples of short-term program planning. But while there are some aspects of short-term programming which are unique, the questions and issues involved in the planning, implementation, and assessment of ALL programs, of whatever duration, are remarkably congruent.

Determining Need

Many faculty and administrators assume that few programs "out there" are truly appropriate to the needs of "our" institution. This may or may not, in fact, be true. In any event, before embarking on what—as the following case histories illustrate—is a complex and expensive task, the following questions should be weighed carefully:

- Have you defined carefully your specific program needs?
- Have you surveyed all other available options that might satisfy this need?
- Is the need immediate or long range? Are you responding to immediate pressure by an individual or department, or is the new program a carefully researched institutional priority?
- Have you carefully examined the motivation behind those individuals or groups who support new program development?
- Are there any individuals or groups on campus that might be hostile or uncooperative to a new program? Would this severely hamper the development of a program?
- Does the need grow naturally out of your existing on-campus academic program?

Gauging Your Resources

Even if you have established that a definite need exists, you should face squarely the issue of resources:

- Do you have the necessary expertise—academic and logistical—on campus to develop a new study abroad program?
- Do you have faculty and departmental support from the discipline(s) to be represented in the program?
- Are you sure that you have a constituency on campus that will provide long-term support for a program?
- Is the institution fully committed to the program at the highest level?
- Do you have the financial resources available for program start-up? For continuing the program if sufficient numbers are not reached? For how long would your institution support a deficit venture?

If you must seek outside support—academic, logistical, or financial—to begin the program, are you convinced that this support will be adequate to carry the program through to implementation?

Exploring the Territory

If you have the need and sufficient resources on campus, the next phase is determining the resources available at the program site. These resources will determine the location and often the shape of your program—whether a free-standing branch campus, something partially or fully integrated into an existing institution, or some sort of reciprocal and direct exchange. Consider the following:

- Does the area possess what appears to be long-term political and/or financial stability?
- Does a strong, ongoing institutional base exist within the program area?
- What contacts do you have in the area? Have faculty from your institution studied or lived in the program area?
- What sort of support will your institution have to provide? Academic? Logistical? Financial? Cultural?
- What steps do you need to take to ensure local support for your program?

These many issues regarding the opening phases in program development are hardly exhaustive, but they are critical. They must be squarely faced in the process of determining if a program should be established at all. Once the programmatic need has been firmly established, attention can be turned to the many, many hard specifics involved in setting up the program.

Ironing Out the Details

As the three following examples amply show, a myriad of tasks must be performed to set up the program. These include but are not limited to the following:

- establishing curricular, credit, and grading correspondences between disparate systems;
- entering into contractual arrangements with foreign universities, other institutions, and governments; following the correct protocol (Who signs the contract?);
- setting admissions standards and defining the process;
- securing housing, office space, classroom space, study space, library resources, and so forth;
- dealing with visa, health, safety, and student social issues;
- setting budgets, handling finances, and so forth; and
- hiring faculty and staff.

Publicity and Promotion

All programs require publicity—even those with a captive group for recruitment. For programs without a built-in base, this phase is critical because almost all programs that are tuition driven will have to

- publish brochures, fliers, and posters, and then distribute them on campus;
- mail materials to other colleges (if you are seeking students from elsewhere); plan and execute off-campus recruitment plans; and
- promote the program by meeting with faculty and students (see Chapter 8, "Promotion and Publicity").

Evaluation

Programs must be periodically evaluated, and the system for such evaluation should be built into the program-planning process (see Chapter 18, "Program Evaluation").

▌ Three Case Histories

The Dickinson College Program in Toulouse

By Jack Henderson

In September 1984 the first group of junior-year students, most of them French majors, began the academic year at the Dickinson College Study Center in Toulouse. Their arrival at our new language-based junior year abroad (JYA) program marked the end of a long, complex planning process.

During the previous two decades, French majors and other students with strong French-language preparation had spent one or both semesters of their junior year in France, participating in several high-ranking academic programs sponsored by individual U.S. colleges and universities or by two consortia of institutions with which we had formal links. Those 18 to 25 students per year seemed to have the best possible options—programs providing a variety of academic offerings, different locations in France among which to choose, and preferential admissions in some cases.

However, as the number of students studying abroad in the early 1980s swelled nationally, there were increased pressures on available slots in established JYA programs. At the same time, the number of our own French majors continued to grow, creating keener competition for admission into the highest-quality programs. The very best continued to be accepted; a small but disturbing number of qualified students found that their options were severely limited.

Even more troubling, perhaps, was the unevenness of our majors' academic experiences overseas. They returned to campus for their senior year equipped with diverse levels of language ability, analytical skills, and exposure to course content. Without direct input into, or control over, their junior year academics, we had difficulty designing a senior-year curriculum that was coherent and appropriate for all. We became convinced that the integrity of our major was at stake and that we needed to create our own program in France.

The necessary expertise to design and implement a new program existed in our own department. We had both French and U.S. faculty members of different ages and at various points in their careers. All had lived and traveled widely in France; all were knowledgeable about study abroad.

In addition, our department benefited from Dickinson's strong support for international education in general and study abroad in particular. The department's needs and aspirations were recognized by both the college administration and faculty from other disciplines. So, working with colleagues from all the language departments and across the curriculum, we designed a multifaceted institutional grant proposal in international education. The result was two grants from the National Endowment for the Humanities, that provided, among other things, the start-up funds for our own program in France. (Support for our proposed JYA program was so strong that the administration had pledged start-up monies from college funds had the grant not been received.)

In designing our program, members of the department fashioned clear goals for academic content and design.

1. A first-rate overseas study component was seen as essential to provide continuity with our on-campus academic program.

2. Experience had clearly demonstrated the superior linguistic and cultural attainments of students who had spent a full academic year in France rather than only one semester. A full-year program was thus deemed mandatory.

3. Partial academic integration of our students in the French educational system was seen as highly desirable. We therefore arranged for our students to take a portion of their coursework at a French university.

4. In our desire to maximize the students' linguistic and cultural integration into French life, we arranged private housing with French families.

5. Because institutional financial aid monies had not previously been applicable to study in France, we built into our program budget an annual contribution to the on-campus financial aid budget, thereby ensuring that all academically qualified students could participate in our program, regardless of financial need.

The task of choosing a location in France was extremely important if we were to realize the goals just enumerated. In addition, discussion surrounded the following issues: first, we agreed that an urban environment would offer the greatest exposure to French culture, the most opportunities for student internships, and the widest range of family contexts in which to house our students. Second, it seemed to us imperative to identify a site not already saturated with American JYA programs.

We recognized important benefits to be gained by establishing strong interinstitutional links between our institution and a French university. Such a linkage would

- provide local university courses in various academic disciplines, including French, in which to place our students;
- encourage interaction between our students and their French peers through opportunities to join university associations, sports teams, and other kinds of extracurricular activities;
- provide access to university faculty who could teach our core courses for us and with whom we might arrange faculty exchanges with the Carlisle campus; and
- attract highly qualified French university students, who could visit Carlisle, live in our French House on campus, and assist the department in its language laboratory and cocurricular activities.

We sought advice from officials at the French Cultural Affairs Office in New York. They suggested possible universities and gave us the names of key contacts. We also made use of professional contacts that our department members had at other French universities. We identified several possible sites before narrowing them down to two. In the process, we learned that officials at the University of Toulouse had been making corresponding inquiries in the United States.

Upon learning that a four-person delegation from Toulouse was planning to visit the United States, we invited them to Dickinson to discuss possible joint ventures. After a short, productive visit, the delegation invited us to visit their campus in Toulouse to meet faculty and administrators. These exchanges laid the groundwork for what was to become a long-range partnership.

Up to this point, we had spent about eight months in the discussion and planning stages. We now began the task of implementation by drawing up a chart of tasks to be accomplished on both sides of the Atlantic, many of them of a nitty-gritty nature, along with month-by-month deadlines and a designation of person(s) responsible for each task.

Among the tasks were the following:

1. Members of our department made three more visits to Toulouse to negotiate details of our formal agreements with two branches of the University of Toulouse. They also collected syllabi (where available) and visited classes in order to identify courses appropriate for American students.

2. Meetings with local faculty and administrators identified professors to teach in our program and helped to arrange for a visiting guest professor from Toulouse in Carlisle the coming academic year.

3. We established our program's legal status (as an association) in France, took photographs for the future program brochure, and established necessary banking arrangements.

4. We were careful to cultivate contacts with key representatives of the city government, as well as cultural and civic organizations (such as Association France–Etats Unis, the local chamber of commerce, and the *syndicat d'initiative*).

5. We met with representatives of French and international corporations with links to the United States and thus likely to be interested in an American educational presence in Toulouse.

6. We began to recruit families for our students through classified ads in the local newspaper plus using personal contacts established in our visits.

7. In locating a "home" for our program in Toulouse, we researched various options, including renting classroom and office space from the university (which was in short supply), renting necessary space on the open market, or purchasing property for a permanent center. We preferred the third option because it provided both permanency and an identifiable location. We were, of course, guided in our decision by our college treasurer's knowledge of the international financial market, as well as by advice given by members of the board of trustees.

The college purchased and began renovations on a villa in a parklike residential setting on the Canal du Midi. These transactions required considerable paperwork and time to hire an attorney, to secure legal documents including powers of attorney, to hire an architect and a contractor, and to supervise the conversion of a former private home into an academic center. We had to purchase furniture, office equipment, supplies, and an automobile for the director's use, as well as to arrange for telephones and other utilities. Although our students would have access to university libraries as well as to the municipal library, we sought to assure easy availability of basic materials by setting up our own modest library with multiple copies of key reference works.

Fortunately, the building was large enough to provide an apartment for our director on the top floor in addition to classrooms, a library, student study facilities, a small computer-equipped writing center, lounge, reception area, and office space on the lower two floors. At the time, the U.S. dollar was unusually strong; the result was an important investment that has since increased sharply in value.

8. Staffing concerns also occupied our attention. As noted above, we believed strongly that continuity between the home campus and the year abroad could best be assured by rotating all members of our department into the Toulouse directorship in two-year cycles. The director's responsibilities were designated as one-half teaching and one-half administrative, a model that had worked well for the college in other overseas settings. To assure permanency and continuity on-site, we hired a native administrative assistant on a nearly full-time basis. Her duties include occasional secretarial work. But, more important, she performs many ongoing, routine, time-consuming (and often bureaucratic) tasks.

We also contracted the services of an accountant to oversee bookkeeping and to pay salaries, social security taxes, and other financial obligations. Finally, as noted earlier, to teach our core courses, we recruited and hired local faculty whom we pay on an hourly basis, according to the French university pay scale for their position. We arranged orientation meetings with them to explain the art of syllabus writing, American course expectations, grade conversion, and the like.

While all of this was happening over a period of seven or eight months in Toulouse, we were no less busy in the United States. We designed our JYA core curriculum, to be taught for our students only, as a logical extension of the on-campus academic program by providing (a) a coherent integration of the study of language, literature, and civilization; (b) a logical progression from sophomore to junior to senior years; and (c) coordinated use of course materials both in Carlisle and in France. These courses were duly approved by the college's Committee on Academic Program and, eventually, by the faculty as a whole.

We drew up a program budget, with expenditures to be made in the U.S. listed in dollars, and those to be made overseas in francs. We determined that the program's comprehensive fee, including airfare, should be less than the on-campus fee so that the actual cost to parents of the year in France would be less, or no more, than a year spent on the main campus.

Responsibilities for recruitment, selection, and orientation of students were shared by department members. One person was designated as the on-campus coordinator and served as contact person for potential applicants. We held information meetings and published a brochure describing the program in detail and noting the prerequisites we had established: good academic standing, junior-class status, good physical and emotional health, completion of a French literary analysis course, and appropriate mastery of the French language (such as an intermediate-high rating on the ACTFL/ETS Oral Proficiency test).

Completed applications included recommendation forms from faculty in French and other departments; applicants were also interviewed by the coordinator. Admission decisions were made at department meetings. After acceptance, each student was paired with a student returned from France to facilitate the orientation process. Group orientation meetings in the spring semester were supplemented by a Toulouse Program Orientation Handbook sent to participants and their families.

By the time the first group of students arrived in Toulouse, nearly everything was in place. The first year was not without a few hitches. But overall, our careful planning had resulted in a highly successful program.

The University of California System Program in Indonesia

By Henry Weaver

The primary reason for a university (or, in our case, a university system) to begin a program overseas should be to expand and diversify its academic program. Faculty at the University of California (UC) encouraged the Education Abroad Program (EAP) to open a program in Indonesia to allow increased opportunities for UC students to learn the Indonesian language, for area studies, and for study of the arts in Indonesia. We were also aware that Indonesia, the fifth most populous country in the world, had almost no study abroad programs.

Fortuitously, the California legislature had just acted to make development into the Pacific Rim a state priority. It made funds available to provide incentive scholarships for students and to facilitate faculty exchanges. At the request of the university president, EAP developed a five-year proposal for increasing programs in the Pacific Rim. With resources available, a program in Indonesia became part of the larger Pacific Rim planning.

Most academic interest in Indonesia came from three campuses of the University of California where Indonesian was being taught (Berkeley, Santa Cruz, and Los Angeles). Berkeley taught several years of Indonesian; Santa Cruz taught two quarters; and a student at UCLA could study the language on a special basis. At the request of EAP, the South and Southeast Asia Center at Berkeley helped to set up consultations with many UC faculty throughout the system. Its own interest was primarily in the social sciences and the language. At Santa Cruz and UCLA a network of involvement with Indonesia also existed, though primarily in the arts. Students were already involved in field work in music, dance, and theater. Faculty on different UC campuses therefore had different but complementary interests, contacts, and innovative ideas for an Indonesia program abroad.

We researched the relative standings of the major universities in Indonesia, including their ability to teach the language to foreigners. What we learned reinforced the conclusion that visits to the University of Indonesia might be necessary, as well as to the principal teacher-education university in Jakarta, and to several institutions in Bandung, Bogor, Yogyakarta, and Denpasar. Malang was not investigated because other U.S. universities were already active there.

Ford Foundation representatives and an Indonesian who formerly taught at UC confirmed most of the information that we had gathered. In Indonesia, higher education is controlled by the ministry of education, and national concerns are taken into consideration in designing exchanges. Contacts with the director of higher education were made on the first visit.

In addition to looking at course availability, quality of instruction, and library resources, each university visit also examined practical living needs: What were the options for students' living and eating quarters? What would they cost? How could they be arranged? What were the health conditions, and what medical resources were available?

As a public system, UC is committed to exchange relationships, so the cost consideration began with a discussion of how the university could meet the needs of the host university. Would it be best for students from the host country to go to the United States as undergraduates or as graduate students? Would they seek degrees, or be able to earn credit that would transfer back? Would faculty exchange or training be desired? Were there currency controls that limited the way in which exchange-related payments could be made? What steps would be necessary for approval of tentative programs within the host university and beyond?

At the time of the first field investigation, the broad strokes of the academic program we wished to establish were clear, but there were a lot of specific concerns:

- High-quality language instruction was essential. Since some UC campuses offered no Indonesian language, coursework would need to be available at the beginning level as well as at more advanced levels.
- We needed courses in the social sciences, including area studies.
- Some students needed courses in music, dance, art, and theater, ideally in various locations, since the gamelan, for example, is played quite differently in West Java, Central Java, and Bali.
- What support systems did UC students in Indonesia need to function at a satisfactory academic level and with due concern for their physical needs?
- How could we ensure that evaluation of students' work would be forthcoming in adequate time and in a usable form to get credit recorded on their transcripts?
- How would we gather the information that the academic senate uses to examine each course in which students enroll?
- Would enough students participate in the program to make it cost-effective to place a UC professor in the field to take care of these details, or would a local liaison be available to do the job?

After extensive investigation, a rather complex UC program emerged. Gadja Mada University, in Yogyakarta, was chosen as the primary contact, and a summer language program was arranged. Here seemed to be an institution with a progressive attitude. It was well administered and had an openness to new ideas. Institutions specializing in the arts were available in Yogyakarta, Bandung, and Denpasar. Padjadjaran University in Bandung could also be entered for some fields of study.

- Students could come from any UC campus and study at three different levels.
- Students with no Indonesian would be encouraged to begin in the summer, find a method of language maintenance during the next year, and then return for a full year the following summer.

- For students staying the full year, the summer study would be an intensive language program (ILP). The rest of the year could be taken in regular courses taught in Indonesian by continuation at Gadja Mada or by transferring to one of four other institutions.

The plan for the Indonesian program was presented to an all-university committee of the faculty senate, which oversees the Education Abroad Program. The plan was then submitted to the Board of Regents for approval before drawing up contracts. When these were executed by the university counsel, they were submitted to the Indonesian universities involved. After these institutions had ironed out some differences from the original planning, they presented the contracts to the Indonesian ministry of education for approval. When these steps were completed, the contracts were signed and the program was ready to begin.

Meanwhile, the EAP office on each campus needed to get enough detail to be able to recruit and counsel prospective students. This called for information fliers and, later, printed brochures. Scanty information about a fledgling program is always a source of frustration to the counselors in campus offices, who need to respond to detailed questions from students.

Once applications were received, each campus office arranged for faculty to interview prospective participants as a part of final selection. The systemwide EAP office then arranged transportation, visa information, health insurance forms, and all the usual details involved in getting students to the foreign site.

Procedures for submitting actual courses to the faculty senate for approval, getting students registered into the courses, and recording their grades onto the transcripts were well established at UC, so these procedures were followed routinely. The UC Study Center in Indonesia was responsible for translating the Indonesian grading system into UC grades.

Finally, after the program was under way, steps were undertaken to correct our first-year problems. This involved considerable rearrangement of the ILP because some of the agreed-on methods did not materialize. The process of evaluation and change will continue as long as the program operates.

The Institute for European Studies Program in London

By Tom Roberts

The Institute for European Studies (IES), based in Chicago, administers programs on behalf of a nationwide consortium of colleges and universities, both private and public. Issues of program development are complex and require the consensus of a variety of constituencies at many points in the process. The following account illustrates the processes undertaken to establish a new program. Since the London program was established, IES has expanded to include programs in Asia and is now known formally as the Institute for European and Asian Studies.

Several members of the consortium had, over a two- to three-year period, expressed an interest to IES in developing a new program in Great Britain. At the time, very few British universities were interested in accommodating U.S. undergraduates. The issue of whether to establish a British program was brought to the curriculum committee, which consists of representatives of several consortium members. They decided to undertake a broad survey of all IES member institutions to determine "new program interest"—not limited to Britain.

Although quite reasonable and conservative, this procedure is not without drawbacks. Where immediate investment of institutional resources is not in question, institutional interest in off-campus programs ranges widely. So, although the survey results indeed indicated agreement that Great Britain would be a good place for a new program, the survey also produced a long list of other desirable program sites. The survey did help, however, to narrow the issue a bit. The committee's next step was therefore to examine the actual range of available administrative capability—taking geography, academic experience, and budget into account.

Most of the staff were, by academic background, specialists in either the humanities or social sciences. This meant that attempts to set up a program with a science or engineering bias would have proven difficult. The geographical and academic issues impinged on the budgetary—it was clearly most economical for IES to establish an arts-based program somewhere in Europe. Other factors included political stability and what other high-quality programs currently existed.

It was agreed that IES should not develop programs in areas where good study abroad options were already available. Too many programs inevitably result in lowered academic standards in all programs offered in that country. The committee concluded, however, that few good programs (of the sort it was envisioning) were operating in Great Britain at the time. It was further decided to locate the program in London because of its many resources. The committee recommended to the full consortium at its annual meeting the establishment of a London program. The issue was formally proposed and ratified by the full body. The committee and staff were then authorized to proceed with the development of the program.

The program's precise curricular nature was worked out over a period of several months. The IES consortium consisted of close to 40 colleges and universities nationwide—mostly small, liberal arts schools, but with a few larger, more broad-based institutions as well. Academic resources were available for a program with almost any curricular bias. Ultimately, the program's shape was dictated by (1) IES staff resources (i.e., academic expertise); (2) student interest, as determined by a survey (results were somewhat inconclusive but showed a slight preference for a program in the social sciences); (3) a historical bias of IES toward social science–based programs; (4) contacts overseas, who were largely faculty at the London School of Economics and Political Science.

Working with a subcommittee made up of faculty from the disciplines to be represented in the program, the curriculum committee studied the issue of ideal program length. At this time students were leaning toward semester-long programs, as opposed to a full year. The committee found that there were numerous opportunities for a full academic year of study at several British universities; fewer options existed for the many students who could not afford to be abroad for this amount of time.

The IES staff includes a stateside director of program development (who also serves as staff representative to the curriculum committee) and a talented group of program directors of existing IES European programs. These European-based directors possessed not only expertise in administering programs but also academic contacts in London. This was particularly true of the director of IES Vienna, who was born and educated in Britain and well connected with academic circles in London. These contacts proved invaluable in establishing and shaping the program, especially in recruiting faculty.

IES custom is to use only indigenous faculty to teach in its programs. Initial interviews were carried out in London by the director of program development and the Vienna IES director. All appointments were screened and ratified by the curriculum committee, which also reviewed and approved all course syllabi, descriptions, and reading lists. During this process of faculty selection and course approval, a fair amount of interchange took place between the U.S. academics (mainly the members of the subcommittee) and their British counterparts concerning course content. Under discussion were the level of the course (in this case upper-division work because all IES programs were geared to junior-year students), contact hours, length of course, credit weightings, and grading.

During this period the IES director of program development and the director of the Vienna program worked out many of the program's logistical details, such as (1) arranging for student housing; (2) finding office space for the program administrator; (3) resolving tax and legal issues; and (4) locating classroom space and library resources, which are critical to a free-standing program. It was decided to provide students membership in the Senate House library of the University of London and the library of the London School of Economics. In addition, a small textbook and reference library would be established on the program premises; classes would also be held at this site.

The committee then turned its attention to the selection of a program director. IES believes strongly in directors who are able to commit to a long-term tenure. Another criterion was solid academic qualifications because the director would need to deal effectively with the local British faculty. The director also should be sensitive to the needs of American students and the requirements of the U.S. system. Most important, however, was IES's conviction (born out of long experience) that the tasks of running an overseas program are demanding and specialized; they take time to master. Long-range continuity in this post was therefore seen as essential.

It is almost impossible to find a U.S. academic who not only has appropriate qualifications but would also be willing to leave an American college or university position for an extended period. Given these facts and criteria, an indigenous academic seemed the only appropriate course—though, as with any appointment, finding the right person was most difficult. Once selected, the director was put through a training program that included a visit to the campuses of several IES consortium members in the United States and some time at the administrative headquarters of IES in Chicago. The newly chosen director also spent an extended period at an IES center in Europe watching an experienced program director in action.

As the program was taking shape, the process of publicizing this new IES offering began. Within a consortium, the very process of program development is an element in the publicity of the program. But this notice is never enough on its own. IES staff prepared brochures and posters for nationwide distribution, as well as arranged for specific on-campus promotion by representatives of the consortium. Such promotional efforts were judged to be especially important because IES has no direct access to students on campus or the recruiting advantages of the campus-based programs. Yet, to ensure selectivity while providing sufficient numbers of students to make the program financially viable, it must attract a large number of applicants. Few programs, however administered (excluding those specially funded from nontuition sources), will long be tolerated at a deficit.

As may be evident from this discussion, the program-development process within a consortium is long and fairly expensive. The planning stages of the programs took from four to six months, preparation of the programs another similar period; publicity did not start until the planning phase was finished and required a lead time of eighteen months. The total elapsed time from the initial idea being broached to the curriculum committee until the first students began studies overseas was more than two-and-a-half years.

■ Further Considerations

The preceding case studies are success stories. Planning for these programs worked well at least in part because their organizers were sensitive to the political, fiscal, and policy issues within their own institutions or groups of institutions. Some of the factors that have caused some otherwise well-planned efforts to founder are discussed in the following paragraphs.

Politics and "Turf"

It would be almost impossible to put too much emphasis on knowing your institution. The more you are able to establish friendly and supportive relationships with faculty, administrators, advisers, and ssupport staff, the more likely it is that your planning will be successful. You need to know which instructors have vested interests in specific areas. You need to know how committee members, program evaluators, and potential program leaders are perceived by colleagues, and department chairs. There may be times when you will need to tread very carefully (see Chapter 2, "The Education Abroad Office in Its Campus Context").

Money Matters

As suggested earlier, economic realities are a prime planning factor. Programs do not live and die on their pedagogy or overseas glories alone. Deans, presidents, and those who oversee the budget must be convinced that any new—or for that matter ongoing—program makes economic sense for the institution. The burden of proof for this is likely to be put squarely on your desk. Although you probably do have the advantage of the best information on actual costs, your priorities are not necessarily those of the decision makers.

Administrators are likely to think that education abroad programming invariably means a loss of money to the institution: a "tuition export." If students are over there, they are not paying salaries or filling beds at home. This perception is perhaps more strongly held at private colleges and universities that consider themselves to be fee-driven, but public institutions also depend on fees paid for on-campus study.

Further, if this is the case, it follows that education abroad must be "frivolous"—something the institution can afford to become involved with only peripherally (for example, summer programs; programs that cannot be applied toward a major or even perhaps general-education credit; or programs to which financial aid does not apply). Your institution may think programs should be limited to honors students, or it may impose other severe limits on enrollment. Horrendous bureaucratic obstacles are often erected in front of students so that only the most determined can surmount the obstacles. In such cases, overseas education—along with your own professional status—is marginalized.

Enlightened Self-Interest

"International" (like its frequent institutional bedfellow, "multicultural") is a current buzzword. Every university and college in the country is giving lip service to it by rewriting mission statements, producing flashy catalogs, revising the curriculum, recruiting foreign students, and the like. Your job is to turn cheap talk into concrete action by convincing your colleagues that over the next ten years there are going to be several hundred truly enlightened schools that provide access to international experience. If yours is not among them, it will not be truly competitive, and admissions and retention will be a problem.

You need not play Cassandra, but it is important to use your informed awareness of what is going on at other institutions (to which your own compares itself) to warn of the consequences of being left out of this true national and international development. Calling education abroad "a growth stock in a stagnant industry," Craufurd Goodwin and Michael Nacht in their book, *Abroad and Beyond: Patterns in American Overseas Education*, conclude with the following observation:

> Above all, leaders of American academe should recognize that this is a fast-moving field they ignore at their peril. If they do not act to their own advantage in a timely fashion, not only will they miss opportunities but their competitors will surpass them. The continued dynamism of the field is so great that a laggard institution cannot simply say, "Let's wait till the dust clears and then pick the best." The dust shows no sign of settling any time soon,

and if an institution is not in there with the others who are stirring it up, it will have little opportunity to gain the understanding needed for sensible action later on. (p. 118)

Seen in the context of long-range institutional planning, the investment of economic resources in sound education abroad programming can be seen as wise.

Faculty Development

The financial investment in education abroad programming can also be presented as having multiple benefits for faculty members. As shown above, new programs inevitably require faculty input and guidance. While some faculty participate in planning and administration as a way to enrich the education of their students, most also see it as an opportunity to make meaningful lasting contacts with colleagues and cultures elsewhere in the world. Short-term program leadership positions become available, and new opportunities for research and exchange emerge. Involved and committed faculty reap personal and professional rewards.

Faculty who have led or taught in overseas programs are much more willing to introduce new international dimensions into the courses they teach on campus. They are also more likely to encourage students who have studied abroad to utilize what they have learned into their campus studies. Thus, the investment in education abroad programming is also an indirect investment in the intellectual development of faculty, and in internationalizing the curriculum. It is your job to make sure that your administration sees these benefits (see Chapter 3, "Faculty Roles").

Exploring Diverse Economic Models

There is great diversity in the way U.S. colleges and universities enroll and charge students for education abroad. In some cases, education abroad is always considered an "extra," something beyond normal degree costs and credits—an attitude that contributes to the perception that overseas study is an elitist activity. In other instances—such as the University of California example above—students pay normal tuition for any educational experience and receive normal credit and full financial aid. Between these extremes, there are many variations. One of the latest trends, at many private colleges and universities is to charge full home-campus tuition (sometimes including fees, room, board, and so forth, but also ensuring both that all financial aid "travels" and that the costs of each student's degree are the same) whatever a particular program might cost and whether or not it is sponsored by themselves or some other institution, agency, or consortium—thus effectively charging for institution approved "credit."

Education abroad programming at some colleges is seen as a money-maker for the university—especially if overseas fixed costs can be kept lower than home-campus costs and student numbers remain high. In these cases, the education abroad budget may be incorporated into the overall institutional budget in the same way as are those of an academic department or the library. Fairly often, an office can cover such things as its own salaries from program revenues, with space and utilities coming out of the institution's general budget. A more general model is for near-ly all program budgets to face the need to break even, with actual pro-gram costs being balanced by tuition revenues. Financial aid monies may or may not be a factor in this equation.

We all know that it costs more to educate a student majoring in chem-istry or engineering than one majoring in literature. It is also true that business professors earn more than art historians. In addition, colleges offer many courses that are underenrolled in relation to the real costs necessary to teach them. Yet undergraduates, whatever courses they choose, almost always pay the same tuition, and these variations in costs are seen as something any self-respecting institution must, within limits, do in order to offer a full and diverse curriculum.

If we follow this institutional logic to its fair conclusion, it follows that education abroad programming should be viewed much as chemistry or business are, not as an "extra" that must pay for itself, down to the final penny. Not every dean will buy this argument, and its effectiveness relies to some degree on the conviction you and others (including students) can muster. It should certainly be tried. Also worth arguing are the other potential financial benefits to the institution: in admissions, in retention, and in enhancing the career prospects of its graduates.

Evidence is mounting, moreover, that students who have studied abroad turn into very loyal alumni of the institution, eternally grateful for having had this opportunity and likely to become strong supporters of alumni-giving campaigns.

Budgeting

You should also try to fight for enough internal budget flexibility to be able to balance an inexpensive program—in, for instance, Mexico or the Caribbean—against more expensive programs—in, for instance, Japan or Africa. Summer or short-term programs (even those that are not as academic and may appeal to a wider constituency) may need to make up for the losses on academic year programs. Even if the realities are that your institution sees any financial support it gives as a type of subsidy, there remain ways to return revenues and balance different kinds of programs against each other to achieve fiscal balance.

∎ Sources for Additional Support

No one else's fiscal model is likely to be entirely appropriate for your institution, but exploring other models can be very useful. Any one of them may have a line item for a kind of revenue or expense that you have not thought to include in your own financial planning. What matters in the end, however, is that you remain proactive in the budget process and that you take the initiative to present to your colleagues alternative ways to implement desired policies and essential, appealing programs. Not to do this is to lose some control over your professional role and to miss opportunities to translate what you know into programs that benefit your entire institution.

NAFSA literature, conferences, professional development workshops, and the consultant referral service all offer other resources for program planning. The preconference workshop "Study Abroad 201: Developing and Managing Study Abroad Policies and Programs," which also has a highly detailed accompanying handbook, is one particularly useful instrument.

16

Program Designs And Strategies

Contributors: Heidi M. Soneson, Cheryl Lochner-Wright, and Joseph Navari

In education abroad circles it is a truism that no perfect program exists—none, that is, that is exactly right for every single student. Its corollary is that almost any program might offer the right match for at least some students. The same thing may be said about institutions: the "perfect" program cannot be defined in the abstract, but rather is one that matches institutional resources, needs, and educational philosophy with the interests and welfare of a significant number of students.

B ecause not all of your students are alike, it may be necessary to establish a variety of programs to meet their differing needs. There are valid reasons to consider offering programs of varied duration, from a summer program to a year-long overseas opportunity, since in both academic and economic terms, what individual students can afford is likely to be quite different. Because some students are bolder and more adventurous than others, you probably need to have some programs that are more interculturally demanding; but you will probably also need some program options aimed at providing more initial shelter and nurture for those who need more time before they plunge into the local overseas culture. Some students need particular courses which they know will fill home-campus requirements; others are more eager to take courses in new areas.

Finally, there will always be students seeking the challenge of learning new skills of value beyond the academic world and those who wish to experience living and learning independently, on native terms, whether or not they earn credit. Building multiple study (and work) abroad opportunities will not only enable you to meet the needs of a diverse student body, it will also encourage students to consider more than one education abroad opportunity during their academic career.

As the previous chapter demonstrates, there are many ways to set up and structure education abroad programs, each requiring lots of forethought and hard work to establish and maintain. The purpose of this chapter is to describe the major types of program designs now in use. The potential academic, intercultural, and economic advantages, as well as the corresponding drawbacks of each design, will be presented. Once you are familiar with the pluses and minuses, costs and benefits, of different sorts of programs, you should be able to decide which features are most appealing and appropriate for your institution and its students. This dialectical discussion is intended to assist you in setting up new programs of your own or making adjustments in existing ones, in each case so that they serve some particular proportion of your students. It will also assist your office in advising your students on how to choose programs that best suit their needs and interests.

❚ Programs Sponsored by Your Own Campus

Branch Campus/Study Center Models

A branch campus or study center is a program designed by your campus to allow students to take courses they need from the campus curriculum while abroad. A branch campus, by definition, is set up to offer a wide variety of courses that fulfill general home-campus degree requirements, while a study center often has a more narrow curricular base, perhaps focusing on a particular academic discipline such as French or eastern European studies. Both, however, offer home-campus-like studies in a foreign setting. Because such programs are largely separate from foreign institutions, they are also sometimes referred to as "island," "unintegrated," or, from those who do not favor such separation, "ghetto" programs. Basic characteristics of the branch campus/study center model are described below.

Participants

Students in these programs come primarily from your institution—though some models allow participants from other U.S. institutions to apply, also. Students from the host culture are rarely involved in the academic program, as it is designed to fulfill U.S. degree requirements.

Admission Requirements

Your campus sets the admission requirements for the program, both for your students and for any off-campus applicants. Requirements often include a minimum GPA, completion of a certain number of credits, or specific course prerequisites. Application procedures vary greatly but may include an essay or interview in addition to a completed application form.

Faculty

Faculty are hired by your institution to teach the courses overseas. The program may provide faculty development for your regular faculty chosen to teach in the program. You may also hire local instructors to teach specific courses. There is often a resident director chosen from your campus faculty who both teaches and acts as the on-site administrator/adviser for the program.

Academics

Courses are from your regular campus curriculum. There may be specialty courses offered only abroad, such as a regional studies course focusing on the host culture. Unless the program focus is language/culture, the language of instruction is typically English. Students often take one course in a language of the host country as well. Your institution's calendar (summer/quarter/semester/academic year) is retained, with accommodation made for host country holidays.

Facilities

You will generally need to rent classroom, office, and faculty workspace either from a local educational institution or from a hotel or youth hostel.

Housing

Housing may also be in rented facilities, or, in some cases, your campus may wish to buy a local facility. However, efforts are sometimes made to place students with local families, thus lessening the "island" effect of the academic program. This is particularly important (perhaps crucial) in language programs, as it gives students the opportunity to apply their language skills in an everyday setting.

Program Costs

Program costs generally include tuition, fees, and room and board. Required excursions, such as field trips related to a particular class, are also included. Some programs include airfare; others provide students with fare information and, where possible, a group-flight option but do not require students to work through the program for travel arrangements.

Advantages of a Branch Campus/Study Center Model

This model of study abroad has several strong points. The first is a high degree of institutional control, which is advantageous for faculty, administrators, and students. Because the program is developed by your campus, all campus units involved in study abroad have input into the finished product. Since all courses come from the campus curriculum, there is no question of how courses transfer and no evaluation of unfamiliar transcripts. Campus academic standards in terms of instructional time, class attendance, method of examination, and grade scale remain the same. The program is tailored to your academic calendar. All of these factors are helpful in marketing the program to students who need to know exactly what major or graduation requirements they are fulfilling, as well as how participation is likely to affect their GPA.

A second advantage is that such programs can accommodate large groups of students—anywhere from 10 to 200, depending on the structure. Because all the students going to the particular program can attend the same orientation programs and are required to hand in the same paperwork, individual advising time can be less than for more individualized programs. Placing an equivalent number of students directly into a foreign host institution is often nearly impossible.

Faculty involvement is another strength of branch campus models. Teaching overseas is faculty development, and it may be possible to have faculty on loan from their department, thus holding down program costs. Aside from giving the faculty member the opportunity to teach and sometimes conduct research in a new environment, this type of arrangement can increase general campus support for education abroad, provided the faculty member has a good experience. You now have an advocate in the classroom who talks to students about study abroad from personal experience.

Finally, branch-campus models attract students who may not have the independence or self-confidence to participate in a less structured type of overseas study. First-generation college students, students from rural areas, or students who have simply never thought of themselves as the type to go abroad may consider the idea if they have an option that does not require them to dive head-first into an immersion experience but rather provides them with their "home island" from which to explore as they become comfortable in the host culture.

Drawbacks of the Branch-Campus Model

Of course, each of these advantages has its opposite. Institutional control and a high level of faculty involvement imply strong support of education abroad on campus. If this support does not exist, you will need to build it before launching many programs of this type. Without the cooperation of campus support offices such as the registrar, admissions, business services, and financial aid, you may find that you need to duplicate services offered by these offices specifically for study abroad students.

A high level of control also means a high level of responsibility. In order to run an effective branch-campus program, you need a dependable overseas liaison who can make all necessary local arrangements. Even if you send a resident director with the program, having an on-site liaison who can deal with arrangements that need to be made between semesters for orientation, housing, or excursions is critical. You should also be prepared to work with students, and their parents, who expect that a program designed, operated, and staffed by your campus will truly have all of the amenities of home. Attempting to meet such expectations of a U.S. campus overseas may more than offset the time group programs save in individual advising.

If your programs depend on faculty involvement, you will need to identify departments and individual faculty members who are dedicated to study abroad. This process may include identifying and working to remove roadblocks to faculty participation, such as teaching overseas not being recognized as valuable in tenure decisions. In addition, current cutbacks in higher education may make it more difficult for you to gain support of deans and department heads, particularly if part of your strategy for holding down costs in study abroad programs includes having faculty loaned to the program—that is, having their salary paid through regular channels and not by program participants. This development can make branch-campus models expensive for participants.

Finally, although proponents of the island format argue that it is beneficial for students who might not participate in a more integrated experience, others disagree. The contention is that direct, daily interaction with the host culture is a key to the academic and personal development students experience while studying abroad. By providing a buffer zone for the students, the branch campus lessens the potential impact of study abroad, making it more of an extended tourist experience and less of a true life experience in the host country.

Integrated Models: Exchanges and Direct Enrollment

In almost diametrical contrast to the previous model, which in essence exports an American campus to a foreign country, integrated study abroad program designs facilitate participation of U.S. students in the educational system of the host country. In short, such models facilitate direct enrollment. Although students may take regular coursework, they bypass much of the regular admissions process of the host institution and are not really matriculated for degree studies in the same way native students are. Still, to enroll in a wide range of regular university courses, they must have the requisite academic background and the language skills to participate fully in the foreign educational environment.

In some cases, bilateral or multilateral exchanges can bring about short-term direct enrollment at both ends. In this case, each institution both sends and receives a limited number of students. (A full description of reciprocal options is included later in this chapter.) In other cases, institutions organize integrated programs at selected overseas institutions in one or more countries, for qualified students. There may or may not be an on-site adviser for the U.S. students. In the case of reciprocal exchanges, with a campus adviser at each end, such support services may not add to overall costs. Basic characteristics of the integrated study abroad model are described below.

Participants

If the program is an exchange between your institution and an institution or institutions abroad, participants will most likely be from your campus. On rare occasions, an exchange agreement will allow you to accept students from other institutions as well. At the site abroad, your students may become part of a larger group of international exchange students or be classmates with students from the host country, or both. In the case of integrated programs that are not exchanges, other students in residence may come from a variety of institutions.

Admission Requirements

Admissions requirements are set by the foreign institution, or, in the case of exchanges, agreed upon by the participating institutions. A typical exchange arrangement allows you to conditionally accept students to the program but gives the host university the final admission decision. In return, you will review the applications of the students they wish to send to you. Requirements often include a minimum GPA, completion of a certain number of credits, and/or specific course or language prerequisites. Many foreign institutions require U.S. students to have junior standing. Application procedures vary greatly but may include an essay or interview in addition to a completed application form. In the case of integrated programs that are not exchanges, overseas institutions may or may not be flexible. Some leave the selection of a limited number of participants to the U.S. institution, which is responsible for ensuring that all necessary requirements such as language ability or academic standing are met by each participant.

Faculty

Students take regular classes from instructors at the host university, who judge their academic performance by local standards.

Academics

Courses are chosen from the host campus curriculum. Foreign universities are generally less wedded to a fixed curriculum because the academic degree is earned more by passing cumulative examinations than by fulfilling curricular requirements and accumulating course credits. Your institution therefore may need to institute some form of preprogram course selection advising for participants, based on coursework that has been hitherto available. Students and advisers thus need to be flexible in the preapproval process, as it may not be clear until students arrive at the host university precisely what courses are being offered.

Students usually need to be proficient in the language of the host country in order to do coursework in its higher education institutions. For those needing some in-country brush-up work, an intensive language course may be offered prior to the beginning of the semester, and some tutoring may be available during the term. With the advent of ERASMUS, however, more western European institutions are offering some courses from their regular curriculum in English. This is especially true in the Nordic countries, in the Netherlands, and in certain countries in Africa and Asia with a British colonial heritage. In these instances, U.S. students can partake of a wide range of regular courses, doing all their reading and writing in English, alongside native students and other visiting students.

Grades are typically given on the scale of the host university, with a transcript sent to your campus. Your institution is responsible for establishing a policy and system for translating these grades into home-campus equivalencies or employing a pass/fail system. The course titles, credits, and grades that will appear on the student's transcript are also ultimately up to your registrar and faculty.

The program will run on the academic calendar of the host institution. Full-year programs were the norm in this model at one point, but, again, with the increasing mobility of European students through ERAS-

MUS, as well as growing semesterization in the U.K., many institutions now allow one-semester options.

Facilities

Students will have available to them all of the facilities available to regular students at their host institution. In many cases, there will be an international education office on campus with special responsibility for foreign students, or a faculty member who is the designated adviser for exchange students. This person/office may offer an orientation program at the beginning of the semester and can generally refer students to resources they need throughout the academic program. U.S. students should be forewarned that "student services" as a philosophy of higher education is a largely American phenomenon.

Housing

Housing is often in university dormitories, usually with other international students as well as students from the host country. The dormitories are generally self-catering, with shared kitchen facilities provided. Homestay and apartment options are sometimes available. Some institutions abroad, however, are not able to guarantee university housing, due to shortage of space or separate administration of student housing. In such cases, students are advised to arrive several weeks early in order to find housing. Most universities will have some form of housing office, but not all do.

Program Costs

In the case of exchange programs, tuition and fees, and sometimes room and board are paid to your institution. You use these funds to provide the same benefits to the international students who come to your campus on the program, while your students receive the benefits abroad. No funds are exchanged between institutions. With an integrated program that is not an exchange, an inclusive or partial program fee is generally negotiated through institution-to-institution discussions, to cover on-site tuition and fees (plus, in some cases, the costs of extra administrative services).

Advantages of Integrated Models

A clear strength of an integrated model is the level of immersion students experience in the host culture. Even if there is an international office students can turn to for advice, the details of their daily life are left to them. They learn to navigate a new academic system and foreign society with minimal assistance. When they need help, they are apt to turn to host-country peers for guidance, building social relationships in the process. Such experiences promote a deeper understanding of the host culture, and the impact of such an experience can be long-lasting.

Exchanges represent an attractive economic option, as the costs of direct enrollment can be often quite low, depending obviously on how much the foreign university is subsidized by its taxpayers, and by its geographic location—France and Sweden, for example, are more costly than Ecuador or Zimbabwe because the cost of living in Europe is higher. But if an exchange agreement includes tuition, fees, room, and board, your student pays the same basic costs that she would pay at home, making the only significant additional expense international airfare. Because students use the facilities of the host institution, little administrative overhead is required for your institution to maintain.

If it is not an exchange arrangement and if your campus or the host institution adds a surcharge for direct enrollment opportunities, costs to students obviously are higher, but the costs to your institution may be lower than for a branch-campus program.

Another strength of the integrated university model is that it puts all of the resources of the foreign institution at a student's disposal. Exchange students can typically take any courses for which they have the necessary prerequisites, even if host-country students are limited in course choice by their major or the particular college to which they have been admitted. This may afford students the opportunity to fulfill requirements in a variety of areas. It may also offer an international opportunity to students in areas such as the hard sciences or other disciplines rarely represented in group programs.

Drawbacks of the Integrated Model

Integrated programs are not for everyone, and can be totally inappropriate or unappealing for certain types of students. Because students participating in such programs often need to fend very much for themselves, the programs will only appeal to students who are already fairly independent and self-confident. If, in addition to being on their own in a new academic system, students must also operate in a second language, such an option can be very intimidating. Many students will thus self-select out of study abroad if an integrated model is the only choice.

A second issue is that students may find it difficult to integrate into the new culture, even if social integration is necessary for survival. Friendship has different connotations in many cultures than it does in the United States, and short-term, casual acquaintance/friends may be less common. Because the American student will only be at the host university for a short time, be it a quarter, semester, or year, host-country students may not go out of their way to befriend such visitors. American students may therefore find themselves by default in a social group of other Americans, or perhaps other international students, much the way they would on a group program—and, worth noting, in the same sort of foreign student ghetto found on many U.S. campuses.

Although the wide range of course offerings may be appealing, it carries its own difficulties. Because students may not know until they arrive abroad exactly which courses will be offered in a given term, they need to plan for many different options before they depart. It is often impossible for an academic adviser to determine how various courses will transfer back without seeing a course outline or syllabus, which again may not be available until the student registers for classes abroad, if then. Therefore, students who need to fulfill specific requirements in a given term may choose not to participate in an integrated program.

If students register for courses that were not discussed in advance, they, as well as several faculty/staff members, may need to go through a lengthy evaluation process to determine credit transfer. (Though e-mail communications may change this. See Chapter 7, "Computerizing Operations.") If your institution only grants pass/fail credit for work on exchange programs, this may deter students who can only take a limited number of such credits in their major. On the other hand, if grade equivalencies are applied, students may not participate because of uncertainties about how an unfamiliar academic system will affect their GPAs. Delays in receiving transcripts are relatively common. Such delays may affect everything from financial aid to registration for the next semester.

Finally, integrated programs are time-intensive on each end. Because each student is, in effect, planning an individualized study abroad program, advising time is high. If this time is not invested prior to the student's participation, then it will often be required to sort out the results after the time abroad. Because many of the advising issues are beyond the scope of the typical education abroad office, they may require the assistance of personnel throughout the institution, from the registrar to the academic dean.

Hybrid or Mixed Models

As we have seen, each of the antithetical program models discussed above has distinct and inherent advantages and drawbacks, at least as considered in the abstract. Each also is best suited to the needs of certain types of students and works ideally in certain types of situations, but not in others. Noting these strengths and weaknesses, many programs have been developed that attempt to combine the cultural advantages of more integrated programming with the pragmatic strengths and conveniences of branch campuses. In addition, hybrid designs have evolved from programs that began as branch campus (which have added opportunities for students to interact with the host culture) and integrated models (which have seen the necessity of providing more on-site support services or perhaps preliminary language courses). Hybrid programs therefore are often offered in cooperation with a foreign institution, as a sort of joint venture at, but are not necessarily fully of, this institution.

Often, all that is added to an integrated program is a U.S. on-site adviser, usually a faculty member familiar with the country and its higher education system, someone who can assist students with academic and personal problems, as needed. Such support services, in another variation, can be provided by the host institution (for an extra fee) by someone who is designated by it as an adviser or tutor to the U.S. students. This person may or may not have teaching duties but is otherwise responsible for the care and well-being of American students, assisting them toward increasing integration into their new studies and social life.

Other mixed-model designs include offering one or more program tracks, each geared for students of differing backgrounds and motivations. These consist of courses developed specifically for program participants. Sometimes this means language preparation only. In other instances, it would involve general background course work, coupled with the option of taking one or two regular university courses at the same time, or, in a year program, during the second semester. Another variation, is to set up tutorials or discussion groups for visiting students; these can be independent or connected with particular lecture courses. In each instance, the idea is to allow students to move toward cultural integration at their own pace.

Sometimes the foreign institution on its own develops a semi-integrated program for U.S. (and frequently other international) students, providing a set of courses for foreigners around a particular theme. These courses are usually taught in English, although there may also be "language and civilization" courses for students with some proficiency in the host language. Students with good proficiency and students staying long enough to improve their language skills, are allowed into regular university courses, from the beginning or when they are ready.

In some cases, there may be a reciprocal agreement that allows host university students to enroll in these special courses (e.g., to practice their English), or in which the host institution earns exchange spaces at your institution in return for allowing your students to enroll in regular university courses. This special curriculum and the faculty who teach it are usually described in university promotional materials, so credit transfer and equivalency issues can be determined prior to participation. Participants need to adjust to a new academic system, but faculty in such programs are generally more aware of, and accommodating towards, this adjustment than they might be in regular university classes.

Hybrid programs at their pragmatic best represent concerted and successful efforts to maximize the advantages and minimize the disadvantages of both 'island' and 'integrated' program models, as discussed above. They will not satisfy institutions that wish to have their students only participate purely in regular overseas university course work and social life, and prepare them fully to be able to do so. Nor, on the other extreme, will they satisfy institutions which feel the necessity of maintaining full curricular and economic control over what students study and how they live overseas. Further, what is possible in one country and university system is simply not possible in others, and what an American institution may wish to accomplish, may turn out to be simply not affordable or practical. Another barrier is language; full integration at the University of Istanbul is not possible for students who do not know university-level Turkish; yet setting up a program that offers no Turkish and keeps U.S. students at a distance from their native counterparts and the cultural richness of Turkey is also unthinkable.

Because most institutions are not at the polarities of the island/integration spectrum described in the first two sections of this chapter, hybrid program models of often ingenious and exciting varieties probably represent the mainstream of U.S. study abroad programming. Each offers an institutionally defined blend of cultural enrichment of a sort not possible at home with interfaced academic demands for learning of a sort which is creditable toward undergraduate degree studies.

Independent Study

The fourth generic program design for education abroad is institutionally sponsored, approved, and directed independent study. In this case, your institution makes no effort to set up classroom instruction of its own, or to arrange for matriculation in a foreign institution, or to combine these program approaches in some hybrid format. Rather, students assume the responsibility of learning largely on their own, carrying out a project usually designed and pre-approved for potential credit beforehand in consultation with your faculty and evaluated for academic credit when they return to your campus. Such individual undertakings may provide students with opportunities to develop particular technical, artistic, or career skills not pursuable at home or in a standardized program.

The duration and intensity of such an experience may be as short as a few weeks or as long as six months. It can be done by itself, or to supplement or extend a more formal mode of study. In all cases, however, this sort of learning is only possible overseas if your institution considers it not only broadly "educational," but potentially worthy of its degree credit.

Under this independent-study rubric can fall such things as:

- language-immersion experiences (usually short-term) with or without formal study, but evaluated on the home campus on the basis of a demonstrated gain in proficiency;
- scientific research projects, designed beforehand, but carried out "in the field" or in a laboratory, with or without an on-site supervisor, but evaluated by appropriate home campus faculty on the basis of demonstrated evidence, usually in a report and analysis of findings;
- library research, perhaps in the humanities or social science areas, stemming from holdings uniquely available overseas, and resulting in a lengthy critical or scholarly paper;
- working, with or without teachers or mentors, in theatre, the plastic or visual arts, music performance, creative writing, photography, or art forms, the quality of which can be judged by the quality of artistic products or performance, upon return.

Faculty

The faculty supervisor can be someone at your campus and/or at the overseas study destination. If this is not a member of your own faculty, it is generally necessary to approve the person for adjunct status, or engage an institutional faculty member to jointly oversee the project. The faculty supervisor is responsible for working with the student to establish the guidelines of the research to be conducted, clarify the requirements that must be completed in order to receive academic credit, and assess the student's work upon its completion.

Supervision

Independent learning abroad can, as the above represents, take a myriad of forms. At its purest, students work entirely on their own while they are overseas, or perhaps maintain contact with home campus faculty supervisors through periodic reports—now made even more feasible via e-mail linkages. But in many instances, it is possible for students or institutions to arrange formal or informal on-site supervision and guidance.

Academics

Students conduct independent research, carry out a plan of study, or undertake some type of internship or work experience related to their formal studies, but they do this while living abroad. Students are expected to gather information and perspectives, synthesize them, do further reading and analysis, and at some point present what they have learned for credit assessment. Projects can vary greatly in duration, but student resources, not the time required for research and writing, will almost always determine the amount of time spent abroad.

Practical Arrangements

Students are in charge of making logistical preparations, including identifying a particular study destination and corresponding with prospective hosts. If he needs to gain formal admission to a host institution (agency, laboratory, library, studio, natural preserve, etc.) in order to carry out the project, this must also be his responsibility. Housing and meals will depend on the nature of the project, its setting, and duration.

Other types of support services (e.g., transportation, visas, police registration, insurance, etc.) are also largely the responsibility of participants, but students will still depend, to some degree, on what the education abroad office can offer in the way of information and advice.

Program Costs

Most institutions that allow students to earn independent study credit have a per-credit fee schedule that should apply to overseas studies as well. Otherwise, students are responsible for all other costs: airfare, housing, meals, in-country transportation, plus any tuition fees or costs charged by a sponsoring institution or agency. Some institutions process financial aid for such arrangements, while others do not. In general, independent study is one of the cheaper forms of education abroad.

Advantages of Independent Study

For a student who is willing to make the proper preparation and arrange adequate support beforehand, then invest the time and energy to gather together what they have learned at the end, an independent study project can produce truly impressive work. Significant cross-cultural learning can take place, particularly where cooperative activity, either research or work, occurs with host-country nationals.

In most cases, this model requires only minimal assistance from the education abroad office. Because students work in cooperation with faculty members to establish project goals, a time frame, required written work, and the grading procedure, your job may be only to help students learn how to prepare to go abroad. Once the student returns to campus, he or she again works primarily with the faculty member to complete the necessary requirements. Credit is usually awarded under the rubric of "individual study" in the faculty adviser's department.

Drawbacks of Independent Study

Relative to other types of education abroad, few students will be attracted to this type of opportunity, though strong institutional support can increase the numbers. Only the best students are capable of undertaking truly independent research abroad. Maturity, discipline, superior background in the research area, language proficiency, organization, cross-cultural skills, patience, and stamina are only some of the essential qualities they will need to possess.

For most undergraduates, independent projects are difficult to develop, and faculty who are called on to support these efforts are often skeptical of their outcomes. Unless overseas contacts are knowledgeable, the body of data that a student wishes to study may not exist, or may not exist in an accessible form. If an independent-study project requires no regular and daily contact with the host culture, as for example in library research, opportunities for cross-cultural learning can be reduced.

The problem of supervision is often cited as the principal weakness of independent study abroad. Supervision of a research project abroad is difficult in the extreme for someone from the home campus, and faculty are often reluctant to supervise projects abroad unless they know the student well. In addition, faculty may be reluctant to undertake this added responsibility on top of their regular workload.

▮ Field Study/Experiential Programs

Field study experiences are organized out-of-classroom projects that enable students to deepen their understanding of another culture by living and working in it for a period of time. A field study experience may be as short as one week or as long as six months. In all cases, however, the experience is designed as a credit-bearing one requiring reflection and critical assessment in addition to the out-of-classroom experience.

A field study program can take several forms. The program may consist primarily of the field study experience with writing assignments and debriefing sessions scheduled at key intervals. In other cases, it may consist of a faculty-led group program in which students conduct independent research projects in the local community and meet periodically with the faculty member to discuss their experiences. Yet another model may offer a credit-bearing internship as one of several courses to be taken as part of a more traditional classroom-based study abroad program.

Participants

Participants may come from your own campus or from many different campuses. For longer field study programs, participants should be mature students who have studied abroad previously or participated in a domestic experiential program.

Admission requirements

Admissions standards will vary depending on the nature and duration of the field study experience. In general, students need to have a tolerance for ambiguity, as field study experiences are rarely fixed or entirely predictable activities. Each student's experience and tasks will vary depending on the interests of the student and the availability of a suitable activity on-site. If the field study experience takes place in a country where a language other than English is spoken, students must be competent in the language.

Faculty

The faculty and administrative staff for field study experiences can be quite limited or more extensive in accordance with the nature of the program. A single faculty member may lead a group of students overseas to conduct archeological investigations or to visit sites to study the architectural features of various buildings and monuments. In this case, the faculty leader works with the participants to establish guidelines for the written assignments, oversees the student projects on site, and determines the appropriate credit and grade for each student's work.

In the case of credit-bearing internships, the cast of players may include one or more of the following: (1) a site supervisor at the agency where the student will be placed who provides guidance and support to the interning student; (2) an internship placement coordinator who negotiates the internship placements on behalf of the study abroad program; (3) an instructor who helps structure the intern's academic learning and who assesses that learning for purposes of credit; and (4) the home-campus program staff who administer the study abroad program that offers the internship. In some cases a single individual may fulfill several of these functions.

Academics

To offer meaningful and challenging experiential programs, the student's tasks and responsibilities must be clearly outlined. For an experience to be creditworthy, a substantial amount of critical reflection must also take place. To achieve these goals, students are usually required to outline their interests and their methods in advance of the program. Once overseas, the students and the participating agencies should develop a project or set of tasks that can be accomplished during the time period allotted. In addition, a syllabus should outline the requirements the student must complete to receive credit for the experience, the meetings that will take place, any additional readings or lectures, and grading procedures.

Facilities

Field study experiences often do not require formal facilities. If an accompanying course is required as part of the experience, then a classroom setting may have to be established in advance. In all other cases, the facilities will be the setting of the students' field study experience.

Housing

Housing will depend on the nature of the program. If the program consists of internships in a rural setting, homestays can be an ideal option that will enhance the student's interaction with the host culture. In the case of a short-term group program, housing usually consists of hotels or youth hostels. For field study experiences that are part of a larger academic study abroad program, housing in student dormitories at the local university may be possible and allow for continued contact with the host culture.

Program costs

Costs will vary depending on the nature of the program. For short-term group programs, the student program cost may include the expenses associated with sending an accompanying faculty leader. Tuition costs for each student would also be part of the program fee, but housing, air fare, and meals may be left to the students. In more elaborate administrative structures overseas, the salaries of the various players would be reflected in the program fee paid by each student.

Advantages of the field study/experiential model

The field study model offers participants the unique opportunity to apply the theoretical concepts learned in a more traditional academic setting to a "hands on" experience. Field study programs also provide students the opportunity to integrate more fully into the daily world of the host culture, thereby enriching their understanding of the country in which they are living and studying. Because field study programs are not necessarily tied to an overseas academic institution, there is greater flexibility when establishing program dates and duration. This can allow you to structure a program to meet the particular needs of students on your campus. In the case of countries that experience frequent campus closures due to funding problems or political tensions, the field study experience can provide the best way to offer students a meaningful and academically credible activity at that location. As part of a comprehensive set of study abroad opportunities on your campus, field study programs offer an important complement to classroom-based learning overseas. In the case of an internship, the field study experience also provides students with the unique opportunity to conduct extensive research and apply their knowledge to a focused and concrete set of activities. As field study programs often do not require a classroom, there is also great flexibility in terms of the location of the program at a given site, and there is the added ability to conduct the program at multiple sites or in multiple countries.

Drawbacks to the field study/experiential model

Because field study experiences often involve multiple players, a breakdown in responsibilities can occur, leaving the student frustrated and occasionally without clear purpose. In the case of internships, the work experience can be tremendously productive or quite menial, depending on the amount of time the agency can afford to invest in the intern. In some cases, students discover that a particular research project or internship experience is no longer realistic to pursue or no longer of interest once they arrive overseas. This can result in a period of uncertainty, as the student and the internship supervisor explore alternatives. Field study experiences also run the risk of minimal end results, either because the student does not complete the assignments required or fails to take the reflective activities seriously. For students who prefer a more structured learning environment, field study experiences can lead to frustration, because they require significant student initiative and effort as well as the flexibility to accept changes.

■ Programs Sponsored in Cooperation with Others

In order to maximize study abroad opportunities in the face of increasingly limited resources, cooperatively run programs can offer attractive alternatives. Two types of consortially organized programs are currently being used by many American colleges and universities. The first, often called a *partnership consortium,* is created when two or more American institutions join forces to operate one or more programs abroad for the students of all member institutions. The second type, often called an *agency consortium,* is run by an independent organization that acts on behalf of member colleges and universities to set up and help administer one or more programs abroad. The relative advantages and disadvantages of these two types of consortia will be considered individually. Consortial programs are especially useful in serving student, curricular, or geographical needs for which, on a given campus, insufficient numbers exist to support a program of its own.

Partnership Consortia

Partnership consortia are structured in different ways. In some cases, two or more institutions share in the operation and governance of a study abroad program, and each member shares equally in the obligations and benefits of the program. The terms of the partnership are usually determined by a formula that regulates the numbers of students participating from the cooperating institutions and the financial obligations of each.

By sharing resources and operational responsibilities, more viable and effective study abroad programs can be possible. In other cases, there is a lead institution which manages the operation of the program, but a limited number of additional institutions endorse the program for their students and participate in a more limited way in the direction and structure of the program.

Basic Characteristics

Students in these programs are generally exclusively students from the member institutions, although nonconsortium students may also be eligible to participate under certain agreements. Students from the member campuses are recruited and encouraged to participate in this program as if it were a program organized by the home campus.

Admission Requirements

Member institutions coordinate admission standards for the program. Special arrangements are made by the member campus to facilitate credit and financial arrangements for participating students, and application procedures are generally coordinated to meet the needs of each member institution.

Faculty/Staff

Depending on the model, faculty may be pooled from the various campuses, drawn from only one campus, or hired in the host country. In some cases, overseas staff are also hired to perform the administrative and academic aspects of the program.

Academics

The academic structure of consortial programs can vary widely, depending on the goals of the program. All of the program types mentioned above, with the exception of independent study, can be organized on a consortial basis in order to broaden the pool of applicants and thereby sustain the program. The challenge for the consortium model is to coordinate credit arrangements with each of the member campuses. Some campuses may only allow for transfer credit if there is a lead institution organizing the study abroad program, while other institutions will make arrangements for their students to remain officially enrolled on the home campus while participating in the consortium program. Careful coordination in advance is generally necessary in order to ensure that participants receive credit upon completion of the program.

Facilities

Overseas facilities will vary widely, depending on the kind of program offered and the resources available. In some cases, you will need to rent classroom and faculty workspace, while in other cases the program may participate in an existing overseas academic structure and program. Depending on the nature of the consortium, it may be necessary to have additional staff in place to coordinate the needs of the member campuses and facilitate regular meetings of the key campus coordinators.

Housing

Depending on the program, housing may be in overseas campus housing, in homestays, or in special housing designed specifically for the consortium program. The type of housing provided will depend on the goals of the program and its duration overseas.

Program Costs

Most consortium models structure program costs to be affordable to all member institutions. If there is a special administrative fee normally charged to outside students, this fee is usually waived or reduced for consortium participants. In some cases, the consortium institutions may decide to establish a reserve fund for miscellaneous administrative costs or to enable a limited exchange agreement for students from the host institution overseas. In this case, a special administrative fee for the consortium program may be created. Other institutions charge full home-campus tuition and fees.

Advantages of the Partnership Consortium

The pooling of students is an obvious advantage of this model because a single institution might not have sufficient numbers of students to mount a program on its own. This may be particularly important when an institution wishes to operate a program in a country that may be relatively unknown and unpopular with students, but nonetheless is important. The same can be said for the sharing of faculty resources.

Where faculty go abroad as resident directors or instructors, it is always better to have a larger pool from which to select a staff. One campus may have strong faculty expertise in the history of a particular geographic area but be lacking in political science or anthropology. By coordinating varied patterns of expertise from among a number of institutions, stronger study abroad programs are possible.

There is also a slight advantage in having a group of students abroad from a variety of American institutions. The mix may help prevent the American group from becoming too ghettoized. Insofar as learning takes place between peers, diverse rather than homogeneous groups are preferred. Working together also provides some leverage when negotiating with foreign institutions over costs, facilities, courses, and support services.

The reduction of fixed program costs (as they are spread out over a larger number of student participants) tends to be the greatest strength of consortially operated programs. But fixed and variable program costs must be identified, and the percentage of fixed costs isolated relative to the total cost in any particular program. Fixed costs are those that a program must pay regardless of the number of students who participate (e.g., the costs of teachers, administration, and facilities overseas). Variable costs are those tied directly to each student participant (e.g., tuition, transportation, books and supplies, insurance, meals, excursions, cultural events, and lodging).

In general, where fixed costs are high relative to total cost, a consortial program will usually save money for the sponsoring institutions, but probably not for students. Where fixed costs are low relative to total costs (or nonexistent as is the case in some direct enrollment programs based upon reciprocity), it makes no difference financially whether a program is consortially organized so long as institutions can find students to go.

Drawbacks of the Partnership Consortium

With the added offices and individuals involved in the operation of such programs, information often does not get where it needs to be in a timely manner. In addition, because institutions play a governance role in the operation of these programs, more time is required to generate the information necessary for program operations. The problem of good communication is compounded if the cooperating institutions are geographically distant. Holding joint predeparture orientation programs, for instance, becomes difficult if not impossible.

Consortially organized programs often involve the loss of some autonomy on the part of each participating college, and governance can be cumbersome. Institutions may not, for example, be able to send all the students they would like because the numbers of participating students are often governed by an agreement among all the members. Representatives of the participating institutions must meet periodically to set policies and in some cases to select students and/or resident faculty or staff.

A number of principles have therefore emerged for governing consortially organized programs. The most common is to have the program administered out of a fixed office or location. This location could rotate or remain at one of the cooperating institutions. In either event, all program-abroad matters are addressed to this central administrative office. If resident directors are sent abroad from the participating institutions, the directorship often rotates among the member institutions. Frequent changes in personnel or administrative operations at any institution, however, can also significantly compound even routine communication difficulties.

Agency Consortia

The second type of consortium gives over to an independent agency (a nonprofit or profit-making organization) the responsibility for much of the logistical and academic details of establishing and maintaining one or more programs abroad. In this type of consortium, the agency works with the host institution to arrange housing, and provides orientation and ongoing support services. It sometimes conducts one or more pre-departure orientation programs. In addition, some agencies coordinate the academic program and the transfer of credit, working with member institution representatives. The agency may be responsible for hiring resident directors (with the approval of member institutions) and monitoring the program on a regular basis. Programs run in this way can follow any number of models: independent campuses for member-institution students only, direct enrollment into a foreign institution, or hybrid curricula that include both special and regular university coursework.

Advantages of the Agency Consortium

Regardless of the overseas program design, the agency consortium model has several domestic advantages. Membership in a consortium offers program choices far beyond those that your institution is able to provide, especially if you work for a small college or a larger institution with limited commitments to education abroad programming. Participating institutions are relieved of the burden of making the logistical arrangements abroad, and, in the case of branch-campus programs, finding a faculty member each year who is willing to accompany the students abroad.

Because the central organization is also responsible for establishing and maintaining the programs abroad, students at the participating institutions have ongoing access to a wide variety of possible study sites, while the education abroad office can focus on advice, recruitment, orientation, and other campus support. The agency can also effectively ensure that on-site orientation programs, advising, and classes meet the specific agreed-upon standards of participating institutions and the personal and academic needs of students.

The costs of membership in an agency consortium vary quite a bit. Some consortia bring together public colleges and universities with reasonably low tuition; others cater to private colleges and universities; some are established so that both public and private institutions find benefits. Some consortia have set a fee for the program, which includes all costs including the airfare, orientation program, room and board, and excursions; others fix fees for only room, board, and tuition. Those with reciprocal agreements have participating students pay fees to the home institution, in addition to an administrative fee to the central organization. This feature is quite attractive to state institutions with low in-state tuition rates. Several agency consortia have special financial aid for qualified students.

Drawbacks of the Agency Consortium

Most agency consortia require an annual membership fee, and in some cases this is significant, especially if few of your students participate. In addition, there is usually a per enrollment administrative fee that is passed on to students, increasing their costs. If fees are set on the basis of private college tuition, public college students often find the costs unaffordable.

In addition, the home institution does not have complete control over the selection and placement process. In some cases, only a few students from each participating institution are eligible for certain programs. Where the consortium places students at several sites abroad, students may not be placed at the institution of their choice or even placed at all. In sum, the admissions process can be lengthy and complex, and the results not always pleasing or easy to explain to students.

Finally, because most consortia operate by consensus, with the agency simply administering decisions, a given institution will not have its way on all matters. Your program can easily get caught between consortium policy and the preferences of your administration, and matters such as the course content, the structure of the program, or the calendar can be divisive issues. If a given institution finds itself continually at odds with other members, however, it can withdraw.

Reciprocally Organized Programs/Direct Exchanges

Any of the study abroad program models described above may be organized reciprocally. Reciprocity means, very simply, that two educational institutions, one American and one foreign, agree to some form of student exchange, or student-faculty exchange. Usually this swap involves an equal number of individuals taking each other's places over equal periods of time.

Originally, exchange programs between universities were based on the principle of student-for-student, with each paying room, board, and tuition at his or her home institution and no monies changing hands. In practice, however, many universities have found it difficult to send an equal number of students in both directions within the same period. Consequently, a variety of exchange mechanisms have been developed that are not limited to the student-for-student exchange. Thus, reciprocity may now also involve asymmetrical numbers of students and unequal periods of time spent abroad; it may also include faculty members as well as students.

Reciprocity can occur only if each institution is able and willing to accept students without an actual payment of tuition. This is possible in some countries where higher education is free to foreign students. It is also possible in many private American institutions that, through appropriate accounting procedures, can register a student without a tuition payment, and at many American state institutions where tuition may be waived on the basis of reciprocal agreements calling for an exchange of "equal service" and not equal numbers of students. But not all American colleges or universities are set up to accommodate this necessity.

Typically, reciprocity also requires that participants pay directly for their room, board, and personal expenses. Obviously, many students from developing countries cannot participate in these types of exchanges without further funding. Another condition is that special services costing extra money not be required beyond those which an institution regularly offers to its current foreign students. Thus, students needing significant language training or health care, for example, might not find either, and therefore not be able to participate. However, when each host institution is already servicing large numbers of foreign students, the cost of educating several more may be marginal.

Imaginative planning (and bookkeeping) sometimes means that the body or dollar balances called for in reciprocity agreements can be spread out over several years. This variation allows a system of credits and debits to develop and provides time for the cooperating institutions to balance these credits or debits by sending more or fewer students in particular years, depending on the credits or debits that have accumulated. This adaptation works very well, particularly where room-and-board costs are covered directly by the participating students.

Some reciprocal agreements are based on allocations of money, rather than an exchange of students. Under these agreements one of the cooperating institutions agrees to generate X dollars for each student it sends abroad, and to reserve that amount to support students coming from the partner institution. This kind of mechanism can easily be combined with those adaptations where uneven numbers of students are being exchanged. This approach simplifies the question of equity and provides great flexibility to the institution that has received monetary credits in a foreign country. The institution can send students, but it may wish to use the credits to support a single faculty member at the partner institution or to buy equipment, library materials, and so forth. Obviously, these types of agreements must be specific about how financial credits can be used, because in most instances they do not represent actual funds that can be spent for salaries or library books.

Advantages of Reciprocal Programs

Reciprocal exchange agreements afford significant advantages. Where costs of launching stand-alone programs might be prohibitive, direct exchanges present reasonably low-cost alternatives. In countries where currency controls restrict the numbers of students studying abroad, programs organized reciprocally can provide some relief. There are also significant nonfinancial advantages. Reciprocity gives each institution a stake in the relationship, so that each works harder to make sure it succeeds. This networking tends to create additional activities, in some cases developing into additional programs (often for faculty), further strengthening the links between the two institutions. Finally, reciprocity in education abroad programming diversifies the student body on your campus and contributes to the international education of students who do not study abroad. Because exchange students are only on campus for a short period of time, they are often eager to become as involved as possible. When you are planning your predeparture sessions for outgoing students, exchange students can be a valuable resource.

Drawbacks of Reciprocal Programs

Reciprocal exchanges demand additional staff time to administer the details of hosting incoming students. This includes admissions, visas, orientation, housing, registration and continuous academic and administrative support while the international students are on campus. Good communication between the participating institutions is also essential to resolve difficulties or confusion regarding academic expectations, financial arrangements, or administrative support. Depending on the available technology and the general economic or political situation overseas, effective communication can become a significant challenge.

17

Work Abroad And International Careers

Contributors: Jane Cary and William Nolting

Education abroad programming will probably always be dominated by credit-bearing study programs. But students learn in different ways and have many different needs, only some of which can be satisfied by educational programs that are purely academic in their structures, methods, and values. As an alternative to academic programs— or to expand their international experience—many students are now seeking work opportunities abroad, in part because of their belief in the intrinsic educational value of such experiences, in part because of economic advantages they provide, and in part for career preparation. All of these motivations are valid and need to be supported by advisers and institutions.

Education abroad includes both academic and experiential programming. This chapter focuses on the possibilities open to students and recent graduates for working abroad. "Work abroad" means immersion in an international work environment for the primary purpose of the experience itself, whether professional or not, whether for academic credit or not. "Work abroad" as we use the term does not include career-related assignments overseas through an employer, nor does it include permanent jobs abroad. By design, work abroad is temporary, lasting anywhere from a few weeks to two or three years, and it may or may not be related to specific career goals.

Programs for working abroad have a tradition paralleling that of study abroad. Volunteer programs known as "workcamps" started 75 years ago in Europe; in 1996 the Fulbright teaching program celebrated its 50th anniversary and the Peace Corps its 35th; two large worldwide internship exchanges (IAESTE and AIESEC) were founded in 1948, and the CIEE Work Abroad program started in the 1960s. Recently, however, interest in working abroad has exploded in the United States, and this is now arguably the fastest-growing sector in education abroad. Articles on working abroad have appeared in major news magazines.

Although the number of programs listed in the IIE education abroad guides increased by about one-third from 1991 to 1996, work abroad listings (indexed in IIE under internships, practical training, student teaching, and volunteer/service) more than doubled, and account for almost one-fourth of all listings in the 1996 edition. Tens of thousands of people participate in work exchanges annually, and it is unfortunate that they are not included in statistics of educational exchange (credit-bearing programs excepted).

A number of reasons lie behind this increased interest in work abroad: students' preference for a nonacademic cultural-immersion experience; their desire to live abroad inexpensively and independently for an extended period of time; the ambition to return overseas after a previous study- or travel-abroad experience; and the desire to prepare themselves for an international career. Although many colleges have been quick to incorporate internship or service-learning components into study abroad programs, fewer institutions have been proactive in establishing advising offices and support services that provide genuine encouragement and counseling for the full range of work abroad options. Those that do so include a broad spectrum of top-ranking universities, liberal arts colleges, and state and community colleges. At many institutions, however, students must still fend for themselves.

Despite the fact that work abroad programs are accessible to students from any college or university, work abroad has been relatively neglected at many colleges and universities because it falls into the bureaucratic cracks. Traditional study abroad offices have refrained from promoting work abroad opportunities because they do not view such programming as their responsibility. Most define their domain as providing access to credit-granting academic opportunities. Although it might seem logical for career-planning offices to handle work abroad advising, such offices frequently lack the international expertise needed to advise in this area. It would behoove both study abroad and career offices to familiarize themselves with these experiences, as the job market is beginning to demonstrate that such experience is good career preparation in an increasingly internationalized economy.

Setting aside questions of "turf," the bulk of this chapter has a practical rather than theoretical focus. It is intended to introduce the education abroad adviser to the great number of work abroad options available to students and recent graduates and to areas of possible cooperation with campus career offices. Please refer to the annotated bibliography in the appendix for a complete overview of the resources available. You are of course encouraged to share the bibliography and this chapter with your campus career office colleagues and, of course, with students.

■ Work versus Study Abroad: Similarities and Differences

One of the best arguments in favor of education abroad offices advising on work abroad options is simply that some of the most significant benefits of a study abroad experience (as detailed below), are also among the main benefits of a work abroad experience. Indeed, some would argue that these goals can be even more fully realized in programs that are not specifically set up to meet American academic credit criteria.

Cultural Immersion

Most work abroad settings are, almost by definition, "full immersion." The work abroad participant is likely to be the only American, or one of just a few, working and living in a fully indigenous setting. Whereas most study abroad students have to work hard to break out of an often comfortable American enclave where English is spoken and familiar customs and mores prevail, work abroad students have no choice but to do what the locals do.

Personal Development

Growth in self-confidence and independence, in tolerance and empathy, in flexibility and adaptability, and in pragmatic know-how and cultural insight is likely to be as great or greater than in most study abroad settings. Most work settings offer less hand-holding and well-intentioned oversight. Although this independence can be stressful, most students adapt readily, discover inner resources, and later name this challenge as one of the primary benefits of their experience.

Cross-Cultural Learning

The opportunity to meet host-country nationals is assured in most work settings. What is different, however, even from full-immersion study abroad settings, is that one is more likely to experience differences of social organization, such as class and cultural distinctions, than would be likely in the relatively elite, homogeneous, and loosely organized environment of university life. The significance of work in the everyday life of another culture, relations between managers and workers, and forms of gender, ethnic, or class discrimination may be very different from that experienced in the United States. First-hand experience of such differences often becomes a rich basis for later study or career work that involves other cultures.

Language Learning

Classroom learning tends to be passive and is largely a solitary endeavor. In a work setting, social interaction is almost always a given. The give-and-take—the immediate feedback—of a workplace can be enormously beneficial in learning a foreign language. Most work abroad participants demonstrate dramatic gains in their language skills. It should be emphasized, however, that this holds true for those already possessing a solid foundation in the language, equivalent to at least two years' study at the college level. And one is probably more likely to learn the slang or dialects associated with everyday life than formal academic language.

Relevance to Academic Major

For students with certain majors, internships abroad can be more readily arranged than study abroad. In engineering, for example, few study abroad opportunities exist in the core curriculum because of problems in matching courses at overseas universities. Yet engineering internships are available in the summer for juniors, seniors, and graduate students, who can go on paid internships without delaying their graduation date. Relatively few work opportunities exist in the humanities, except in related applied fields. An English major can teach English as a foreign language. A history or political science major might do a parliamentary internship, while an art major could, if fortunate, act as a guide for a famous European museum or help restore a damaged painting. In an effort to combine the best of the academic and work models, many colleges have begun to build evaluated-for-credit field experiences into their study programs. These experiences may take the form of job placements before or after a study term, volunteer activity during the academic year, or a field-based independent study built around an internship.

Grade Point Average

If a university selects "academic rigor" as the only institutional goal of its students' overseas experience, the types of opportunities open to students will be limited, as will the types of students who are able to take advantage of programs. Students with higher GPAs are admitted to traditional study abroad programs, and those with lower GPAs are often not—even though some evidence suggests that a high GPA is not the primary factor in ensuring maximum educational gain abroad. Attitude, practical experience, and motivation are seen as being of equal or even greater importance than GPA in selection for work abroad programs. Thus, a wider range of students can qualify for work abroad than for study abroad.

Timing of Participation

Work abroad tends to attract slightly older and more intellectually and socially mature students. Although most students who study abroad do so during their junior year, most work abroad participants go after the junior year, after graduation, or as graduate students.

Location

A majority of work abroad participants, like study abroad students, choose western Europe. However, the numbers of Americans who are working abroad in eastern Europe, Asia, and in many developing countries far exceeds the numbers of Americans who are studying abroad in these regions.

Costs and Benefits

Cost is one area in which study and work abroad differ significantly. Most work abroad options are substantially less expensive than study abroad options for the same location and length of time (except for university-sponsored study-work programs, which have the advantage of eligibility for financial aid). Some students may object to the notion of having to *pay* to work, as will be the case to participate in many internships abroad. This is where the savvy study abroad adviser can talk about making an investment in one's future job marketability!

Not-for-credit work abroad does not necessarily delay graduation because it is often done in the summer or after graduation. True, there may be opportunity costs—either lost time when one could be earning credit toward an advanced degree, or lost income compared with what one might be earning in a job back home. But one can argue that the latter options carry their own cost of a lost opportunity compared with working abroad, particularly because the majority of work options are limited to students or the young and unattached.

▮ Advising for Work Abroad

Advising for work abroad is more complex than advising for study abroad, as discussed in Chapter 10. Although you need not become a walking encyclopedia, it will be extremely useful for you to be familiar with the main issues, organizations, and resources in work abroad. Ideally, you should make a variety of sources available to students (see bibliography) inasmuch as the field has no single exhaustive directory comparable to the IIE guides for study abroad. A library of the most important guides for work abroad, mentioned in the text, consists of about a dozen inexpensive books.

There are many available work abroad options with respect to time, location, and so forth. But an unrealistic wish, such as a paid philosophy position in Paris, may simply be impossible to fulfill. The following are essential considerations to cover when advising for work abroad because they will clarify possible options. Each raises issues of "reality testing," of which the prospective work abroader needs to be aware. Be sure to use this section together with the following section, "Types of Work Abroad."

Working Abroad Legally

A work permit is required in any country to pursue legal paid employment—a fact of which most students seem unaware. "Off the books" work is possible, but this limits the type of work to the lowest-paying jobs and puts the individual at risk for exploitation, on-the-job injury without legal recompense, and deportation. Visas permitting work are usually far more difficult to get than visas for study or tourism, because jobs-for-citizens-first is an issue (as it is in the United States). Special work-exchange programs, such as those detailed below, are an important exception to this rule. Unpaid work, whether in an internship or volunteer capacity, may not require a work permit, and some types of work compensated primarily in room, board, and spending money, such as au pair work, can be exempted from the need for a regular work permit.

If students have skills possessed by few citizens of the host country, a work permit may be obtained, depending on the particular country's regulations. Very few recent graduates are in this exceptional position, however, except when applying for jobs teaching English as a foreign language, where simply being a native speaker of English may be treated as a unique qualification in some instances.

Where Are the "Best" Places?

Options can be highly country-specific. In western Europe, for example, numerous programs exist for paid short-term work in some countries (Britain, Ireland, France, Germany), but are scarce in others (Spain, Italy). In Asia, eastern Europe and countries of the former Soviet Union, teaching English as a second language (TESL) is most likely, though at vastly differing rates of pay. In developing countries, volunteer organizations and study-work programs offer virtually the only realistic option for U.S. students and recent graduates to work in these economies.

What Are the Real Costs and Benefits?

Students are also usually unaware of a basic economic fact: the great disparities in living standards around the world. They may be surprised to learn that they cannot expect an American-level salary when working in a formerly communist country or in a developing country—indeed, the cost of an airplane ticket may exceed a local citizen's annual salary! Thus, working abroad may in fact cost something, especially in less-wealthy countries—and in these countries, a U.S.-funded "volunteer" experience such as the Peace Corps (which covers all expenses and pays a $5,400 stipend at the end of two years) may be the best-paid job available to a recent graduate. Even in wealthy western Europe, Americans participating in paid work programs such as Council Work Abroad will probably be able to save less than they would with a summer job at home, simply because of the additional costs involved in traveling abroad and settling into a new environment.

When Is It Best to Work Abroad—As an Undergraduate, Graduate Student, or an Alumnus?

Some work abroad programs are open only to those with student status (or recent graduates), such as the Council Work Abroad programs and internship programs offered by IAESTE or the U.S. State Department. Other work abroad programs are open only to those who have a bachelor's degree, such as most programs for teaching English abroad and long-term volunteer programs. Internships with certain well-known international organizations (such as the United Nations) and corporations (such as Proctor & Gamble) may prefer graduate students or those with graduate degrees.

Duration—Or, How Long Can I Work Abroad?

Work-abroad programs last anywhere from a few weeks (volunteer workcamps), to a summer or semester (internships and short-term work abroad), to one or two years (teaching English or volunteer organizations). Permanent work abroad will be extremely difficult for most individuals to arrange, except for those possessing professional skills that are in high demand.

How Can I Link My Work Abroad to Academic Credit and Career Considerations?

Most work abroad is not directly linked to a career field—as indeed, most study abroad is not—but can provide overseas experience, which would be one of several steps toward an international career (see careers section, below). Prospective teachers might consider teaching English, or alternatively, language and area studies majors might teach English as a means to improve their knowledge of a culture. Those interested in issues concerning developing countries would certainly want to consider a long-term experience with the Peace Corps or a similar organization.

Internships, by definition, should provide experience in a particular career field. Undergraduates can receive credit for working abroad through tuition-charging academic internship programs. Such programs offer the greatest choice in terms of location and subject. Students need to check their own institution's policy toward credit for internships or other experiential learning. Unfortunately, graduating seniors rarely need academic credit, and paid internships are even more rare abroad than in the United States. Note that the student who asks for an "internship" abroad may in fact not have any specific career focus and often simply wants some kind of work abroad experience.

An internship in the United States with an international organization might be another option worth mentioning. Paradoxically, students may face a choice between gaining overseas experience in a job with little specifically "international" content, or having an internship in the United States involving international issues and working with American colleagues.

What Are Foreign Language Proficiency Requirements?

Even "nonprofessional" jobs (work in restaurants, *au pair* work) will require a level of foreign language proficiency considered by Americans to be intermediate or advanced—a fact that many students may not know. Conversely, for most overseas English-teaching positions, knowledge of the host-country language is not required although it would definitely facilitate cultural integration.

Is Previous Work Experience Required?

Any type of experience beyond the purely academic is a plus when applying for work abroad programs. Obviously, for technical positions (such as engineering internships) there is no substitute for academic training—

but even in this case prior work experience is advantageous. For a parliamentary internship, prior experience working for a local politician or even in student government would be viewed positively. For positions teaching English as a foreign language, previous experience as a tutor or conversation partner would prove valuable.

What Are Citizenship Requirements?

Some work-exchange programs, such as those of CIEE or CDS, are limited to U.S. citizens or permanent residents; U.S. government internships are usually limited to U.S. citizens, as is the Peace Corps. One option for non-U.S. citizens is the organization IAESTE, which can arrange for work permits in a third country outside the United States. Study-internships and unpaid internships rarely have citizenship restrictions.

Types of Work-Abroad Programs

Programs make working abroad far easier than trying to line up a job abroad on a student's own initiative—analogous to the difference between using a study abroad program and directly enrolling in a foreign university. Given the severe restrictions imposed by most countries on work by foreigners, special work exchanges make feasible that which would otherwise be difficult, if not impossible. For advising purposes, it is useful to categorize work abroad programs into four types: (1) internships, (2) short-term paid work, (3) teaching, and (4) volunteering. We name here a few major organizations, especially if they are unique (function, longevity, reputation), but there are hundreds more listed in the resources in the bibliography. For an alternative approach, that of making contacts while studying abroad to create one's own overseas job later, see the final section.

Internships

Advising highlights:

- Most direct connection to career tracks
- Wide range of location and discipline, equaled only by volunteer options
- Paid internships fairly rare

Internships can be found through three routes. First, colleges and universities offer study-internship programs which charge tuition and grant academic credit; these number in the hundreds and are available in countless disciplines. Second, special reciprocal internship exchange organizations such as the Association for International Practical Training (IAESTE/AIPT), AIESEC, CDS, and the American-Scandinavian Foundation offer paid internships, usually in business or technical fields. Third, corporations, governments, and international organizations may be willing to take on interns (often unpaid); some, such as the U.S. State Department, have large formal programs.

Advantages

Internships give insight and, occasionally, entry into international careers. Even those who "try out" a career this way and decide against it feel the experience is extremely valuable. Some internships offer a group experience, either in classes or organized social activities. Academic credit and financial aid may be available for many university-sponsored internships.

Disadvantages

Assignments are sometimes very demanding, leaving little time to explore the local culture. Conversely, some internships involve excessive busy work at the expense of professional tasks, or may simply lack structure. The intern may have to demonstrate initiative before being given responsible assignments. Study-internship programs sometimes do not guarantee an internship placement. In some settings, social contacts may be limited to older professionals uninterested in socializing outside the workplace. U.S. government internships overseas will be in an all-American environment.

Application Requirements

The selection process may be somewhat to extremely competitive, and the "fit" between an applicant's background and the job may be as important a factor in the selection as a good academic record. Excellent command of the relevant foreign language is often essential if the internship is in a non-English-speaking country. Prior related work experience is very helpful. Watch for early application deadlines (November 1 for summer State Department interns)!

Duration

Summer or semester-length internships are typical; a few are longer.

Location

Although most international internships are located in Europe or the United States, a great many are available in other locations worldwide.

Sample Sponsoring Organizations

- Universities: Hundreds of study-internship programs are offered by universities and are readily accessible in the IIE and Peterson's study abroad guides, which are indexed for internships.
- Reciprocal internship organizations: AIESTE/AIPT (technical, scientific, agricultural, and hotel management; 4,000+ placements worldwide, of which a few hundred are Americans); AIESEC (business; 5,000+ placements, but entry possible only through campus chapters); American-Scandinavian Foundation (technical); and CDS (business and technical positions in Germany).
- Government, corporations, and international organizations: U.S. State Department (1,000+ internships, half of these abroad); Proctor & Gamble; CNN; United Nations (New York or Geneva). Internships with the named organizations are very competitive, sometimes for graduate students only, and often unpaid.
- Nongovernmental organizations (NGOs): Many NGOs offer internships at their U.S. offices or, for the well-qualified, overseas. The Overseas Development Network acts as a clearinghouse for NGO internships.

The most useful guides to internships include IIE's study abroad guides (more work abroad listings than Peterson's); *Directory of International Internships,* Michigan State University; *The Internship Bible,* Princeton Review; *International Internships and Volunteer Programs,* Worldwise Books. All of these are recommended because there is surprisingly little overlap in their listings.

Several universities have established World Wide Web sites that list work abroad options offered by many institutions:

- http://www.cie.uci.edu/~cie/iop (University of California, Irvine, by Ruth Sylte). Extensive work abroad listings by type, extensive links, and "how-to" guide for using the Internet to research overseas options.
- http://www.istcp.umn.edu (University of Minnesota ISTC, by Richard Warzecha). Searchable directories include study abroad, volunteering, internships.
- http://www.umich.edu/~icenter (University of Michigan International Center, by William Nolting). Descriptive articles with links.

Short-Term Paid Work Abroad

Advising highlights:

- Work is typical of summer jobs anywhere, such as restaurant, temp work, or childcare (au pair), though enterprising students do find professionally relevant work
- Ordinary work in an extraordinary environment
- Best chance of paying one's way abroad for a short time, although there will be up-front costs
- Participants report satisfaction with the degree of self-sufficiency they have achieved
- Rapid improvement in foreign language skills (where applicable)
- Locations primarily in western Europe

There are essentially three options for short-term paid work. One is to go through CIEE Work Abroad, a unique reciprocal program that provides work permits and assists students in finding their own jobs. The second option would be to apply to one of several organizations that offer job placements overseas. Thirdly, students can attempt to find their own job while abroad; work permit programs such as those listed below can help remove one of the major obstacles to getting an offer.

The CIEE Work Abroad Program

The CIEE Work Abroad Program can procure a short-term work permit (three to six months) that allows students or recent graduates to enter a specific country and seek work of any kind. Outside this unique program, work permits can be obtained only after receiving a job offer, which would usually not be forthcoming without a work permit!

With around 6,000 U.S. participants annually (and far more overseas students coming to work in the United States), this is the single largest work abroad program. CIEE Work Abroad administers reciprocal exchanges with a limited number of countries: Canada, Costa Rica, France, Germany, Great Britain, Ireland, Jamaica, New Zealand (check with CIEE for changes in participating countries).

CIEE charges $225 (1997) for the work permit and for assistance from its overseas counterparts in finding a job and accommodations. How much students earn depends very much on the economy of their chosen country; CIEE provides reliable income figures in its literature. Students should be advised to take along $800 to $1,000 to tide them over until the first paycheck. Participants in Britain, and perhaps Ireland, France, Germany, or Canada, may be able to cover their expenses and save. This is much less likely in the other countries, which have much lower wage levels (or high airfare, in the case of New Zealand). Note that CIEE's ISIC and Bailey scholarships can be used for work abroad.

- *Advantages.* Permits can be used for any type of work, including professional-type work. Nearly all jobs involve total cultural immersion because colleagues at work are nearly always local citizens. Social contacts tend to be with people from a variety of class backgrounds. Since students find their own jobs, they have control over their employment situation, and credit themselves with success. Although jobs are not guaranteed, few participants fail to find a job; average job-search time is four to ten days, depending on the country. Application is noncompetitive.

- *Disadvantages.* The uncertainty of arriving without a job deters some students (and parents). Even under the best of circumstances, the stress during the job and apartment hunt can be high.

- *Application requirements.* Applicants must have carried at least an eight-credit-hour load (undergraduate or graduate) in the semester prior to participation. Two years' study of the appropriate language is required for Costa Rica, France, and Germany. Participants must be U.S. citizens, though some countries allow U.S. permanent residents to participate. Allow one month between application and receipt of the working papers.

Other Permit Programs

Other organizations can also assist individuals in getting a permit, typically for up to 18 months, but they require that the individual have a job offer first. Those seeking positions can let potential employers know that the employer would be relieved of the burden of obtaining the work permit, which will increase the chances of getting a job offer. In practice, an employee is rarely hired sight unseen; therefore these permits are most useful for those participating in a work abroad program who want to stay longer (although a return to the United States for the new permit is necessary), or for cases in which an individual has the necessary connections—perhaps made during a study abroad experience, through alumni, or even through e-mail contacts—to land a job offer.

These organizations—all of which also arrange for internship placements, as mentioned above—include the AIPT/IAESTE, with placements in more than 70 countries; The American-Scandinavian Foundation, for Scandinavian countries; and CDS, for Germany.

Placement Programs

It is possible to be placed into a paid short-term overseas job with the assistance of a number of organizations. We mention here several reputable, established U.S.-based programs. Fees range from around $300 to $1,500 (1997). The main *advantage* of this kind of program—that is, the prearranged job—is also the main potential *disadvantage* in the event of an unsatisfactory placement. Agencies should be willing to furnish names of past participants.

- Center for Interim Programs (since 1980)—worldwide; offers database of 2,400 nonacademic but structured opportunities.
- InterExchange (since 1971)—nonprofit; Europe; offers positions in English teaching, resort jobs, skilled and unskilled farm work, internships, and au pair.
- International Cooperative Education Program (since 1971)—Europe and Asia; paid "entry level" internships that require knowledge of a foreign language.
- World Learning, Au Pair/Homestay Abroad—a branch of World Learning/School for International Training; Europe; *au pair,* homestays.
- Worldwide Internships and Service Education (WISE)—nonprofit; Europe; community service, internships, working farm guest, *au pair,* homestays, language immersion.

Another option would be volunteer workcamps—see Volunteering, below.

Work Without a Permit

Working for pay without a work permit is illegal. The illegal worker is without any legal protection from exploitation, or in the event of injury on the job, and may be deported if discovered by the authorities. Student travelers do occasionally find casual work without a permit, usually of a menial and low-paying variety, but it is generally not recommended.

Most Useful Guides to Short-Term Paid Work Abroad

Copies of the invaluable *Council Work Abroad Participant's Handbooks* can be requested by college offices; these are otherwise available only to individual participants. The magazine *Transitions Abroad* is best for up-to-date overviews. For the adventurous individual who wants to find a job on-the-spot, Susan Griffith's *Work Your Way Around the World* is the ultimate source, though its advice, from a British perspective, may occasionally be misleading for Americans who wish to work in countries of the European Union (EU citizens can legally work in any member country). See also World Wide Web sites (above, Internships section).

Teaching English as a Foreign Language
Advising highlights:
- One of the most accessible long-term (one- to two-year) options for recent graduates
- Locations primarily outside of western Europe
- Teaching or tutoring experience before going highly recommended

In the late 1980s and early 1990s, political changes in eastern Europe and strong economies in East Asia created a booming market for teachers of English as a foreign, or second, language (known variously as TEFL, EFL, TESL, or ESL). Anyone whose native tongue was English could travel to these regions and land a job within days. This is no longer the case due to market saturation in popular destinations, such as Prague and Tokyo, and higher standards for teachers. Although teaching EFL remains one of the most accessible options for long-term work abroad, most positions now require a bachelor's degree and some experience teaching or tutoring English, even if only as a volunteer. Teacher placement programs and agencies can match the novice teacher with locales that still need EFL teachers.

Salaries vary, as usual, depending on the local economy. Positions in east Asia (Japan, Taiwan, Korea) can pay very well. If the position has been arranged by a sponsoring organization, airfare may be included and housing—otherwise scarce and expensive—provided. If the position is found on-site, beginning expenses can be very high, including airfare, housing (deposit of several months' nonrefundable rent), and a trip to another country to obtain a work permit.

In areas with less-wealthy economies, such as eastern Europe, China, and most of Africa and Latin America, pay can be high by local standards, but low in absolute terms, making these in effect volunteer positions. Living expenses may be covered, but not the cost of airfare. Many volunteer organizations provide placements, sometimes also providing training.

Advantages
Teaching English is one of the few long-term overseas positions available to new graduates. Considerable cultural-immersion is possible, especially for those who have some knowledge of the host country's language before going abroad.

Disadvantages

Most of the working day is spent speaking English, which makes learning the host country's language difficult. For those with little knowledge of the host country's language, friendships tend to be mainly with other English-speaking expatriates. Many programs give only limited training and on-site support; prospective teachers should bring their own teaching materials.

Application Requirements

In most cases, a bachelor's degree is required, and applicants must be native speakers of English. Formal TEFL credentials are rarely required (outside western Europe) though some TEFL tutoring or teaching experience is a big advantage; volunteering as a tutor for one's own university's English program for foreign students is an easy way to get experience. No knowledge of the host country's language is usually required, though this actually may prove to be a disadvantage in the long run.

Duration

Nearly all positions are for at least one year. A few summer- or semester-long placements are available.

Locations

Most positions are in East Asia (Japan, Taiwan, Korea, China) or eastern Europe. Some are also available in Latin America and Africa. In western Europe, TEFL positions are very competitive even for experienced teachers with formal TEFL credentials.

Sample Sponsoring Organizations

- Governments: The U.S. Peace Corps places EFL teachers. The Japanese English Teaching (JET) program—4,000+ positions annually—recruits EFL teachers through Japanese consulates.
- Fulbright English Teaching Assistantships: Available in France, Germany, Korea, and Taiwan, future teachers preferred.
- Universities: Earlham College (Japan), Princeton-in-Asia (most of Asia), Western Washington University (China) have well-organized programs that place teachers into paying positions.
- Private language schools: Several chains recruit from the United States for their overseas branches, including AEON and GEOS (Japan) and Hess (Taiwan).
- Volunteer organizations: Many nonprofit organizations assist in

placing TEFL teachers abroad. Teachers will be expected to cover the cost of airfare and a placement fee. Examples include The Central Europe Teaching Program, Foundation for a Civil Society, Volunteers-in-Asia, WorldTeach.

Most Useful Guides to Teaching English Abroad

Dozens of excellent books exist on this topic (see bibliography), most specific to regions or countries. Two with worldwide coverage are: *Teaching English Abroad* (published by Transitions Abroad), lists U.S.-based programs; Susan Griffith's *Teaching English Abroad: Talk Your Way Around the World* is very comprehensive, but its information on western Europe, from a British perspective, is useful mainly for European Union citizens. See also Web sites (above, Internships section).

Professional Teaching Positions in Overseas K-12 Schools and Universities

A different realm of possibilities exists for those with certification to teach in kindergarten through high school: teaching in Department of Defense (DOD) schools at overseas U.S. military bases; or teaching in private international schools, which are English-language schools for the offspring of expatriate diplomats and businesspeople. The easiest way to land a position in these schools is to attend one of the special job fairs for international schools. Major fairs are held in February, and a few smaller fairs take place in June. For more information, contact the two largest job fair organizers: International Schools Services and University of Northern Iowa. Another job placement service, Search Associates, offers the International Schools Internship Program, which recruits "teaching interns" (certification not necessary) for overseas K-12 schools.

The Fulbright Scholars program offers overseas assignments for up to one year for university-level teaching or research, and the Fulbright Teacher Exchange does the same for community college and K-12 teachers. The Civic Education Project (CEP) sends holders of recent advanced degrees to teach in eastern European universities.

Volunteer Work Abroad

Advising highlights:

- Defined not by pay or lack of it, but by service at the grassroots level
- Work is with citizens of the host country
- Excellent career preparation for those interested in developing countries or nongovernmental organizations

Traditionally, volunteer work abroad has been seen as service work, helping the underprivileged and powerless. Though this is still true, today most volunteer organizations see their role as one of solidarity with indigenous peoples, helping them to achieve their own goals. Sponsoring organizations run the gamut from the U.S. government's Peace Corps to nonsectarian, nongovernmental organizations (known as NGOs, or private voluntary organizations—PVOs) to religious organizations—the latter may be either virtually indistinguishable from NGOs, or they may have a more missionary focus.

Volunteering is not necessarily defined by lack of pay. The Peace Corps, for example, covers all expenses, provides training and on-site support, and pays a "resettlement allowance" of $5,400 (1996) at the end of the two-year assignment. This benefit package far exceeds local wage levels in most developing countries. Other, mostly religious-based organizations also support volunteers willing to make this lengthy a commitment. Even the short-term volunteer projects known as work-camps provide room and board. But many programs are unpaid or charge a fee to cover the costs of supporting the volunteer. College-based "service-learning" programs combine volunteering with coursework and provide academic credit in return for tuition. CIEE's ISIC and Bailey grants can be used for volunteering abroad, and community groups (such as service or religious organizations) may be willing to help fund a volunteer's expenses.

Advantages

Volunteers are needed for a huge variety of work, ranging from the unskilled to the professional, in nearly all areas of the world. Volunteering is frequently the only realistic possibility for working in developing countries, and can provide essential career preparation for those interested in development or relief work—unfortunately, a growing field in these times. Most volunteers live and work with ordinary local people, rather than with the host country elite, other Americans, or other foreigners.

Disadvantages

Service work is not for everyone. Idealistic persons in particular may be frustrated at being able to do little about conditions they would like to see changed; successful volunteers tend to combine idealism with other goals, such as the desire to learn about other cultures. *How to Serve and Learn Abroad Effectively: Students Tell Students,* published by Partnership for Service Learning, gives excellent guidance for those considering service work. Culture shock can be severe for sojourners to developing countries. Not every volunteer organization has a good support network.

Application Requirements

These vary widely depending on the organization, length, and type of assignment. For example, screening for the Peace Corps is thorough and the application process can take nine months to a year. Organizations offering such long-term positions often want volunteers with highly developed skills. For other positions such as workcamps, applications are noncompetitive, on a first-come, first-served basis. Organizations affiliated with religious groups may insist on membership in the religion or at least a willingness to examine the particular belief; in this case applicants should be sure to find out whether or not proselytizing would be expected as part of the overseas assignment.

Duration

Most workcamps last two to three weeks in the summer. Other volunteer possibilities may last from a few weeks to two or three years.

Locations

Short-term possibilities, such as workcamps, and a few long-term ones are available in Europe. The vast majority of long-term positions, and some short-term positions, are in developing countries—primarily in Africa, Latin America, and South and Southeast Asia, with relatively few possibilities in East Asia.

Sample Sponsoring Organizations

- Government: Peace Corps (3,500-4,000 new volunteers annually). For the United Nations Volunteer Program, applicants who are U.S. citizens also apply through the Peace Corps.
- Academic institutions: Brethren Colleges Abroad; Goshen College; Partnership for Service Learning; University of Minnesota Studies in International Development.
- Nonsectarian volunteer organizations: Amigos de las Americas; Earthwatch; Los NiZos; Mobility International; Operation Crossroads Africa.
- Religious-affiliated organizations: American Friends Service Committee; World Zionist Organization; Brethren Volunteer Service; Jesuit Volunteer Corps; Mennonite Central Committee (these are all nonproselytizing).
- Short-term workcamps: Council International Volunteer Projects; Volunteers for Peace (VFP).

Best Guides to Volunteering Abroad

Volunteer! (CIEE)—a must-have; *The Peace Corps and More; Travel Programs in Central America.* See also Ann Halpin's searchable database, located at the University of Minnesota Web site (see Internship section, above).

∎ International Career Paths

There is a distinct difference between working abroad for a short while and actually establishing an international career. Many of the options covered in this chapter and in the work abroad bibliography are available to those with little previous work experience and are not especially competitive. Most students who go abroad, either for work or study, do not necessarily want an international career—at least they do not intend to work overseas for the rest of their lives. What these students consciously seek is a serious, nonacademic cultural-immersion experience; career considerations are secondary. However, many who return from an extended period of working abroad do in fact go on to develop an international career, often by pursuing graduate study or a professional degree in business, public health, or medicine, engineering or natural resources, law, or international relations, to name a few. Such a career, however, may or may not entail living overseas.

Ironically, Americans in international careers are usually based in the United States. In addition, international careers are notoriously competitive. Even an entry-level position may require a combination of education in a discipline related to the career, for example a master's degree in business administration; career-related work experience; overseas experience; and knowledge of one or more foreign languages. Not surprisingly, in view of this complexity, preparation for an international career often takes place in several stages, as the following chart shows. Those interested in an international career should start by researching it thoroughly in the guides listed in the work abroad section of the bibliography. We also recommend contact with an institution's alumni in international careers for the purposes of information interviewing.

Five Typical Patterns of International Career Development

Pattern 1

- Peace Corps volunteer
- Graduate school in the United States

- Private voluntary organization
- Agency for International Development or the State Department (sometimes followed by work in a *public multinational*)

Pattern 2

- College year abroad
- Small international educational organization
- *Master's degree*
- Larger international educational organization
- A foundation or a U.S.-based university (as a director of international programs)

Pattern 3

- *B.A./B.S.*
- *Several years' experience in consulting, investment banking, economic analysis, etc.*
- Business school
- Trainee in a multinational corporation
- Overseas assignment #1 (one or two years after trainee position)
- Overseas assignment #2 (two to four years after overseas assignment #1)
- U.S.-based assignment
- Possible future overseas assignments

Pattern 4

- International studies major
- Foreign service exam *(no longer offered annually, but only as personnel are needed)*
- Foreign service officer in series of overseas posts (two-year cycle)
- Washington, DC, post
- Other overseas posts (may either stay in the foreign service or move into work for an educational or private voluntary organization or for another branch of the U.S. government)

Pattern 5

- Study of technical field (e.g., engineering, agriculture, health)
- Five to ten years of domestic experience

- Project team member with an international consulting firm on a series of overseas contracts
- Independent consultant to U.S. government agencies, multinational corporations, or international private voluntary or educational organizations

SOURCE: Howard Schuman, *Making It Abroad: The International Job Hunting Guide,* 1988 (New York: John Wiley, 1988), 135B136. Reprinted by permission of John Wiley & Sons, Inc. (Italics mark additions by chapter's authors.)

The Student's Role in Planning a Work Abroad Experience or an International Career

As an adviser, you may be excited or appalled by all the information you would need to master if you were to become completely informed about all the resources that exist for this area. Ideally, this information should be readily available to students through your office and/or via the campus career center. Most career centers now see their campus role as that of offering student counseling as well as placement services. They hope that the lessons they impart about career planning and job search strategy will remain with students well after graduation. If one assumes that career planning and preparation occur throughout one's life, it makes sense to use a student's study abroad experience as a jumping-off point for career exploration, too.

In this chapter, work abroad is presented as an alternative, or a complement, to study abroad. Indeed, often study abroad advisers see students twice: when they are sophomores, seeking advice about study abroad opportunities, and then again when they are seniors, so inspired by their time abroad that they are seeking assistance to plan another foreign excursion. The two experiences are thus rather naturally conjoined.

There is much your office can and should do to help your students integrate their overseas studies into their career preparation. There is even more your students can do to help themselves before, during, and after their study abroad experience, to plan their own work abroad experience and to explore their international career options. We suggest that each study abroad adviser who provides a predeparture orientation include a handout similar to the following. Advisers should work with the campus career office to ensure that the proper career "lingo" for that campus is employed, and that the campus's own process is reflected correctly:

Checklist for Students Studying Abroad Who May Be Interested in Working Abroad or in an International Career

Before you go...

❏ Make a list of alumni living in the city/country where you'll be.

❏ Talk with current students who are back from your study site. Did any of them work or perform an internship while there?

❏ If yes, did they do it during the semester or after? How did they arrange it?

❏ Read the sections of all the "work abroad" books that mention the country/city where you'll be.

❏ Read back issues of *Transitions Abroad* magazine.

While abroad...

❏ Maintain a "contacts" notebook. Include the name, address, and phone number, and if available, the e-mail address of every interesting professional you meet.

❏ Contact the alumni whose names and addresses you collected. Meet them at their place of business or socially. Express your interest in staying on after your program of study ends to work, or your interest in returning after graduation.

❏ Check out the local "yellow pages" and scan the daily paper's want ads for future reference. What types of jobs seem to be available?

❏ Look for schools that teach English and go check them out. What qualifications/credentials do the teachers have?

❏ If in a homestay, talk with adults in the family about the local economy. Take every opportunity to meet the family's friends and extended family to network.

❏ Practice, practice, practice the local language. Speak with "natives" in all walks of life constantly. Read the local and national papers and periodicals.

❏ When you encounter older Americans living in that city, introduce yourself. Make polite inquiries about where they are employed, and how they obtained their positions.

❏ Pay attention to the cost of living there as opposed to the United States. Figure out how much money you would need to live there.

❏ Have a friend come to the Career Center to pick up (domestic) summer job and internship information for you if you plan to return to the U.S. immediately after you study abroad.

❏ If graduate study in that country might be an option, get application information while you're there. Go directly to the universities to gather this information.

When you return...

❏ Go to the Career Center for a description of services for job hunting seniors. Attend all relevant job-hunting workshops.

❏ Learn whether firms with offices abroad recruit on campus. Don't be surprised to learn that you'll need to work in the U.S. first!

❏ Ascertain whether you will need a higher degree to obtain the job you want. What graduate entrance exams are required? Where in the U.S. or abroad can that degree be earned?

❏ Make time to gather and peruse short-term and more permanent work abroad resources.

❏ Prepare your resume. Make sure it dynamically describes your experience abroad and language skills. Prepare one resume for U.S. employment and another for employment abroad.

❏ Keep in touch with the contacts you gathered abroad. Write to them, stating your serious interest in returning to work in that country after graduation (if you are serious).

❏ Investigate short-session programs that teach the Teaching of English as a Second Language. Will they help with job placement?

❏ Determine your financial situation. Must you earn money before you go? How long can you afford to live abroad?

❏ Find a buddy with whom to job hunt. Two heads are better than one, and you can share leads and contacts.

▮ Organizations Mentioned in This Chapter

The following organizations were discussed in this chapter. The bibliography in the Appendix provides contact information for more work abroad programs.

AEON Intercultural Corporation, 203 N. LaSalle St. #2100, Chicago IL 60601; (312) 251-0900; http://www.aeonet.com

AIESEC (International Association of Students in Economic & Business Management), 135 W. 50th St. 20th Floor, New York NY 10020; (212) 757-3774; aiesec@aiesec.org; http://www.aiesec.org

AIPT (Association for International Practical Training) / IAESTE, 10400

Little Patuxent Pkwy Suite 250, Columbia MD 21044-3510; (410) 997-2200, fax (410) 992-3924; aipt@aipt.org; http://www.aipt.org

American Friends Service Committee, 1501 Cherry St., Philadelphia PA 19102; (215) 241-7141, fax (215) 241-7026; info@afsc.org; http://www.afsc.org

American-Scandinavian Foundation, 725 Park Ave., New York NY 10021; (212) 879-9779, fax (212) 249-3444; asf@amscan.org

Amigos de las Americas, 5618 Star Lane, Houston TX 77057; (800) 231-7796 or (713) 782-5290, fax (713) 782-9267; info@amigoslink.org; http://www.amigoslink.org

Brethren Colleges Abroad, Manchester College, North Manchester IN 46962; (219) 982-5238, fax (219) 982-7755.

Brethren Volunteer Service, 1451 Dundee Ave., Elgin IL 60120; (847) 742-5100, fax (847) 742-6103; cdb_bvs.parti@ecunet.org

CDS International, 330 Seventh Ave., New York NY 10001; (212) 497-3500, fax (212) 497-3535; cdsintl.org; http://www.cdsintl.org

Center for Interim Programs, P.O. Box 2347, Cambridge MA 02238; (617) 547-0980, fax (617) 661-2864; interim@thecia.net; http://www.thecia.net/users/interim/index.html

Central European Teaching Program, Beloit College Box 242, 700 College St., Beloit WI 53511; (608) 363-2619, fax (608) 363-2689; mullenm@beloit.edu, http://www.beloit.edu/~cetp

Council Work Abroad / Council International Volunteer Programs, CIEE, 205 E. 42nd St., New York NY 10017-5706; (888) COUNCIL; http://www.ciee.org

CEP (Civic Education Project), P.O. Box 205445, Yale Station, New Haven CT 06520-5445; (203) 781-0263, fax (203) 781-0265; cep@cep.yale.edu; http://cep.nonprofit.net

CNN, Turner Broadcasting System, One CNN Center, P.O. Box 105366, Atlanta GA 30348-5366; (404) 827-1700.

Department of Defense Dependents Schools, 4040 N. Fairfax Drive, Arlington VA 22203-1634; (703) 696-3269.

Earlham College, Institute for Education on Japan, Drawer 202, Richmond IN 47374-4095; (317) 983-1324.

Earthwatch, 680 Mt. Auburn St., Watertown MA 02272; (800) 776-0188, fax (617) 926-8532; info@earthwatch.org; http://gaia.earthwatch.org

Foundation for a Civil Society, Masaryk Fellowship Program, Suite 609,

1270 Avenue of the Americas, New York NY 10020; (212) 332-2890, fax (212) 332-2898; 73303.3024@compuserve.com

Fulbright English Teaching Assistantships, U.S. Student Programs Division, IIE, 809 United Nations Plaza, New York NY 10017-3580; (212) 984-5330; bcagney@iie.org; http://www.iie.org

Fulbright Teacher Exchange Program (K-12 & community college), U.S. Information Agency, 600 Maryland Ave. SW, Room 235, Washington DC; (800) 726-0479 or (202) 401-9418; http://www.usia.gov.

Fulbright Scholars (university teaching), Council for International Exchange of Scholars (CIES), 3007 Tilden St., Suite 5 M, Washington DC 20008-3009; (202) 686-4000; info@ciesnet.cies.org; http://www.cies.org

GEOS Language Corporation, Ontario Simpsons Tower, Suite 2424, 401 Bay St., Toronto Ontario M5H 2Y4, Canada; (416) 777-0109, fax (416) 777-0110.

Goshen College, International Education, 1700 S. Main St., Goshen IN 46526; (219) 535-7346, fax (219) 535-7319; http://www.goshen.edu/sst/International.html

Hess Language School, 4 Horicon Ave., Glens Falls NY 12801; phone/fax (518) 793-6183; http://www.hess.com.tw

IAESTE (International Association for the Exchange of Students for Technical Experience), see AIPT above; (410) 997-3068.

InterExchange, 161 Sixth Avenue, New York NY 10013; (212) 924-0446, fax (212) 924-0575; interex@earthlink.net

International Cooperative Education Program, 15 Spiros Way, Menlo Park CA 94025; (415) 323-4944, fax (415) 323-1104; icemenlo@aol.com

ISS (International Schools Services), P.O. Box 5910, 15 Roszel Road, Princeton NJ 08543-5910; (609) 452-0990, fax (609) 452-2690; edustaffing@iss.edu; http://www.iss.edu.

JET (Japan Exchange and Teaching Program), Embassy of Japan, 2520 Massachusetts Ave. NW, Washington DC 20008; (800) INFO-JET or (202) 939-6772.

Jesuit Volunteers International, P.O. Box 25478, Washington DC 20007; (202) 687-1132, fax (202) 687-5082; jvi@gunet.georgetown.edu; http://guweb.georgetown.edu/jvc

Los Ninos, 287 G St., Chula Vista CA 91910; (619) 426-9110; losninos@electriciti.com; http://www.electriciti.com/~losninos

Mennonite Central Committee, 21 S. 12th St., Akron Pa 17501; (717) 859-1151, fax (717) 859-2171; mailbox@mcc.org; http://www.mbnet.mb.ca/mcc

Mobility International USA (MIUSA), Box 10767, Eugene OR 97440; (541) 343-1284, fax (514) 343-6812; miusa@igc.apc.org

Operation Crossroads Africa, 475 Riverside Dr., Suite 830, New York NY 10027; (212) 870-2106, fax (212) 870-2055; ocainc@aol.com

Overseas Development Network, 333 Valencia St., Suite 330, San Francisco CA 94103; (415) 431-4204, fax (415) 431-5953; odn@igc.org

Partnership for Service Learning, 815 Second Ave., Suite 315, New York NY 10017; (212) 986-0989, fax (212) 986-5039; pslny@aol.com

Peace Corps, PRU Box 941, Washington DC 20526; (800) 424-8580; http://www.peacecorps.gov

Princeton-in-Asia, 224 Palmer Hall, Princeton NJ 08544;

(609) 258-3657, fax (609) 258-5300; pia@phoenix.princeton.edu

Proctor & Gamble, Internship Program Manager, P.O. Box 599, Cincinnati OH 45201-0599; (513) 983-1100.

SCI-International Voluntary Service, 5474 Walnut Level Road, Crozet VA 22932l; (804) 823-1826, fax (804) 823-5027; sciivsusa@igc.apc.org

Search Associates / International Schools Internship Program, P.O. Box 636, Dallas PA 18612; (717) 696-5400, fax (717) 696-9500.

United Nations, Coordinator of the Internship Program, Room F 2590, New York NY 10017; (212) 963-4437, fax (212) 963-3683.

United Nations Volunteers (see Peace Corps); (202) 606-3370; http://www.peacecorps.gov/

University of Northern Iowa, Overseas Placement Service for Educators, SSC #19, Cedar Falls IA 50614-0390; (319) 273-2083, fax (319) 273-6998.

University of Minnesota Studies in International Development, 106 A Nicholson Hall, 216 Pillsbury Dr. SE, Minneapolis MN 55455-0138; (612) 625-3379, fax (612) 626-8009; global@maroon.tc.umn.edu

U.S. State Department, Student Intern Program, Recruitment Division, Box 9317, Arlington VA 22219; (703) 875-4884; http://www.state.gov

VFP (Volunteers for Peace), 43 Tiffany Road, Belmont VT 05730; (802) 259-2759, fax (802) 259-2922; vfp@vermontel.com; http://www.vfp.org

Volunteers-in-Asia, Haas Center for Public Service, P.O. Box 4543, Stanford CA 94309; (415) 723-3228; via@igc.apc.org

Western Washington University, China Teaching Program, Old Main 530A, Bellingham WA 98225-9047; (360) 650-3753, fax (360) 650-2847; ctp@cc.wwu.edu

WISE (Worldwide Internships and Service Education), 303 S. Craig St., Suite 202, Pittsburgh PA 15213; (412) 681-8120, fax (412) 681-8187; wise+@pitt.edu; http://www.pitt.edu/~wise

World Learning/Au Pair, 1015 Fifteenth St. NW, Suite 750, Washington DC 20005; (202) 408-5380.

WorldTeach, Harvard Institute for International Development, One Eliot St., Cambridge MA 02138-5705; (617) 495-5527, fax (617) 495-1599; worldteach@hiid.harvard.edu; http://www.hiid.harvard.edu/programs/wteach.htm

World Zionist Organization, 110 E. 59th St., New York NY 10022; (800) 27-ISRAEL, fax (212) 755-4781; usd@netcom.com; http://www.wzo.org.il

18 Program Evaluation

Contributors: Ronald Pirog and Patricia C. Martin

The evaluation of overseas study programs is multifaceted, time-consuming, and never-ending. The first step to an effective evaluation process is the establishment, within the mission statement of the home institution, pedagogical guidelines and goals for international education by which all programs can be measured. The criteria on which the evaluation depends should be consistent as possible across programs, although the methods of assessment will vary according to the variety of sources of information that are available. Adequate staff time and funds should be allocated to the process, so that evaluation is an integral part of the planning and operations of the study abroad office. You should also work closely with colleagues at your institution, across the United States, and with those overseas. The successful program evaluation relies on many sources of information and has as its reward the benefit that study abroad gives to your students and your institution.

The task of evaluating overseas education programs is understandably complicated. First of all, the sheer number of programs available (and the promise of more to come) adds to the formidable task of keeping current and seeing programs in relation to each other. Second, there are so many different types of programs in existence, ranging from U.S.-planned and -run traditional "island" programs and branch campuses to direct enrollment in foreign universities and exchanges—as well as experiential, service-learning, and internship programs. This superabundance of numbers and types makes the task extremely difficult—especially if one wants to compare the quality of one to another (see Chapter 16, "Program Designs and Strategies").

In addition, the spread of overseas programs beyond western Europe and into countries where the education system is not as familiar to U.S. campuses, exacerbates the challenge even more. Fact-finding site visits to such locations are expensive and time-consuming due to the distances involved. Yet further challenges are presented by the fact that study abroad programs are likely to embrace a far greater range of pedagogical approaches and structures than most campus-based academic programs. Many would assert, for instance, that the degree of experiential learning that takes place overseas is of a different order from what is possible at home. The question is how to "value" this, especially in relation to academic credit.

Evaluation becomes even more complex when one takes into account the fact that what may be seen as the ultimate rationale for study abroad—that it is unique and worthwhile *because* it presents learning modes and opportunities *not* available on the home campus—may be seen as its very deficiency by some faculty observers. For example, a program may get high marks because it complements or supplements work done on the home campus and thereby conforms to the institution's curriculum and academic standards. Yet another measure of a program's quality may relate to its ability to present entirely new and different academic, cultural, and personal experiences. This latter aspect is typically regarded as integral to the ideals of education abroad and may in fact be deemed as highly significant by program participants. Thus, the very qualities which make a given program special to some, make it questionable in the eyes of others.

The larger problem is that these singular elements are often not readily and systematically understood (or, if understood, not fully appreciated) precisely because they are introduced through a "foreign" system of learning, and are part of a different academic culture. Moreover, the results of learning carried out through initiative and personal involvement may be difficult to grade or otherwise assess when transferred back to the system of the home institution. As a result, the success of the (foreign) academic experience may even be seen as suspect by U.S. faculty members or others involved in the process of assessing program quality. This can be seen either as "U.S. academic chauvinism" or as "upholding U.S. academic standards."

Nevertheless, in spite of the aforementioned complexities, the need to evaluate programs (those run by one's own institution and/or those sponsored by others) remains crucial. This ongoing task provides a vital service to the home institution and to the individual student. Before beginning the task of evaluation, however, it is imperative that an institution (or education abroad office) first develop a systematic approach to evaluating programs so that the same standards can be applied to all.

As stressed in previous chapters, in developing this approach to assessing program quality, you need to ensure that your institution has established pedagogical guidelines and goals for international education—ideally, as part of its mission statement—and to make certain that an assessment of the effectiveness of education abroad is prominent in any campuswide review process. At the same time, international educators must be aware of how education abroad fits into this stated mission because without such a frame of institutional reference the task of evaluating overseas study programs will be incomplete and be conducted in isolation from the academic goals of the institution.

So, whether your institution has one program or a number of programs, whether your institution works from a limited list of "approved" programs or your students participate solely in programs sponsored by others, there must be an institutional commitment to program evaluation. As part of this commitment, certain aspects of programs should be evaluated each semester or year, and a thorough overarching examination of programs should be conducted on a three- to five-year cycle. Such a thorough evaluation naturally requires the budgeting of time and money, but without it the process will be haphazard or inconclusive. Moreover, without this attention to evaluation, the identification of any weaknesses will go unnoticed which may have serious consequences in regard to the effectiveness and reputation of a program.

This chapter will provide some basic guidelines to assist you in the process of evaluating overseas study programs. The first section focuses on *internal or institutional self-evaluation*; i.e., what needs to be done to evaluate programs sponsored by your own institution. The second section focuses on the *external evaluation* whereby evaluating programs sponsored by other U.S. colleges and universities and consortia, foreign universities, and agencies is the primary objective. The third will discuss particular *problems and guidelines* for assessing direct enrollment opportunities that function usually without benefit of an intermediary.

Although your institutional standards should be the same during the evaluation process, the methods used to evaluate the various types of programs are likely to differ.

∎ The Internal Evaluation

In establishing a regular approach to self-evaluation, specific objectives, evaluation criteria, and assessment procedures must be identified in the context of the institutional mission statement. The following general discussion of program evaluation will provide some concrete examples. Obviously, specific criteria and evaluation procedures will differ from one institution to the next in accordance with its own particular goals and objectives. Regardless of the scope of the evaluation or the level of institutional commitment, an institutional self-assessment should be an ongoing, regularly scheduled, systematic, and integral part of any institution's education abroad programming.

Criteria

Evaluation criteria must be general enough to allow for flexibility but specific enough to give the assessment a concrete direction and focus. The following are general criteria included in most institutional guidelines:

- Does the program help to fulfill the institution's overall mission, general goals, and strategic plan—i.e., does it do what it promises?
- What inherent academic quality or distinction does the program provide?
- Is the program's pedagogical methodology compatible with its defined goals?
- Is the program comparable in academic rigor to the home institution?
- To what extent does the program complement or supplement (rather than duplicate) coursework available at the home institution?
- What distinct advantage is given for basing the program abroad?
- What rationale is offered for the program's particular location?
- How desirable is such a program, given the institution's academic mission and the mission of cross-cultural education in general—i.e., what is the level of need and usage?
- How does the program fit into the overall array of overseas study programs offered by your institution (e.g., for a given geographic area and in regard to language study options or available academic subjects in general)?
- How effective is the program design in meeting the prescribed objectives of the program?

- To what extent does the program take advantage of the features and resources unique to education abroad, such as the level of integration into the host institution's academic and student life, the length of time spent abroad, and the nature and degree of exposure to the host culture and language?
- How available and adequate are the resources and support services abroad to ensure a viable program of high academic quality?
- What is the level of student and faculty interest and commitment in maintaining this particular kind of program?

Each of these general criteria can be further refined. In their very useful guide to program evaluation, *Study Abroad Programs: An Evaluation Guide* (May 1979), the Task Force on Study Abroad of the American Association of Collegiate Registrars and Admissions Officers (AACRAO) and NAFSA present program evaluation criteria in the form of 89 specific questions. These criteria are grouped into four general areas:

1. Basic Information:
   - The adequacy and accuracy of printed materials
   - The clarity of the program's objectives and the ways that the program and its location and resources contribute to the fulfillment of those objectives
   - Admissions requirements, their relation to the program's objectives, and the ways in which they are enforced
2. Academic Aspects:
   - How does the curriculum contribute to fulfilling the program objectives? How does it benefit from the host environment? How does it compare with the home curriculum in terms of level and degree of difficulty?
   - What are the qualifications and attitudes of the faculty teaching the courses abroad?
   - What are the academic resources (e.g., library and laboratory facilities, language labs, etc.)? How do they support the program's curriculum?
3. Interaction with the Host Culture:
   - Predeparture materials and on-site orientation sessions: are they adequate?
   - To what degree does the program promote and facilitate student interaction with the host culture?

Administrative Aspects:

- What is the extent and adequacy of administrative support at the home campus?
- How effective is the on-site support structure, including the resident director and administrative support staff?
- How is the program affiliated, if at all, with the host institution?
- Are housing and meal arrangements adequate?
- Are there sufficient support services (for example, personal and academic advising and health—both medical and psychological—services)?
- How much does the program cost and what will this include or not include? How accurate is the cost information available to the students?
- Are the travel arrangements adequate?

4. Sources of Information:

   In order to conduct an effective and thorough evaluation, you and your colleagues will need to solicit input from a wide variety of sources: survey questionnaires, interviews with returning students, on-site faculty and staff, the home campus's faculty and academic units, the study abroad staff, and outside evaluation teams. This approach is especially crucial in the early years of a program when a review can provide an opportunity to identify and correct problem areas.

Survey Questionnaires

One method of obtaining information is to send out survey questionnaires to all students immediately upon their return from abroad—these may be mailed to the home address or put in the campus mailbox for the return to campus. These questionnaires, also referred to as program evaluation forms, can be a useful way to gather information systematically on the many aspects of the overseas experience. When designing such a survey, it is important to consider the method of tabulating the results as well as the method of compiling and distributing the results.

A word of caution: Although it is tempting to produce a lengthy document, you must consider how much time a student may be willing to devote to this activity as well as how much time and resources you have to devote to this task. You may wish to choose one particular aspect of the program each year to better obtain feedback.

Similarly, you need to make the decision whether it is a requirement that the program receive a completed questionnaire from each participant and what can be done to ensure compliance. Some universities make the completion of the evaluation form mandatory, subject to the reporting of program courses on the student's transcript. A wise person once commented, however, "You can make them fill them out, but can you make them do so responsibly?" Ideally, the survey questionnaire should be considered an educational tool for the returning student; i.e., an instrument used to synthesize the various aspects of the total experience. Another way to achieve this goal is to have students write an essay upon their return, as a type of capstone to their experience.

Minimally, the evaluation form is a useful resource to obtain material for the orientation of future participants, as well as providing the home institution with much needed data. When making use of this information, it is necessary to ask permission from individual students before sharing comments beyond the study abroad staff or others responsible for collecting the data.

In 1986, NAFSA's Field Service division, with support from USIA, funded a seminar at Pennsylvania State University to develop a survey instrument for collecting information from returning study abroad participants. Forms based on the survey have been adapted for use at many institutions. Several examples can be found in *Forms of Travel: Essential Documents, Letters, and Flyers for Study Abroad Advisers*, ed. Judith W. Carr and Ellen Summerfield (Washington, DC: NAFSA, 1994).

Returning Students

Although survey instruments can be useful, they also have their limitations. Another method to obtain information is to invite returned students to a welcome-back get-together, at which time all aspects of the experience can be discussed. Students should also have the opportunity to schedule a personal interview in order to discuss (perhaps anonymously) issues or problem areas more personal in nature, thus not fitting for a group discussion forum.

This method of interviewing individual students, however, may cause another set of difficulties. The criteria students use to judge the value of their experience is likely to be quite different from those used to determine its creditworthiness. Sometimes these criteria are quite visceral (e.g., how much "fun" they had or how many new places they visited). More often, students are eager to reflect searchingly on how they have grown, how they see the world differently, how alive they felt when they were abroad, how they have a new sense of direction, or even how good it was just to get away from the routine of the home campus for awhile.

Such responses may or may not be relevant to an evaluation of the academic and administrative content of the program. Moreover, whatever a student's immediate conclusions, they are quite likely to change with time. For example, students overseas can sometimes remember the home campus as a place where problems were solved easily, forgetting that they endured, at times, as much frustration on the home campus as they later experienced on the study abroad program.

All of which is to say that if our professional and personal concerns are with the total educational value of the overseas experience, we should not rush to easy and oversimplified judgments. Thus it is recommended that the interviewer be prepared for the interview with specific questions (some of which may be prompted by information already obtained from the survey responses), and students should be encouraged to volunteer whatever information they consider relevant and significant.

Reports from On-Site Staff

The international programs office should receive periodic as well as annual reports from its on-site staff. The resident director or coordinator can identify problem areas and provide an insider's perspective on the relative success of the program. Resident directors should be provided with a set of criteria for program evaluation that include the nature and effectiveness of the following aspects:

- on-site orientation programs (arrival and predeparture)
- field trips and excursions
- extracurricular programs
- academic program, internships, grading practices/standards, credit transfer, effectiveness of instruction
- academic resources, facilities, library resources
- measurement of progress in language acquisition
- homestays
- health and safety issues
- on-site student program evaluations

Note: It is also important to schedule periodic visits by the resident director (and possibly other on-site staff) to the home campus in order to review policies and procedures and to learn more about the standards and goals of the home campus. This is especially true if the resident director is not a regular member of the home institution. This step can also make the evaluation process run more smoothly.

Site Visits

Site visits are an essential component of any ongoing self-evaluation. You, or someone from your office or from the advisory committee on international programs, needs to make periodic visits to each program sponsored by your institution. This is done to ascertain that acceptable levels of administrative and logistical support are being maintained, and to nurture rapport with, and elicit support from, the host faculty and staff. Provisions should also be made, either through the resident director or via a faculty representative visiting from the home institution, to assess course compatibility in terms of content and academic quality.

Faculty Oversight

It is one of the recurring themes of this publication that faculty should be involved in all stages of education abroad programming and advising. Your advisory committee, or a special campus academic program committee made up of faculty and administrators (and even student representatives), should be involved in any review. But whatever form the committee takes, its perspective on the extent to which specific overseas study programs are compatible with and fulfill the home institution's academic mission is fundamental (see Chapter 3, "Faculty Roles").

The curriculum may be reviewed from a variety of perspectives, depending on the criteria established by the institution for overseas study programs. Criteria can include, but are not limited to the credentials of teaching faculty, course content (description/syllabi/reading list), course contact hours and credits, program courses versus courses at the host (or other) institution, and how often students are assessed, i.e., the grading policy.

In addition to evaluating the curriculum, other aspects that should be taken into consideration by the campus advisory committee are: previous program reviews (for point of reference and/or comparison), enrollment trends, profiles of student participants, and faculty concerns and interests.

Outside Evaluators

Every effort should also be made to obtain the services of an outside evaluation team as a way of providing an objective cross-check of the institution's internal review at least every three to five years. As an example, the Commission on Higher Education of the Middle States Association of Colleges and Schools (CHE/MSA) has been providing a study abroad evaluation service to its member institutions since 1981. A CHE/MSA evaluator reviews all the pertinent written information about the program, then visits the program site for a day or two during its actual oper-ation—it is very important that any on-site evaluation take place when it is "business as usual."

During the site visit, the evaluator interviews as many students, facul-ty, and administrative staff members as possible and tries to assess a wide range of activities, including promotion and recruitment, selection and admission, orientation, any relevant financial aspects of the program, and the fit between, the curriculum and the mission and objectives of the home institution. The evaluator also talks to faculty about their percep-tions of the program; students are asked about their perceptions of the faculty and their overall experiences, both academic and cross-cultural. The evaluator then prepares a written report for submission to the home institution's chief executive officer and study abroad office.

The NAFSA Consultant Referral Service is an excellent source of sea-soned professional expertise, and other professional consultation within the field of international educational exchange is also available. CIEE also provides an evaluation service to its members, and informal arrange-ments are possible within many consortia.

Longitudinal Studies

Whether or not a particular study abroad program meets certain criteria can only be evaluated over a period of time. In this light, the study abroad office can work in conjunction with career planning and placement and alumni relations' staff to develop a method to track the progress of stu-dents after graduation. If the broader mission of overseas study programs is to prepare students to function and work across national boundaries, then the evaluation process should include assessing whether language and cultural acquisition along with practical experiences abroad have contributed to the attractiveness of program participants as job candi-dates. One of the first and most complete assessments of long-term effects of study abroad is the publication *Study Abroad: The Experience of American Undergraduates* (Greenwood Press, 1990) by Jerry S. Carlson, Barbara B. Burns, John Useem, and David Yachimowicz.

Studies of this nature provide much needed information for the assessment of whether overseas study programs have the predicted and desired outcome. Over time this information can help the direction of study abroad programming while providing data on outcomes that is extremely useful in the promotion of study abroad on campus.

Follow-Up

Clearly, maintaining the quality and integrity of a program is a never-ending process; as a consequence, no program review is complete without adequate follow-up, nor is any program without room for change or improvement. For example, a program you and others considered nearly perfect one year may be seen to be a near-disaster the next. Any number of factors can contribute to the relative success or failure of a program in a given year, as well as to perceptions about it—keeping current is a must.

By drawing on as many different sources as possible to ensure adequate cross-checks and differing perspectives, the program evaluation process must carefully interpret all available information in light of clearly defined institutional criteria. Only then can the institution make appropriate judgments or necessary changes. Given the dynamic conditions and circumstances surrounding education abroad, every program must be considered a potential subject for revision and refinement. A systematic approach to self-evaluation and follow-up will help the institution maintain effective programs that fulfill its goals.

▌ Evaluating External Programs

When U.S. students who study overseas are enrolled in programs sponsored directly by their own institutions, there is a good measure of home-campus control over academic and economic matters. It also means that when an institution concludes, through its own internal evaluation, that a program is not working well, it can be changed or dropped. However, few institutions can offer all the programs its students might be interested in. Even campuses with many of their own programs have to consider allowing at least some students to look elsewhere. And, many campuses, especially small ones, offer few or no programs of their own, so all students seeking an education abroad experience must participate in outside programs. This makes the task of evaluating external programs a primary concern for all involved.

Unfortunately, given the current number and range of programs, there is no easy way to approach assessment. Even compiling a list of approved programs can be a laborious task. Most reputable U.S. institutions, consortia, and agencies do their own evaluations, but the results are usually not widely available. Nor is it very feasible for you to do site visits, even brief ones, to every program your students are interested in. If you can find the time, money, and energy to visit those programs abroad used frequently by your institution, however, such an undertaking would be very worthwhile. Some organizations and agencies regularly sponsor such opportunities. Most, however, do not.

What can often face an adviser in a minimally staffed office is increasing quantities of study abroad brochures all painting a very positive picture of the promised experience. When other factors, such as student motivation, wish-fulfillment, and perhaps gullibility are added, an adviser's job in trying to confidently evaluate programs and provide relevant advising services is challenging indeed. There are some guidelines, however, that can help in identifying programs that meet both the interests of an institutions' students and that institutions' academic goals.

Criteria

The general criteria discussed above for evaluating your own programs ought to be equally applicable for judging external programs. In both cases the questions concern the criteria of comparable quality and suitability: Are the academic standards of the overseas program comparable to those of the home campus? Does the program offer something unique and important that cannot be obtained at the home institution? Does the program provide a truly intercultural experience or just a different setting? Are students properly fed, housed, and counseled? Is student performance adequately and fairly judged? If programs are seen to duplicate any of your own programs in curriculum, location, or emphasis, an additional criterion might take into consideration comparative overall quality or perhaps cost.

In the case of the programs that compete with your own offerings, there should probably be compelling academic reasons for approving, or recommending, participation in an external program—if a choice has to be made. In programs of comparable quality, however, economic considerations that benefit students may occasionally conflict with economic considerations that impact your own program and institution.

Sources of Information

Obtaining enough reliable, objective information about external programs can be a frustrating part of the evaluation process. Nevertheless, you should still be able to assess the quality of external programs and get the answers you, your colleagues, and your students need, if you take a systematic approach to evaluating the information at hand.

Guides

At the earliest stages of assessment, you will often need a succinct and accurate overview of the full-range of aspects related to a program. The IIE and Peterson's guides provide this. Although this information is furnished by sponsors and may not be absolutely accurate in every particular detail, the guides do their best to keep it current, to define carefully what its terms mean, and to be impartial. No qualitative questions can be answered by these listings, but hard information can be obtained. So, it is important that you know how to interpret what is written.

Program Materials

Perhaps understandably in the age of consumerism and hype, materials sent to your campus (or available on the World Wide Web) by other universities, consortia, and agencies trying to interest you and your students in their programs are likely to be unbalanced mixtures of hard information and soft sell. The current level of verbal and visual hyperbole is very sophisticated. Let the reader beware! At the same time, respectable programs provide good, ample, detailed information in their materials. Nevertheless, brochures, fliers, posters, web pages, even perhaps videos must be examined critically. At the same time, do not hesitate to contact program sponsors and ask them to send copies of course materials, program handbooks, acceptance letters, cost estimates, orientation materials, and the like to aid in the process of evaluation.

Some institutions set up procedures whereby advisory or academic program committees review materials before a decision is made to allow students to participate in a particular program. This makes it easier to evaluate the program when the student returns, because the actual experience abroad can be compared with the printed materials. Other campuses initially evaluate courses for (major, minor, or elective) credit, often granting only temporary approval until the student returns with course materials and copies of all work completed. Some campuses provide self-help guides to assist students in evaluating their needs.

Program Representatives

Many programs (even some foreign universities) send representatives to campus to discuss their programs. If you have the opportunity to host such a visit, a great deal of useful information and insight can be gained. To make the most out of this visit, you should make sure that you have first reviewed all relevant materials, including any available student evaluations, in order to be able to get at matters that are not clear or to discuss current developments in the program or on your campus. If you have questions or concerns, this is the time to bring them up. If the representative cannot answer a particular question, make sure that ultimately it is answered, or draw your own conclusions about why it is not. It is worthwhile being open and honest with your questions; some program representatives are very knowledgeable about their programs but also are aware that some students would not be suited and will honestly discuss other programs; other program representatives are more like salesmen for a particular product.

In addition to your own private conversation, it also can be very helpful to arrange for the program representative to meet with your advisory committee, appropriate faculty in key departments, and perhaps the academic dean. Often representatives also wish to hold general information meetings with interested students. Unless this is impossible (e.g., there may be a conflict of interest in regard to your own programs), you should support this initiative as a way for students to learn more about the program. Any former participants and/or visiting foreign students from the country in which the program is located might also be invited. As with reading program materials, it is important to consider what is and is not said in these meetings.

Student Evaluations

As in the case of an internal evaluation of programs, reading the evaluations of, and conducting interviews with, students who have returned from a program overseas can be invaluable. Unlike the situation with your own programs, where you have access to a vast amount of collective opinion, it is unlikely that student assessments of external programs will be voluminous, at least for a given semester or year.

A word of caution: try not to give too much weight to any one student's evaluation, positive or negative; the more readings you have, the closer you get to an objective view. But do check evaluations from previous years to determine any patterns of change. It is also accepted practice to request evaluations from students at other institutions or from the program itself. When serious discrepancies or concerns arise from these comparisons, further discussions with students or with the program sponsor, or even with the program itself are in order.

Using Students as Test Cases

If the desired information about a particular overseas program is not forthcoming, it is sometimes necessary to use one student as a "test case." Obviously, you need to be frank with the student about credit prospects. When the student returns and the record is available for review, a decision will then have to be made about whether to approve the program, place it on an informal "worry list," or drop it altogether from future consideration. Prudence dictates, of course, that a single student's evaluation be weighed together with the insights of colleagues, the opinions of students at other universities, or by initiating contact with the program directly.

Contact with Colleagues

Making contact with trusted colleagues at comparable institutions is another valuable resource in the evaluation process. In some regions, where numerous advisers from similar types of colleges or universities are geographically proximate, occasional meetings can be held several times a year for the purpose of comparing notes on programs. Too-public discussions about particular programs (for instance at NAFSA conferences or SECUSS-L over the e-mail network) are prone to cause hard feelings and also in some cases can lead to legal complications. Conversely, open and free discussions about how to improve the general quality of education abroad programs and programming are essential.

Other Sources of Information

- A survey of one's own campus to learn whether a faculty member or other person may already have knowledge about the program in question, may have visited the site in question, or may plan to be in the area on sabbatical and could visit a site or sites.
- Foreign students on campus may be familiar with programs in their country or be willing to visit a certain program upon their return home.
- Students who are overseas (studying or just traveling) might be able to visit a particular site or meet with students from other programs and share their impressions.
- Parents who plan to visit children on a particular program might be contacted as well to solicit their impressions.
- Alumni living overseas might be willing to visit a site in their area.

▌ Direct Enrollment

Most of what has been said thus far pertains to overseas programs sponsored by U.S.-based institutions or organizations. The process of evaluating overseas programs becomes much more difficult and complicated when a student intends to enroll directly into a foreign institution or program without going through an intermediary sponsor.

Criteria

Direct enrollment will require a somewhat different set of criteria for the evaluation process than is used for U.S.-administered or -sponsored overseas study programs. If students are directly matriculated, the evaluation, in effect, represents an assessment of a foreign educational institution, or at least a single foreign university. If they are in a special program, set up for foreigners, different problems may arise. One problem is that information about course offerings and services provided may not be available in a predetermined or timely fashion. In fact, students will often be required to obtain the needed information and send it to the home institution if any kind of assessment is to take place.

Sources of Information

Office of Foreign Student Affairs

Fortunately, an increasing number of foreign institutions have set up international program offices to deal with overseas students. Contact them directly and ask them to send a catalogue and other literature. Many of these universities also send representatives to the U.S. on campus visits; request a visit to your campus. As a result of these visits, many overseas institutions are becoming more aware of U.S. students' needs while abroad as well as policies about grade assessment and credit transfer.

Overseas International Education Organizations

Organizations, such as the Japanese Association for Foreign Student Affairs (JAFSA), the European Association for International Education (EAIE), NAFSA's professional educator group for overseas educational advisers (OSEAS), the Australian Association for International Education (AAIE), the British Universities Transatlantic Exchange Association (BUTEX), and others that are counterparts to NAFSA can provide valuable information about contacting overseas institutions during the process of evaluating direct enrollment schemes.

The American Association of Collegiate Registrars and Admissions Officers (AACRAO)

An organization such as AACRAO provides information about the transferability of work done (i.e., credit and transcript evaluation) through direct enrollment at foreign institutions. Your colleagues in the admissions office and the registrar's office might also be able to provide some assistance. There are also a number of private organizations (and consultants) that specialize in evaluating transcripts from foreign institutions;

while this sort of credential evaluation is usually for foreign students, it can be applicable for American students who have studied in a foreign university.

Contact with Colleagues

Attendance at the regional and national conferences of NAFSA (or at one or more of the abovementioned overseas counterparts) can provide an excellent setting for discussing program evaluation in connection with direct enrollment. You can often locate colleagues from U.S. institutions (ideally comparable to your own) who have a program at or otherwise send students to the institution and can provide the information that you will require for your evaluation. What is more, you will usually be able to establish direct contact with the representatives of foreign institutions.

Other Agencies

Another approach, though more time consuming and cumbersome, is to check with the accrediting agencies of the country in question (e.g., the ministry of education), the U.S. embassies/consulates in that country, the U.S. Department of Education, or with the many handbooks dealing with the subject of evaluating overseas institutions.

Other Sources of Information

Your institution may have a guest student from the overseas institution in question who would be more than willing to discuss details with you. Similarly, faculty members on your campus may have knowledge about the institution or are in touch with colleagues from the overseas institution.

Your main objective in all of these approaches is to use whatever method or resource is available to ensure that the program meets the two basic criteria of comparable quality and suitability.

19 Legal Issues

Contributors: Robert Aalberts and Gary Rhodes

It is naive and dangerous to assume that education abroad advising and program administration exist in a vacuum, apart from the legal context of U.S. higher education. Acknowledging that overseas programs and those who work with them are indeed legally bound by the same rules and parameters that guide domestic programs, however, is only a first step to wisdom. Wise international educators should take a variety of steps to reduce actual risks to participants and legal risks to the institution. This involves seeking the help of campus legal counsel and risk-management personnel to understand and minimize institutional legal exposure.

We live in litigious times. Many Americans, both in their public and private affairs, are apprehensive about, and feel vulnerable to, the threat of lawsuits—as do most U.S. institutions and the people who run them. College and university life, from a legal standpoint, is complex enough. But when a foreign dimension is added, concerns are likely to grow. Anything far away and foreign may seem, to an isolated campus administrator, inherently more risky. But, until recently, potential legal issues related to education abroad advising and programming have not received much attention.

This neglect may owe something to the tendency of international educators to accentuate the many positives of study and work abroad and to the fact that there have been remarkably few documented instances of legal difficulties for institutions or programs over the years. This does not mean that no problems have occurred, but rather that they have been not been publicized—for a variety of institutional reasons. Under the circumstances, it behooves education abroad advisers and administrators, on behalf of their institutions, to become more aware of potential legal *good phrase!*

issues and take steps to lessen danger to their institution, through prudence and planning.

As discussed elsewhere in this book, students in education abroad programs may face some potential risks to their health and safety. Although it is tempting to dismiss those risks by noting the greater dangers facing students on college and university campuses and in U.S. domestic life, several serious liability issues related specifically to education abroad programming must be recognized and addressed. The recent expansion of programs into nontraditional geographical areas—particularly in developing countries, where health and political risks are assumed, often incorrectly, to be greater than in traditional study locales in western Europe—has also increased concerns. But true security is less a matter of what happens where than of *being prepared for the worst* wherever and whenever it might occur, and in doing everything possible to make sure that it does not happen.

The death or injury of a student or staff member poses the greatest potential cost to institutions. In the past few years, cases of serious illness and injury on study abroad have included drowning, malaria, leishmaniasis, and a fall from a cliff during an excursion. In the spring of 1996, a chartered bus taking a group of U.S. students to the Taj Mahal in India ran off the road, killing four American students and injuring numerous others. Apart from the human sorrow they cause, such accidents can result in very expensive lawsuits and jeopardize the future of programs.

Even threats of terrorism and civil unrest can seriously damage a program's future. In 1986, in the wake of the *Achille Lauro* cruise ship hijacking and the terrorist murder of American tourists at the Rome and Vienna airports, at least three education abroad programs were discontinued or interrupted, though most continued, albeit with enhanced security procedures. Two years later, some programs were halted in the Middle East, parts of South America, and China when violence erupted in these troubled areas. The terrorist bombing of Pan Am Flight 103 brought terrorism to the forefront with the deaths of study abroad students on their return to the United States. Several years later national attention focused on the killing of an American Fulbright student in South Africa. In 1995 a U.S. student in Russia died after being thrown out of a dormitory window, reportedly by local hoodlums. More recently an American student was killed by terrorists on a bus in Jerusalem.

The striking feature of these harrowing events is that, even though the statistical chances of Americans—soldiers, business people, diplomats, tourists, or students—being attacked by terrorists or caught in civil disturbances are indeed small, the fear of violence and danger abroad (compounded by vivid news reports) can quickly impair and even destroy years of hard work and dedication in putting together a fine educational program.

It is therefore vitally important for institutions to be aware of the difference between real and perceived dangers, and in all cases to recognize their legal obligations and responsibilities when they develop or maintain education abroad programs for their own and other students. Whether harm is caused by acts of nature or by human carelessness, institutions are seen as being responsible for putting program participants in its way. Simple disclaimers signed by students before they depart may provide little legal protection if negligence on the part of the program or institution can be established.

But natural catastrophes or political strife are not the only problems that can result in expensive legal action. In point of fact, the litigation that has recently been bedeviling colleges and universities has centered less on physical injury or death than on a host of other contractual matters: admissions standards and criteria, student misbehavior and appropriate discipline, misunderstandings over the nature of the academic program, disagreements over what is included in the program fee, and other more mundane but essential details.

▌ The Law and Education Abroad—Some Basics

Education abroad advising and programming does not exist apart from the legal strictures and constraints that apply to U.S. higher education, even if the center of the student experience occurs on foreign shores. It is hard, in fact, to identify any area of administration or advising, domestic or foreign, that is not in some way affected by U.S. law. In addition, your institution and students are responsible for knowing and respecting the laws of any country where your programs operate or students are sent.

Almost every college and university has a person or an office responsible for institutional risk management and insurance. In addition, all institutions employ legal counsel—on their payroll or on call—who formally advise the institution on how to reduce risks and avoid damaging legal situations. If the institution faces legal action, such individuals provide legal representation in and out of court.

As an adviser or administrator you should have a basic understanding of the legal issues related to education abroad. Such knowledge will help you to work effectively with the individuals on your campus who are responsible for formulating institutional policies and procedures that limit legal exposure. In this joint endeavor, institutional legal counsel and risk management officers should become your closest colleagues.

Working with such colleagues, you should endeavor to become familiar with at least the basic concepts of effective and prudent administrative practice in relation to the following concepts, doctrines, and statutes:

Age Discrimination in Employment Act; affirmative action policy; alternative dispute resolution; Americans with Disabilities Act of 1990; alcohol liability; assumption of risk; Campus Assault Victims Bill of Rights; choice of forum and choice of law; comparative negligence; constitutional law, including freedoms of speech, religion, assembly, and press; conflict of interest; contract law; defamation of character and libel; Drug Free Schools and Communities Act of 1989; drug-free workplace; duty of landowner to maintain safe premises; duty to protect invitees; duty of landowner to control third persons; duty of reasonable standard of care; duty to supervise; Family Educational Rights and Privacy Act; due process, procedural and substantive; financial aid guidelines, federal and state; unreasonable search and seizure; harassment, sexual and racial; high-risk vs. risk-limited activities; Higher Education Act of 1965; *in loco parentis* and special relationships; individual and institutional liability; insurance, major medical, evacuation, repatriation; international agreements/treaties; legal audit; negligence; nonprofit organization tax status; personal injury; potential dangers and risks; prior restraint; private vs. public institution regulations; Rehabilitation Act of 1973 (Section 504); student disciplinary process and procedure; Student Right to Know and Campus Security Act; Title IX requirements; Title VI of the Civil Rights Act of 1964; Title VII of the Civil Rights Act of 1964; tort liability; transportation liability.

None of the above were developed specifically with regard to overseas study. But if you become familiar with what domestic legal compliance means, the legal issues pertaining to education abroad will become clearer. Advisers and administrators should take advantage of the expertise of student- and academic-affairs administrators in these regards.

Look at features of your program and match them to relevant administrators on your campus. This will assist you in getting advice on how to deal with potential problems in those areas. Maintaining consistent policies and procedures on campus and abroad is something to aim for. Only through your continuing communication with the many administrative arms of your institution can your programs operate effectively.

As argued elsewhere, education abroad represents an overseas extension and diversification of U.S.-degree studies and career preparation. Study abroad programs are covered by domestic higher education law because American colleges and universities are supported, to varying degrees, by state revenues. Both public and private institutions receive federal funding through direct grants and loans to students who qualify for them, as well as for research and special programming. Even at private universities, more than 60 percent of students might be receiving financial aid in the form of grants and subsidized loans from state and/or federal government.

Because many students participating in study abroad programs remain registered at their home campus and use U.S. government aid, federal and state law remain relevant. Institutions cannot ignore U.S. law simply because the actual programs take place elsewhere. It is certainly the case that many students and parents assume that students will have the same support and protection of the college or university while abroad. Program publications and communications may seem to assure parents and students that programs are perfectly "safe."

The legal principle of *stare decisis* (or "let the decision stand") directs legal experts to look at previous decisions for legal precedent. While there is not much established legal precedent with regard to education abroad in particular, U.S. higher education law in general may provide legal precedent that can give guidance to those looking for direction in developing education abroad policies and procedures. Two major bodies of law—those related to contracts and torts—are particularly relevant for students and faculty in a study abroad program.

Contract Law

Contracts regulate myriad relationships from the mundane to the most consequential. If constructed properly and with foresight, contracts are able to regulate legal relationships and prevent or mitigate problems. Education abroad programs often involve complicated relationships and issues. A program's continuing viability depends on your knowing and respecting these issues and articulating them in program agreements and formal contracts. All documents that could be interpreted to provide a contract or agreement between your institution and a foreign (or domes-

be careful w/ marketing DO'g info

tic) partner institution, as well as with student participants, therefore need to be developed in conjunction with, and with the clear approval of, institutional legal counsel.

The use of promotional brochures and advertisements constitutes one area with the greatest potential for contractual difficulties. Promotional language used to describe a program, it is often argued, implies a contractual relationship. By promising more than the program can deliver, or even by appearing to offer something of value to students, study abroad programs can raise expectations. When these are not met, breach of contract suits may result.

A well-settled rule of contract law is that ambiguous or misleading language is construed against the party who writes it. Materials describing a program should pay heed to this rule by being honest and specific in describing accommodations and support services. One way to be clear about potential hidden costs is to include a question about costs in your evaluation—then listen to what students say and recycle it into your materials. Cost is a decisive factor for students choosing a program, so all program expenses should be clearly stated in the program literature—including, for example, side excursions, entertainment, events, and so forth, that require extra money.

Contracts can be used to shift risks not only to other universities and businesses but also to students through the use of releases and disclaimers. If a program includes high-risk activities like scuba diving or mountain climbing, the program literature dispensed to students should describe the dangers involved. Further, document your discussions of risk with your students not only to demonstrate that the institution is passing along a consistent message but also to ensure that the students understand. To be clear that specific risks are shifted to students, for example, the program can insert releases and disclaimers in contracts drawn up for them to see and sign.

Materials given to students should include health and safety information and resources for the country where they will be studying. Such material should identify program-related activities and distinguish these from living and traveling independently of the program. When a student is a minor, it is important that the parents or guardians sign all important documents as well.

Another contract law issue concerns the relationships with the many parties that supply the program's goods and services. Education abroad programs may, for example, contract with local educational or other

356

institutions for use of their facilities, with local transportation companies for bus and car service for side excursions, with other colleges, universities, and organizations, as well as with travel agencies providing transportation and other logistical help. It is important first to find out all you can about all organizations you choose to work with. Second, the contracts should articulate the limits of each institution's responsibility.

In all these relationships, one of the most important functions of a contract should be to allocate risk and responsibility among the parties. In the case of any misunderstandings, a contract can clarify which institution was responsible for which details. For example, if a university contracts with a local travel agency for services and the agency is negligent in providing the agreed-upon services, the university itself may be the one sued first by any aggrieved parties. In fact, a plaintiff's attorney is likely to attempt to sue anyone and everyone connected in any way with a mishap.

If the university must later pay the court's judgment or a portion of it, a contract clause that states that the agency will reimburse or indemnify the university can greatly facilitate the recapture of lost monies. Contracts detailing which party bears what risks and responsibilities are greatly preferable and much more efficient than relying on the outcome of expensive, prolonged litigation. Education abroad programs should inspect their contract language with an experienced attorney. While this should be done to protect and limit your institution's liability, the detailing process can also clarify the responsibilities of each organization to ensure effective program administration.

The legal status of the education abroad program can also influence your institution's legal exposure. A program may be a joint venture or a mutual exchange program with a foreign university; it may be incorporated as a foreign corporation under the laws of the host country; it may be part of a U.S. consortium supporting students from various institutions; or it may be a unit of a U.S. college situated in a foreign locale. Each type of legal status possesses different vulnerabilities with respect to legal and political risks, expenses, and control.

For example, if your university creates its own foreign corporation in Italy, it could ultimately be shielded from a large U.S. judgment because the Italian corporation could be found liable. Under contract law, the Italian corporation could be the party having contracts with suppliers of goods and services. However, the Italian corporation would have to be created and operate under Italian laws. It would probably be required to hire local accountants and lawyers, file tax returns, and involve local citizens in the corporation's governance. In contrast, a transferred foreign campus structure generally allows your university more autonomy from local laws and officials but exposes it to the legal environment of the litigious United States. In the abstract, all sorts of program models and structures are possible. Each has pros and cons, and these need to be investigated thoroughly before contracts are signed.

Additional Clauses

Other doctrines in U.S. law define the legal relationship between the college or university and its students. Invoking such doctrines in contracts with students may provide the institution some protection. Clauses pertaining to choice of forum and choice of law, in fact, appear routinely in contracts and have been effectively used by businesses engaged in international transactions for years.

Choice of Forum

This clause clarifies which jurisdiction—usually a state or country—will be the setting of a lawsuit under the contract, should one arise. For example, a program in Italy sponsored by a university in, say, Colorado would likely choose the State of Colorado as its forum. A plaintiff would have to commence the suit in Colorado, even if he resided in Georgia. If this clause were not in the contract, the student might be able to sue the Colorado university in Georgia, or even in Italy. Such ambiguity puts the institution at a great strategic and procedural disadvantage.

To survive legally, the forum clause must be "reasonable"; that is, it must be designed to create predictability and efficiency in prosecuting a case. In most litigation arising in an international studies program, the selection of the host university's state would likely satisfy the legal demands of reasonableness.

Choice of Law

A choice-of-law clause can also be an important feature of contracts between students and programs. This clause would select which jurisdiction's law should apply in any litigation that might ensue between parties. Again, the Colorado university would almost certainly choose Colorado law. The familiarity and predictability of applying its own law obviously benefits the university and its lawyers in defending or prosecuting a case. The absence of the clause can give rise to very complicated procedural issues within an area of law called "conflicts of law." Depending on a number of factors, a mountain-climbing accident in Italy involving a Colorado university program and a plaintiff from Georgia might require the application of Italian tort law, a set of circumstances that any university counsel would wish to avoid.

Alternative Dispute Resolution

Finally, a program may wish to insert a clause requiring one of several methods of alternative dispute resolution (ADR) to resolve legal conflict. International business agreements routinely call for contractual disputes to be decided by a panel of arbitrators in a certain forum using the laws of a certain country. The same can be done in an education abroad program.

The most common examples of ADR are *arbitration and mediation.* An arbitration clause generally requires the decision of the arbitrator(s) to be binding on the parties, with almost no chance of appeal. Arbitration creates closure. Mediation, on the other hand, is a totally voluntary action in which the mediator seeks to downplay differences between the disputants and effect a compromise. The disputants, however, are not bound unless they agree to be. The application of a certain rule of law is not necessary in either situation, although arbitration agreements often specify the laws of a certain jurisdiction.

ADR is almost always quicker, cheaper, and more efficient than litigation. It is becoming the preferred method of resolving disputes in many traditional areas of the law, including product liability, environmental law, securities, labor and employment law, as well as international business law. Unfortunately, and somewhat puzzlingly, ADR clauses are found in few study abroad agreements. Institutions should consider adding one to bring their agreements up to current standards.

Tort Law

Although breaches of contract law can create significant legal problems for education abroad programs, their potential for devastating a program's future is not as great as that of "torts." Tort law, like the breach of a contract, involves "civil wrong." It covers wrongful acts that result in injury, loss, or damage. Violations of tort law almost always bring significantly greater damages than do violations of contract law, which are measured solely in terms of demonstrable economic losses).

To illustrate the relative risks of contract violations and torts, if a court finds that a student was led to believe—due to ambiguous language in a program brochure—that she was to have a side excursion to Rome as part of the overall program, and then found out, on site, that there was an extra charge for this trip (which she had not budgeted), the court might determine her loss to be the dollar value of the trip. But if a student goes mountain climbing, gets lost, suffers hypothermia, and dies, and it is later ruled that she was not sufficiently warned about foreseeable perils unique to the mountains in which she was climbing, a court judgment on her behalf might result in damages against the program and/or the sponsoring institution that could run into the millions. Under tort law, in short, the damages are not only actual economic losses (such as medical expenses and loss of income) but general compensatory damages for pain and suffering and even, in rare situations, punitive damages.

Intentional Tort

There are various kinds of torts. The commission of an intentional tort involves actions consciously inflicted by one person on another, resulting in injury to the recipient's body, property, or reputation. Examples include assault and battery, false imprisonment, and defamation. Intentional torts are unlikely to be committed in an international studies program. In one of the only reported education abroad cases, *Furrh v. Arizona Board of Regents* (676 P.2d 1141 Ariz. App. 1983), the University of Arizona and one of its professors were sued for "false imprisonment." The professor had tied up a mentally ill student who risked great physical harm to himself by repeatedly running away from an isolated biology field camp in the Mexican desert, the site of the program. The university and the professor were exonerated.

Tort of Negligence

Torts of negligence are the most commonly litigated tort in the United States and within higher education. A tort of negligence consists of four elements, all of which the plaintiff must successfully prove: duty, breach of the duty, proximate cause, and injury. These elements are discussed below. The most frequent tort situations in which American institutions of higher learning are sued include transportation-related liability, athletic events, liability stemming from buildings and equipment, and failure to prevent criminal acts. With regard to education abroad programs, negligence most often involves allegations of insufficient institutional counsel to participants or staff about dangers inherent in the program's foreign environment—natural, social, political, cultural, and legal.

To mitigate allegations of negligence, certain common-sense steps can be taken. For example, when contracting with a local transportation company, the company's safety record should be examined and advice sought from other study abroad program personnel and from locals. Premises should also be closely scrutinized for problems. For example, warnings will obviously be written in the language of the host country. Since many Americans students speak no foreign language, they may not become aware of these dangers. Security concerns ranging from petty crimes to terrorism may also be great in a foreign land. Staff should be vigilant for suspicious-looking outsiders. Some programs have hired security personnel to do this for them. In areas susceptible to terrorist activity, students might be warned to stay away from known American hangouts, to dress more like locals, and generally to keep a low profile.

The Elements of Negligence: Duty, Breach of Duty, Proximate Cause, Injury

Duty is defined as an obligation recognized by law. Generally the obligation is created as a reaction to the specific facts of a case brought to a court, which then sets a precedent and binds future courts. Through the passage of decades and centuries, cases evolving through the common law system of the United States (sometimes based on earlier cases in England) have created a great many obligations or duties that are now firmly rooted in the legal system. For example, it has been established under American common law that a school has a duty to maintain safe premises and equipment.

A duty is determined when the risk in question is deemed to be foreseeable through the objective eyes of "a reasonably prudent person in a similar situation." Thus, if a reasonable person would have foreseen that inadequate lighting in a campus parking lot might result in a physical attack on a night student leaving the campus at ten o'clock, a duty exists to protect students from such an attack by providing adequate lighting.

When considering the question of duty, institutions should pay special attention to what is said by returned students on their program evaluation forms. If their comments raise issues or identify deficiencies—for example, concerning the safety of the premises or sexual harassment by a staff member or professor—and these questions are not promptly addressed and resolved—the institution will be in a particularly vulnerable position if a subsequent participant brings a claim of injury resulting from a deficiency identified previously.

A duty can also be created by misrepresentation. Thus, if your program brochure lauds a safe environment, courts may rule that you have a duty to provide such an environment. Recently, a student sued a consortium, a college, and a resident director on the grounds that the program flyer erroneously stated that there were no health or safety risks in the country where the program took place. Institutions have a duty not to make misleading promises about their activities abroad.

In Loco Parentis

The doctrine of *in loco parentis* is making a small comeback after losing influence in previous decades. Primarily due to a number of cases in the 1980s, courts now generally accept the idea that at the very least colleges and universities owe their students a safe environment. This relatively new and distinctive duty, the courts have specifically noted, constitutes a "special relationship" in residentially based higher education that is even greater than what landlords traditionally owe their tenants. This duty is based on the foreseeability of harm on the part of the institution on behalf of its students; it obliges institutions to take steps to limit potential harm. For this reason, institutions have been increasing their security staffs, adding lighting, and taking other precautions to comply with this enlarged view of their duty.

Because education abroad programs are often seen as a transplanted version of what applies in the United States, more stringent security measures and other precautions may be in order. Some observers believe the "special relationship" has an even greater impact on foreign study programs owing to the unique milieu and to student expectations that they will be provided a safe environment in lands strange to them. (Evans, 1991, 303). Study abroad programs, almost by definition, bring students with limited understanding of other countries and cultures to unfamiliar places. Some programs take place in countries where U.S. students may not speak one word of the local language when the program begins.

Many students and parents understandably expect that a program bringing students to a place where they cannot be expected to act as independent adults has a unique obligation to protect them, and the courts might agree. But because education abroad is designed to foster greater personal and intellectual maturity among program participants, being overprotective of students while they are abroad is not the answer. Education abroad programs must strike a balance through sensible program planning, careful one-on-one student advising, a judicious admissions process, materials that are open and thorough in describing the program and its social and cultural setting, and superior predeparture and postarrival orientation programs.

Breach of Duty

Once a duty has been determined to exist, a standard of care is established. If it is ascertained that a reasonably prudent person would have foreseen an attack on a student due to a lack of lighting at a program site abroad, then the university's failure to provide the lighting means it breached its duty to the student because it did not meet the acceptable standard of care. This is a particularly challenging standard abroad as many of the more interesting cultural, historical settings may of course not be particularly well illuminated—nor, more to the point, is this anything the U.S. program can do much about. It is important, therefore, to develop an appropriate minimum standard of what care can be provided, and of course to provide prudent counsel.

If an institution breaches its duty by falling below this standard, it leaves itself open to being found "at fault." Being at fault, however, does not yet mean that one is legally negligent. From a legal standpoint, two more elements must be proven.

Proximate Cause

The element of proximate cause is proved by demonstrating that the breaching of the duty led directly to the victim's injury. This is sometimes referred to as the "but for" cause. Put another way, had there been lighting the student would have been safe. Moreover, to meet the proximate-cause criterion the injury the plaintiff suffered cannot be too remote from the cause of the injury. For example, if the student's mother suffers heart failure upon hearing the news of the attack, the university cannot be found responsible for the heart failure.

Injury

Finally, the victim must suffer actual injury—either physical or mental damages, or damage to property or reputation. Successful plaintiffs may not only recover their losses (for example, for medical expenses or lost wages) but also may receive compensation for the pain and suffering they have had to endure. The total amount awarded by the court for full damages can be considerable. How much is eight hours of pain and suffering from hypothermia worth in terms of dollars? If the award is left in the hands of juries, the amount of the award can be quite unpredictable.

▌ The Liability of Advisers and Administrators

Anyone whom a plaintiff believes is even partially responsible for a grievance can be sued—requiring the defendant to mount a legal defense. To protect both the institution and its staff, it is vital that campus-based administrators and advisers, as well as those who travel overseas to lead programs, understand that what defines "appropriate and inappropriate personal and professional behavior" on campus (often formally stated in campus handbooks) also applies overseas. The "Standards of Professional

Practice" of NAFSA's Section on U.S. Students Abroad (SECUSSA), and the NAFSA Code of Ethics, can provide additional and detailed guidance with regard to the work of international education advisers and administrators (see Chapter 1, "Being an Education Abroad Professional").

Beyond that, it is vital that you know the campus process that will support you in the event of legal action. Find out from your legal counsel what constitutes negligence in various circumstances. Whether you should have the further protection of a personal liability policy is up to you—you may wish to seek advice on this point apart from that provided by your institutional counsel. It should be noted that the record of education abroad professionals being involved in civil lawsuits over something said or done in the course of their duties is very limited.

Your office may or may not serve as a resource center for information about other institutions' programs. If it does, this raises the question of whether your institution's liability extends to any and all programs your students may choose to enroll in. At present, this point is hazy, though aggrieved parties are frequently encouraged by their attorneys to go after any and all who may have had a role, however marginal, in their difficulties. To reduce the risk of potential legal trouble, it is wise to give approval only to programs about which you possess direct and current knowledge and which do everything possible to reduce their own liability. This will lessen the likelihood that your students will have a negative experience and reduce the risk that they will hold you responsible if things go awry.

In discussing with students or colleagues programs run by other institutions and organizations do not make comments that might leave you open to charges of defamation. Again, see SECUSSA's Standards of Professional Competence for guidance. This does not mean that you cannot discuss what seem to you to be negative features of programs (including your own), but rather that you voice your concerns only when they are relevant to advising students and are based on adequate and objective evidence. Further, your judgments should not be idiosyncratic or arbitrary; instead, they should be based on the institutional criteria and policies you have developed in conjunction with your faculty and administration to approve programs for your students' participation.

▎ Managing Legal Risks

There are a number of ways to manage the legal risks discussed above. Primary among these, as emphasized above, is of course to know your programs (and those of others) backwards and forwards and to discuss them thoroughly with your institution's wisest and most informed minds. These individuals can advise you on ways to reduce any threats they represent. You can and should eliminate all programs that seem, in fact, unduly risky. You can make changes in your own programs to eliminate trouble spots. And you can provide legal cover by making sure that program participants receive and acknowledge warnings about anything dangerous or risky. There are contractual ways to manage risks as well; these are discussed earlier in this chapter. A more formal way of knowing what might need to be done to protect yourself, your programs, and your institution is a formal legal audit of each of your programs.

The Legal Audit

Risk cannot be managed until it is identified. Legal issues should be studied before they become problems so that university counsel can be engaged in a timely manner instead of being put in the position of rescuing the study abroad office from a situation that might have been avoided. The idea behind a legal audit comes out of preventive law, which emphasizes limiting liability and avoiding legal action by taking appropriate prior actions. In a legal audit, your institution's general counsel—or a lawyer hired for the purpose in coordination with the education abroad staff—reviews all of the university's current education abroad programs, policies, and procedures.

The legal audit is a tool for reviewing current policies and procedures to determine what parts of your programs embody a "reasonable and prudent" standard of care and which need to be upgraded. The aim is to identify anything that may not be effective or that could leave the institution vulnerable to future legal action.

The audit examines each program against a compliance checklist. It is likely to include items such as accreditation, insurance policies, contracts and linkage agreements, advertising and promotion, admissions standards and procedures, emergency response planning, cancelation policies, student behavior policies and grounds for dismissal, personnel policies, budgets, cash transfers, accounting procedures, student records, consent and disclaimer forms, orientation and predeparture information, and program evaluation procedures. The legal audit, when completed, provides an impetus and rationale for taking corrective or preventive action. This, in turn, should result in a list of areas that need immediate, short-term, and long-term action.

Release or Disclaimer Forms

A program may also wish to have students read and sign a release or disclaimer detailing the specific risks involved, not just those posed by physical hazards. If a student becomes aware of such risks, the university may be at least partially, if not totally, protected from a tort claim under the doctrine of "assumption of risk." Although some U.S. jurisdictions disfavor releases or disclaimers as a violation of public policy, they can still be effective tools in defending a case, particularly if they are worded clearly and precisely. When students who are legally minors are allowed to participate, it is important that parents and legal guardians also sign and receive copies of relevant forms and materials. Signing disclaimer forms can also have the effect of discouraging petty lawsuits.

Dealing with Emergencies

You must be prepared for the worst. Institutions should develop effective crisis-management policies and procedures that enable them to respond immediately and effectively to emergencies facing administrators and students. The importance of insurance coverage for major medical care abroad and in the United States, as well as for evacuation and repatriation of remains, cannot be overstated.

If an accident does occur, it is crucial to investigate what happened on site as thoroughly and quickly as possible so as to establish a verbatim record that contains the facts of the incident. Memories can often be faulty, so accurate and timely notes offer an important degree of credibility. It is also important to have an emergency response plan in place, detailing all that needs to be done overseas and on campus. This will include establishing lines of communications with students, parents, legal counsel, investigative authorities, and other appropriate campus personnel. Having published and discussed the safety risks involved in program participation will not only aid your institution should litigation arise, but also it may expedite a more moderate settlement or even discourage someone contemplating a suit.

Bibliography

Aalberts, R. J., and R. B. Evans. 1995. "The International Education Experience: Managing the Legal Risks." *Journal of Legal Studies Education* 13 (1):29–44.

Aalberts, R. J., K. D. Ostrand, and K. C. Fonte,. 1986. "The University, the Law, and International Study Programs." Continuum 50:59–67.

Aalberts, R. J., and K. D. Ostrand. 1987. "Negligence, Liability and the International Education Administrator." *Journal of the Association of International Education Administrators* 7(2): 153–163.

Barr, M. J. et al. 1988. *Student Services and the Law: A Handbook for Practitioners.* San Francisco: Jossey-Bass.

Brown, A., and A. O. Kandel. 1991. *The Legal Audit: Corporate Internal Investigation.* New York: Clark Boardman Callahan.

Burling, P. 1992. *Managing the Risks of Foreign Study Programs.* Boston: Foley, Hoag & Eliot (One Post Office Square, Massachusetts, 01209).

Evans, R. B. 1991. "A Stranger in a Strange Land: Responsibility and Liability for Students Enrolled in Foreign Study Programs." *Journal of College and University Law* 18(2):299–314.

Kaplin, W. A., and B. A. Lee. 1995. *The Law of Higher Education: A Comprehensive Guide to Legal Implications of Administrative Decision Making.* Third ed. San Francisco: Jossey-Bass.

Millington, W. G. 1979. *The Law and the College Student: Justice in Evolution.* St. Paul, Minn.: West Publishing.

Moore, D. 1993–1994. "Faculty and Students Abroad Pose Unusual Risk Management Problems." Report. Washington, D.C.: University Risk Management and Insurance Association.

Rhodes, G. M. 1994. "Legal Issues and Higher Education: Implications for Study Abroad: Key Issues for Institutions and Administrators." Ph.D. diss., University of Southern California.

Rhodes, G. M., and R. J. Aalberts. 1994. "Liability and Study Abroad: 'Prudent' Policies and Procedures Are the Best Insurance." *Transitions Abroad*

Rhodes, G. M., and W. G. Millington. 1994. "Avoiding Liability in Study Abroad: Home Campus and International Campus Concerns." *NAFSA Newsletter* 45 (March): 3, 44, 46.

IV

Part Four

Appendixes

Getting on with the Task:
A National Mandate for Education Abroad
*Report of the National Task Force on Undergraduate
Education Abroad (1990)*

Resources for Education Abroad: A Bibliography
Contributors: William Nolting and Clay Hubbs

Index

List of Contributors

Getting on with the Task: A National Mandate for Education Abroad

Report of the National Task Force on Undergraduate Education Abroad (1990)

In June 1989 NAFSA invited the Institute of International Education and the Council on International Educational Exchange to join in forming a National Task Force on Undergraduate Education. This report and its recommendations are the result of the task force's work.

T he role of the United States as a leader among nations is changing rapidly. Despite our position of international leadership for almost fifty years, we are ill-prepared for the changes in business, manufacturing, diplomacy, science and technology that have come with an intensely interdependent world. Effectiveness in such a world requires a citizenry whose knowledge is sufficiently international in scope to cope with global interdependence.

—Advisory Council for International Educational Exchange, Educating for Global Competence. p.1.

Task Force Purpose and Focus

At the very moment when dramatic changes in the world cause our nation to re-evaluate priorities and to search for policies and alignments which will serve our people in the new century, our position of international leadership among nations is rapidly shifting. The extraordinary events of 1989 rank as markers of human history comparable to those of 1848, 1914, and 1945. Without warning, the comfortable dimensions of the present convulsed and the world transformed itself in unimagined ways. Many of the goals of more than forty years of American foreign policy were realized in a matter of months. The United States, the Soviet Union, Europe, indeed the entire world, grapple with fundamental role changes as we all enter this new period in history, one that is full of possibility and hope.

Yet, in the United States, optimism about this new world is tempered by anxiety created not only by uncertainty about events still to unfold but also by our ability to rise to these new challenges. There is abundant evidence that our citizens are not well prepared for the international realities ahead. By any measure, whether it be comparisons of foreign language proficiency, tests of geographic literacy, or availability of specialists to advise government or business regarding eastern Europe or other distant but important parts of the world, the level of international knowledge and understanding in our country is wanting. In comparison with others, we as a people are poorly educated to deal with the political, economic and social issues which we will face in a new global era that will not measure strength primarily in terms of military preparedness.

In fact, for the past several years, there has been growing acknowledgement that education must provide more international content and lead to greater sensitivity and understanding. For undergraduates at our universities and colleges, a serious educational experience in another country brings cross-cultural understanding and international learning not achievable through almost any other approach. Opportunities for such experience abroad are still confined to a small fraction of American undergraduates, mainly upper middle class, and still focus predominantly on western Europe and on study of the humanities and social sciences. Study abroad opportunities largely neglect the rest of the world and internationally important professional fields. At a time when American citizens and professionals in most fields require much more international knowledge, the narrow scope of undergraduate education abroad constitutes a grave neglect of extremely important needs and limits opportunities to a select few.

It was to address this situation that the National Association for Foreign Student Affairs (NAFSA) invited the Council on International Educational Exchange (CIEE), and the Institute of International Education (IIE) to join it in forming the National Task Force on Undergraduate Education Abroad. The Task Force was established in June 1989 and adopted the following mandate:

- To make undergraduate study and other academically related experiences abroad a higher national priority, with particular reference to such specific needs as increasing financial support, greater diversity of opportunity and program participation, and the assurance of program quality.

- To initiate and introduce language in existing legislation that will facilitate and expand undergraduate study abroad, develop new legislation at the state and federal levels, and explore and support nonlegislative/governmental avenues of funding.
- To develop an action agenda for the exchange field and the broader higher education community and involve these constituencies in the advocacy and implementation of the Task Force's recommendations.

Crucial to the work of the Task Force were the accomplishments of the "Bartlett Committee," a nationally distinguished group appointed by CIEE and named for its chair, Thomas A. Bartlett, to review and make recommendations on future priorities for study abroad. We, the members of the Task Force, fully support the priorities set forth by that committee in its 1988 report, "Educating for Global Competence," and have defined as our own agenda advocating and facilitating their implementation. Chief among them are: a major expansion of undergraduate education abroad, greatly increased access for minority and other underrepresented students, and correction of the grossly disproportionate involvement of Western European program sites compared to all the rest of the world.

Although the Task Force expects to function actively for only a year, making undergraduate education abroad a higher national priority will require the ongoing support of many. Crucial to this effort will be the follow-up activities of the sponsoring organizations: CIEE, IIE, and NAFSA as well as others involved in the process. If such efforts are catalyzed by the Task Force and some progress achieved before its work is done, the substantial commitment of our sponsors will have been well justified.

The establishment of the National Task Force reflects and should strengthen the mounting awareness that study abroad is one of the most effective means to achieve international education for undergraduates and the internationalization of colleges and universities. Although in the past undergraduate study abroad may have in some instances been deficient in academic substance and lacked institutional and national support, its importance is now beginning to be more widely recognized in the United States. Some recent events and trends reenforce this development.

In reaching its conclusions the Task Force benefitted and drew on a large number of recent studies and reports which have targeted the need to strengthen international education and exchange. Our primary inspiration came from the earlier mentioned CIEE report, "Educating for Global Competence." The more significant recent studies and reports which represent the mounting awareness of the value of an international educational experience are listed in the reference section.

One of these studies, however, should be mentioned here because of its findings on the results of study abroad. A five-country, five-year study, for which the U.S. report was published in summer 1990, compellingly documents the major impacts of study abroad in terms of students' international learning, interests, and career aims: the U.S. students substantially increased foreign language proficiency; after their sojourn abroad their knowledge of their host country increased dramatically, as did their interest in and knowledge of international affairs; a majority of the American study abroad returnees planned on careers that would benefit from the knowledge and perspectives gained from their period abroad. [Ed. note: This report was published in two volumes by the European Cultural Foundation as *Study Abroad Programmes*, ed. by Barbara B. Burn, Ladislav Cerych, and Alan Smith; and *Impacts of Study Abroad Programmes on Students and Undergraduates*, by Susan Opper, Ulrich Teichler, and Jerry Carlson. Both volumes are available from Jessica Kingsley Publishers, 118 Pentonville Road, London, N1 9JN, United Kingdom.]

An additional and important point of further reference for the Task Force was its understanding of the impressive educational goals of ERASMUS, the European Community program aimed at ensuring that by 1992, 10 percent of EC university students can afford and will have a significant study abroad experience in another EC country. ERASMUS will prepare European students not only for the professional, commercial, technical, linguistic, academic, and diplomatic needs of a united Europe, but also for performing effectively in the world market of ideas and trade. According to the most recent data available, hardly two percent of American undergraduates study abroad for academic credit, a percentage far below the ERASMUS goal of 10 percent by 1992. In the view of the Task Force, American higher education must also vigorously meet this latter challenge.

While focussing on the undergraduate level, the Task Force explicitly recognizes the importance of opportunities for study and other experiences abroad at all levels of American education, from secondary school to graduate school and postgraduate research; for students, teachers, and scholars. But we believe that it is the internationalization of the undergraduate experience which can have the greatest impact on American

374

society in terms of lifelong interests and values. Moreover, while the main emphasis of this report concerns formal study abroad programming organized and overseen by colleges and universities or by consortia of higher education institutions, the Task Force is convinced that international work or service experiences, as well as other forms of immersion in the daily life of a foreign culture, can contribute greatly to a student's formal academic and/or preprofessional education and understanding of the world, even if this educational gain is not measured in terms of academic credit.

Summary of Recommendations

The work of the Task Force has resulted in five major recommendations. Each recommendation is treated in more detail in one of the following five chapters, and they are presented here in summary form. Taken together, they will greatly enhance the contribution of overseas study abroad programs to the internationalization of the higher education experience of undergraduates.

Expansion of Education Abroad

By the year 1995, 10 percent of American college and university students should have a significant educational experience abroad during their undergraduate years. Achieving this will require substantial growth in the number and type of opportunities provided and a more pervasive integration of education abroad into institutional strategies aimed at strengthening the international dimension in U.S. higher education.

Increased Diversity

As numbers and opportunities are expanded we urge that greater diversity be a major goal for all aspects of education abroad: greater diversity in participating students, in foreign locations, and in types of programs.

Curricular Connections

The study abroad experience must be integrated into regular degree programs in many different fields including professional schools. In some fields, study abroad should become a requirement, for example, for future foreign language teachers in elementary and secondary schools.

Major Inhibitors

A variety of factors inhibit expansion of numbers and diversity in undergraduate education abroad. Some are historical; others are tied to negative perceptions. We urge that all be vigorously addressed. They include:

- Insufficient institutional commitment to international education.
- Negative views of some faculty members.
- Restrictive curricular requirements.
- Foreign language deficiencies.
- Inadequate study abroad support services on campus and abroad.
- Inadequate information about education abroad opportunities and their relative quality.
- Financial regulations and shortfalls.

Financial Options

While lack of money is not always the main obstacle to program development or student participation, expanded funding from both private and public sources will be essential if the academic community is to diversify the types of institutions, students, and experiences involved in study abroad in the years ahead.

I Expansion of Education Abroad

In order to enhance the impact of study abroad on the internationalization of U.S. colleges and universities, the goals set forth in "Educating for Global Competence" must be implemented. Chief among them is: participation in study abroad by 10 percent of all undergraduates by 1995, and, for the longer term, 20 to 25 percent by the year 2008, two decades after the CIEE committee completed its report. The rationale for these goals merits repeating:

> It is absolutely essential that college students cultivate an informed and sensitive awareness of those parts of the world in which more than half the global population lives....
>
> The intensely interdependent nature of the world community and the challenges to American competitiveness mean that we need to increase the competence of students in their knowledge of other countries and their abilities with foreign languages.

An educational experience in a foreign setting certainly contributes significantly to this increased knowledge and competency, and yet, according to IIE figures, the number of students receiving credit for studying abroad in 1987–88 was only 62,341. Although this figure omits data from some non-responding institutions, it nevertheless documents that only a tiny fraction of America's more than 12.5 million college and university students have a study abroad experience.

The expansion of education abroad is urgent for the following reasons:

- The impact of study abroad is far greater if substantial numbers of students rather than the occasional few participate. Only then does the experience produce important multiplier effects on home campus curricula and teaching and on students' academic and personal goals and achievements.
- Americans must, like their European and Japanese student counterparts, learn to function professionally across national boundaries. The United States cannot afford to lag in preparing future professionals for the internationally involved careers that await them.

The National Task Force strongly urges American colleges and universities to integrate study abroad into their institutional strategies for strengthening not only international education but also the quality of their overall academic programs. Study and other educational experiences abroad, as part of the internationalization of undergraduates programs, should play a much more central role in what colleges and universities are all about: in their missions and goals, in their institutional structures and policies, in their educational programming and planning, and in their allocations of staff and other resources.

II Increasing Diversity

Ensuring that at least 10 percent of U.S. students have an educational experience abroad requires more than mere linear increases in what now exists. Recruiting more undergraduates must involve a wider spectrum of students studying in a wider range of geographic destinations and new and different program models.

Geographic Locations

The overwhelming dominance of western Europe in U.S. study abroad programming, while historically understandable, is no longer compatible with the nation's needs in international education. To function as citizens and professionals in a shrinking world, American students should learn about all of it, not just the Anglo-European countries. At the same time it must be recognized that study abroad in many countries and regions outside of western Europe can present American students with a variety of difficult challenges: unfamiliarity with the host country's culture and language(s); enormous competition among host country students; a limited number of places in higher education; major differences in accommodations, student services; different approaches to teaching and learning; smaller libraries and fewer academic facilities; and unfamiliar student social interaction. These kinds of differences make it especially important to revise program models for study abroad and to develop new ones, especially for Third World country sites.

The National Task Force urges as a short-term target that undergraduate study outside of western Europe be expanded to at least one-third of all study abroad students. At present more American undergraduates study in the United Kingdom alone than the total of all in Asia, Africa, the Middle East, and Latin America. To reach this new goal, these major world regions must see a doubling of American undergraduates pursuing education abroad.

Minority Student Participation

Efforts to expand the number of undergraduates who study abroad must address the lack of diversity among them. Traditionally American study abroad students have come from affluent, middle or upper class, white, professional families rather than from the broad spectrum of American society. Even though minority enrollments in American colleges and universities have increased overall by 8 percent in 1984-86, and in 1986 represented 10 percent of all four-year college students, minority participation in study abroad has increased little, representing only a tiny fraction of all undergraduate study abroad students.

Because, as stated in "Educating for Global Competence," "it is clearly in the national interest to have internationally skilled students from the widest possible range of backgrounds," recruiting the underrepresented minorities, especially blacks and Hispanics, to study abroad calls for special measures, not least of which may be special funding.

III Developing Program Approaches

Forging Curricular Connections

The existence of few or no connections between home campus curricula and what students study abroad is an important deterrent to study abroad for American students. Students who do not study abroad give as reasons their perception that it did not fit with or was not required by their major, might prolong their degree period, and was not encouraged or was even explicitly discouraged by their faculty advisers.

Study abroad can enroll substantially more undergraduates only if it is clear that their studies abroad will both earn them academic credit and will be treated as an integral part of their degree program and an asset to it. In particular, a study abroad period should be treated as part of, rather than apart from, their studies for their major. It is ironic that in the United States where the academic credit system facilitates the recognition of studies done elsewhere, students in many disciplines find this difficult or impossible with respect to requirements for their major. In western Europe, even with only an incipient system of academic credit, ERAS-MUS enables many EC students who study in another EC country to have their work treated as an integral part of their home campus degree.

In order to strengthen study abroad's connections with home campus curricula, the following steps are needed:

- Students should have greater access to information on study abroad opportunities, including specific courses, in order to plan their study abroad far enough in advance so that it can be incorporated into and not extend their degree period.
- American faculty members and undergraduate advisers should have sufficient information on courses their students wish to take abroad to counsel them on courses that will count towards the degree and to encourage them to study abroad.
- To integrate study abroad more closely into home campus curricula and reduce the sense of alienation many returnees experience on returning to campus, faculty should attempt to build on students' international learning, developing or modifying courses in which such students tend to enroll.
- Colleges and universities should encourage an academically related experience abroad as an option in all degree programs.

Subjects Throughout the Curriculum

If more students are to have educational experiences abroad, program opportunities must become much more varied in subject or discipline focus. Rather than being primarily in humanities and social sciences fields, education abroad opportunities must be targeted across disciplines. Obvious fields are public health, education (including practice teaching abroad), architecture, environmental studies, and hotel and travel administration, but business and engineering, because of their large enrollments and the rapid internationalization of careers in these fields, must also be priorities.

Major constraints to including study abroad in such fields as engineering and business are the tight curricular requirements, including sequencing, which leave little flexibility for students. The Task Force believes, however, that early and careful planning should, given faculty encouragement, enable more of these students to study abroad. The fact that some professional schools in the United States not only make it possible but encourage their majors to study abroad suggests that this is indeed a realistic goal.

New Models

In expanding study abroad to encompass 10 percent of all undergraduates and diversify both participants and destinations, merely replicating and multiplying current program models is unrealistic and inappropriate. For students who are older, of minority background, employed (46.5 percent of full-time students under 25 years are employed at least part-time), are disabled, or have limited funds, study abroad often is not perceived to be an option. The needs of such students are mostly ignored by the more typical study abroad models and structures. The Task Force cannot prescribe the new models for greatly expanded and diversified education abroad. These must be developed pragmatically by individual institutions, consortia, or other appropriate organizations. However, features to consider include more short-term stays, flexible language requirements, "no-fee swapping" of students between U.S. and foreign institutions, and built-in student work or service components that reduce costs.

An important model for diversifying education abroad is work experience in another country which puts students in close contact with the local people and culture. Undergraduate student interest in work experiences abroad is increasing rapidly and certainly at a faster rate than study abroad program participation. Nevertheless, little interest in support for these students has been shown by much of the international education and academic communities, who confine their attention to academic programs and may wrongly dismiss experiential learning as of little educational value. Internships, various types of cooperative education arrangements, voluntary service and independent study/research projects are among approaches which could either generate academic credit or be academically or professionally relevant to degree programs at the home institution.

For students preferring to work abroad rather than pursue formal courses, whether for reasons of finance or other motivation, the many opportunities now available, for example through CIEE and the various other organizations which facilitate work abroad, should be brought to students' attention, and be further expanded. Other possible models would be service in an undergraduate Peace Corps, working as undergraduate teaching assistants in schools or colleges abroad, or participating in workcamps and other kinds of volunteer activities.

IV Attacking Major Inhibitors

The Task Force identified seven factors which stand in the way of expansion of and improved quality in undergraduate study abroad. While there is some overlap among them, each impediment is sufficiently separate from the others to call for a different treatment and strategy, either at the institutional level or more broadly. They must be addressed.

First, the lack of institutional commitment to a strong international dimension in undergraduate education is a serious impediment at some colleges and universities. Without such a commitment—that is, a determination to adjust and tune undergraduate learning to the multicultural and global realities of the decade ahead—there will be little institutional encouragement for students to study abroad and for faculty members to organize new programs.

National associations and organizations are helping to build commitment, reinforced by an impressive array of national commission pronouncements, state governors' recommendations and the general search for excellence in education. Many institutions, in spite of strained financial circumstances, are studying their international educational needs, often in the context of a review of the core undergraduate curriculum.

Substantial momentum now exists toward attaining a greater international dimension in higher education. For example, a recent national initiative, the Coalition for the Advancement of Foreign Languages and International Studies (CAFLIS), consists of 160 regional and national organizations, both large and small, seeking to improve international education and enhance the nation's competence to deal with global issues. Yet, there are still some colleges and universities which have not embraced such commitments and others which have done so superficially. The Task Force encourages the faculty and students at these institutions to push hard for a more vigorous international commitment, one which includes undergraduate study abroad as a means to accomplish curricular and educational ends.

The strategy will vary among colleges and universities, faculties, departments, and disciplines. The authors of a report which canvassed a cross-section of institutions in four selected states note the following:

We were struck repeatedly by the importance of a charismatic leader in galvanizing a campus to focus on and undertake study abroad. Usually the key person is the president, but it also may be a provost, dean, state governor, system chancellor, or even some dynamic senior faculty member. Enormous resources are not required to make study abroad work; what are usually lacking where such a program does not exist are vision, a sense of commitment, and a clarion call to action.

We urge persistence on the part of those who are already committed, but whose institution may be laggard. Persistence, enlisting internal and external allies, pushing for creation of a review committee and strategic planning to take advantage of opportunities and normal information flow are all important. These endeavors must be taken with a thorough knowledge of and sensitivity to the institution's governance structure.

Even with general institutional commitment, attitudes of individual faculty and those prevailing in some departments can be a problem, sometimes even a severe obstacle to forming new programs or encouraging student participation. The explanation for lack of faculty support includes such inglorious reasons as inertia and the egocentric "what's in it for me?" Less crass but equally parochial—and more prevalent—is the attitude among some faculty, even those who ought to be among the strongest proponents of study abroad, that study abroad deprives them of their best students, actually taking students out of their classrooms and reducing their full time equivalent statistics. But, by far the most frequent cause of lack of faculty interest in or opposition to study abroad programs is that they are not perceived to be relevant to or supportive of what faculty do. Faculty often do not recognize the academic legitimacy of the students' activities abroad. In support of their position, faculty members cite student reports selectively, for example, those asserting that students' experience abroad was not as rigorous academically as their experience on the campus.

One approach to winning the support of faculty is to design study abroad programs with particular faculty in mind and to begin to plan new programs with them. For example, professional-school faculty who typically are suspicious of study abroad opportunities because they perceive them as detracting from preprofessional training should be asked to identify the off-campus experience that might enhance the preparation of students in his or her field. Responses that point toward greater knowledge of Japanese culture or business practices, or the implications of the European Community in 1992 for U.S. society should become the starting point for planning a new course or a program in Japan or Europe. Faculty should participate in program planning, course design, and site selection, and then help fit the program into the curriculum and form part of an advisory committee to the program. Faculty can be similarly involved in programs calling for direct enrollment in foreign institutions or the design of appropriate internships. Quite naturally they will become advocates for such study abroad experiences in their classrooms and potential future resident directors, as well as academic advisers to students returning from abroad. Most important, they will become the legitimizers of the program on campus to their more parochial colleagues, to hesitant administrators and to doubting parents.

A more interesting challenge and one that requires more imagination is to involve the faculty who teach international subjects but who have not traditionally been associated with study abroad programs, for example, a professor of international relations or security studies. Again, the key is to begin with the faculty member's professional interests and concerns. The result might be a program designed around a theme—e.g., the European Economic Community, NATO, international security in a world of declining great power competition—at a site identified by the professor where colleagues are doing quality work on the subject and where broad opportunities may exist for students' exposure to key officials and participants.

In short, faculty members must become convinced that some learning of their subject matter may well take place in a foreign setting. Not all will become convinced; nor should they, since much subject matter is indeed better taught at home. But getting them involved at a formative stage is an important step.

Curricular issues in various forms comprise a third inhibitor and were addressed in the preceding chapter.

A fourth inhibiting factor, closely related to curricular issues, is the national problem of language deficiencies. Study abroad is an important tool for attacking this serious national deficiency. New program development in other than English, Spanish or French speaking locations is not always easy but should be undertaken. This is especially true because the overseas study program has tended to be viewed from a traditional liberal arts viewpoint, i.e., overseas study as the domain and mainly serving the needs of Eurocentered language, literature and arts majors. Creative thinking and planning will result in broader curricular focus for study abroad and include a language and culture component.

The point is that higher education must break out of its inhibiting mold. The benefits of study abroad to other fields and situations must be seen; for example, programs in China can provide excellent learning situations for English-speaking American undergraduate students even if their introduction to the Chinese language is modest. There is much to be learned in China from English-speaking Chinese lecturers and English texts about Chinese subjects, and through an accompanying U.S. faculty member. The same is true in Japan, the Middle East and the USSR. There are also many sites outside Europe where French and Spanish language can profitably be explored in other cultural contexts, specifically those of Africa and Latin America. In general, much more can be done to structure programs which are not so dependent on language skills and the needs of language and literature programs. Faculty in architecture, history, business, government, social work, engineering and many other fields can develop sound programs for students who do not speak the local languages.

In fact, properly structured, an experience can serve to introduce students to language study.

At some universities, mainly those with little tradition of encouraging study abroad, there is a serious deficiency of support services to facilitate recruitment and flow of students. The Task Force considers this to be the fifth substantial inhibitor of faculty and student initiative. This deficiency may also extend beyond the U.S. campus to the situation abroad where facilities may be weak and support service minimal.

There should be an office available on campus to assist, advise, and encourage both faculty and students. Professional study abroad personnel should be included in any initiatives to strengthen involvement in study abroad. Such an office can provide the leadership, working with departments, to expand and diversify undergraduate study abroad. The study abroad professional can assure full consideration of options and encourage adequate coverage of language and culture studies in new programs. The absence of such a unit, and the resultant lack of attention to professional and support services, slows down growth of quality programs locally and participation of students in externally sponsored programs.

Even with adequate support services on campus, weak support arrangements in some areas abroad prevent expansion of program sites. This is particularly true in Third World locations where suitable living facilities may be in very short supply, where health problems may exist or personal security may be a concern. Obviously, there are locations which are still inaccessible to U.S. undergraduate students and may be so for some years to come. But there are many which are suitable and can become available through proper planning, cooperation among U.S. institutions and organizations and with colleagues in the foreign setting.

In some cases, reciprocity—such as interinstitutional exchanges of students—is the key. In others, the presence of U.S. students and faculty will be seen as especially welcome. A combination of initiative and persistence will overcome the problems in many locations abroad. In some cases new investment in facilities may be needed; in others, elaboration of potential benefits in both directions and patient negotiation will be sufficient. If study abroad locations are to be diversified, such patience combined with healthy persistence will certainly be needed. Consortia and networking schemes are part of the solution to this inhibitor, and ways must be found to put them in place.

Lack of accurate and adequate information about the opportunities and realities of undergraduate study abroad opportunities can serve as another significant inhibitor. There is so much incomplete or misleading information available that those concerned with providing a good flow of accurate information on all aspects of undergraduate education abroad must be particularly alert and active. Unfortunately, there are some programs in existence which deserve criticism; but these are the great exception. They are easily offset by examples of learning experiences abroad which surpass the experience of those who study only on campus. Frequently, the value of study abroad can be seen both in the academic learning that takes place, and also in an enhanced self-confidence and sense of personal direction which serves the individual student better than, perhaps, any other single undergraduate experience.

Lack of timely, accurate information can affect the judgment of faculty at the departmental level as well as that of those in the administration of the university. Therefore, both must be targets of any information campaign. The best instigators of such campaigns are those on campus who are committed to the expansion of the international dimension, and particularly, overseas study abroad opportunities. Their allies are the similarly committed, national organizations armed with data.

The study abroad support unit on campus should be the main force in spreading the good word about opportunities available. If no such office exists, it remains to others who are committed within the faculty or the administration and in national organizations to be sure that program information is widely available and that the distortions of the past are corrected.

Another target of accurate information flow must certainly be the "consumer"—the undergraduate student. Undergraduate study abroad is serious academic business and it must be portrayed that way, not as an academic holiday. Furthermore, the student who seeks information about opportunities offered by national consortia or by other universities should have ready and adequate information. A support services office on campus should be the source for such information.

It is also important that parents as well as students understand the plus and minus factors related to any specific program of study abroad. There are certain costs, but there are certainly overwhelming benefits in most such study situations, and these must be communicated effectively to families and supporting individuals. Outreach beyond the confines of the institution is essential. The insecurity caused by reports of terrorist activity, or a sense of hostility toward Americans abroad, can be easily overstated and parents can draw the wrong conclusion from newspaper headlines. Those concerned about accurate portrayal of the foreign situation must certainly be alert to problems, but also find ways to counter them with timely and realistic appraisals.

The seventh inhibitor is the shortage of funds for exploring and establishing new programs and for supporting some students. The chapter which follows deals directly with available options and recommends actions.

V Addressing Financial Options

The problems of finance should be considered from several perspectives and levels.

Institutional Issues

Fortunately, most colleges and universities allow their students who participate in study abroad programs organized by their home campus to receive financial aid. However, it is still common to find institutions which do not allow financial aid for programs sponsored by other institutions, to find private institutions where students cannot use institutional aid for study away from the home campus, or to find that only some kinds of federal aid are allowed for support of study abroad.

These situations clearly deter undergraduates from study abroad. Colleges and universities that are fully committed to undergraduate education abroad will take action to ensure that their study abroad students are entitled to and receive at least the same level of financial support abroad—federal, states or private—as at the home campus (institutional commitment is also reflected in the faculty reward system and in support services and program funding relating to study abroad).

We applaud the approach of the University of California system and some other institutions which assume that just as costs for study at UC are supported by the university, so should they be when UC students study abroad. Furthermore, the UC system funds much of the cost of hosting "reciprocity students" from partner institutions abroad in order to assure UC student access to classrooms abroad. This UC approach contrasts with that of other institutions which expect study abroad to be self-funded by students or even revenue-generating for the U.S. institutions. Where the latter viewpoint prevails, it is a painful indicator of the low priority accorded to study abroad. If study abroad is to gain more priority, colleges and universities ideally should invest institutional resources in the activity.

The wide range of financial models suggests that where there is a will, there is a way. The task may be more difficult at low tuition public universities in contrast with higher tuition institutions. But if study abroad ranks as a high enough priority, no institution for financial reasons should have to deny its undergraduate students an opportunity to study abroad for credit either in a university-managed program, or through a well-planned and managed consortium program, or independently. Any institution can design affordable programs, assure that support services are sufficient, that exploratory funding is available, and that student aid funds are useable if needed.

Government Support at State and National Levels

State and federal support for undergraduate study abroad has been limited and, when available, over-regulated. At the federal level there are several issues. Statutory and regulatory limits prevent students who study abroad from receiving aid without major delays, bureaucratic obstacles, or other disincentives. Federal aid does not normally take into account that study abroad may involve extra costs compared to study at the home campus, just as laboratory studies for the science student may require extra expenditures. Even though it is in the national interest that study abroad involve more diverse students and sites abroad, almost no public funding now is targeted to that need.

In light of these and related circumstances, the Task Force recommends a careful review and modification of regulations, specifically:

- Existing statutory and regulatory limits which discourage or prevent undergraduate study abroad should be revised to facilitate undergraduate education in other countries and reflect sensitivity to the special needs of students participating in it;
- Federal law and regulations relating to student financial aid should ensure that the extra costs of study abroad, when applicable, are taken into account in determining students' awards;
- Federal eligibility requirements should be revised to allow more aid to study abroad students because most cannot work while studying abroad;
- Federal appropriations to institutions which do not allow students to use the aid for which they are eligible for study abroad should be restricted or made conditional on the institution's assuring the availability of this aid.

Moving beyond federally-funded financial aid regulations, at the federal level, the National Task Force has reviewed existing legislation and programs which involve or are pertinent to undergraduate education abroad in order to identify what might best advance the field. As part of this we were concerned whether at a time of budget deficits nationally, we should focus on including a larger or new undergraduate study abroad dimension within existing programs, or advocate new federal legislation and funding in support of this field. The Task Force decided to do both, as is set forth below.

- The Fulbright Student Program, almost entirely graduate, should be expanded to provide a few highly targeted awards for undergraduate study abroad, with priority to diversifying student participation, nonwestern destinations, and underrepresented disciplines. Another important target group are graduating seniors, for whom Fulbright awards can serve to attract and facilitate a talented and more diverse study abroad pool.
- The International Student Exchange Program (ISEP) which provides an excellent study abroad model offering cost-effectiveness, reciprocity, and diversity, should be continued and expanded, especially in the developing, nonwestern world.

388

- The Group Projects Abroad program of the U.S. Department of Education, which encourages international and foreign language education for current and future teachers and emphasizes sites outside of western Europe should encourage the inclusion of undergraduates as program participants, especially the underrepresented minorities.
- There are a number of provisions of the Higher Education Act, Title VI, which deserve attention, especially in the months leading up to its reauthorization in 1991. The Foreign Language and Area Studies (FLAS) Fellowship Program under the Department of Education (Title VI) should give more opportunities to undergraduates for study abroad, especially for study of "critical" languages and in nonWestern countries (though allowable under the program, very few awards have been made for undergraduate study abroad). Title VI, Section 604, the Undergraduate International Studies and Foreign Language Program, should be revised to authorize support for study abroad, especially that which is closely related to on-campus foreign language and international studies curricula funded under this program. Title VI, Section 605, authorized but not yet funded, in granting funds to higher education institutions for intensive summer language courses, should include among eligible participants advanced foreign language students as well as teachers. Title VI, Sections 612 and 613, of the Higher Education Act, in encouraging more internationalization in business studies and programs, should give strong encouragement to internships abroad for undergraduates in business/foreign language fields.
- PL 480 legislation, which authorizes a percent of sales of American commodities abroad and paid for in local currency to be used towards the costs of U.S. programs abroad, should make support of undergraduate study abroad a priority.
- A variety of federally-funded programs, mostly administered by the U.S. Information Agency to support undergraduate education abroad, such as the Youth Exchange Initiative, the Bundestag Program with the Federal Republic of Germany, the Samantha Smith Program, and so on, should be reassessed in order to ensure adequate participation by minority and other underrepresented students.
- The University Affiliation Program of USIA should include, as a consideration in funding applications, the U.S. university's intention to

make study abroad or student exchange an element in the interinstitutional relationship.

In addition to the above measures, the Task Force views as essential and urgent a new federal initiative to implement the objectives described above, including:

• Providing a substitute or work/study option for income earned while working in the United States (at present, students rarely can be approved for work abroad while studying);

• Supporting nontraditional, minority and other underrepresented students to study abroad, and among them students aspiring to programs focused in the Third World/developing countries.

The Coalition for Advancement of Foreign Language and International Studies (CAFLIS) has issued its action plan, which calls for expanded study abroad and urges creation of a new entity to help orchestrate and support major improvements in international education over the next decade. As this new national initiative takes shape and funding becomes available, we urge attention to study abroad needs.

Corporate Role

Prompted by concerns for international competence, developments such as Europe 1992, and the accelerating internationalization of business and industry, the interest of U.S. corporations in promoting greater awareness among their staff of the cultures, languages, and ways of doing business of other countries has sharply increased in recent years. Even though the subsidiaries of many U.S.-based firms hire host country nationals as local managers, more and more U.S. corporations are acknowledging needs for internationally trained recruits.

In seeking more support for undergraduate study abroad, colleges and universities should take the above trends and concerns into account and seek more assistance from the private sector. This should apply especially for programs which enable business students to become competent in other languages and knowledgeable about other cultures. Such assistance might take the form of financial contributions by U.S. firms to such programs or providing funded internships or other practical experience opportunities with their operations abroad. Such assistance should also be sought for programs abroad for engineering undergraduates because of the rapid internationalization of this field.

Third World Debt

The huge debts which some countries now owe to banks in the United States and other developed countries must be considered a possible source of funding for new overseas study programs. The "debt-for-development" or "debt-for-environment" programs which have been studied, planned, and in a few cases, actually launched, suggest to those of us concerned with building new study programs in diverse areas that a "debt-for-study" theme would also be appropriate. In fact, the U.S. Department of Commerce issued a report on just such a possibility as part of the department's desire to increase U.S. competitiveness, in this case through educating American students in a foreign setting.

These large debts are found in countries which offer great potential for diverse new educational programs—for example Brazil, Mexico, Argentina, and some countries of Africa. The existence of these multibillion-dollar funds are a real problem but they also pose a challenge. Can we find a way to use them for educational purposes, namely the establishment of new opportunities for U.S. students to study in these countries? And can such programs offer some benefit to other concerned parties as well? We believe that if properly designed they offer such possibilities and are clearly worth the effort.

At this time, most transfers of debt to serve development, environment, or educational purposes are not being offered as gifts. The debt funds must be negotiated and purchased, presumably at a greatly discounted rate. The currency must be used in the country of origin, not converted to U.S. dollars or other hard currency. But that is precisely where study abroad programs encounter most operating expenses—in the foreign setting—so the restriction should be manageable.

Since students pay hard currency for undergraduate study, they provide a source of funds to buy discounted debt currency. Their payments make it feasible to use debt funds to underpin study abroad programs. Of course, an outright gift of such funds to create an endowment fund locally would be better, but is probably unrealistic at the present time. Use of purchased debt funds could result in lower costs to the students, reduced debt totals, and improved educational opportunity.

Without providing detail here, we recommend that those involved in discussions of debt usage for worthwhile purposes keep U.S. undergraduate study in mind. The Task Force has already started to discuss such possibilities with relevant persons and believes it to be feasible and certainly desirable.

VI Towards Action

We have recommended two broad goals—significant expansion of and greater diversity in education abroad programs—and three routes towards realizing them. These three are to align study abroad programs more closely with the undergraduate curriculum, to attack the identifiable, widespread inhibitors to growth and diversity, and to refine and improve the financial base for study abroad.

These five recommendations, as elaborated in this report, lend themselves to concerted, organized effort at the national, state, and institutional levels. We urge that at each level the community concerned with undergraduate study abroad work through existing organizations to move strategically on these goals. Where organizations do not exist, they must be created or the task absorbed within some other entity. We urge a direct approach to these goals as an important part of the broad effort to internationalize higher education and to produce well-educated leadership for the twenty-first century.

At the national level, this will mean that existing organizations concerned with education abroad must ally with others to see that it is incorporated in all initiatives to educate for global competence. Education abroad must be placed on the agendas of national association meetings, including college and university presidents, area studies and discipline-based organizations, professional education associations, and others. Included in this effort might be the entity proposed by the Coalition for Advancement of Foreign Languages and International Studies. All of these groups and organizations should, in concert and individually, seek to bring a better understanding of the importance of study abroad in a quality program of international education.

These alliances should be a part of a broader and more activist strategy to advance study abroad than has been present in the past. As the Higher Education Act moves towards reauthorization in 1991, education abroad as a component of Title VI should be prominent. It should be promoted within each of the varied strands of financial support for higher education, for example, as a part of broader minority student participation. An activist stance, one allied with other groups, will bring higher visibility for the study abroad field as its leaders increasingly work with legislative and executive branch leaders on issues related to expansion and diversity goals.

At the state level, action is critical because most public institutions of higher learning derive a large share of their revenues from state governments and because private corporations frequently link their political activities and their philanthropic work to the communities in which they are located. Action at the state level by those committed to the goals of this report should focus on those organizations that comprise the political environment in which educational policy decisions are made. Obviously, this includes the official bodies that formulate educational policy for the state and establish the budgets for public institutions.

The objective must be to convince officials at the state level that study abroad is an integral and valuable part of higher education. study abroad advocates should seek to place study abroad in all state processes such as higher-education legislation, budgets, or university support arrangements that deal with international education. The report of the National Governors Association should be viewed as a foundation—and justification—for bold actions.

Equally important, action should be directed at civic groups and corporations. Together these constitute the largest portion of the constituency for international education in the private sector at the state level. Without their support, it will be difficult to convince state governments to make study abroad a matter of priority in the policy process. The goal is to create a grass-roots mandate for study abroad. Many corporate leaders are already on record nationally as favoring international education. The state level action plan should focus on winning the explicit support of corporate leaders for study abroad. Local corporations and civic groups can play an important role in convincing state officials and institutional administrators that study abroad is integral to our efforts to prepare the coming generation for the challenges they will confront. Fortunately, state and regional level organizations which support international education are generally well-positioned to lead these study abroad efforts.

Much of what we are recommending must become part of the action agenda at the institutional level. We urge that leaders of colleges and universities where international education, including study abroad, is not yet a priority appoint a task force to develop strategy to accomplish this goal. In pursuing the goal, academic leadership should forge alliances with appropriate interest groups and individuals within and beyond their institutions in order to maximize the effectiveness and impact of their efforts.

While there is no single model for strengthening study abroad, among the many possible strategies for action at the institutional level are the following.

- Allocate institutional funds to study abroad as a legitimate and significant instructional offering, and make it an important target for institutional fund-raising.
- Encourage and accord appropriate recognition to faculty involvement with and contributions to study abroad, including student advising, program development, and the integration of study abroad into the home campus curricula.
- Take such measures as may be required to assure that students who study abroad are not penalized with respect to financial aid, and endeavor to provide special assistance to minority and other students underrepresented in study abroad so that they have equal access to it.
- Establish/strengthen a central office to develop, monitor, and coordinate international education, including study abroad, with appropriate staffing and other resources. The nature of the central office will vary, but the essential need for such leadership is increasingly apparent.

These national, state, and institutional activities and strategies fall in various ways within our five recommendations. Each of the five calls for specific actions, including the formation of political alliances, direct debate, and other tactics at each level. These actions will take different form and substance from one institution and locality to another. But we have suggested the ways they can be approached, recognizing the need to vary the pattern and strategy within our diverse system.

Whatever the variation, those committed to internationalizing higher education and, specifically, expanding and improving study abroad, must now get on with the task. Never before has the need been so apparent, nor the opportunity greater.

References

A partial list of recent reports and publications on the value of educational experiences abroad appears here, as well as those references footnoted in the text of this report.

America in Transition: The International Frontier. Report of the Task Force on International Education, Washington, D.C.: National Governors' Association, 1989.

Boyer, Ernest. *College.* New York: Harper & Row, 1987.

Burn, Barbara B., Jerry S. Carlson, John Useem, and David Yachimowicz. *Study Abroad: The Experience of American Undergraduates.* Greenwood Press, 1990.

Educating for Global Competence: The Report of the Advisory Council for International Educational Exchange. New York: Council on International Educational Exchange, 1988.

"Exchange 2000: International Leadership for the Next Century." Washington D.C.: The Liaison Group for International Educational Exchange, 1990.

Financial Aid for Study Abroad: A Manual for Advisers and Administrators. Edited by Stephen Cooper, William Cressey, and Nancy Stubbs. Washington, D.C.: National Association for Foreign Student Affairs, 1989.

Goodwin, Craufurd D. and Michael Nacht. *Abroad & Beyond: Patterns in American Overseas Education.* Institute of International Education Research Report. Cambridge: Cambridge University Press, 1988.

"Improving U.S. Competitiveness: Swapping Debt for Education." A Report to the Secretary of Commerce, U.S. Department of Commerce, International Trade Administration, Washington, D.C.: U.S. Department of Commerce, 1988.

"International Competence: A Key to America's Future." A Plan of Action of the Coalition for the Advancement of Foreign Languages and International Studies, Washington, D.C.: CAFLIS, 1989.

"International Cooperation in Business Education." A Wingspread Conference Report. Edited by Stephen J. Kobin. New York: Council on International Educational Exchange, 1989.

Lambert, Richard D. *International Studies and the Undergraduate.* Washington, D.C.: American Council on Education, 1989.

Nation at Risk. Washington, D.C.: National Committee on Excellence in Education, 1983.

Open Doors: 1988-89: Report on International Educational Exchange. Edited by M. Zikopoulos, New York: Institute of International Education, 1989.

"Renewing the National Commitment to International Understanding through Educational and Cultural Diplomacy." Washington, D.C.: National Association for Foreign Student Affairs, 1989.

"Study, Work and Travel Abroad: A Bibliography." Washington, D.C.: National Association for Foreign Student Affairs, 1989.

Members of the Natational Task Force on Undergraduate Education Abroad

Peggy Blumenthal
Vice-President, Educational Services
Institute of International Education—New York
809 United Nations Plaza
New York, NY 10017

Barbara B. Burn, Associate Provost
Director, William S. Clark International Center
Clark Hill Road
University of Massachusetts—Amherst
Amherst, MA 01003

Jack Egle
President and Executive Director,
Council on International Educational Exchange
205 East 42nd Street
New York, NY 10017

Mary Anne Grant
Executive Director,
International Student Exchange Program
1242 35th Street, N.W.
Washington, D.C. 20057

Ralph H. Smuckler
Dean and Assistant to the President
International Studies and Programs
Michigan State University
211 Center for International Programs
East Lansing, MI 48824-1035

Joseph Tulchin
Director
Office of International Programs
University of North Carolina—Chapel Hill
Chapel Hill, NC 27514

Resources for Education Abroad: A Bibliography

Contributors: William Nolting and Clay Hubbs

T his annotated directory of resources—including books, videos, and internet sites of value to education abroad advisers and administrators and their students—has been compiled at the request of NAFSA's Section on U.S. Students Abroad (SECUSSA).

The first section identifies resources useful to study abroad advisers and administrators in their professional work. The second section lists resources for study, work, and travel abroad libraries of use to students and advisers alike. The third section gives contact information for organizations with two or more resources listed; most of these provide free publication catalogs and have home pages on the World Wide Web.

Resources preceded by two asterisks (**) are judged to be essential for even small education abroad libraries and would also be the best ones with which to begin when researching options. Resources preceded by one asterisk (*) are considered to be useful for a broad audience and belong in a well-stocked library. Resources without an asterisk may be useful for a specific audience, such as students and faculty in area studies or law or medicine.

This list is meant to be *used*, so complete contact information (including fax numbers, internet addresses, and web sites) is given, along with the latest known edition and its 1997 cost. With this information, it should be easy to inquire about new publications, future editions, or changes in prices.

This bibliography was compiled by William Nolting, Director of International Opportunities, University of Michigan International Center, 603 East Madison, Ann Arbor, MI 48109-1370; tel: 313.764.9310; fax: 313.647.2181; e-mail: bnolting@umich.edu; and Clay Hubbs, Director of International Studies, Hampshire College, and editor of *Transitions Abroad*, Amherst, MA 01004-1300; tel: 413.256.3414; fax: 413.256.0373; e-mail: cah00@hamp.hampshire.edu *or* trabroad@aol.com, http://www.

transabroad.com. We welcome suggestions and updates. Finally, we grate-fully acknowledge the work of Catherine Gamon and Heidi Soneson, and before them, Lily von Klemperer, on previous editions of this bibliogra-phy, as well as more recent suggestions received through SECUSS-L by NAFSA members too numerous to mention.

I. Resources for Advising and Administration

General Resources

The Advising Quarterly. Subscription: $40 ($50 overseas) from AMIDEAST.
   Quarterly dealing with trends and developments in international edu-cational exchanges with the Middle East.

AIFS Advisors' Guides. Various authors and dates. American Institute for Foreign Study. Free from AIFS, 102 Greenwich Ave., Greenwich, CT 06830; tel: 800.727.AIFS; fax: 203.863.6009.
   Guides by and for education abroad advisers cover topics such as pro-moting ethnic diversity, reentry, health, nontraditional education abroad, political advocacy, and administrative issues.

** Catalogs of publications from organizations and publishers specializ-ing in international education: Council on International Educational Exchange (CIEE); Institute of International Education (IIE); Impact Publications; Intercultural Press; NAFSA: Association of International Educators.
   Essential for staying up-to-date. Check their web sites, too. (See con-tact information in Section III.)

* *CIEE Occasional Papers.* Various authors and dates. Available from CIEE. Costs range from $3 to $10. Papers 1–19 are bound in a single vol-ume that costs $16.
   These 31 reports focus on various aspects of the education abroad field, including studies on U.S. student populations overseas, partici-pation of minorities in education abroad, faculty exchanges, interna-tional business programs, the nature of international education, and essential considerations for developing successful programs in the developing world.

Designing Sustainable Educational Linkages with Institutions in

Developing Countries. Karen Jenkins. 1995. 32 pp. NAFSA. $10 from NAFSA.

This practical guide to establishing programs with developing countries outlines the five steps of program development and gives examples of successful programs.

* *Educational Associate.* Included in IIE's institutional membership fee.

IIE's membership newsletter, published five times a year, provides a chronicle of trends and resources in international education, with a focus primarily on foreign student issues.

Film and Video Resources for International Exchange. Lee Zeigler. 1992. 34 pp. NAFSA. $6.50 from Intercultural Press.

Descriptions and ordering information for over 200 documentary videos and films of interest to study abroad advisers, foreign student advisers, and ESL instructors on U.S. campuses.

** *Forms of Travel: Essential Documents, Letters and Flyers for Study Abroad Advisers.* Judith W. Carr and Ellen Summerfield. 1994. 242 pp. NAFSA. $20 members, $24 nonmembers from NAFSA.

From NAFSA Study Abroad 101 workshops nationwide, this collection of forms and information materials, developed by education abroad offices, covers topics such as the application process, financial aid, travel documents, medical insurance, housing, orientation, and reentry.

International Dialing Guide, AT&T. Free upon request; tel: 800.222.0400; fax: 800.805.6663.

How to make international calls from the United States or abroad. Includes dialing codes worldwide.

** *International Educator.* NAFSA. Quarterly magazine. $24 per year in the United States; $36 in Canada and Mexico; $48 elsewhere; or included in NAFSA membership fee.

Essays on major issues and trends in international education.

* *International Exchange Locator: A Guide to U.S. Organizations, Federal Agencies, and Congressional Committees Active in International Educational Exchange.* Alliance for International Educational and Cultural Exchange. 1996. 192 pp. $29.95 plus shipping from IIE.

Key information on nearly 100 organizations responsible for the exchange of over 100,000 U.S. and foreign nationals annually. Contact information on congressional committees and federal agency officials that deal with exchange issues.

* *NAFSA Cooperative Grants Model Programs List.* Free from NAFSA.
Describes dozens of successful programs initiated by education abroad and international student offices with assistance from NAFSA COOP grants; full reports available. Education abroad examples include peer adviser and reentry programs, workshops and handbooks focusing on women and minorities abroad, guides to internships and volunteering abroad, and using the World Wide Web for researching overseas options. Provides inspiration for programming ideas or applying for a grant.

** *NAFSA's Guide to Education Abroad.* William Hoffa, John Pearson. 1997. NAFSA. $36 members, $45 nonmembers from NAFSA.
This indispensable reference for education abroad offices provides both an overview of principles and practices and detailed information and advice for advisers. Includes bibliography on work, study, and travel; case histories; program evaluation guide.

** *NAFSA Membership Directory: Institutions and Individuals in International Educational Exchange.* 1997. Biennial. 196 pp. NAFSA. $25 members, $75 nonmembers from NAFSA.
The essential reference for finding colleagues and institutions in international educational exchange.

** NAFSA *Newsletter.* NAFSA. Published 8x/year. Included in NAFSA membership fee.
Explores the latest developments in international educational exchange, carries in-depth examinations of issues and articles on practical applications of knowledge in the field, and provides commentary on governmental actions.

* *Update.* Monthly. CIEE. Free ($12/year outside United States and Canada).
CIEE's monthly newsletter reports on study, work, and volunteer programs and conferences organized by the CIEE. Covers developments in the field of international educational exchange. Includes book reviews.

Adviser's Resources: Diverse Populations

* *Black Students and Overseas Programs: Broadening the Base of*

Participation. CIEE. 1991. 80 pp. $10 plus shipping from CIEE.
  Addresses the issue of underrepresented groups in education abroad. Practical and positive advice by faculty, administrators, and students. Authors include Johnnetta Cole, Holly Carter, Robert Bailey, and Margery Ganz.

BMCPIE-L. E-mail group for NAFSA's Black and Multicultural Professionals in International Education (BMCPIE). Subscribe free by sending a message reading "subscribe bmcpie-l (your full name)" to: listserv@uga.cc.uga.edu; leave subject field blank.
  E-mail announcement group for advisers interested in promoting greater involvement of minorities in international education.

* *Careers.* 1997. Video, 30 minutes. Charlayne Hunter-Gault, director. Available for the cost of shipping from: Nicole Morris, The Global Center, 1600 Broadway Suite 700, New York, NY 10019; tel: 212.246.0202; fax: 212.246.2677.
  Video aims to increase minority awareness of international career opportunities, and is intended for high school and college audiences. Features on-site interviews with African-Americans, Latinos, Asian-Americans and Native-Americans who are working in international settings.

* *The Handbook for Women Abroad.* Jane Wemhoener, ed. 1991. 61 pp. Available from Kenyon College, Office of International Education, Gambier, OH 43022; tel: 614.427.5637. Ask for price.
  Features first-hand accounts by women who studied, worked, and traveled worldwide. Topics include feminism, sexual harassment, religion and gender, friendships and dating, and host family dynamics. Project was sponsored by a NAFSA COOP grant.

* *Increasing Participation of Ethnic Minorities in Study Abroad.* 1991. CIEE. Free.
  A brochure to assist advisers in increasing enrollments of underrepresented minorities.

New Manual for Inclusion of Persons with Disabilities in International Exchange Programs. Mobility International USA (MIUSA). 1996. Contact MIUSA for price.
  Includes information on accessibility, organizations to assist people with disabilities, and checklists to identify specific needs of participants with disabilities.

* *A World of Options: A Guide to International Exchange, Community Service and Travel for Persons with Disabilities.* Christa Bucks. 1996. 659 pp. Mobility International USA (MIUSA). Contact MIUSA for price.
A comprehensive directory of international exchange, study, and volunteer opportunities for people with disabilities.

Adviser's Resources: Reports on the State of Education Abroad and Calls for Advocacy

Abroad and Beyond: Patterns in American Overseas Education. Craufurd Goodwin and Michael Nacht. 1988. 133 pp. Cambridge University Press. $13.95 paperback.
Goodwin and Nacht's IIE-sponsored analysis contains discussion of the issues study abroad presents to U.S. higher education and the consequent policy decisions administrators face.

Advocating International Programs to Campus Decision Makers. Kerry O'Connor and Gail Ferrari. NAFSA. 1996. $18 (nonmembers) or $15 (members) from NAFSA.
Provides an overview of strategies successfully used by international educators to advocate within their own institutions on behalf of programs for international students and education abroad.

America in Transition: The International Frontier. Report of the Task Force on International Education, National Governor's Association. 1989. 95 pp. Item #08031, $10.95 plus $4.95 shipping from NGA Publications, PO Box 421, Annapolis Junction, MD 20701-0421; tel: 301.498.3738; fax: 301.206.9789.
The first and only national gubernatorial consensus on international education.

Educating Americans for a World in Flux: Ten Ground Rules for Internationalizing Higher Education. American Council on Education, Commission on International Exchange. 1995. 16 pp. $8 including shipping from ACE.
Forty-five college presidents present a challenge to their own and other 2- and 4-year institutions on changes essential in U.S. higher education to meet the challenges of globalization.

Educating for Global Competence: The Report of the Advisory Council for International Educational Exchange. CIEE. 1988. 28 pp. $5 plus shipping from CIEE.

This report by an advisory group of leaders in education, business, and government (chaired by Thomas A. Bartlett, chancellor of the University of Alabama), reviews the state of study abroad and makes recommendations for the future.

Educational Exchange and Global Competence. Richard Lambert, ed. 1994. 294 pp. CIEE. $20 plus shipping from CIEE.
An in-depth look at the relationship between international exchange and "global competence," based on the remarks of speakers at the 1993 CIEE conference.

Exchange 2000: International Leadership for the Next Century. The Liaison Group for International Educational Exchange. 1990. 12 pp. Free from the Alliance for International Educational and Cultural Exchange, 1090 Vermont Ave., NW, Suite 720, Washington, DC 20005; tel: 202.371.2070; fax: 202.371.2190.
A post-Cold War perspective on international exchange and changing global needs.

Getting on with the Task: A National Mandate for Education Abroad. Report of the National Task Force on Undergraduate Education Abroad (NAFSA, IIE, CIEE). 1990. Reprinted as an appendix in NAFSA's *Guide to Education Abroad.*
Summarizes studies to date and makes recommendations for expanding education abroad, increasing diversity, making curricular connections, inhibitors to be addressed, and funding education abroad.

Global Preparedness and Human Resources: College and Corporate Perspectives. Sally Ann Law and Tora K. Bikson. Rand. 1994. 84 pp. $13 from Rand Distribution Services, 1700 Main St., PO Box 2138, Santa Monica, CA 90407-2138; tel: 310.451.7002; fax: 310.451.6915; e-mail: order@rand.org. Study summarized in the Winter 1995 issue of NAFSA's *International Educator.*
Study of 16 corporations and 16 academic institutions assesses what skills are needed for professionals to be competitive in a global workforce according to corporations, and ways in which academic institutions can best prepare their students for success in a global economy.

In the International Interest: The Contributions and Needs of America's International Liberal Arts Colleges. Report of the International 50 Liberal Arts Colleges. 1991. 87 pp. Free from the Office of the President, Beloit College, 700 College St., Beloit, WI 53511; tel: 608.363.2201.

Highlights the considerable contribution of 50 leading liberal arts colleges to international studies and education abroad, and makes recommendations for further strengthening the international dimension of a liberal arts education.

International Studies and the Undergraduate. Richard D. Lambert. 1989. 168 pp. American Council on Education. $17.50 including shipping from ACE.

Reviews the state of study abroad, foreign language instruction, and international studies, and notes that the "growth and validity of international studies cannot depend on actions within the field itself," but requires a strong commitment at the top and throughout the institution.

Missing the Boat: The Failure to Internationalize American Higher Education. Craufurd Goodwin and Michael Nacht. 1991. 130 pp. Cambridge University Press. $49.95 (hardcover only) plus shipping.

An in-depth look at the international experience of U.S. faculty, commissioned by the Council for the International Exchange of Scholars. An appraisal of the personal and professional benefits and risks of faculty travel abroad.

Open Doors 1994/95. IIE. Annual. $39.95 plus shipping from IIE.

Definitive statistics from IIE's annual survey of the numbers of foreign students studying in the United States as well as the number of U.S. students studying abroad. Note that the study abroad statistics from *Open Doors* are reprinted in IIE's *Academic Year Abroad.*

Overcoming Barriers to Study Abroad: The Case of New York State. New York State Task Force on International Education. 1995. 75 pp. plus appendices. Free from Cornell Study Abroad, Cornell University, 474 Uris Hall, Ithaca, NY 14853-7601; tel: 607.255.6224; fax: 607.255.8700.

Reports results of a survey of New York colleges and universities about participation in education abroad, and obstacles to same. Gives seven recommendations for expanding education abroad, from issues to be addressed by individual campuses to suggestions for statewide cooperation.

Adviser's Resources: Research on Education Abroad

These studies attempt to measure the effects of education abroad upon participants. Many offer suggestions to administrators for improving program effectiveness.

Encounters With Difference: Student Perceptions of the Role of Out-of-Class Experiences in Education Abroad. Michael R. Laubscher. 1994. 126 pp. Greenwood Press. $52.95 plus $4 shipping from Greenwood Publishing Group, Inc.

Through in-depth interviews with study abroad participants, this study seeks to illuminate a powerful element of education abroad, and to show how programs can assist students in maximizing their learning from these experiences. Includes literature review and bibliography.

Journal of Studies in International Education. CIEE and European Association of International Education (EAIE). To be published twice yearly beginning in 1997. Subscriptions available from CIEE.

Will publish research, essays, and reviews concerning international education.

Frontiers: The Interdisciplinary Journal of Study Abroad. Annual. $12 per issue from Frontiers, Boston University, International Programs, 232 Bay State Rd., Boston, MA 02215; tel: 617.353.9888; fax: 617.353.5402.

A forum for research-based articles on study abroad.

Research on U.S. Students Abroad: A Bibliography with Abstracts. Edited by Henry D. Weaver. 1989. 113 pp. CIEE. $12 plus shipping from CIEE. Also available (free) in searchable format at University of Southern California's web site, http://www.usc.edu/dept/overseas/bib.html. Updates planned for the web version.

A comprehensive listing of studies through 1987 on U.S. students studying or working abroad. It contains approximately 250 detailed abstracts by Barbara B. Burn, Jerry S. Carlson, Jürgen C. Kempff, Judith N. Martin, and John Useem.

Students Abroad: Strangers at Home. Norman L. Kauffmann, Judith N. Martin, and Henry D. Weaver. 1992. 208 pp. Intercultural Press. $19.95 plus shipping from Intercultural Press.

Examines the study abroad experience from the student's point of view and provides a theoretical frame for understanding the effects of a study abroad experience on students, along with recommendations for increasing effectiveness of programs.

Study Abroad: The Experience of American Undergraduates. Jerry S. Carlson, Barbara B. Burn, John Useem, and David Yachimowicz. 1990. 243 pp. Greenwood Press. $55 plus $4 shipping from Greenwood Publishing Group, Inc.

Landmark study by a team of American and European researchers on the effects of study abroad on students' learning and development, contrasting students who study abroad with those who do not.

Study Abroad: The Experience of American Undergraduates in Western Europe and the United States. CIEE Occasional Paper No. 28. 1991. 64 pp. Available from CIEE for $6.

Integrating Study Abroad into the Undergraduate Liberal Arts Curriculum: Eight Institutional Case Studies. 1991. Greenwood.
Reports on the practical measures taken by eight U.S. participating institutions in response to the study.

Impact of Study Abroad Programmes on Students and Graduates. 1990. *Study Abroad Programmes.* 1990. Jessica Kingsley (London).
These books examine the impact of study abroad on European participants.

Adviser's Resources: Credit Transfer and Evaluation of Programs Abroad

See also the sections on directories of universities (worldwide and region-specific).

International Admissions Bibliography. NAFSA/ADSEC. 1995. 16 pp. Free single copy from NAFSA.
Reviews current resources on how to evaluate and transfer credit from overseas institutions.

Recording the Performance of U.S. Undergraduates at British Institutions: Guidelines Toward Standardized Reporting for Study Abroad. David Rex and Thomas Roberts, ed. 1988. 9 pp. NAFSA. $8 members, $12 non-members plus shipping from NAFSA.
Guidelines for officials at British educational institutions for reporting the academic performance of U.S. study abroad students.

Transcripts from Study Abroad Programs: A Workbook. Eleanor Krawutschke and Thomas Roberts, ed. 1986. 59 pp. NAFSA. $8 members, $12 nonmembers plus shipping from NAFSA.
Workbook provides guidelines for those determining credit transfer and equivalencies for U.S. students abroad.

Transfer Credit Practices of Selected Educational Institutions. 1996–98. American Association of Collegiate Registrars and Admissions Officers (AACRAO). $25 members, $40 nonmembers from AACRAO, One Dupont Circle, NW, Suite 330, Washington, DC 20036-1110; tel: 202.293.9161; fax: 202.872.8857; internet: http://www.aacrao.com.

Lists acceptance practices of one "reporting institution" in each state regarding transfer credit completed at other colleges and universities in that state. Indicates whether institutions are members of regional accreditation associations. Also lists selected institutions outside the United States, with an indication of their accreditation status. AACRAO has numerous other publications specifically on evaluation of international credits.

Adviser's Resources: General Cross-cultural

In addition to the following, there are other cross-cultural reference materials of potential use to an education abroad adviser or library, many of which are country- or culture-specific. Intercultural Press is the most comprehensive source of such materials.

American Cultural Patterns: A Cross-Cultural Perspective. Edward C. Stewart and Milton J. Bennett. 1991 (originally 1972). 208 pp. Intercultural Press. $16.95 plus shipping from Intercultural Press.

Contrasts the assumptions and values of mainstream American culture with other cultures of the world. Analyzes patterns of perception, thinking, behavior, and belief which characterize culture in four major categories: form of activity, form of social relations, perception of the world, and perception of the self.

Applied Cross-Cultural Psychology. Richard Brislin. 1990. Sage Publications. $26 (paperback) from Sage.

Introduces applications of cross-cultural psychology. Themes include ethnocentrism, culture-general vs. culture-specific approaches, cultural awareness, and cultural differences.

The Art of Crossing Cultures. Craig Storti. 1990. 136 pp. Intercultural Press. $15.95 plus shipping from Intercultural Press.

Analyzes the personal challenges inherent in the cross-cultural experience, based on psychological and communication theory as well as on the perceptions of some of the world's greatest writers.

The Basic Works of Edward T. Hall. Original dates of publication 1959–1983. Anchor/Doubleday. $36.80 (entire set only) plus shipping from Intercultural Press.

A collection of cross-cultural works by Edward T. Hall: *The Silent Language, The Hidden Dimension, Beyond Culture,* and *The Dance of Life.*

Crossing Cultures Through Film. Ellen Summerfield. 1993. 197 pp. Intercultural Press. $16.95.

Examines how films can be used by international educators, especially in the context of cross-cultural discussions. Analyzes and discusses over seventy classic films.

Culturgrams: The Nations Around Us. 1996–97. Brigham Young University, Kennedy Center for International Studies. $75 postpaid.

Culturgrams provide clear and concise information on customs and courtesies, lifestyles, people, and history and government of 153 nations. They provide a quick overview for prospective travelers.

Human Behavior in Global Perspective: An Introduction to Cross-Cultural Psychology. Marshall H. Segall, Pierre R. Dasen, John W. Berry, and Ype H. Poortinga. 1993. 448 pp. Allyn & Bacon. $37.95 from Allyn & Bacon, 160 Gould St., Needham Heights, MA 02194; tel: 617.455.1200; internet: http://www.abacon.com.

A review of the history and present state of the major issues in cross-cultural psychology. Examines culture, cognition, personality, and social behavior within a cultural context. The last section of the book focuses on cultures in contact and cultural change.

InterActs. Series edited by George W. Renwick. Various dates from 1985-present. Intercultural Press. Various prices.

Each book in this series analyzes how Americans and nationals of another country or culture see and do things differently, and how these differences affect relationships. Cultures featured to date include: Arab, Australian, Chinese, East European, Filipino, Israeli, Japanese, Mexican, Russian, Spanish, Thai.

Intercultural Interactions: A Practical Guide. Richard Brislin, Kenneth Cushner, Craig Cherrie, and Mahealani Yong. 1995, 2nd ed. 379 pp. Sage Publications. $25.95.

A cross-cultural orientation and training manual based on techniques developed at the University of Illinois. The practical suggestions are accompanied by theoretical essays.

Learning Across Cultures. Gary Althen, ed. 1994. 197 pp. NAFSA. $16 members, $19 nonmembers from NAFSA.

> Collection of essays provides an up-to-date overview of cross-cultural theories and practice. Writing on topics from counseling student sojourners ("revisiting the U-Curve of adjustment") to cross-cultural training, the contributors include Judith N. Martin, Margaret Pusch, Janet and Milton Bennett, Kay Thomas, Gary Althen, and others.

On Being Foreign: Culture Shock in Short Fiction. Edited by Tom Lewis and Robert Jungman. 1986. 293 pp. Intercultural Press. $17.95 plus shipping from Intercultural Press.

> Anthology provides insights into culture shock and cross-cultural adjustment through the eyes of fictional characters from twenty short stories by such authors as Borges, Conrad, Crane, Hesse, and Kipling.

Toward Multiculturalism: Readings in Multicultural Education. Jaime Wurzel. 1988. 240 pp. Intercultural Press. $24.95 plus shipping from Intercultural Press.

> A selection of 19 articles that examine behaviors in a variety of cultures, illuminating both the dynamics of multiculturalism worldwide and the nature and challenges of multiculturalism in the United States.

Transcultural Study Guide. 1975 (reprinted 1987). 155 pp. Volunteers in Asia. $7.95 from VIA, Box 4543, Stanford, CA 94309; tel: 415.725.1803; fax: 415.725.1805.

> A series of questions designed to help students make the most of an educational experience abroad.

The Travel Journal: An Assessment Tool for Overseas Study. Nancy Taylor. CIEE. 1991. Occasional Paper on International Educational Exchange No. 27. $5 plus shipping from CIEE.

> Practical guide to writing and evaluating student travel journals.

Adviser's Resources: Predeparture Orientation and Reentry

* Back in the USA: Reflecting on Your Study Abroad Experience and Putting It to Work. Dawn Kepets. 1995. 34 pp. NAFSA. $5 plus shipping.

> A workbook intended to help returning students put their cross-cultural experiences into perspective. Also provides an adviser's outline for a reentry workshop using this workbook.

BAFA BAFA. R. Garry Shirts. 1977. Simile II. $255 plus shipping from Simile II, PO Box 910, Del Mar, CA 92014; tel: 619.755.0272.
   A simulation game of intercultural experience, in which participants assume the roles of two different cultures.

Barnga: A Simulation Game on Cultural Clashes. Sivasailam Thiagarajan and Barbara Steinwachs. 1990. SIETAR International. $21.95 plus shipping from Intercultural Press.
   Participants play a simple card game in small groups and experience simulated culture-shock. The game allows players to feel as if they are entering a different culture.

Cold Water. Noriko Ogami. 1987. $150 for purchase, $50 for rental, from Intercultural Press.
   Videotape consisting of interviews with a number of foreign students deals with issues of cross-cultural adjustment and with values. Can be used in predeparture orientations for U.S. students as well as in other cross-cultural training situations, and is accompanied by a facilitator's guide.

Cross-Cultural Reentry: A Book of Readings. Clyde N. Austin. 1986. 284 pp. ACU Press. $14.95 from ACU Press, ACU Station, PO Box 8060, Abilene, TX 79699; tel: 915.674.2720.
   Collection of 25 articles deals with reentry issues in general, issues related to specific groups, and strategies for reducing reentry stress. Includes exercises and other materials for use by individuals or in workshops and seminars.

Education for the Intercultural Experience. R. Michael Paige, ed. 1993. 344 pp. Intercultural Press. $25.95.
   Includes articles from an earlier volume edited by Paige, *Cross-Cultural Orientation: New Conceptualizations and Applications,* and from a special issue of the *International Journal of Intercultural Relations,* "Theories and Methods of Cross-Cultural Orientation." Focus is on the emotionally challenging nature of intercultural experience and training methodologies for orientations.

The Exchange Student Survival Kit. Bettina Hansel. Intercultural Press. 1993. 128 pp. $13.95 plus shipping.
   Covers issues from cultural baggage to culture shock and reentry. Although the book is based on high-school students' experiences, it may be useful for any kind of student exchange.

Going International® films and videotapes. Copeland Griggs Productions. $350 for purchase; $75 for rental; $25 to preview, plus postage and handling for nonprofit organizations. Available from Copeland Griggs, 5616 Geary Blvd., San Francisco, CA 94121; tel: 800.210.4200.

Seven films and videotapes examine different aspects of cross-cultural experience from the perspective of individuals who have lived abroad as well as professionals in the field of cross-cultural communication. Developed for business use. Some may be useful in predeparture or reentry sessions for college students; check production dates.

International Student Reentry: A Select, Annotated Bibliography. Leiton Chinn. 1992. 48pp. NAFSA. $8 members, $12 nonmembers from NAFSA.

Comprehensive annotated reviews of a vast variety of materials, from workshop models and simulations to research and theory. Those of particular interest for education abroad are noted in reviews.

A Manual of Structured Experiences for Cross-Cultural Learning. Edited by William W. Weeks, Paul B. Pedersen, and Richard W. Brislin. Intercultural Press. 1979. 133 pp. $9.95 plus shipping.

Fifty-nine exercises, long used by cross-cultural trainers, designed to stimulate learning in multicultural groups. Sections include clarification of values, identification of rules, recognition of feelings and attitudes, and community interaction.

* *Survival Kit for Overseas Living: For Americans Planning to Live and Work Abroad.* L. Robert Kohls, ed. 1996 (3rd ed). 181 pp. Intercultural Press. $11.95 plus shipping.

Provides a series of practical, do-it-yourself exercises for Americans planning to live and work abroad. Offers guidelines on how to set objectives for an overseas experience, how to become a foreigner with style and understanding, how to get to know your host culture, and how to combat culture shock.

Theories and Methods in Cross-Cultural Orientation. Edited by Judith Martin. Special edition of *International Journal of Intercultural Relations.* Vol. 10, no. 2. 1986. Pergamon Press. Out of print, but available in libraries.

This series of articles addresses theoretical issues related to cross-cultural orientation and training. Several of these are reprinted in the Paige volume, *Education for the Intercultural Experience.*

World within Reach: A Pre-Departure Orientation Resource for Students

Planning to Study or Work Abroad. Work/Study Abroad Network. 1995. Video, 55 minutes. $120 from Intercultural Press.

Video produced by a consortium of Canadian universities features interviews with students and advisers. It provides 5 segments: Predeparture Preparation, Academic Environment, Host-Culture Awareness, Culture Shock, and Coming Home. A user's guide suggests ways in which advisers can use the video with individuals or groups.

Writing Across Culture: An Introduction to Study Abroad and the Writing Process. Kenneth Wagner and Tony Magistrale. 1995. 154 pp. $19.95 plus $3 shipping from Peter Lang Publishing Inc., 275 7th Ave., 28th Floor, New York, NY 10001; tel: 800.770.5264; fax: 212.647.7707.

Recommended by the authors for predeparture reading, this book discusses culture shock and coming to terms with it through writing an "analytical notebook," achieving cultural- and self-understanding in the process.

II. Resources for Students and Advisers: Study, Work, and Travel Abroad

Guides to Study and Work Abroad, Worldwide

This section includes some of the most often-used books in education abroad libraries.

** *Academic Year Abroad.* Sara J. Steen, ed. 1996. Annual. 650 pp. IIE. $46.95 postpaid from IIE, or included with IIE membership. Also available as a searchable database accessible to IIE members on IIE's web site, at http://www.iie.org.

Authoritative and comprehensive directory of over 2,300 semester and academic year programs offered by U.S. and foreign universities and private organizations. Indexed for fields of study and location, with special indexes for cost; graduate, professional and adult courses; internships, practical training, student teaching, and volunteer work. Companion volume to *Vacation Study Abroad.*

Advisory List of International Educational Travel and Exchange Programs. Annual. $8.50. Council on Standards for International Educational Travel, 3 Loudoun St. SE, Leesburg, VA 22075; tel: 703.771.2040; fax: 703.771.2046.

Lists programs for high school students which adhere to CSIET's standards and provides valuable information for prospective exchange students, host families, and schools.

* *Alternative Travel Directory: The Complete Guide to Work, Study and Travel Overseas.* Clay Hubbs, ed. 1997. Annual. 400 pp. $23.95 from Transitions Abroad.

A compilation of directories of resources and programs for "life-seeing travel," learning abroad, and working abroad which appeared in the previous year's issues of *Transitions Abroad* magazine; useful for non-subscribers. Index for geographic area.

Archaeological Fieldwork Opportunities Bulletin. Annual in January. Archaeological Institute of America. $15 ($13 for AIA members) from Kendall/Hunt Publishing Co., Order Dept., 4050 Westmark Dr., Dubuque, IA 52002; tel: 800.228.0810; e-mail: aia@bu.edu.

A comprehensive guide to excavations, field schools, and special programs with openings for volunteers, students, and staff worldwide, for academic credit or experience.

Architecture Schools: Special Programs. Martin Moller, ed. 1996. Annual. 60 pp. $12.95 including shipping from the Association of Collegiate Schools of Architecture, 1735 New York Ave. NW, Washington, DC 20006; tel: 202.785.2324; fax: 202.628.0448.

Lists more than 100 study abroad programs sponsored by U.S. collegiate schools of architecture as well as short-term programs in the United States.

* *Basic Facts on Study Abroad.* IIE, NAFSA. New edition expected in 1997. Single copies free from IIE, or $35 per 100.

Basic information for students interested in an educational experience abroad.

** *Directory of International Internships: A World of Opportunities.* Compiled and edited by Charles A. Gliozzo, Vernieka K. Tyson, and Adela Peña. 1994 (new edition expected 1997–98). 168 pp. Available for $25 prepaid including shipping from Michigan State University, Attn: International Placement, Career Services and Placement, 113 Student Services Bldg., East Lansing, MI 48824; tel: 517.355.9510, ext. 371; fax: 517.353.2597; e-mail: pla14@msu.edu.

Based on a survey of 4,000 organizations, this directory describes a variety of overseas experiential educational opportunities for academic credit, for pay, or simply for experience. Cross-indexed by both location and subject. The original edition was developed with support of a NAFSA COOP grant.

The Directory of Work and Study In Developing Countries. Toby Milner. 1997. 256 pp. Vacation Work. $16.95 from Seven Hills.
A comprehensive guide to employment, voluntary work, and academic opportunities in developing countries worldwide. Intended for a British audience, it may omit some organizations of interest to Americans.

"How to Read Study Abroad Literature." Lily von Klemperer. 1976. Reprinted in IIE's Academic Year Abroad and Vacation Study Abroad and in NAFSA's *Guide to Education Abroad.*
What to look for in ads for study abroad programs.

* *The High-School Student's Guide to Study, Travel, and Adventure Abroad.* Richard Christiano, ed., CIEE. 1995. 308 pp. St. Martin's. $13.95 plus shipping from CIEE.
Describes over 200 programs for high school students, including language programs, summer camps, homestays, study tours, work, and volunteer opportunities. Indexes by program type and location.

Home from Home. Central Bureau for Educational Visits and Exchanges. 3rd edition, 1994. 224 pp. $18.95 plus shipping from IIE.
Compiled from a comprehensive database used by U.K. government agencies, this guide contains details on homestays, home exchanges, hospitality exchanges, and school exchanges worldwide. Information on school exchanges pertains primarily to high school. Includes profiles of organizations by country.

* *The Peace Corps and More: 120 Ways to Work, Study, and Travel in the Third World.* Medea Benjamin. 1993 (new edition forthcoming, 1997). 107 pp. Seven Locks Press. $6.95 from Global Exchange.
Describes 120 programs that allow anyone to gain Third World experience while promoting the ideals of social justice and sustainable development.

* *Peterson's Study Abroad: A Guide to Semester, Summer and Year Abroad Academic Programs.* Peterson's Guides. 1996. Annual. 955 pp. $26.95 plus $6.75 for shipping.
Detailed information on over 2,000 study abroad programs worldwide. Less than half the number of listings in the IIE guides, but slightly more information in each; a useful supplement. Includes essays on credit, financial aid, nontraditional destinations, internships and volunteering, and traveling (also for those with disabilities). Indexes for field of study, location, host institutions, and internships.

Planning for Study Abroad. IIE. 1989. $53.95 (members $26.95) postpaid from IIE.

Advising video that presents basic information on study abroad from students acting as peer counselors.

Smart Vacations: The Traveler's Guide to Learning Abroad. CIEE. 1993. 320 pp. St. Martin's Press. $14.95 from CIEE.

Directory of programs for adults lists study tours, opportunities for voluntary service, field research and archaeological digs, environmental and professional projects, fine arts, and more.

Sojourns. 1995. Regularly updated. Canadian Bureau for International Education (CBIE).

A searchable computer database of 2,000 work and study opportunities worldwide. Contact CBIE for purchase information.

The Student's Guide to the Best Study Abroad Programs: Where to Go from Those Who Know! Greg Tannen and Charley Winkler. 1996. 336 pp. Pocket Books/Simon and Schuster Inc. $12.00 from Simon and Schuster, 1230 Avenue of the Americas, New York, NY 10020.

Begging the question of what program is "best" for whom, the authors choose 50 college-level programs they consider "best," and provide excerpts from interviews with participants. While the questions posed are good ones, this selection of programs is highly arbitrary, and there is only disparaging reference (no titles) made to other resources.

Study Abroad. UNESCO. Vol. 29, 1995. 1150 pp. $29.95 plus $4 shipping from UNIPUB, 4611-F Assembly Drive, Lanham, MD 20706; tel: 800.274.4888; fax: 800.865.3450.

Describes approximately 4,000 international study programs and sources of financial assistance in more than 100 countries.

* *Taking Time Off: Inspiring Stories of Students Who Enjoyed Successful Breaks from College and How You Can Plan Your Own.* Colin Hall and Ron Lieber. 1996. 288 pp. The Noonday Press. $12 from Farrar, Strauss and Giroux, 19 Union Square West, New York, NY 10003.

Thoughtful book gives reports of individuals who studied abroad or interned, worked, volunteered, or traveled both abroad and in the United States. Contains useful directories to other resources.

** *Transitions Abroad.* Bimonthly magazine available from Transitions

Abroad, Dept. TRA, PO Box 3000, Denville, NJ 07834; tel: 800.293.0373; e-mail: trabroad @aol.com. $24.95/6 issues.

This is the only U.S. periodical that gives extensive coverage to all varieties of education abroad, from study, working, and volunteering abroad to socially responsible independent travel.

** *Vacation Study Abroad.* Sara J. Steen, ed. 1996. Annual. 430 pp. $36.95 plus shipping from IIE, or included with IIE membership. Also available as a searchable database accessible to IIE members on IIE's web site, at http://www.iie.org.

Authoritative and comprehensive guide to over 1,800 summer and short-term study programs sponsored by U.S. and foreign organizations and language schools in over 60 countries. Indexes by fields of study and location with special indexes for cost; graduate, professional, and adult courses; internships, practical training, student teaching, and volunteer work. Companion volume to *Academic Year Abroad.*

What in the World is Going On? A Guide for Canadians Wishing to Work, Volunteer or Study in Other Countries. Alan Cumyn. 5th edition, 1996. CAN$20 including shipping from the Canadian Bureau for International Education (CBIE).

A comprehensive listing of study and work abroad possibilities. Addressed to a Canadian audience; some listings restricted to Canadian citizens. Indexed by country and field. Invaluable for Canadian advisers and students.

The Whole World Guide to Language Learning. Terry Marshall. 1990. $15.95 plus $2 shipping from Intercultural Press.

Guidelines on how to learn a language while abroad.

Work, Study, Travel Abroad: The Whole World Handbook 1994–95. Lazar Hernandez and Max Terry, ed. St. Martin's Press. 1994. 605 pp. $13.95 plus shipping from CIEE.

Useful background information and overview of opportunities for study, work, and travel worldwide for college students. Lists only programs of CIEE members; these listings now dated. Contact CIEE for any plans for revision. Indexes for country and field of study.

* *A World of Options: A Guide to International Exchange, Community Service and Travel for Persons with Disabilities.* Christa Bucks. 1996. 659 pp. Mobility International USA (MIUSA). Contact MIUSA for price of this new edition.

Comprehensive guide to international exchange, study abroad, volunteer service, and travel for persons with disabilities.

Internet Resources for Study and Work Abroad, Worldwide

Although not as comprehensive as published directories (with the exception of the IIE home page), these sites do provide, at their best, links to relevant organizations around the world and information too recent to be found in books.

World Wide Web Sites

The World Wide Web is experiencing explosive growth, so any listing must be incomplete. Try using standard search tools such as AltaVista or InfoSeek (these two seem the most useful), and search for the names of organizations, or experiment with key words such as TESL, TESOL, ESL (for Teaching English) or other desired field and country. Here are a few excellent starting points.

** http://www.iie.org
  Institute of International Education. Provides information about services and publications offered by IIE, including Fulbright scholarships. IIE's directories of education abroad programs, *Academic Year Abroad* and *Vacation Study Abroad,* and IIE's scholarship directories can be accessed at IIE's home page by individuals at institutions that are members of IIE.

* http://www.nafsa.org
  NAFSA: Association of International Educators. Essential professional resources for advisers and administrators in international education, though not a directory of overseas programs.

* http://www.cie.uci.edu/~cie/iop/
  University of California-Irvine, International Opportunities Program (IOP). Ruth Sylte. One of the most comprehensive sites on the web. Provides directories of U.S.- and non-U.S.-based study abroad programs, and extensive guides for working abroad. Also features a "how to" manual for students and advisers, "The World At Your Fingertips," on using the Internet to research and prepare for overseas experiences (developed with funding from a NAFSA COOP grant).

* http://www.istc.umn.edu/
  University of Minnesota, International Study and Travel Center (ISTC).

Richard Warzecha. Excellent searchable database for study abroad, low-cost study abroad, scholarships, and a volunteer abroad directory.

* http://transabroad.com
  Transitions Abroad home page. Clay Hubbs, Jason Whitmarsh. Has directories of resources for study, work and educational travel abroad, and selected articles from Transitions Abroad.

* http://www.ciee.org/
  Council on International Educational Exchange (CIEE)/Council Travel. Information on study, work, and volunteer programs offered through CIEE only, as well as services offered by Council Travel (ISIC student IDs, etc.).

http://www.petersons.com/
Peterson's Education Center, Study Abroad Sector. A listing of study abroad programs. Lacks the detail of Peterson's published guide.

http://www.studyabroad.com/
Studyabroad.com. A commercial listing of study and work abroad programs. Not comprehensive.

E-Mail Discussion Groups ("lists")

To sign on to any e-mail list, send a message to the LISTSERV address where the group is based, along with a SUBSCRIBE command in the body of the message. For example, to subscribe to the SECUSS-L e-mail list:

1. Send e-mail message to: listserv@listserv.acsu.buffalo.edu.

2. Leave <subject> section blank, and in <message> section, type only:
   SUB SECUSS-L yourfirstname yourlastname yourinstitution

3. Send the message, and you will shortly receive a confirmation message (in this case from SECUSS-L) with full information about the group. *Save it for instructions!*

** SECUSS-L, SUB request to: listserv@listserv.acsu.buffalo.edu.
Essential discussion group for university education abroad advisers. List managers are volunteers of NAFSA's MicroSIG team, acting on behalf of the SECUSSA team. Searchable SECUSS-L archives are located at http://listserv.acsu.buffalo.edu/archives/secuss-l.html.

** INTER-L, SUB request to: listserv@vtvm1.cc.vt.edu.
Essential for U.S. university advisers working with foreign students,

418

though sometimes esoteric for others due to much discussion on immigration regulations. Possible to subscribe for specific topics such as SECUSSA. Often dozens of messages daily. List managers are volunteers.

PCORPS-L, SUB request to: listserv@cmuvm.csv. cmich.edu.
Discussions by returned and potential Peace Corps volunteers, on the Peace Corps experience, developing countries, etc. Updates on positions. Lively (a dozen messages daily) and informative. Owner: Elliot Parker, Central Michigan University.

JET-L, SUB request to: listserv@listserv.arizona.edu.
Discussions by returned and prospective JET participants (teaching English in Japan); moderate activity. Owner: Michael McVey.

CIE-NEWS, SUB request to: listserv@uci.edu.
Twice-monthly announcements—not a discussion group—of overseas opportunities for study, work, internships, teaching, research and volunteering (or see web site, above). Owner: Ruth Sylte, University of California–Irvine.

Directories of Universities, Worldwide

These expensive directories, found in most college libraries, can be valuable for researching options not listed in study abroad directories, such as direct enrollment (e.g., for Fulbright or Rotary scholarship recipients) and degree programs. The directories can also lead you to information on contacting institutions, and evaluation of credit from overseas institutions. See also region-specific directories.

Commonwealth Universities Yearbook. Compiled by the Association of Commonwealth Universities. 71st edition, 1995. 2,200 pp. Two-volume set. $235 plus $6 shipping from Stockton Press.
Detailed profiles of universities in all 34 of the Commonwealth countries, including Africa, Asia, the Americas, and the Pacific Rim, with comprehensive listings of degree programs and a register of 230,000 academic and administrative staff. Useful for researching options for direct enrollment and degree programs in universities in which the language is often English.

International Handbook of Universities. 14th edition, 1996. Biennial. 1,350 pp. $245 plus $6 shipping. International Association of Universities.

Distributed in United States and Canada by Stockton Press.
Entries for more than 5,700 universities and other institutions of higher education in 170 countries and territories. Listings include descriptions of academic departments, language of instruction, admission requirements, fees, student enrollments. Contact information includes addresses, telephone, fax, and e-mail.

World Academic Database CD-ROM. 1996. $435 plus $6 shipping from Stockton Press. Combines the 14th edition of *International Handbook of Universities* and the 20th edition of *World List of Universities* with additional information from TRACE.
One of the most complete sources of information on higher education around the world.

World List of Universities. International Association of Universities. 1995, 20th edition. 1,100 pp. $160 plus $6 shipping from Stockton Press.
Addresses, telephone, and fax numbers of over 9,000 institutions of higher education worldwide.

The World of Learning. 1996. Annual. 2,025 pp. Europa Publications Ltd. $415 plus postage from International Publications Service, c/o Taylor & Francis Group, 1900 Frost Rd., Suite 101, Bristol, PA 19007; tel: 215.785.5800; fax: 215.785.5515; e-mail: bkorders@ tan.tfpa.com.
This authoritative guide lists over 26,000 institutions of higher education by country, gives names of staff and faculty, and includes information such as language of instruction and academic calendar. It also provides information on a broad spectrum of international organizations and associations (learned societies, research institutes) involved in education throughout the world.

Funding for International Activities, Worldwide

Note that relatively few scholarships are available for undergraduate study abroad; advisers should work with their financial aid offices to ensure that financial aid is available for study abroad. Also see region-specific resources.

Annual Register of Grant Support. 1996. Annual. 1,275 pp. R.R. Bowker, division of Reed Reference. Available for $199.95 plus shipping from Reed Reference Publishing Co., 121 Chanlon Rd., New Providence, NJ 07974; tel: 908.464.6800; fax: 908.665.6688; e-mail: info@reedref.com. Available in most college libraries.

A comprehensive listing of scholarships, fellowships, and grants; some chapters are devoted to international affairs and area studies, as well as international studies and research abroad.

* CIEE Scholarships for Undergraduates.
ISIC Travel Grants for Educational Programs in Developing Countries. Covers transportation costs for undergraduates to study, work, or volunteer in developing countries. Students at CIEE member institutions are eligible. Bailey Minority Student Scholarships cover transportation costs for undergraduate students of color to study, work, or volunteer with any CIEE program. Contact CIEE toll free at 888.COUNCIL for applications.

Dan Cassidy's Worldwide College Scholarship Directory, 4th edition. (Formerly *International Scholarship Directory*. Daniel J. Cassidy.) 1995. 249 pp. $19.95 plus $3.50 shipping from Career Press, Inc., 3 Tice Rd., PO Box 687, Franklin Lakes, NJ 07417; tel: 800.CAREER.1 or 201.848.0310.
Information on private sector funding sources for undergraduate study. Oddly, this volume's geographical index lists the United States as the country of study for all but a handful of these listings.

Dan Cassidy's Worldwide Graduate Scholarship Directory. Daniel J. Cassidy. 1995. 400 pp. $26.99 plus $3.50 shipping from Career Press (above).
Directory of private sector funding sources for graduate study; same drawback as the above directory from the same source.

Fellowship Guide to Western Europe. Gina Bria Vescovi, ed. 1989. 113 pp. Available for $8 plus $2 shipping prepaid by check to "Columbia University-CES" from Council for European Studies, 808-809 International Affairs Bldg., Columbia University, New York, NY 10027; tel: 212.854.4172; fax: 212.854.8808.
Scholarships and fellowships for use in Western Europe, mostly for graduate study. Chapters for general listings; fellowships for women; specific fields of study; specific countries. One index for names of organizations.

Fellowships in International Affairs: A Guide to Opportunities in the United States and Abroad. Gale Mattox, ed. 1994. 195 pp. Women in International Security. $17.95 plus $3 shipping from Lynne Rienner Publishers, 1800 30th St., Suite 314, Boulder, CO 80301; tel: 313.444.6684.
Well-researched directory of fellowships and grants for international

relations; most for graduate and postdoctoral students or professionals. Indexes for level of study, geographic specialization, and non-U.S. applicants.

Fellowships, Scholarships, and Related Opportunities in International Education. 1995. 100 pp. Available for $10 postpaid from Center for International Education, 1620 Melrose Ave., University of Tennessee-Knoxville, Knoxville, TN 37996-3531; tel: 423.974.3177; fax: 423.974.2985.
Describes fellowships and scholarships for study and research abroad, primarily at the graduate level. Indexes for field of study and country.

* *Financial Aid for Research and Creative Activities Abroad 1996–98.* Gail Ann Schlachter and R. David Weber, ed. 1996. Revised every 2 years. 440 pp. $45 plus $4 shipping from Reference Service Press.
Lists 1,300 funding sources available to support research, professional development, teaching assignments, or creative activities. Sources mainly for graduate students, postdoctorates, professionals; relatively few for undergraduate and high school students. Indexes for level of study, location, subject.

* *Financial Aid for Study and Training Abroad 1996–98.* Gail Ann Schlachter and R. David Weber, ed. 1996. Revised every 2 years. 275 pp. $38.50 plus $4 shipping from Reference Service Press.
Lists 1,000 funding sources available to support formal educational programs such as study abroad, training, internships, workshops, or seminars. Sources for high school students, undergraduate and graduate students, and postdoctorates; some for professionals. Indexes by level of study, location, subject.

* *Financial Aid for Study Abroad: A Manual for Advisers and Administrators.* Stephen Cooper, William W. Cressey, and Nancy K. Stubbs, eds. 1989. $12 nonmembers, $8 members plus $5 shipping from NAFSA.
Not a directory of scholarships, this volume for administrators tells how to use primarily federal sources of financial aid for study abroad programs for undergraduate students, and how to utilize this information to help shape institutional policies. Still useful for its sound advice on working with campus financial aid offices. The Manual also includes updated descriptions of regulations.

Financial Aid Information Page (NASFAA), http://www.finaid.org/. Available free on the World Wide Web. Not available in hard copy.
World Wide Web home page of the National Association of Financial

Aid Administrators includes sections on financial aid and scholarships for study abroad.

** *Financial Resources for International Study: A Guide for U.S. Nationals.* Marie O'Sullivan and Sara Steen, eds. 1996. 280 pp. Institute of International Education. $39.95 plus shipping from IIE.

Authoritative and comprehensive directory based on a survey of over 5,000 organizations and universities in the United States and abroad. Lists funding sources available to support undergraduate, graduate, post-doctorates, and professional learning abroad from study and research to internships. Indexes by level of study, subject, organization name.

Guide to Funding for International and Foreign Programs. 1994. 316 pp. $85 plus $4.50 shipping. *Grant$ for Foreign and International Programs 1995–96* (Guide #10). 1995. 345 pp. $75 plus $4.50 shipping. Both available from The Foundation Center, 79 Fifth Ave., New York, NY 10003; tel: 800.424.9836; fax: 212.691.1828; internet: http://fdncenter.org; also available in major libraries nationwide.

Guide to Funding describes how to research and approach foundations for funding institutions' international programs; *Grant$* lists 6,300 grants given to organizations in the two preceding years. The Foundation Center publishes numerous other directories from its comprehensive and up-to-date database on foundations and corporate giving programs.

A Guide to Grants, Fellowships and Scholarships in International Forestry and Natural Resources, No. FS-584. Damon A. Job. 1995. 114 pp. USDA-U.S. Forest Service. Available free from the USDA-U.S. Forest Service, International Forestry Division, 1049 14th St. NW, Franklin Court Bldg, Washington, DC 20090-6538; tel: 202.273.4695.

Particularly useful for students of the environment and natural resources; includes many listings for overseas study and research.

* *Fulbright and Other Grants for Graduate Study Abroad.* Annual. Applications free from IIE, USIA Fulbright, U.S. Student Program, 809 United Nations Plaza, New York, NY 10017-3580; tel: 212.984.5330; internet: http://www.iie.org or http://www.usia.gov.

Scholarships for graduating seniors and graduate students, as well as qualified English teaching assistants. Currently enrolled students should apply through their own college, others should apply through IIE. Application deadline is typically in October or a month earlier through campus offices.

* *Fulbright Scholar Awards Abroad: Grants for Faculty and Professionals.* Applications free from Council for International Exchange of Scholars, 3007 Tilden St., NW, Suite 5M, Washington, DC 20008-3009; tel: 202.686.4000; e-mail: info@ciesnet.cies.org; internet: http://www.cies.org or http://www.usia.gov.

Information and application for university-level opportunities for lecturing and research abroad; most positions require doctoral degrees and/or three years of professional experience. 1996 deadlines for 1997–98: May 1 (Western Europe, Canada); August 1 (rest of world); November 1 (international education administrators); January 1 (NATO scholars).

The Grants Register 1995–97. Lisa Williams, ed. 1994. Biennial. Revised in December. 786 pp. St. Martin's Press, Inc. $95.

Lists scholarships, fellowships, prizes, and other sources of financial aid for professional and academic work beyond the undergraduate level. Has an index for traditional academic disciplines, but lack of geographic and other indexes hampers this volume's usefulness for education abroad.

Guide to Grants and Fellowships in Linguistics, 1994–96. 73 pp. $5 plus $1.50 shipping, prepaid only, from Linguistic Society of America, 1325 18th St., NW, Suite 211, Washington, DC 20036-6501; tel: 202.835.1714; fax: 202.835.1717.

Grants and fellowships primarily for graduate students and faculty, many for overseas use, offered by institutions, associations, foundations, and U.S. government agencies.

* *Money for International Exchange in the Arts: A Comprehensive Arts Resource Guide.* Jane Gullong and Noreen Tomassi, ed. 1992. 126 pp. IIE. $14.95 plus shipping from IIE.

Lists grants, fellowships, and awards for individuals and organizations in the creative arts, as well as exchange programs, artists residencies and colonies, most of which will not be found in other directories.

* *Rotary Foundation Ambassadorial Scholarships.* Information available from The Rotary Foundation of Rotary International, One Rotary Center, 1560 Sherman Ave., Evanston, IL 60201-3698; tel: 847.866.3000; fax 847.328.8554.

Information about Rotary scholarships for study abroad, available to undergraduates and graduates who are unrelated to a member of Rotary. Application possible only through local Rotary Clubs.

Application deadlines vary locally and may be as early as one and a half years ahead of the desired date for going abroad.

World Arts: A Guide to International Arts Exchange (home page). Free on the World Wide Web at http://arts.endow.gov. Not available in hard copy.
  Guide by the National Endowment for the Arts to organizations that provide funding and other support for artist exchanges.

Region-Specific Directories of Study and Work Abroad Programs, Scholarships, and Universities

Additional information is available from the cultural or educational offices of embassies and consulates. For listings check the NAFSA directory under District of Columbia, or the Electronic Embassy, http://www.embassy.org. OSEAS advisers can sometimes help with education abroad questions, and may be contacted through INTER-L.

Africa/Middle East

* *African Studies WWW*, University of Pennsylvania (home page). Free on the World Wide Web at http://www.sas.upenn.edu/African_Studies/AS.html. Sandra Barnes, ed. Continuously updated. Not available in hard copy.
  Outstanding compilation of links to African and African-American information. Using phrase "study abroad" with this home page's search engine produces a list of study abroad programs.

* *AMIDEAST's Guide to Study Abroad in the Middle East* (home page). Free on the World Wide Web at http://www.amideast.org. Kate Archambault, ed. Continuously updated. Not available in hard copy.
  Excellent source for up-to-date information about study abroad throughout the Middle East and North Africa; project initially funded by a NAFSA COOP grant.

Beyond Safaris: A Guide to Building People-to-People Ties with Africa. Kevin Danaher. Africa World Press, Inc. 1991. 193 pp. $12.95 plus shipping from Global Exchange.
  Tells how to build and strengthen links between U.S. citizens and grassroots development efforts in Africa; brief chapters on volunteering and studying abroad.

Directory of Graduate and Undergraduate Programs and Courses in Middle East Studies in the United States, Canada, and Abroad. Biennial. $10

members, $20 nonmembers. Published by Middle East Studies Association of North America, University of Arizona, 1643 E. Helen St., PO Box 210410, Tucson, AZ 85721; tel: 520.621.5850; fax: 520.626.9095.
  Directory published by the main U.S. professional association for Middle East area studies; includes study abroad programs.

* *Complete Guide to the Israel Experience.* Annual. Available from the World Zionist Organization, 110 E. 59th St., 3rd Floor, New York, NY 10022; tel: 800.274.7723; fax: 212.755.4781; e-mail: usd@netcom.com; internet: http://www.wzo.org.il.
  Information on study and volunteer work opportunities in Israel.

* *Higher Education in Israel: A Guide for Overseas Students.* 1991–95. (Revision planned for 1997.) 160 pp. Free upon request from Committee for Overseas Students, Council for Higher Education in Israel, PO Box 4037, Jerusalem 91040, Israel; tel: 011.972.2.663131; fax: 011.972.2.660625.
  Describes degree and study abroad programs of all universities in Israel. Lists U.S. offices to contact for further information.

Opportunities in Africa. African-American Institute. 1993. (Revision planned for 1997.) 24 pp. $3 prepaid including shipping from Interbook, 130 Cedar St., New York, NY 10006; tel: 212.566.1944; fax: 212.566.1807.
  Addresses for information on study abroad, scholarships, volunteering, teaching, and educational travel. Interbook also distributes *Africa Report,* a bimonthly magazine published by the African-American Institute.

Sustaining Linkages Between U.S. and Southern African Universities: An Analysis and Inventory. Ann McKinstry Micou. 1995. 134 pp. IIE. $10 plus shipping.
  Includes extensive listings and descriptions of exchanges between U.S. and South African universities.

Asia–China

* *China Bound: A Guide to Life in the PRC.* Revised. Anne Thurston, for the Committee on Scholarly Communication with China. 1994. 252 pp. $24.95 plus $4 shipping from National Academy Press, 2101 Constitution Ave., NW, Lockbox 285, Washington, DC 20055; tel: 800.624.6242; fax: 202.334.2451; internet: http://www.nap.edu.
  Updated classic on studying and teaching in the People's Republic of China. Invaluable for university students, researchers, and teachers.

Chinese Universities and Colleges. Chinese Education Association for International Exchange. 2nd edition, 1994. 760 pages. $75 plus $4 shipping from IIE.

Comprehensive directory profiles 1,062 higher education institutions in the Peoples' Republic of China. Contact information included.

* *Living in China: A Guide to Teaching and Studying in China Including Taiwan.* Rebecca Weiner, Margaret Murphy, and Albert Li. 1991 (new edition, February 1997). 304 pp. $16.95 from China Books and Periodicals, Inc., 2929 24th St., San Francisco, CA 94110; tel: 415.282.2994; fax: 415.282.0994; e-mail: chinabks@ slip.net.

Contains descriptions of study abroad programs offered by universities and U.S.-sponsored programs. Also lists hundreds of possibilities for teaching English in China and Taiwan, along with practical advice on living and working there.

* *The Yale-China Guide to Living, Studying, and Working in the People's Republic of China, Hong Kong, and Taiwan.* 1996. 40 pp. $6.25 including shipping, prepaid only, from The Yale-China Association, Inc., Box 208223, New Haven, CT 06520-8223; tel: 203.432.0880; fax: 203.432.7246; e-mail: ycassoc@minerva.cis.yale.edu.

Profiles selected host-country and U.S.-sponsored study abroad and intensive language programs.

Asia–India

Studying in India. Published by Indian Council for Cultural Relations. Free from Indian consulates and embassies.

Basic information and advice on studies and research in India's many educational and scientific institutions.

Universities Handbook (India). Biennial. Available from: Association of Indian Universities, AIU House, 16 Kotla Marg, New Delhi 110002, India.

Overview of courses of studies, faculty members, degrees, library, and research facilities.

Asia–Japan

ABCs of Study in Japan. Association of International Education. Free from the Embassy of Japan, 2520 Massachusetts Ave., NW, Washington, DC 20008; tel: 202.939.6700.

Information on study and research at Japanese universities and graduate schools.

427

Academic Focus Japan: Programs and Resources In North America. Gateway Japan. 1994. 647 pages. $45 plus $5 shipping from Gateway Japan, $35 nonprofits, $15 students from Gateway Japan (checks payable to National Planning Association).

Profiles 160 academic programs, scholarships, and research opportunities in North America for Japanese area studies.

Academic Year in Japan. The Japan-United States Educational Commission. 1995. 118 pp. $20 from NAFSA.

Step-by-step practical guide to studying in Japan, based on the experience of Fulbright scholars.

Directory of Japan Specialists and Japanese Studies Institutions in the U.S. and Canada. Patricia G. Steinhoff, ed. The Japan Foundation. 1995. $50 plus $8 shipping ($12 non-U.S.) from The Association for Asian Studies, 1 Lane Hall, University of Michigan, Ann Arbor, MI 48109; tel: 313.665.2490; fax: 313.665.3801; e-mail: postmaster@aasianst.org.

Guide to Japanese area studies programs and faculty in North America. Also available: *Survey of Japanese Studies in the United States: The 1990s.* $15 plus $4 shipping.

* *Japan: Exploring Your Options—A Guide to Work, Study and Research in Japan.* Gretchen Shinoda and Nicholas Namba, ed. 1995. 437 pp. Gateway Japan. $20 ($15 students) plus $5 shipping from Gateway Japan (checks payable to National Planning Association).

The most comprehensive directory of study abroad, degree programs, cultural and homestay programs, scholarships, research, internships, and teaching opportunities in Japan. An essential resource.

Japanese Colleges And Universities, 1995–97. Association of International Education, Japan (AIEJ) and Monbusho, Ministry of Education, Science, Sports, and Culture. 1995. Biennial. 395 pp. Available to institutions from the Association of International Education, Information Center, 4-5-29 Komba, Meguro-ku, Tokyo 153 Japan; fax: 011.81.3.5454.5236; internet: http://www.aiej.or.jp.

A directory of degree and short-term programs (latter in English) offered by Japanese institutions and open to foreign students. Produced by AIEJ, a government-sponsored organization that assists with exchanges. Available free from AIEJ: *Index of Majors; Japanese Language Institutes in Japan; Scholarships for International Students in Japan; Student Guide to Japan.*

Australia

A Guide to Australian Universities: A Directory of Programs Offered by Australian Universities for International Students. Magabook Pty. Ltd. 1995. 168 pp. Free from Magabook Pty. Ltd., PO Box 522, Randwick, NSW Australia 2031; tel: 011.61.2.398.2.5555; fax: 011.62.2.399.9465; e-mail: info@magabook.com.au; internet: http://www. magabook.com.au.

    Profiles of universities and their degree programs. Also: *Studies in Australia: A Guide to Australian Study Abroad Programs.* Magabook Pty. Ltd. 1995. Both are published for promotional purposes; listings incomplete.

Good Universities Guide to Australian Universities, International Edition. Dean Ashenden and Sandra Milligan. 1996. Available from DW Thorpe, 18 Salmon St., Port Melbourne VIC 3207, Australia; fax: 011.61.3.9245.7395; inquire about cost.

    Profiles and rankings of Australian universities.

* *Studies in Australia: A Guide for North American Students.* 1996. Free from Australian Education Office, Australian Embassy, 1601 Massachusetts Ave., NW, Washington, DC 20036; tel: 800.245.2575 or 202.332.8285; e-mail: aeosec@cais.com; internet: http://www.psu.edu/research/aeo.

    Official information on year-long, semester, and summer programs; undergraduate, graduate, medical, and law degrees; scholarships and financial aid information (for both U.S. and Canadian citizens); internships. Also free: *Summer Study in Australia.*

Study Abroad in Australia: A Handbook for North American Students, Guidance Counsellors, Financial Aid Advisors and Study Abroad Staff. Annual. Free 30 page booklet from IDP Education Australia (North American Office), 5722 S. Flamingo Rd., #303, Cooper City, FL 33330; tel: 954.424.9255; fax: 954.424.9315; e-mail: auststudy@aol.com.

    Guide to study abroad published by a consortium of 33 Australian universities, supported by the Australian government's Australian Education Office.

Universities in Australia: The Complete Students Guide. Michael Dwyer and Kate Marshall. 1993. 317 pp. $17.95 from Financial Review, 201 Sussex St., Sydney NSW 2000, Australia; e-mail: afr@afr.com.au.

    In-depth university profiles.

Canada

Awards for Study in Canada. Free from Canadian Bureau for International Education (CBIE).
>Awards and traineeships open to foreign nationals. Also available from CBIE: *Destination Canada: Information for International Students* (free); *International Student's Handbook* (CAN$12).

Directory of Canadian Universities. Biennial. Free from the Association of Universities and Colleges of Canada (AUCC), Publications Office, 151 Slater St., Ottawa, Ontario, Canada K1P 5N1.
>Details on Canadian universities and program offerings.

European Continent: Central and Eastern Europe, Russia and the Newly Independent States

Directory of Programs in Russian, Eurasian, and East European Studies. American Association for the Advancement of Slavic Studies (AAASS), 8 Story St., Cambridge, MA 02138; tel: 617.495.0677; fax: 617.495.0680.
>The most comprehensive source of information available on U.S. and Canadian university programs, on-campus and abroad, in Russian, Eurasian, and East European studies. New edition available in 1997.

International Research and Exchanges Board (IREX) Grant. Opportunities for U.S. Scholars. Annual. Free from International Research and Exchanges Board, 1616 H. St., NW, Washington, DC 20006; tel: 202.628.8188; e-mail: irex@irex.org; internet: http://www.irex.org.
>Descriptions of scholarships for study abroad, academic exchange programs, and special projects administered by IREX in the Baltic States, Central and Eastern Europe, Mongolia, and the successor states of the former Soviet Union.

* *The Post-Soviet Handbook: A Guide to Grassroots Organizations and Internet Resources in the Newly Independent States.* M. Holt Ruffin, Joan McCarter, and Richard Upjohn. 1996. 393 pp. University of Washington Press. $19.95 plus $4 shipping from Center for Civil Society International, 2929 NE Blakely St., Seattle, WA 98105; tel: 206.523.4755; fax: 206.523.1974; e-mail: ccsi@u.washington.edu; internet: http://solar. rtd.utk.edu/~ccsi/ccsihome.html.
>Comprehensive guide to U.S. and host-country organizations involved in "institution building" in the former Soviet Union; many of these assist with academic, professional, and volunteer exchanges. The CCSI web site provides updates.

REESWeb: Russian and East European Studies, University of Pittsburgh (home page). Free on the World Wide Web at http://www.pitt.edu/~cjp/rees.html. Karen Rondestvedt. Continuously updated. No hard copy version available.

> Click on "Academic Programs and Centers" for listings of language and study abroad programs. Links to other REES area studies centers and information.

Where Walls Once Stood: U.S. Responses to New Opportunities for Academic Cooperation with East Central Europe. Mary E. Kirk. 1992. 110 pp. IIE. $7 plus shipping from IIE.

> A comprehensive listing of exchange agreements as of 1992 between universities in the United States and East Central Europe. *Continental Responsibility,* 1994, also from IIE ($11), lists exchanges between Western and Eastern European universities.

European Continent: Western Europe

All Europe

* *The EARLS Guide to Language Schools in Europe 1995.* Jeremy J. Garson, ed. 312 pp. $23.95 from Cassell, 215 Park Ave., S., 11th Fl., New York, NY 10003; tel: 800.561.7704; fax: 703.689.0660.

> Covers the 14 most popular European languages, including Russian. The guide profiles selected schools for each major language and gives details of specialized and general courses for children (ages seven and up), teenagers, adults, and business people.

Higher Education in the European Community. Brigitte Mohr and Ines Liebig, eds. 6th edition, 1990. Kogan Page. $32.50 plus $3.25 shipping from Oryx Press, 4041 N. Central Ave., #700, Phoenix, AZ 85012-3397; tel: 800.279.ORYX; fax: 800.279.4663; e-mail: info@oryxpress.com; internet: http://www.oryxpress.com.

> Information on study in 12 EU nations. New edition planned.

* *The International Education Forum* (home page). Free on the World Wide Web at http://www.csc.fi/forum. By John Hopkins, Tampere University, Finland. Not available in hard copy.

> Comprehensive and up-to-date information on universities and international exchange throughout Europe. Contains the ORTELIUS database (subscription only) on higher education, the NEXUS database of Overseas Advisers, and links to professional organizations such as the European Association for International Education (EAIE).

431

Austria

Austria: Information for Foreign Students; German Language Courses for Foreign Applicants and Students in Austria; Summer Courses in Austria – "Campus Austria." Available free from the Austrian Cultural Institute, 950 3rd Ave., 20th Floor, New York, NY 10022; tel: 212.759.5165.

Annual publications by the official Austrian Foreign Student Service (ÖAD).

France

* French Cultural Services Information: The following publications are free from French Cultural Services, 972 5th Ave., New York, NY 10021; tel: 212.439.1400; fax: 212.439.1455 This office may direct you to a regional office.

* *French Courses for Foreign Students.* Annual. Free from the French Cultural Services. List of French universities and language centers offering summer and year courses for foreigners.

I am Going to France 1995–96. CROUS. 220 pp. Extensive overview of university degree programs also includes lots of practical information useful for any student.

Studies in France. Basic document outlining various possibilities for study in France, including direct enrollment at French institutions.

* *Studying and Working in France: A Student Guide.* Russell Cousins, Ron Hallmark, and Ian Pickup. 1994. 314 pp. $17.95 from Manchester University Press. (Distributed in the United States by St. Martin's Press.)

Useful, detailed information on directly enrolling in French universities and language courses; one brief chapter on working.

Germany

CDS International. Free brochures from CDS, 330 Seventh Ave., New York, NY 10001; tel: 212.497.3500; fax: 212.497.3535; e-mail: cdsintl.org; internet: http://www.cdsintl.org.

Descriptions of paid study/internship programs offered by CDS for high school and college students and professionals.

* Information from the German Academic Exchange Service: *Scholarships and Funding for Foreign Students, Graduates, and Academics in Germany; Sommerkürse in Bundesrepublik Deutschland* (summer language and culture courses); *Postgraduate Courses in Germany; Studying in Germany–Universities; Study in Germany–Colleges of Art and Music.* Each publication revised annually. Available free from the German Academic Exchange Service (DAAD), 950 Third Ave., 19th Floor, New York, NY 10022; tel: 212.758.3223; fax: 212.755.5780; e-mail: daadny@daad.org.

Complete information about studying in Germany from its official exchange office.

Spiegel Spezial: Welche Uni ist die Beste? Special edition number 3, 1993 of *Der Spiegel.* Available for DM7.50 from Spiegel-Verlag, Versandservice, Postfach 2600, 74170 Neckarsulm, Germany; fax: 011.49.7132.969190.

Survey-based rankings for reputation and quality of teaching in German universities (overall and by discipline), with student comments. In German.

Netherlands

Study in the Netherlands. Annual. 100 pp. Free from NUFFIC, PO Box 29777, 2502 LT The Hague; fax: 011.31.70.426.03.99; e-mail: mknaapen@nufficcs.nl; internet: http://www.nufficcs.nl.

Official directory of all study abroad and degree courses (most taught in English) open to foreign students in the Netherlands. Also available from NUFFIC: *Living in Holland*; *The Education System of the Netherlands*; and more.

Scandinavia

Information from Scandinavian Ministries of Education: The following publications (and more) are available free from the embassies and consulates of each country, or from the Nordic Council of Ministers, Store Strandstraede 18, DK-1255 Copenhagen K, Denmark; fax: 011.45.33.96.02.02. *Norden: Higher Education and Research in the Nordic Countries* (overview of higher education systems); *Higher Education in Norway*; *Studying in Denmark*; *Study in Finland–University Sector*; *Swedish in Sweden*; and *Courses in English at Swedish Universities.*

Each publication lists courses of interest to foreign students, often taught in English.

* *Study in Scandinavia 1996–97.* Annual. 45 pp. Free from the American-Scandinavian Foundation, 725 Park Ave., New York, NY 10021; tel: 212.879.9779; fax: 212.249.3444; e-mail: asf@amscan.org.

Directory of summer and academic year programs (most are taught in English) sponsored by U.S. and host-country universities for high school and college students, and others interested in Scandinavia. Includes work and volunteer opportunities.

433

Spain

* *Courses for Foreigners in Spain Sponsored by Spanish Institutions;
American Programs in Spain; Study in Spain* (entering the Spanish uni-
versity system). Available from the Education Office of Spain, 150 5th
Ave., Suite 918, New York, NY 10011.

Latin America/Caribbean

* *After Latin American Studies: A Guide to Graduate Study and
Fellowships, Internships, and Employment.* Shirley A. Kregar and Annabel
Conroy. 1995. $10 (check payable to University of Pittsburgh) postpaid
from: Center for Latin American Studies, 4E04 Forbes Quad, University
of Pittsburgh, Pittsburgh, PA 15260; tel: 412.648.7392; fax: 412.648.2199;
e-mail: clas+@pitt.edu; internet: http://www.pitt.edu/~clas.

An essential resource for anyone with career or scholarly interests in
this region. Packed with useful information, though most listings are
not overseas. Extensive bibliography. Also available, free: * *A Guide to
Financial Assistance for Graduate Study, Dissertation Research and
Internships for Students in Latin American Studies,* 1996.

An International Students' Guide to Mexican Universities. Alan Adelman,
ed. 1995. 122 pp. IIE. $19.95 plus shipping from IIE.

Profiles higher education institutions in Mexico and lists fields of
study. Contains descriptions of aspects of Mexican universities of
interest to the prospective study abroad student. Gives contacts for further information.

Latin America Study Programs Course Guide. 1995. $35 postpaid from
WorldStudy, 9841 SW 73rd Court, Miami, FL 33156; tel: 305.665.5004;
fax: 305.665.7085; e-mail: 74722.32@compuserve.com.

Detailed guide to courses offered at selected universities in Argentina,
Belize, Chile, Columbia, Costa Rica and Ecuador.

Mexico: Oportunidades de Empleo. 1996. Annual. Available from
American Chamber of Commerce of Mexico, Lucerna 78, Col. Juárez,
06600 México, D.F.; tel: 011.52.5.724.3800; fax: 011.52.5.703.3908 or
011.52.5.703.2911.

Lists private-sector internships in Mexico for Mexican and U.S. students.

* *Travel Programs in Central America, 1995–96.* Ann Salzarulo-McGuigan
and Carolyn Martino, eds. 1995. Annual. 91 pp. $8 postpaid from San
Diego Interfaith Task Force on Central America (IFTF), c/o Ann

Salzarulo-McGuigan, 56 Seaview Ave., North Kingston, RI 02852 (written orders only).

Comprehensive guide to over 250 programs sponsored by U.S. and host-country organizations for short- and long-term study and volunteer service in all fields. Essential for finding options located in this region.

United Kingdom and Ireland

* *The BUTEX Directory; The BUTEX Guide to Graduate Study in the UK.* British Universities Transatlantic Exchange Association (BUTEX). Annual. Each guide approximately 90 pp. Free from BUTEX Secretariat, International Office, University of Plymouth, Drake Circus, Plymouth, Devon PL4 8AA UK; fax: 011.44.1752.232014; e-mail: jarandall@plymouth.ac.uk.

Guides by a consortium of 80 UK universities provide information about undergraduate study abroad opportunities (BUTEX Directory) and graduate degrees in Britain, along with complete contact information including e-mail and web addresses.

Graduate Study and Research in the U.K. The British Council, Education Information Service, 3100 Massachusetts Ave., NW, Washington, DC 20008-3600; tel: 202.898.4407; fax: 202.898.4612; e-mail: study.uk@bc-washingtondc.sprint.com.

Gives official advice on study opportunities in the U.K. at the graduate and research level (not for undergraduate study). Includes program information, addresses, and funding.

The Guide to Postgraduate Study in Britain 1997. 1996. £15 plus £2.50 shipping from The Newpoint Publishing Co. Ltd., Windsor Court, East Grinstead House, East Grinstead, West Sussex RH19 1XA; fax: 011.441.1342.335785.

A comprehensive guide including a range of postdoctoral taught and research degrees.

Study Abroad in Ireland. Annual. Free from Irish Tourist Board, 345 Park Ave., 17th Floor, New York, NY 10154; tel: 800.223.6470.

Academic programs and travel-study tours.

Study in Britain. Free from British Information Services, 845 3rd Ave., New York, NY 10022; tel: 212.752.5747; fax: 212.758.5395; internet: http://britain.nyc.ny.us.

Guide to study abroad and undergraduate degree study.

Times Higher Education Supplement Internet Service (home page). Free on the World Wide Web at http://www.newsint.co.uk/. Also as hard copy articles in back issues of the *THES*, often available in university libraries.
   The (London) Times lists results of official reviews of British universities; universities are ranked by teaching quality and research.

* *The Underground Guide to University Study in Britain and Ireland.* Bill Griesar. 1992. 222 pp. $9.95 postpaid from Intercultural Press.
   Designed to guide the reader through the entire study abroad experience; the only narrative of its kind from an American perspective.

University & College Entrance: The Official Guide. Universities and Colleges Admissions Service (UCAS). 1997. Annual. 1488 pp. £18.95 from Sheed & Ward, 14 Coopers Row, London EC3N 2BH, England.
   Massive official directory of all undergraduate degrees (as opposed to study abroad) offered by British universities and requirements for admission. Includes CD ROM, "STUDYLink UK."

University Courses in Education Open to Students from Overseas 1996–97. £7.50 surface mail from Universities Council for the Education of Teachers, 58 Gordon Square, London WC1H ONT, England.
   Postgraduate courses in education at British universities open to foreigners.

Young Britain. Annual. Free from British Tourist Authority, 557 W. 57th St., New York, NY 10176-0799.
   Information on study, work, and accommodations.

International Internships, Worldwide

These directories list internships located abroad or with international organizations in the United States, and may be for credit or for experience.

** *Academic Year Abroad/Vacation Study Abroad.* IIE. (See Worldwide Overview section.)
   Indexes for internships, practical training, volunteering, and student teaching list over 1,100 programs, most of which charge tuition fees and give academic credit.

* *The ACCESS Guide to International Affairs Internships in the Washington, D.C. Area.* ACCESS. Bruce Seymore II and Matthew T. Higham, eds. 1996. 157 pp. $19.95 plus $5 shipping from ACCESS, 1511 K St., NW, Suite 643, Washington, DC 20005; tel: 202.783.6050; fax:

202.783.4767.
The most up-to-date directory for the city with the most internships in international affairs. Also: *International Affairs Directory of Organizations,* Bruce Seymore II ed., 1992, 326 pp., $30, includes U.S. and overseas organizations.

** Association for International Practical Training (AIPT)/International Association for the Exchange of Students for Technical Experience (IAESTE). Contact them at 10400 Little Patuxent Parkway, Suite 250, Columbia, MD 21044-3510; tel: 410.997.2200; fax: 410.992.3924; e-mail: aipt@aipt.org; internet: http://www.softaid.net/aipt/aipt.html.
This nonprofit organization is uniquely able to assist students in obtaining work permits in some 60 countries for career-related practical training in most fields. It also offers programs for paid internships in engineering and science, tourism, and hotel and restaurant management.

Development Opportunities Catalog: A Guide to Internships, Research, and Employment with Development Organizations. Sri Indah Prihadi, ed. Overseas Development Network. 1993. 1996 insert, $5. 127 pp. $8.95 (students), $10 (individuals) $15 (institutions) plus $1.50 shipping from ODN, 333 Valencia St., Suite #330, San Francisco, CA 94103; tel: 415.431.4204; e-mail: odn@igc.org.
Descriptions of 79 development organizations offering internships or staff positions in the United States, and a few abroad. Indexed by subject and location. Also available from ODN, a nationwide student organization for development issues: *Career Opportunities in International Development in Washington, D.C.* Brian Dunn, ed. 1994. 98 pp. $6 (students), $9 (individuals), $12 (institutions). *Opportunities in Grassroots Development in California.* Wesley Batten, ed. 1994. 89 pp. $7 (students), $10 (individuals), $15 (institutions). *Opportunities in International Development in New England.* Michelle Burts, ed. 1993. $7 (students), $10 (individuals), $15 (institutions). Add $1.50 shipping for each book.

** *Directory of International Internships: A World of Opportunities.* (See Worldwide overview section.)
Indexed by subject and country, this is the only directory to both academic and nonacademic internships located abroad.

Directory of Summer Jobs in Britain. Includes listings of internships in Britain ("traineeships"). The ** *CIEE/ BUNAC Work in Britain Participant's Handbook* is a better source for U.S. students. (See Short-term Work section for both listings.)

* *Guide to Careers in World Affairs.* 1993. (See Careers section.)
Lists internships with some 200 international organizations located in the United States.

* *A Handbook for Creating Your Own Internship in International Development.* Natalie Folster and Nicole Howell. 1994. 98 pp. $7.95 plus $1.50 shipping from Overseas Development Network (above).
How to arrange a position; evaluate one's skills, motivations and learning objectives. Not a directory of opportunities.

International Directory of Youth Internships. Michael Culligan and Cynthia T. Morehouse. 1993. 52 pp. $7.50 plus $3.50 postage from Apex Press, Publications Office, PO Box 337, Croton-on-Hudson, NY 10520; tel/fax: 914.271.6500.
Comprehensive guide to U.N. agencies and U.N. affiliated organizations that regularly use interns and volunteers. Most internships are in the United States and unpaid.

International Health Electives for Medical Students. American Medical Student Association. 1993. $21 (members) or $31 for four-volume set, also available separately, from AMSA Publications, 1890 Preston White Dr., Reston, VA 22091; tel: 703.620.6600; fax: 703.620.5873; e-mail: amsatf@aol.com.
Overseas internships for third- or fourth-year medical students. Related titles: *A Student's Guide to International Health* ($5.50/7.50), and *Cross-Cultural Medicine: What to Know Before You Go* ($5/7), also available from AMSA.

** *International Internships and Volunteer Programs.* Will Cantrell and Francine Modderno. 1992 (new edition expected, 1997). 233 pp. $18.95 postpaid from Worldwise Books.
Well-researched information, much of it not available elsewhere, on programs abroad and in the U.S. which can serve as "stepping stones" to international careers for both students and professionals. Has no indexes.

The Internship as Partnership: A Handbook for Campus-Based Coordinators & Advisors. Robert P. Inkster and Roseanna G. Ross. National Society for Experiential Education (NSEE). 1995. 125 pp. $28 from NSEE.
A comprehensive handbook on how to administer an internship program. Though there is virtually nothing here about internships abroad, its advice on matters such as developing, structuring, monitoring, and evaluating internships for credit could be applied to over-

seas internship programs. Has bibliography of practical and theoretical literature on experiential learning.

* *The Internship Bible.* Mark Oldman and Samer Hamadeh. 1997. Annual. 614 pp. $25 from Princeton Review-Random House, NYC; tel: 800.REVIEW.6 or 212.874.8282; fax: 212.874.0775.

New directory describes in detail paid and unpaid internships offered by more than 900 mostly nonacademic organizations. About 120 of these may offer overseas internships (this is not always made clear), listed in an index for location. Other indexes for field, benefits, level of study, minority programs, deadlines.

The National Directory of Internships. Gita Gulatti and Nancy R. Bailey. National Society for Experiential Education (NSEE). 1995. 673 pp. $29 from NSEE.

Internship directory lists over 900 organizations offering internships, nearly all of which take place in the U.S. Notable for regional listings not found in other directories. Indexes for name of organization, geographic location, and field of interest.

* U.S. Department of State Student Intern Program. Free brochure and application from U.S. Department of State, Student Intern Program, Recruitment Division, Box 9317, Arlington, VA 22219; tel: 703.875.4884; internet: http://www.state.gov.

Nearly 1,000 paid and unpaid internships annually in Washington and abroad. Only for currently enrolled undergraduate and graduate students who will continue studies after the internship; competitive. Deadlines November 1 (Summer), March 1 (Fall), July 1 (Spring).

A Year Between: The Complete International Guide to Work, Training, and Travel in a Year Out. Central Bureau (U.K.). 1994 (new edition, 1997). 288 pp. $18.95 from IIE.

Addressed to a British audience, this book describes over 100 internships, teaching, and volunteer possibilities of up to one year, primarily in Britain and Europe.

Short-term Paid Work Abroad, Worldwide

These are guides to working abroad for pay or payment in-kind, usually not-for-credit and usually in non-career-related jobs.

The Au Pair and Nanny's Guide to Working Abroad. Susan Griffith and

439

Sharon Legg. 1997. 300 pp. Vacation Work. $16.95 from Seven Hills.
  Practical, insightful advice on how to prepare for and find a child care job in another country. Lists agencies worldwide. *Work Your Way Around the World,* below, has some of this information.

** *Council Work Abroad.* Free brochure from CIEE Work Abroad, 205 E. 42nd St., New York, NY 10017-5706; tel (toll-free): 888.COUNCIL; e-mail: wabrochure@ciee.org; internet: http://www.ciee.org. Available free in bulk to institutions.
  Application for paying work exchange programs through the CIEE for college students and recent grads in Britain, Canada, Costa Rica, France, Germany, Ireland, Jamaica, New Zealand, and South Africa. Approximately 6,000 U.S. participants annually. Also:
  ** *Council Work Abroad Participant's Handbooks* can be requested from CIEE at 212.822.2659 by college study abroad or career planning offices; otherwise for program participants only (not for sale).

* *The Directory of Overseas Summer Jobs.* David Woodworth, ed. Annual. 256 pp. Vacation Work. 1996. $15.95 from Peterson's Guides.
  More than 30,000 temporary jobs, paid and volunteer, in over 50 countries: who to contact, pay rates, how and when to apply, etc. Valuable information on work permits required for paid or volunteer work. CIEE (above) and AIPT (see Internships section) can assist Americans in obtaining work permits.

The Directory of Summer Jobs in Britain. David Woodworth, ed. Vacation Work. 1996. Annual. 255 pp. $15.95 from Peterson's Guides.
  More than 30,000 jobs listed, ranging from internships, farming, and hotel work to volunteering. Listings include wages, qualifications, and contacts. Americans need a work permit—contact CIEE or AIPT. The *CIEE/BUNAC Work in Britain Participant's Handbook* (above) is more useful for U.S. students.

Employment in France for Students. 1991. Free from French Cultural Services, 972 Fifth Ave., New York, NY 10021; tel: 212.439.1400; fax: 212.439.1455.
  Work regulations and possibilities. Also free: *Au Pair Work in France.*

* *International Cooperative Education.* Free brochure from ICE, 15 Spiros Way, Menlo Park, CA 94025; tel: 415.323.4944; fax: 415.323.1104; e-mail: icemenlo@aol.com.

Non-profit program offers paid, structured work placements and internships for students who have studied German, French, Italian, Dutch, Finnish, Chinese or Japanese.

Le guide du Job-Trotter en France. Emmanuelle Rozenzweig. 1994. 204 pp. Dakota Editions (France). US$18.95 plus shipping from Ulysses Books, 4176 Saint Denis, Montreal, Quebec H2W 3M5; tel: 514.843.9882; fax: 514.843.9448.
Complete guide to temporary jobs in France. In French.

** *Work Your Way Around The World.* Susan Griffith. 1997. Biennal. 512 pp. Vacation Work. $17.95 plus shipping from Peterson's Guides.
The authoritative (and only) guide to looking for short-term jobs while abroad. Extensive country-by-country narratives include first-hand reports.

* *Working Abroad,* InterExchange. Free brochure from InterExchange, Inc., 161 6th Ave., New York, NY 10013; tel: 212.924.0446; fax: 212.924.0575; e-mail: interex@earthlink.net.
Nonprofit program offers placements for paid work abroad, internships, English teaching, and au pair in Europe.

* *Working Holidays.* 1997. Annual. 382 pp. Central Bureau (U.K.). $18.95 from IIE.
Thoroughly researched information on 101,000 paid and voluntary work opportunities in over 70 countries. Written for a British audience, it sometimes omits relevant U.S. organizations.

* Worldwide Internships and Service Education (WISE). Free brochure from WISE, 303 South Craig St., Suite 202, Pittsburgh, PA 15213; tel: 412.681.8120; fax: 412.681.8187; e-mail: wise@unix.cls.pitt.edu.
Nonprofit program offers experiential learning placements for au pair (Europe), service and internships (United Kingdom), farm work (Norway), and low-cost language immersion programs.

Teaching English Abroad, Worldwide

Most of these directories and programs are intended not for the professional TESL teacher, but for college graduates who are native speakers of English.

* Fulbright English Teaching Assistantships. Applications free from USIA Fulbright, U.S. Student Program, 809 United Nations Plaza, New York,

NY 10017-3580; tel: 212.984.5330; internet: http://www.iie.org.
Currently enrolled students should apply through own college, others apply through IIE. English teaching options for graduates in Belgium/ Luxembourg, France, Germany, Hungary, Korea and Taiwan. Application deadline in October, or one month earlier if through own college.

** Japan Exchange Teaching Program (JET). Free applications available from Office of the Jet Program, Embassy of Japan, 2520 Massachusetts Ave., NW, Washington, DC 20008; tel: 202.939.6772 or 800.INFO.JET. Also available from Japanese consulates.
The largest program for teaching English abroad, with more than 4,000 placements annually. Offers two types of positions in Japan: English-teaching assistantships in secondary schools; Coordinator for International Relations (latter requires Japanese proficiency). Application deadline early December.

* *Japan: Exploring Your Options—A Guide to Work, Study and Research in Japan.* (See Regional Overview section.)
Detailed descriptions of English teaching possibilities, through both U.S.- and Japan-based organizations.

* *Living in China: A Guide to Teaching and Studying in China, Including Taiwan.* (See Regional Overview section.)
Useful tips and hundreds of addresses for anyone who wants to teach English in China or Taiwan.

Make a Mil-¥en: Teaching English in Japan. Don Best. 1994. 176 pp. $14.95 plus $2 (book rate) or $3.50 (first class) postage from Stone Bridge Press, PO Box 8208, Berkeley, CA 94707; tel: 800.947.7271; fax: 510.524.8711.
Guide has up-to-date information on everything from preparation and the job search to settling in.

* *More Than a Native Speaker: An Introduction for Volunteers Teaching Abroad.* Don Snow. 1996. 320 pp. $29.95 plus $3.50 shipping from Teachers of English to Speakers of Other Languages (TESOL).
Comprehensive source of English teaching ideas and techniques.

Native Speaker: Teach English and See the World. Elizabeth Reid. 1996. 93 pp. $7.95 plus $3 shipping from In One Ear Publications, 29481 Manzanita Dr., Campo, CA 91906-1128; tel: 800.356.9315.
Guide by an American who taught English in Latin America; main focus is on teaching tips.

* *Now Hiring! Jobs in Asia.* Jennifer Dubois, Steve Gutman, Clarke Canfield. 1994. 289 pp. $17.95 from Perpetual Press, PO Box 45628, Seattle, WA 98145-0628; tel: 800.793.8010; fax 206.971.3708.

Guide to finding an English teaching job in Japan, South Korea, or Taiwan. Lists U.S. placement organizations and overseas schools. Some information on teaching methods and living abroad. Similar "Asia Employment Program" is direct-marketed through ads in college newspapers for $50 by Progressive Media Inc., PO Box 45220, Seattle, WA 98145-0220; tel: 206.545.7950.

* *Now Hiring! Jobs in Eastern Europe.* Clarke Canfield. 1996. 320 pp. $14.95 from Perpetual Press, above. Similar concept as *Now Hiring! Jobs in Asia.* This is the only book at present with extensive contact addresses for teaching English in Eastern Europe.

O-Hayo Sensei: The Newsletter of Teaching Jobs in Japan. Lynn Cullivan, ed. Contact: Editor, O-Hayo Sensei, 1032 Irving St., Suite 508, San Francisco, CA 94122; fax: 415.731.1113; e-mail: editor@ohayosensei.com; internet: http://www.ohayosensei.com.

Biweekly listings by e-mail, $1 per issue or free on the World Wide Web.

Opportunities in Teaching English to Speakers of Other Languages. Blyth Camenson. 1995. 143 pp. $10.95 from VGM Career Horizons.

Overview of the professional field of Teaching English as a Second Language.

Teach English in Japan. Charles Wordell and Greta Gorsuch. Japan Times. 1992. 212 pp. $18.25 + $5 shipping and handling from Kinokuniya Book Store, 10 West 49th St., New York, NY 10020; tel: 212.765.1461.

Valuable for its realistic reports by experienced American teachers; no job search information.

** *Teaching English Abroad: First-Hand Reports and Resource Information.* 1996. Annual. 95 pp. $9.95 postpaid from Transitions Abroad.

Describes teaching opportunities worldwide by region, legitimate placement organizations, training centers, resource books, first-hand reports. Especially useful for Americans.

** *Teaching English Abroad: Talk Your Way Around the World.* Susan Griffith. Vacation Work. 1997. 368 pp. $16.95 from Peterson's Guides.

The only guide with extensive worldwide coverage (including Western and Eastern Europe, the Middle East, and other regions ignored in other guides), this outstanding volume gives in-depth information on everything from preparation to the job search. Extensive directories of schools.

* *Teaching English in Asia: Finding a Job and Doing it Well.* Galen Harris Valle. 1995. 178 pp. $19.95 from Pacific View Press, PO Box 2657, Berkeley, CA 94702.
   Detailed yet lively overview of teaching English in East and South East Asia with comprehensive teaching tips by a professional teacher. Few contact addresses provided.

Teaching English Guides (Passport Books/In Print Publishing series). Available in the United States from Passport Books (see NTC/VGM listing); elsewhere from In Print Publishing Ltd, 9 Beaufort Terrace, Brighton BN2 2SU, UK; tel: 01273.682836; fax: 01273.620958.
Teaching English in Southeast Asia. Nuala O'Sullivan. Forthcoming, 1997. $14.95. Covers People's Republic of China, Hong Kong, India, Indonesia, Japan, South Korea, Malaysia, Philippines, Singapore, Taiwan, Thailand, Vietnam.
* *Teaching English in Eastern and Central Europe.* Robert Lynes. 1996. $14.95. The only book to date with extensive teaching tips specifically for this region; focus is on Bulgaria, the Czech and Slovak Republics, Hungary, Poland, and Romania.
Teaching English in Italy. Martin Penner. 1996. $14.95. Note that the job search in Italy will be extremely difficult for citizens of non-European Union countries.
Teaching English in Japan. Jerry O'Sullivan. 1996. $14.95.
Teaching English in South and Central America. Forthcoming, 1998. This will be first book to cover this region in depth.
   Books in this British series offer extensive advice by professional teachers on teaching and living abroad. All would be valuable for teachers headed abroad, but the books provide few job search addresses.

TESOL Placement Bulletin. $21/year (United States, Canada, Mexico); $31/year (all other countries). Available only to members of Teachers of English to Speakers of Other Languages (TESOL).
   The best job bulletin for professionally qualified teachers of ESL and EFL. (TESOL also publishes a directory of U.S. schools providing TESOL training: $16.50 for members and $22.50 for nonmembers.)

Teaching Abroad: K-12 and University Level

These directories are for teachers with K-12 or university-level teaching credentials.

* *China Bound: A Guide to Life in the PRC.* Revised. (See Regional Overviews section.)
Invaluable for university students, researchers, and teachers.

College Teaching Abroad: A Handbook of Strategies for Successful Cross-Cultural Exchanges. Pamela Gale George. 256 pp. Longwood (hardcover). $37.50 plus $5.99 shipping and handling from Allyn and Bacon, 160 Gould St., Needham Heights, MA 02194; tel: 800.278.3525.
Thought-provoking yet practical guide to the cross-cultural dimensions of teaching abroad, based on the reports of 700 Fulbright exchange participants. Essential reading for teachers headed overseas.

* *Fulbright Scholar Awards Abroad: Grants for Faculty and Professionals.* 168 pp. Free from Council for International Exchange of Scholars, 3007 Tilden St., NW, Suite 5M, Washington, DC 20008-3009; tel: 202.686.4000; e-mail: info@ciesnet.cies.org; internet: http://www.cies.org/.
Information and application for university-level opportunities to lecture and do research abroad; most positions require doctoral degrees or three years' professional experience. Typical deadlines: May 1 (Western Europe, Canada); August 1 (rest of world); November 1 (international education administrators); January 1, 1997 (NATO scholars).

Fulbright Teacher Exchange: Opportunities Abroad for Educators. Free from the U.S. Information Agency, Fulbright Teacher Exchange Program, 600 Maryland Ave., SW, Room 235, Washington, DC 20024-2520; tel: 800.726.0479; fax: 202.401.1433; e-mail: advise@usia.gov; internet: http://www.usia.gov.
Program descriptions and application for direct exchanges in over 30 countries for currently employed K-12 and community college faculty and administrators. Deadline usually in October.

* *The ISS Directory of Overseas Schools.* Gina Parziale, ed. International Schools Services. 1995. 530 pp. $34.95 from Peterson's Guides, or ISS Inc., PO Box 5910, Princeton, NJ 08543; tel: 609.452.0990; fax: 609.452.2690; e-mail: edustaffing@iss.edu; internet: http://www.iss.edu.
The most comprehensive and up-to-date directory of overseas K-12 schools that hire qualified American teachers.

Overseas Academic Opportunities. Monthly bulletin. $38/year from Overseas Academic Opportunities, 72 Franklin Ave., Ocean Grove, NJ 07756; tel/fax: 908.774.1040.

Openings primarily for new teachers in all K-12 subject areas for jobs where the only language needed is English and state certification is not required.

* *Teach Abroad.* Central Bureau (U.K.). 1993 (new edition, 1997). 192 pp. Available from IIE.

A comprehensive British survey of paid and volunteer teaching opportunities worldwide.

Volunteer Abroad, Worldwide

Volunteer positions may be for academic credit or not-for-credit, paid or unpaid, but all are characterized by an orientation towards service.

* *Alternatives to the Peace Corps: A Directory of Third World and U.S. Volunteer Opportunities.* Phil Lowenthal, Stephanie Tarnoff, and Lisa David. 7th ed, 1996. 88 pp. $9.95 plus $4 shipping from Food First Books, 398 60th St., Oakland, CA 94618; tel: 510.654.4400, book orders 800.274.7826; fax: 510.654.4551; e-mail: foodfirst@igc.apc.org.

Thoroughly researched guide to voluntary service, study, and alternative travel overseas and in the United States with organizations which "address the political and economic causes of poverty." Excellent bibliography.

Archaeological Fieldwork Opportunities Bulletin. (See listing in section on worldwide guides to study and work abroad.)

Most comprehensive American guide to archaeological projects needing volunteers worldwide.

Archaeology Abroad, 31-34 Gordon Square, London WC1H OPY, England.

Three annual bulletins: March, May, and October. Lists worldwide projects and provides details on staffing needs.

Going Places: A Catalog of Domestic and International Internship, Volunteer, Travel and Career Opportunities in the Fields of Hunger, Housing, Homelessness and Grassroots Development. Joanne Woods. 1991 (new edition, 1997). 63 pp. $6.25 postpaid from National Student Campaign Against Hunger and Homelessness, 11965 Venice Blvd. #408,

Los Angeles, CA 90066; tel: 800.NOHUNGE or 310.397.5270, ext 324; fax: 310.391.0053.

Well-researched descriptions of more than 90 organizations and selected graduate programs.

* *How to Serve and Learn Effectively: Students Tell Students.* Howard Berry and Linda Chisholm. 1992. 77 pp. $7.00 from Partnership for Service Learning, 815 2nd Ave., Suite 315, New York, NY 10017; tel: 212.986.0989; fax: 212.986.5039; e-mail: pslny@aol.com.

Reality testing and exploration of motivations for students considering volunteering overseas; not a directory of opportunities. Developed with the assistance of a NAFSA COOP grant.

* *InterAction Member Profiles 1995–96.* InterAction. 1995. 350 pp. $20 members, $40 nonmembers from InterAction Publications, 1717 Massachusetts Ave., NW, Suite 801, Washington, DC 20036; tel: 202.667.8227; fax: 202.667.8236; e-mail: iac@interaction.org. See also http://www.interaction.org/ia, InterAction's World Wide Web clearing-house for volunteer options in the relief and development field, found under "Alliance for a Global Community."

Up-to-date information on 150 U.S. private voluntary organizations in relief and development work. Details which agencies are doing what in which countries. Also by InterAction: *Monday Developments,* bi-weekly job listing in this field, $65/yr for individuals or $275/yr for institutions; *The Essential Internet,* 47 pp., $12.

* *The International Directory of Voluntary Work.* David Woodworth. 1993 (new edition, January 1997). 264 pp. Vacation Work. $15.95 from Peterson's Guides.

Directory of over 500 agencies offering volunteer jobs and how to apply. Most comprehensive listing of volunteer opportunities in Britain and Europe of any directory.

* *International Voluntary Service Guide: Peace Through Deeds, Not Words.* Annual. $3 postpaid from SCI-IVS, 5474 Walnut Level Rd., Crozet, VA 22932; tel: 804.823.1826; fax: 804.823.5027; e-mail: sciivsusa@igc.apc.org.

Describes short-term volunteer options in Europe, Africa, Asia, and North America. Available through SCI-IVS.

** *International Workcamper* (VFP). Free brochure available from Volunteers for Peace (VFP), International Workcamps, 43 Tiffany Rd., Belmont, VT 05730; tel: 802.259.2759; fax: 802.259.2922; e-mail:

vfp@vermontel.com; internet: http://www.vfp.org.

The *VFP International Workcamp Directory* (119 pp.), available each April for $12 from VFP, describes over 800 short-term service placements in over 40 countries available through VFP for the summer and fall of the year of publication. VFP's World Wide Web home page has an outstanding set of links to other volunteer-sponsoring organizations.

* *International Volunteer Projects* (CIEE). Free brochure available from CIEE, 205 E. 42nd St., New York, NY 10017-5706; tel: 888.COUNCIL or 212.822.2695; e-mail: IVPBrochure@ciee.org; internet: http://www.ciee.org. Describes over 600 short-term summer voluntary service options available through CIEE in 23 countries of Europe, Africa, and North America.

Council International Volunteer Projects Directory (82 pp.), available each April for $12 postpaid, describes the workcamps in depth.

* *Kibbutz Volunteer.* Victoria Pybus. 1996. 192 pp. Vacation Work. $15.95 from Seven Hills.

Now the most up-to-date resource on volunteering in Israel. New edition lists over 200 kibbutzim at different sites in Israel; also includes information on work on a moshav and other employment opportunities in Israel.

** *Peace Corps Information Packet.* Free from Peace Corps, 1990 K St., NW, Room 9320, Washington, DC 20526; tel: 800.424.8580; internet: http://www. peacecorps.gov.

The largest U.S. volunteer-sending organization, with around 3,000 placements annually. Two year assignments. One of the best paid job opportunities in the developing world and Eastern Europe for Americans.

* *The Post-Soviet Handbook: A Guide to Grassroots Organizations and Internet Resources in the Newly Independent States.* (See Overviews by Region section.)

Most up-to-date source for organizations which may welcome volunteers.

* *Response: Volunteer Opportunities Directory of the Catholic Network of Volunteer Service.* 1996. 90 pp. Free (donations accepted) from CNVS, 4121 Harewood Rd., NE, Washington, DC 20017; tel: 800.543.5046 or 202.529.1100; fax: 202.526.1094; e-mail: cnvs@ari.net. Directory also online at http://www2.ari.net/ home3/cnvs.

Directory of lay mission opportunities in the United States and abroad. Indexes by type of placement, location, length of stay, etc.

* *Travel Programs in Central America.* 1996. (See Overviews by Region section.)

The most comprehensive listing of volunteer opportunities in this region.

** *Volunteer!: The Comprehensive Guide to Voluntary Service in the U.S. and Abroad.* Richard Christiano, ed. 1995. 188 pp. $12.95 from CIEE.

Detailed descriptions of nearly 200 voluntary service organizations recruiting volunteers for work in the United States and abroad. Organized by short-term and long-term opportunities, with indexes by country and type of work; the best place to start exploring volunteer options.

* *Volunteer Vacations: Short-Term Adventures That Will Benefit You and Others.* Bill McMillon. 1995 (new edition, 1997). 453 pp. $13.95 from Chicago Review Press, 814 N. Franklin St., Chicago, IL 60610; tel: 312.337.0747.

Describes more than 250 organizations sponsoring projects in the United States and abroad. Indexed by cost, length of time, location, type of project, and season. Opportunities from 1 weekend to 6 weeks.

* *Volunteer Work: The Complete International Guide to Medium and Long-Term Voluntary Service.* Central Bureau (U.K.). 1995. 240 pp. Available for $18.95 from IIE.

A thoroughly researched British survey of volunteer possibilities worldwide, with many listings not found elsewhere. Indexed by country and type of work.

International Careers

These are guides to developing a long-term career with an international focus, whether based in the United States or abroad. They typically focus on career fields rather than on specific locations.

The Adventure of Working Abroad: Hero Tales From the Global Frontier. Joyce Sautters Osland. 1995. 269 pp. Jossey-Bass. $25 from Intercultural Press.

Thirty-five American expatriates assigned abroad tell about the perils and opportunities of working in a new culture. Suggestions for employers and employees for preparation, support, and reentry.

** *The Almanac of International Jobs and Careers: A Guide to Over 1001*

Employers. Ronald Krannich and Caryl Krannich. 1994 (new edition, 1997). 334 pp. $19.95 from Impact Publications.

Companion volume to *The Complete Guide to International Jobs and Careers,* this is a comprehensive source of hard-to-find information, tips on other resources, and trends in international employment for Americans.

* *The Canadian Guide to Working and Living Overseas.* Jean-Marc Hachey. 1995. 1000 pp. CAN$47.65 or US$37 postpaid from Intercultural Systems, PO Box 588, Station B, Ottawa, Ontario, Canada K1P 5P7; tel: 800.267.0105, 613.238.6169; fax: 613.238.5274.

The most comprehensive single volume on working and living abroad; listings emphasize Canadian organizations. Americans can benefit from the thorough advice on overseas job searches, and from the most extensive bibliography anywhere, describing 550 publications.

* *Careers for Foreign Language Aficionados and Other Multilingual Types.* Ned Seelye and Laurence Day. 1992. 114 pp. VGM Career Horizons. $12.95.

Mainstream and offbeat jobs for those who want to use a foreign language. Includes profiles.

** *Careers in International Affairs.* Maria Pinto Carland and Michael Trucano, eds. 1996. 320 pp. $17.95 plus $4.75 shipping from Georgetown University Press, PO Box 4866, Hampden Station, Baltimore, MD 21211-4866; tel: 800.246.9606; fax: 410.516.6998.

New edition is the most up-to-date United States overview of international career fields; provides survey-based specifics on major organizations in all international sectors. Highly recommended.

Careers in International Business. Edward J. Halloran. 1995. 97 pp. $12.95 from VGM.

Overview of education for international business and types of opportunities, from employment to entrepreneurship.

Careers in International Law. Mark W. Janis, ed. 1993. 229 pp. $19.95 plus $3.95 shipping from American Bar Association, Attn: Financial Services, 9th Floor, 750 N. Lake Shore Dr., Chicago, IL 60611; tel: 312.988.5522.

Essays on how to plan for a career in international law by lawyers in the field. Also lists ABA-approved study abroad programs.

** *The Complete Guide to International Jobs and Careers.* Ronald L. Krannich and Caryl R. Krannich. 1992. 306 pp. $13.95 from Impact.

The best introduction to strategies and skills for landing an international job, along with listings of resources for researching international employers.

Directory of American Firms Operating in Foreign Countries. 1996. $220 plus $9.50 shipping from Uniworld, 342 E. 51st St., New York, NY 10022; tel/fax: 212.752.0329.

Lists 3,000 American companies with subsidiaries and affiliates in 138 foreign countries. University libraries have this and dozens of other expensive specialized international directories, which are beyond the scope of this bibliography. Impact Publications also carries many of these.

* *The Directory of Jobs and Careers Abroad.* André DeVries, ed. 1993 (new edition, January 1997). 407 pp. Vacation Work Publications. $16.95 from Peterson's Guides.

The only career guide with country-by-country coverage of everything from professional fields to short-term and volunteer possibilities. British publication, but usually includes relevant U.S. organizations.

Directory of Opportunities in International Law. Paul Brinkman, ed. 1992. 204 pp. $20 ($10 for students) from John Bassett Moore Society of International Law, University of Virginia School of Law, Charlottesville, VA 22901; tel: 804.924.3087.

Addresses of law firms, agencies, and organizations with international practices, and a partial list of U.S. law schools that provide international training.

Directory of U.S. Based Agencies Involved in International Health Assistance. 1996. 254 pp. $35 members, $65 nonmembers postpaid from National Council for International Health, 1701 K St., NW, Suite 600, Washington, DC 20006; tel: 202.833.5900; fax: 202.833.0075; e-mail: ncih@ncih.org.

Lists organizations in international health fields, by specialty and location. *Career Network* is the NCIH job bulletin. Subscriptions are $60 for members, $120 for nonmembers.

Employment Abroad: Facts and Fallacies. Rachel Theus, ed. 1993. $7.50 plus $3 shipping from the International Division of the U.S. Chamber of Commerce, 1615 H. St., NW, Washington, DC 20062; tel: 202.463.5460; fax: 202.463.3114; internet: http://www. uschamber.org/.

Stresses the realities of international employment.

Flying High in Travel. Karen Rubin. 1992. 319 pp. John Wiley & Sons. $19.95 from Impact.
Surveys the travel industry. Includes useful resources.

Getting Your Job in the Middle East. David Lay. 1992. 184 pp. DCL International. $19.95 from Impact.
An overview of career possibilities in the Middle East, along with information about Middle East history, culture, and recent events.

Great Jobs for Foreign Language Majors. Julie DeGalan and Stephen Lambert. 1994. 242 pp. VGM Career Horizons. $11.95.
Covers careers that involve foreign languages; advice often inaccurate.

** *Guide to Careers in World Affairs.* Pamela Gerard, ed., Foreign Policy Association. 1993. 421 pp. $14.95 from Impact Publications.
Thoroughly researched information on careers with hundreds of U.S.-based international employers in business, law, journalism, consulting, nonprofit organizations, and the U.S. government. Gives specifics on entry-level qualifications, internships, etc. Excellent annotated bibliography. Highly recommended.

Guide to Careers, Internships, and Graduate Education in Peace Studies. 1996. 71 pp. Available for $4.50 from PAWSS Publications, Hampshire College, Amherst, MA 01002.
Includes information on graduate study, internships, fellowships, and relevant organizations.

* *How to Find an Overseas Job with the U.S. Government.* Will Cantrell and Francine Modderno. 1992. 421 pp. $28.95 postpaid from Worldwise Books.
Comprehensive guide to finding work with the organization that hires the greatest number of Americans to work abroad.

How to Get a Job in Europe: The Insider's Guide. Robert Sanborn. 1995. 546 pp. Surrey Books. $17.95 + $3 shipping and handling from Surrey Books, Inc., 230 E. Ohio St., Suite 120, Chicago, IL 60611; tel: 800.326.4430.
Good source for country-by-country employer addresses (otherwise found in expensive directories). Includes general suggestions for finding a job.

How to Get a Job in the Pacific Rim. Robert Sanborn and Anderson Brandao. 1992. 425 pp. Surrey Books.
Same concept and price as above, but for Asia.

International Affairs Network Web, available free on the World Wide Web at http://www.pitt.edu/~ian/index.html.
 Home page provides information on graduate programs and careers in international relations. No hard copy version available.

The International Businesswoman of the 1990s: A Guide to Success in the Global Marketplace. Marlene Rossman. 1990. 171 pp. $19.95 plus $4 shipping from Praeger Publishers, One Madison Ave., New York, NY 10010; tel: 212.736.4444.
 One of the best descriptions to date of what it's like to work in international business.

* *International Education Career Information*. NAFSA Working Paper #40. 1996. 45 pp. $10 postpaid from NAFSA Publications.
 Excellent overview of careers in international educational exchange, with a good annotated bibliography.

* *International Jobs: Where They Are and How to Get Them*. Eric Kocher. 1993. 394 pp. $16 from Addison-Wesley, Reading, MA 01867; tel: 800.822.6339; fax: 617.944.4968.
 An overview of international career fields and how to prepare for them, along with general information on employers.

International Opportunities: A Career Guide for Students. David M. Kennedy International Center. 1993. 128 pp. $10.95 postpaid from Brigham Young University, Kennedy Center for International Studies.
 Useful guide for the student interested in international career opportunities.

The Job Hunter's Guide to Japan. Terra Brockman. 1990. 232 pp. Kodansha International. $12.95 from Impact Publications.
 Insightful firsthand interviews with Americans working in Japan in various professions.

* *Jobs For People Who Love Travel*. Ronald and Caryl Krannich. 1995. 304 pp. $15.95 from Impact Publications.
 Information for those who want to work the world before settling down, including but going far beyond the travel industry. Explores motivations; 50 myths about jobs involving travel.

* *Jobs in Russia and the Newly Independent States*. Moira Forbes. 1994. 228 pp. $15.95 from Impact Publications.

Provides much-needed help in finding opportunities, from business to volunteer, in this rapidly changing region.

* *Jobs Worldwide.* David Lay and Benedict Leerburger. 1996. 377 pp. $17.95 from Impact Publications.
　Country-by-country examination of employment opportunities; identifies key employers.

Journal of Career Planning and Employment. Periodical published by: National Association of Colleges and Employers (formerly College Placement Council), 62 Highland Ave., Bethlehem, PA 18017; tel: 800.544.5272; available in university libraries.
　Articles by career planning professionals. See especially "Student Dreams and the Real International Job Market," by Jeffrey B. Wood and other articles on international jobs in the November 1992 issue; see also the May 1994 issue.

Live and Work in...(series): *Australia and New Zealand* (1996); *Belgium, The Netherlands, and Luxembourg* (1993); *France* (1994); *Germany* (1992); *Italy* (1992); *Scandinavia* (1995); *Spain and Portugal* (1991). Vacation Work. $16.95 each from Seven Hills.
　Excellent British series for long-term stays. Information on employment, residence, home buying, daily life, retirement, and starting a business. More useful for those on overseas assignment than for those looking for a job.

Living and Working in...(series): *Britain* (1995), *France* (1996), *Spain* (1995) *Switzerland* (1996), *USA* (1995). David Hampshire. Survival Books (U.K.), available in the United States for $21.95 each plus $3.50 per book shipping from Seven Hills.
　Detailed information for long-term stays on everything from working to buying a house. More useful for those on overseas assignments than for those looking for jobs.

* *Making It Abroad: The International Job Hunting Guide.* Howard Schuman. 1988. 168 pp. John Wiley & Sons. May be available from Impact Publications.
　Positive insight into career patterns in various international career fields and employment sectors. Out-of-print, but available in libraries.

Opportunities in Foreign Languages Careers. Wilga Rivers. 1993. 151 pp. $11.95. VGM Career Books.

Discusses the use of languages as an auxiliary skill; also covers teaching languages and working as a translator or interpreter. Short on practical information.

Opportunities in International Business Careers. Jeffrey Arpan. 1995. 150 pp. $11.95 from VGM Career Books.
General overview of careers in international business, with discussion of types of international business degrees and specific business schools.

OPTIONS. Job opening newsletter available for $25 per year (6 issues) from Project Concern's OPTIONS/Service, 3550 Afton Rd., San Diego, CA 92123; tel: 619.279.9690.
Places doctors, nurses, and other health care professionals in Third World countries and underserved areas of the United States.

Special Career Opportunities for Linguists/Translators/ Interpreters. Free pamphlet from U.S. Department of State, Language Services Division, Room 2212, Washington, DC 20520; tel: 202.647.1528; fax: 202.647.0749.

Tax Guide for U.S. Citizens Abroad (Publication 54). Free from Forms Distribution Center, PO Box 25866, Richmond, VA 23260.

* *U.S. Department of State Foreign Service Careers.* Free pamphlet available from Recruitment Division, Department of State, Box 12226, Arlington, VA 22219; tel: 703.875.7490; internet: http://www.state.gov.
Application for the Foreign Service Officer Program. Available from above address (written requests only). Typical application deadline is in October; may not be offered every year. Study Guide to the Foreign Service Officer Written Examination and Assessment Procedure. Invaluable preparation, $9.95 postpaid from FSO Study Guide, Educational Testing Service, Mail Stop 31-X, Princeton, NJ 08541-0001; tel: 609.921.9000.

** *Working in Asia.* Nicki Grihault. In Print Publishing Ltd (UK). 1996. 444 pp. $16.95 from Weatherhill, 568 Broadway, Suite 705, New York, NY 10012; tel: 800.557.5601; fax: 800.557.5601.
This is the first book to give an overview of all work options, from volunteer to teaching to career opportunities, throughout Asia—from the Indian subcontinent to Southeast Asia to Northern Asia. Includes specifics on U.S. and other organizations.

Working in France: The Ultimate Guide to Job Hunting and Career Success à la Française. Carol Pineau and Maureen Kelly. 1991. 194 pp. Frank Books. Useful guide to working in France, focusing on cross-cultural differences in the workplace, written by two Americans who live there. Out-of-print but worth a search.

International Job Listings

Jobs listed in these publications tend to be for those with professional experience and credentials; therefore, these publications are of limited value to students, except for the two marked with asterisks.

* *Global Alternatives.* Monthly listing from the Professional Development Resource Center, School for International Training, Box 676, Kipling Rd., Brattleboro, VT 05302-0676; tel: 802.258.3397; fax: 802.258.3248. Subscriptions (within U.S.) $40/year non-alumni, $30/year SIT alumni (pay by check or money order only).

Each issue lists 80–100 domestic and overseas openings, mainly in the fields of administration, educational exchange, teaching, student services, consulting, intercultural training and refugee work. Internships listed too.

International Career Employment Opportunities. Subscriptions available from 2 months ($29 individuals, $35 institutions) to 2 years ($229 individuals, $350 institutions) from International Employment Opportunities, Rt. 2, Box 305, Stanardsville, VA 22973; tel: 804.985.6444; fax: 804.985.6828; e-mail: intlcareers@internetmci.com.

Biweekly listings of 500–600 international job openings (about half located overseas) organized by career fields: international education; foreign policy; trade & finance; environment; development; program administration; health care. Main listings are for professionals, typically asking for 2 to 5 years or more experience. One section in each issue covers internships; these are nearly all in United States.

International Employment Gazette. $35 for 3 months (6 issues); $55 for 6 months (13 issues); $95 for 1 year (26 issues) from International Employment Gazette, 220 N. Main St., Suite 100, Greenville, SC 29601; tel: 800.882.9188; fax: 803.235.3369.

Each biweekly issue includes more than 400 overseas job openings by region and field. Good for private sector business and technical jobs, though many of these require extensive experience, as well as teaching and volunteer positions.

** *International Employment Hotline.* Will Cantrell, ed. \$39 for 12 issues from Worldwise Books, PO Box 3030, Oakton, VA 22124; tel: 703.620.1972; fax: 703.620.1973.

Monthly reports by an international careers expert on "who's hiring now" in private companies, government, and nonprofit organizations. Lists overseas job openings, both entry-level and mid-career. Each issue has information-packed articles of lasting value on topics such as internships, organizations recruiting for teaching English abroad, and more. An outstanding bargain.

Job Registry, NAFSA: Association of International Educators. 10 issues/year for \$20 members, \$30 nonmembers from NAFSA Job Registry, 1875 Connecticut Ave., NW, Suite 1000, Washington, DC 20009-5728; tel: 202.939.3131.

The best job listing for those interested in the field of international educational exchange.

Travel, Health, and Safety Abroad

Able to Travel: Disabled People Travel the World. Alison Walsh, ed. 1992. 560 pp. Rough Guides/Penguin (see below). \$19.95.

Country-by-country coverage of travel around the world by people with disabilities. First-hand accounts and practical information.

Adventure Holidays. 1997. Revised. 225 pp. Vacation Work Publications. Peterson's. \$15.95.

Lists over 300 organizations that offer alternatives to package tour vacations.

* *AIDS and International Travel.* 1995. CIEE. Single copies free.

Pamphlet provides advice to international travelers on this important topic.

AILA U.S. Consular Posts Handbook. 1996. 225 pp. American Immigration Lawyers Association. \$25 plus shipping and handling from American Immigration Lawyers Association, Publications Department, 1000 16th St., NW, Suite 604, Washington, DC 20036; tel: 202.371.9377; fax: 202.371.9449.

A guide to State Department consular posts. Includes international and domestic addresses, telex and fax numbers, and names of consular officers. The *Key Officers of Foreign Service Posts* is a cheaper alternative.

Background Notes Series. U.S. Department of State. Country updates published irregularly. Available from the U.S. Government Printing Office. $1 each; complete set of current notes is $69; annual subscription for updates is $34. Also free on the State Department web site, http://www.state.gov.

Capsule descriptions of basic features of countries worldwide.

Blue Guides Series. W. W. Norton and Co., 500 Fifth Ave., New York, NY 10110; tel: 800.233.4830 or 212.354.5500.

Guidebooks series features expansive descriptions of art and architecture, but no practical information on transportation, accommodations, or food.

** Centers for Disease Control (CDC), International Traveler's Hotline: 404.332.4559; fax: 404.332.4565; internet: http://www.cdc.gov. To receive regular mailings about international health conditions from the CDC, send written request to Centers for Disease Control, National Center for Infectious Diseases, Division of Quarantine, Mailstop E03, Atlanta, GA 30333.

The federal government's CDC provides the latest and most authoritative information on health conditions and immunizations for travel worldwide. Faxed information for specific countries can be ordered free from the Hotline number.

Diplomatic List. U.S. Department of State. 1996. Revised twice yearly. U.S. Government Printing Office. $5 single copy or $9.50 annual subscription.

Contains the addresses, telephone, and fax numbers of foreign government embassies located in Washington, DC, and includes names and titles of staff members.

** The Electronic Embassy, http://www.embassy.org/
** The Embassy Page, http://www.embpage.org/. Home pages, free on the World Wide Web, continuously updated. Not available in hard copy.

Two outstanding web sites provide direct links to the home pages of embassies and consulates in the U.S. and abroad. Full of specific information, such as entry and visa requirements, and more general information about study, work, and travel abroad.

EuropeBOUND. Brian Hughes. CIEE. Video, 67 minutes. $89 ($79 for member institutions) from CIEE.

Three-part video introduces students to independent, inexpensive travel in Europe.

** *Foreign Consular Offices in the United States.* U.S. Department of State. 1996. Revised twice yearly. $7.50 from U.S. Government Printing Office. Addresses, telephone, and fax numbers of foreign government embassies and consulates located across the United States.

* *Health Check for Study, Work, and Travel Abroad.* NAFSA and CIEE. 1995. Free from CIEE; available in bulk for education abroad offices.
Brochure for students and advisers provides a checklist of health, safety, and insurance issues.

* *Health Information for International Travel.* 1996. Annual. Centers for Disease Control, see listing above.
Authoritative guide to health conditions and immunizations for travel worldwide. Single copy free to international education offices by calling the CDC Hotline (as above). Multiple copies $14 each from the U.S. Government Printing Office.

International Travel Health Guide. Stuart R. Rose, M.D. 1996. Annual. 464 pp. $17.95 plus $5.95 shipping from Travel Medicine, Inc., 351 Pleasant St., Suite 312, Northampton, MA 01060; tel: 413.584.0381; fax: 413.584.6656; e-mail: travmed@travmed.com; internet: http://travmed.com.
A guide to the prevention and diagnosis of illnesses encountered while traveling abroad, from jet lag to tropical diseases. Includes sections on trip preparation and a country-by-country guide listing entry requirements and advisories (similar to information provided by CDC publications, though easier to use).

** *Key Officers of Foreign Service Posts.* U.S. Department of State. 1996. Revised twice yearly. $4.25 single copy, or $5 annual subscription from U.S. Government Printing Office.
Essential publication lists addresses, telephone, and fax numbers of every U.S. embassy and consulate abroad. Also lists names and titles of foreign service officers.

** *Let's Go Series.* Harvard Student Agencies, Inc. Annual. St. Martin's Press. Around $19 each.
By Harvard students, these guides provide exhaustive tips for low-cost travel from the student point of view, including specifics on sights, transportation, accommodations, and food. Titles available for European countries, Central America, Southeast Asia, Israel and Egypt, United States, and Canada.

Living In Series. $4–5 each from Prolingua Associates, 15 Elm St., Brattleboro, VT 05301.

Tips on the customs, language, and lifestyle of France, West Germany, Great Britain, Italy, Japan, Mexico, Spain, and the United States.

* *Lonely Planet Series.* Various dates and prices. Lonely Planet Publications, 155 Filbert St., Suite 251, Oakland, CA 94607; tel: 510.893.8555 or 800.275.8555; fax: 510.893.8563; e-mail: info@lonely-planet.com; internet: http://www.lonelyplanet.com.

A wide array of "travel survival kits" and other guidebooks for "shoe-string" travelers to virtually any country, from Albania to Zimbabwe. Comprehensive information on sights and low-cost transportation, accommodations, and food. Lonely Planet also offers videos on independent travel in developing countries.

Michelin Guide Series. Michelin Travel Publications, Michelin North America, One Parkway South, Greenville, SC 29615; tel: 800.423.0485; fax: 800.378.7471.

Concise yet informative guides for cultural and scenic sights. No information on accommodations, food, or transportation.

* *More Women Travel: Adventures and Advice from more than 60 Countries.* Natania Jansz and Miranda Davies, eds. 1995. 694 pp. Rough Guides/Penguin (see below). $14.95.

Country-by-country information on cultural and social factors which affect women travelers. Includes local contacts for women and first-hand accounts from women who have studied, worked, and traveled abroad.

The Pocket Doctor. Stephen Bezruchka, M.D. 1992. 96 pp. $4.95 from The Mountaineers, 1011 SW Klickitat Way, Suite 107, Seattle, WA 98134-1162; tel: 206.223.6303; fax: 206.223.6306.

A guide to self-diagnosis and treatment of illness for travelers abroad.

* *Rough Guide Series.* Various dates and prices. Rough Guides, Division of Penguin Books, Consumer Sales, Penguin USA, PO Box 999–Dept. #17109, Bergenfield, NJ 07621-0120; tel: 800.253.6476; internet: http://www.hotwired.com/rough.

Series excels in providing very up-to-date cultural, political, and historical insights along with detailed practical information on sights and low-cost transportation, accommodations, and food. Worldwide coverage.

Staying Healthy in Asia, Africa, and Latin America. Volunteers in Asia. 1995. 200 pp. $11.95 from Moon Publications, 330 Wall St., Chico, CA 95928; tel: 800.345.5473; fax: 916.345.6751.

Information for preventing and treating illness and other health problems while traveling in less-developed regions.

Rick Steves' Through the Back Door Series; *Rick Steves' Country Guides* (formerly *2-22 Days*); *Europe 101: History and Art for the Traveler.* Rick Steves. 1996. Annual. Around $19 each from John Muir Publications, PO Box 613, Santa Fe, NM 87504-0613; tel: 800.888.7504 or 505.982.4078; fax: 505.988.1680.

Useful introduction to traveling independently and inexpensively, and planning travel itineraries. PBS video series by Rick Steves on travel in Europe also available.

Tips for Travelers. Bureau of Consular Affairs. Various dates. Available from the U.S. Government Printing Office. $1, with 25 percent discount on orders of one hundred or more.

A series of guides covering visa regulations, health precautions, crime and personal security, and travel restrictions for specific countries or regions worldwide.

* *Student Travels: Magazine for International Travel, Study, and Work.* Fall and Spring. Free from CIEE; available free in bulk for education abroad offices.

Covers rail passes, insurance, work and study opportunities abroad, airfares, car rentals, and other services offered by CIEE and Council Travel. Includes articles by students on their experiences abroad.

** U.S. Department of State Overseas Citizens Services (OCS). Information and emergency hotline; tel: 202.647.5225; fax: 202.647.3000. Department of State homepage for overseas traveler's information: http://www.state.gov.

Provides emergency services for U.S. citizens abroad, country-by-country information on travel conditions (crime, political stability, medical facilities), and visa requirements. The State Department operator, 202.647.4000, can connect you with country desk officers if more detailed information is needed. The home page lists travel advisories and much more, such as travel per diem rates and contact information for U.S. embassies and consulates worldwide. State Department publications are available in hard copy from the U.S. Government Printing Office.

Bookstores Specializing in Travel

Book Passage, 51 Tamal Vista Boulevard, Corte Madera, CA 94925; tel: 800.321.9785 or 415.927.0960; fax: 415.924.3838; e-mail: messages@ bookpassage.com; internet: http://www.bookpassage.com.

Bookpeople, 7900 Edgewater Dr., Oakland, CA 94621; tel: 800.999.4650 or 510.632.4700; fax: 510.632.1281.

Forsyth Travel Library, 9154 West 57th St., PO Box 2975, Shawnee Mission, KS 66201; e-mail: library@forsyth.com; internet: http://www. forsyth.com. U.S. distributor of Thomas Cook rail schedule books.

Phileas Fogg's Books and Maps, #87 Stanford Shopping Center, Palo Alto, CA 94304; tel: 800.233.FOGG (California) or 800.533.FOGG (elsewhere in the United States); e-mail: foggs@aol.com.

Worldwide Books & Maps, 1911 N. 45th St., Seattle, WA 98103; tel: 206.634.3453; fax: 206.634.0558.

III. Organizations and Publishers

The following is an alphabetical list of organizations and publishers that provide two or more of the resources listed in the bibliography.

American Association of Collegiate Registrars and Admissions Offices (AACRAO), One Dupont Circle NW, Suite 330, Washington, DC 20036-1110; tel: 202.293.9161; fax: 202.872.8857; internet: http://aacrao.com.
   Professional association and publisher of guides for evaluating domestic and international transfer credit.

American Council on Education (ACE), One Dupont Circle, NW, Suite 800, Washington, DC 20036; tel: 202.939.9385; fax: 202.833.4760; internet: http://www.ACENET.edu/.
   ACE's Commission on International Exchange has published numerous reports on educational exchange. Contact ACE for the list of ACE International Publications.

AMIDEAST, 1730 M St., NW, Suite 1100, Washington, DC 20036-4505; tel: 202.776.9600; fax: 202.822.6563; e-mail: inquiries@amideast.org; internet: http://www.amideast.org.
   Assists with educational exchange with the Middle East; publications for both foreign student and education abroad advisers.

Brigham Young University, David M. Kennedy Center for International Studies, Publication Services, PO Box 24538, Provo UT 84602; tel: 800.528.6279; fax: 801.378.5882.

Publisher of *Culturgrams* and a guide to international careers.

Cambridge University Press, 40 W. 20th St., New York, NY 10011; tel: 800.872.7423; fax: 212.691.3239.

Publications about the state of international educational exchange.

Canadian Bureau for International Education (CBIE), 220 Laurier Ave. W., Suite 1100, Ottawa Ontario K1P 5Z9, Canada; tel: 613.237.4820; fax: 613.237.1300; internet: http://www.cbie.ca.

Canadian nonprofit association publishes print, database, and video resources for education abroad, as well as information on study in Canada.

Central Bureau for Educational Visits and Exchanges, 10 Spring Gardens, London SW1A 2BN, England; tel: 011.44.171.389.4004; fax: 011.44.171.389.4426.

British nonprofit organization publishes directories on working abroad; most publications distributed in the United States through the Institute of International Education.

Council on International Educational Exchange (CIEE or Council), Council–Pubs Dept., 205 East 42nd St., New York, NY 10017-5706; toll free 888.COUNCIL; fax: 212.822.2699; e-mail: info@ciee.org; internet: http://www.ciee.org.

Publishers of materials on work, study, and travel abroad, especially for students. This nonprofit organization also administers CIEE study abroad programs, Council Work Abroad, and Council Workcamps. Subsidiary Council Travel offers discounted airfares and international ID cards (ISIC, ITIC, Go-25). Add $1.50 (book rate) or $3 (first class) shipping and handling (within U.S.) for each book.

Gateway Japan, National Planning Association, 1424-16th St., NW, Suite 700, Washington, DC 20036; tel: 202.884.7646; fax: 202.265.4673; internet: http://www.gwjapan.org.

Publisher of guides on studying and working in Japan, and on Japanese studies programs in North America.

Global Exchange, 2017 Mission St., Room 303, San Francisco, CA 94110; tel: 800.497.1994 or 415.255.7296; fax: 415.255.7498; e-mail: globalexch@igc.org.

Offers publications on education abroad and solidarity with developing countries. Add $1.75 shipping ($3 first class) for each book ordered.

Greenwood Publishing Group, Inc., 88 Post Road West, Westport, CT 06881; tel: 203.226.3571; fax: 203.222.1502.
Publications include several volumes of research on education abroad.

Impact Publications, 9104-N Manassas Drive, Manassas Park, VA 22111; tel: 703.361.7300; fax: 703.335.9486; internet: http://www.impactpublications.com. Free catalog.
The best one-stop source for international career books published by Impact and many other publishers. Add $4 shipping and handling for the first book ordered, plus $1 for each additional (within the United States).

Intercultural Press, PO Box 700, Yarmouth, ME 04096; tel: 207.846.5168; fax: 207.846.5181; e-mail: interculturalpress@mcimail.com; internet: http://www.bookmasters.com/interclt.htm. Free quarterly catalog.
Publications dealing with cross-cultural issues in settings ranging from academic to business.

Institute of International Education (IIE), IIE Books, Institute of International Education, PO Box 371, Annapolis Junction, MD 20701-0371; tel: 800.445.0443; fax: 301.953.2838; e-mail: iiebooks@iie.org; internet: http://www.iie.org. Free catalog.
Publisher of authoritative directories for study or teaching abroad and financial aid, and distributor of Central Bureau (United Kingdom) publications on working abroad. Add $2 shipping and handling per book on orders under $25; $4 per book for orders over $25; or 10 percent for orders over $100 (within the United States).

Mobility International USA (MIUSA), Box 10767, Eugene, OR 97440; tel: 541.343.1284 (voice and TDD); fax: 541.343.6812; e-mail: miusa@ igc.apc.org.
Publications and videos on including persons with disabilities in international exchange and travel programs.

NAFSA Publications, PO Box 1020, Sewickley, PA 15143; tel: 800.836.4994; fax: 412.741.0609. Free catalog.
Essential publications for advisers and administrators in international educational exchange. For membership information, contact NAFSA: Association of International Educators, 1875 Connecticut Ave., NW, Suite 1000, Washington, DC 20009-5728; tel: 202.939.3103 or

202.462.4811; fax: 202.667.3419; e-mail: inbox@nafsa.org; internet: http://www.nafsa.org.

National Society for Experiential Education (NSEE), 3509 Haworth Dr., Suite 207, Raleigh, NC 27609-7229; tel: 919.787.3263; fax: 919.787.3381.
Professional association publishes a directory of internships and guides for administrators of internship programs.

Peterson's Guides, Inc., 202 Carnegie Center, PO Box 2123, Princeton, NJ 08543; tel: 800.338.3282; fax: 609.243.9150; internet: http://www.petersons.com.
Publisher of guides on study abroad, work abroad, jobs, and careers. U.S. distributor for many Vacation Work (United Kingdom) publications. Add $4.75 shipping and handling for each book or avoid this charge by ordering through a bookstore.

Reference Service Press, 1100 Industrial Rd., Suite 9, San Carlos, CA 94070; tel: 415.594.0743; fax: 415.594.0411.
Publishes directories of scholarships and fellowships.

Sage Publications, Inc., 2455 Teller Rd., Thousand Oaks, CA 91320; tel: 805.499.0721; fax: 805.499.0871.
Publications on cross-cultural topics.

Seven Hills Book Distributors, 49 Central Ave., Cincinnati, OH 45202; tel: 800.545.2005; internet: http://www.sevenhillsbooks.com.
Carries a wide range of travel books and maps from foreign publishers. U.S. distributor for many vacation work publications.

St. Martin's Press, 175 Fifth Ave., Room 1715, New York, NY 10010; tel: 800.221.7945 or 212.674.5151; fax: 212.420.9314.
Publisher of books by CIEE, the *Let's Go* guidebook series, and the *Grants Registry.*

Stockton Press, 345 Park Ave. South, New York, NY 10010-1707; tel: 800.221.2123 or 212.689.9200; fax: 212.689.9711; e-mail: grove@pipeline.com; internet: http://www.stocktonpress.com.
Publisher of directories of universities.

Teachers of English to Speakers of Other Languages (TESOL), 1600 Cameron St., Suite 300, Alexandria, VA 22314; tel: 703.836.0774; fax: 703.518.2535; e-mail: publ@tesol.edu; internet: http://www.tesol.edu.

Professional association publishes guides and job listings for teachers of English.

Transitions Abroad, Dept. TRA, Box 3000, Denville, NJ 07834 (for subscriptions); tel: 800.293.0373. Editorial offices: 18 Hulst Rd., PO Box 1300, Amherst, MA 01004; tel: 413.256.3414; fax: 413.256.0373; e-mail: trabroad @aol.com; internet: http://www.transabroad.com.

U.S. Government Printing Office, Superintendent of Documents, Washington, DC 20402; tel: 202.512.1800; fax: 202.512.2250; e-mail: gpoaccess@gpo.gov; internet: http://www.access.gpo.gov.
   Publisher of U.S. State department materials for overseas travel and the country "Background Notes" series.

Vacation Work Publications, 9 Park End St., Oxford OX1 1HJ, England; tel: 011.44.1865.241978; fax: 011.44.1865.790885.
   Publisher of books on work abroad and international careers; distributed in the U.S. by Peterson's Guides and Seven Hills (each has different titles).

VGM Career Horizons, a division of NTC Publishing Group, 4255 West Touhy Ave., Lincolnwood, IL 60646-1975; tel: 708.679.5500 or 800.679.5500.
   Books on careers. Available through bookstores.

Worldwise Books, PO Box 3030, Oakton, VA 22124; tel: 703.620.1972; fax: 703.620.1973.
   Publisher of books on international jobs and careers as well as the *International Employment Hotline* newsletter.

Bios

List of Contributors to the Second Edition

Additional acknowledgments appear in the Publisher's Acknowledgments in the front of the book.

Robert J. Aalberts is the Ernst Lied professor of legal studies at the University of Nevada-Las Vegas. He earned a J.D. from Loyola University and an M.A. in geography from the University of Missouri-Columbia. Professor Aalberts has written a number of articles dealing with legal liabilities in foreign studies programs including two seminal articles in the mid-1980s which appeared in Continuum and the Journal of the Association of International Education Administrators. Since then he has lectured to various groups on the topic, including several times at NAFSA Region XII conferences. His other legal specialties include employment law and real estate law. Professor Aalberts is currently the editor-in-chief of the Real Estate Law Journal and has also coauthored a textbook, Business and the Law, published by McGraw-Hill Book Co. (4th edition, 1994). He has taught in several foreign studies programs, including the University of New Orleans summer programs in Innsbruck, Austria.

Susan Ansara began her career in international education in the Peace Corps in Tunisia, where she taught ESL. She taught in the linguistics department at SUNY-Stony Brook, established the Intensive English Center there, and was appointed assistant dean of international education with responsibility for study abroad. In 1990 she was named director of international education at SUNY-Oswego where she has since worked. She served as regional chair for Region X and chair of the SUNY Council of Directors of International Education. She holds a B.A. from Wellesley College and an M.A. from New York University. She has held three Fulbright awards, which have taken her to Italy, Germany, and Japan.

Bill Barnhart has been the director of the International Center at the University of Utah for the past 15 years. The center provides services to international students and scholars and sponsors the university's 34 study abroad programs. He has been involved with NAFSA for 18 years, serving as vice president for regional affairs, as chair of the 1990 national conference, on the board of directors, and as chair of membership committee.

M. Archer Brown has worked in the educational exchange field for more than 35 years, currently as deputy executive director of NAFSA: Association of International Educators. Prior to 1978, she was assistant executive director of the Council on International Educational Exchange in New York City.

Jim Buschman is associate director of Syracuse University's Division of International Programs Abroad. He holds a Ph.D. and a Certificate of Latin American studies from the University of Florida, and has lived in Nigeria, Mexico, Brazil, and Germany. Prior to arriving at Syracuse, he worked in study abroad with the School for International Training, Kalamazoo College, and Alma College. He served as the NAFSA MicroSIG liaison for Region V. He has conducted several NAFSA computer-training workshops, and claims proudly that he learned everything he knows about computers while working in international education.

Jane Cary was for ten years the study abroad adviser and associate director of career counseling at Amherst College in Amherst, Massachusetts. She served as SECUSSA Region XI representative, and was SECUSSA national chair from 1993–94. She was a frequent presenter at regional and national NAFSA conferences on topics that integrated the interests of study abroad advisers and career counselors. Upon her family's move to Lawrenceville, New Jersey in June 1996, she became the director of health professions advising at Princeton University. She holds a B.A. in English and theater from Bates College and an M.A. in student personnel administration from Columbia University.

Cynthia Felback Chalou is the assistant director of study abroad at Michigan State University and served as coordinator of study abroad at North Carolina State University from 1985 to 1995. She has held a variety of leadership positions, including SECUSSA chair of Region VII; SECUSSA national team; member of the SECUSSA Task Force on Financial Aid; and member of the International Student Exchange Program (ISEP) Advisory Board. She was a previous contributor to NAFSA's Guide to Education Abroad and is actively involved in the implementation of NAFSA's foundation workshops. She served as a Peace Corps volunteer in Swaziland from 1980 to 1982.

Stephen Cooper is director of academic programs abroad at Louisiana State University, where he teaches speech communication. He has chaired the CIEE Editorial Board and served on CIEE's Board of Directors and Executive Committee. He is a frequent presenter and panel chair at NAFSA and CIEE conferences. Among his publications is the NAFSA book Financial Aid for Study Abroad: A Manual for Advisers and Administrators, which he coedited with Nancy Stubbs and Bill Cressey. He has served on NAFSA's SECUSSA Task Force on Financial Aid since its founding in the mid-1980s. In 1993 NAFSA presented him with the Lily Von Klemperer Award for service in the field of study abroad.

Paul DeYoung is the director of international programs at Reed College. During his 20 years at Reed, which is a member of the International 50 Liberal Arts Colleges, he has developed a comprehensive international framework (overseas study, on-campus international programs, and international student and scholar services) within one office. He was recently elected chair of SECUSSA. He holds undergraduate and graduate degrees from Stanford University and a Ph.D. from the University of Oregon. He is a long-standing member of IIE, NAFSA, and CIEE. He has been a Fulbright grantee to Germany, and he has most recently been researching the impact of reunification on higher education exchanges between the United States and the former GDR.

Valerie M. Eastman is director of off-campus study at Scripps College, a member of the Claremont Colleges. Scripps College administers programs in Ecuador, France, Germany, and Zimbabwe. Prior to coming to Scripps College she worked for the California State University systemwide international programs office. She has been involved in NAFSA activities at all levels. Currently, she is a Ph.D. candidate in education at the Claremont Graduate School.

Janeen Felsing is associate director for overseas study at the University of Oregon. She has a master's degree from the University of Iowa, where she worked for several years as assistant director in the Office of International Education and Services. She has held several positions in NAFSA and its Section on U.S. Students Abroad.

Catherine Gamon is field director for the eastern region of the Department of Campus Relations, Council on International Educational Exchange. Her previous positions include director of study abroad at Bentley College, vice president and director of program development in the College Division of the American Institute for Foreign Study, and coordinator and adviser in the Opportunities Abroad Office,

International Center, University of California, San Diego. She has served in various local, regional, and national positions in NAFSA: Association of International Educators

Margery A. Ganz is an associate professor of history at Spelman College and has served as director of study abroad for the college since 1991, where she previously served as coordinator. She has given numerous talks at NAFSA, CIEE, and IES annual conferences on the subject of minority students and study abroad. Her best known talk, "The Spelman Experience: Encouraging and Supporting Minority Students Abroad," appears in Black Students and Overseas Programs: Broadening the Base of Participation, published by CIEE. She currently serves on Butler University's National Advisory Council and the Academic Council of the Institute of European and Asian Studies. She has also served on CIEE's Board of Directors and Beaver College's National Advisory Board. She won the Lily Von Klemperer Award in 1995.

Joan Gore is associate academic officer for the Council on International Educational Exchange. Over the span of her career she has worked with colleges, universities, and associations on campus and curriculum inter-nationalization and with agencies that have developed and managed exchange programs worldwide. She has been a resident director overseas and worked as a study abroad adviser, administrator, and faculty member. She has developed and presented workshops and programs on a wide variety of topics in the field of education abroad and campus interna-tionalization, including office organization and administration, health issues abroad, financial aid and tuition drain, professional development, and the history of U.S. undergraduate education abroad.

Jack Henderson is director of off-campus studies and an associate pro-fessor of French at Dickinson College, where he directs the operation of 20 overseas study programs. He has been active in international educa-tion and study abroad for more than 25 years. A member of NAFSA since 1973, he has participated in regional and national conferences and has served on numerous task forces. He was a contributor to the 1975 SECUSSA Sourcebook.

Harlan Henson published one of the early studies dealing with student perceptions of study abroad (NAFSA Newsletter, March 1979) while he developed the study abroad program at the University of Illinois-Urbana Champaign. He also expanded study abroad opportunities at the University of Rhode Island, and he is currently establishing a study abroad office and creating programs at Auburn University in Auburn,

Alabama. Henson serves on several national advisory boards and committees and has made numerous presentations at CIEE, CCIS, and NAFSA conferences. After completing field research in India, Henson received his Ph.D. in international education from the University of Illinois. He has taught cross-cultural anthropology and multicultural education at several universities and he consults on the establishment of study abroad offices.

Deborah C. Herrin was until 1997 the deputy director of the International Student Exchange Program (ISEP). She has been a member of NAFSA's Insurance Advisory Committee since 1990, serving as chair since 1992. She has presented on health and insurance issues at NAFSA annual conferences and at the American College Health Associate conference in 1994. She was a member of the SECUSSA team (1993–96), the Task Force on Financial Aid (1992–94), and the Whole World Committee (1992–96). She is now a manager at the Optical Society of America.

William Hoffa, Ph.D. holds academic degrees from Michigan, Harvard, and Wisconsin, and is founder of Academic Consultants International. He is author and editor of numerous professional publications: essays, interviews, book reviews, and reports on education abroad for *Transitions Abroad* magazine and other journals. He has contributed 17 years of active professional involvement within NAFSA, including national election to SECUSSA chair, appointments to other key leadership positions, and presentations at regional and national conferences. Previous positions in the education abroad include being field director of university programs at CIEE, and executive director of Scandinavian Seminar (Inc). Previous to this he served as professor of English and American studies at Vanderbilt University and Hamilton College. During his years as a teacher and scholar he produced extensive publications in literary study and was appointed senior Fulbright lecturer to the University of Jyvaskyla, Finland, and National Endowment for the Humanities fellow to the University of New Mexico.

Clay Hubbs is director of international studies at Hampshire College and editor and publisher of *Transitions Abroad*. After 18 years of teaching modern European literature at Hampshire, he recently retired from teaching to devote full time to international education—advising at Hampshire and editing Transitions Abroad, which he founded in 1977.

Maria C. Krane is assistant vice president for international education and off-campus programs at Nebraska Wesleyan University. A native of Brazil, Maria received her B.A. and Licenciado in English and Portuguese from the Universidade Federal de Santa Maria and completed an M.A.T. in linguistics at Indiana University with the support of a Fulbright grant. For her doctoral thesis at Mississippi State University, Maria developed an internationalization index for liberal arts colleges and identified its correlating factors. Some of her findings were published in the International Education Forum. Other research findings have been presented at NAFSA, ISEP, AIEA, and EAIE conferences. Maria has taught linguistics, ESL, and Portuguese at Brazilian and U.S. universities. She currently serves on the Advisory Board of ISEP, NAFSA's Whole World Committee, and AIEA's Campus Administration and Programs Committee.

Larry Laffrey is the associate director for study abroad at the Center for International Programs at Ball State University in Muncie, Indiana. A NAFSA member since 1981, Larry's experience in international education includes a stint as assistant director of NAFSA Field Service (1985–88) and campus-based study abroad positions in Michigan, Wisconsin, and Alberta. Starting a three-year "work abroad" sojourn at the University of Alberta in 1991, Larry became the first full-time study abroad adviser at a Canadian university. He has served on NAFSA's Membership Committee and the Region V team, and helped launch the Canada SIG. An extended backpacking adventure from Istanbul to Calcutta, wedged between bachelor's and master's degrees from the University of Michigan, was the inspiration for his career path.

Barbara Jo Lantz is a cultural anthropologist with field experience in Latin America and the United States. She first studied abroad to Colombia as an undergraduate anthropology major. She has taught anthropology and writing across the curriculum at Marlboro College, Williams College, Ithaca College, and Cornell University. She is currently acting as assistant dean for first-year students at William Smith College in Geneva, New York and pursuing an M.A. in social work from Marywood College in Scranton, Pennsylvania. At the time of collaborating on the NAFSA education abroad guide, she was assistant dean for international programs in the College of Arts and Sciences at Cornell University.

David C. Larsen, a full-time administrator who started his professional life as an honest educator, has taught at public and private institutions in this country and abroad. He was on high school and university faculties in Maine, was executive director of the Fulbright Foundation in Greece, directed an administrative division of IIE in New York, and the Center for

International Education at the University of Tennessee. Since 1988 he has been vice president and director of the Center for Education Abroad at Beaver College. He joined NAFSA in 1974, and has served on the boards of directors of AIPT, CIEE, the Fulbright Association, and the Fulbright Center.

Michael Laubscher, director of the Office of Education Abroad Programs at the Pennsylvania State University, has had more than twenty-five years of experience in the field of international education. He joined Penn State in October 1971 after four years of active duty as an officer in the U.S. Air Force. He has been a presenter on panels at NAFSA's national and regional conferences and at the conferences of the Council on International Educational Exchange. He holds a doctoral degree in higher education from Penn State.

Cheryl Lochner-Wright is study abroad coordinator at the University of Wisconsin-Eau Claire, where she overseas the administration of the university's 22 programs abroad. Prior to coming to Eau Claire, she worked with exchange programs at the University of Minnesota. She has been active in NAFSA at the regional and national levels as a presenter, a member of the SECUSSA Trainer Corps, and an OSEAS Partnership participant.

Kathy Lutfi is a program director at the Center for Global Education, Augsburg College. She has served as an international student adviser, a study abroad adviser, a faculty adviser, and an EFL teacher with the Peace Corps in Morocco. She received a B.A. in international relations and German from Hamline University and an M.A. in international administration from the School for International Training. NAFSA awarded her a COOP grant and two field study grants to create a symposium, a workshop, and a seminar. She has been a member of the Whole World Committee, Committee on Women International (CWI) co-chair, and NAFSA's Region IV CWI and Minnesota representative.

Patricia C. Martin is the senior overseas program manager and coordinator of student services at the Office of International Programs of the University of Pennsylvania. She has a B.A. from Williams College and an M.A. from the School for International Training. She is a frequent presenter and chair of sessions at NAFSA Region VIII and national conferences. She is coauthor of the report Study Abroad Re-entry Conference: A Model for Regional Cooperation, which resulted from a NAFSA COOP grant. She currently serves on the Board of Directors of the Pennsylvania Council on International Education.

Michael D. Monahan has worked in international education for 15 years and currently serves as director of the International Center at Macalester College in St. Paul, Minnesota. As such, he is responsible for Macalester's Study Abroad and International Student Program. Monahan holds a B.A. in political science and Spanish from the University of Wisconsin-Madison, and an M.A. from the American Graduate School of International Management. He has studied and worked abroad for six years, including directing study abroad programs in Denmark, Ireland, Mexico, and Spain. His educational interests include the internationalization of liberal learning, the interdisciplinary study of globalization, and questions of cultural identity and ethnic conflicts in deeply divided societies. He has undertaken independent study in Sri Lanka and Quebec, and has developed and evaluated study abroad programs in a dozen other countries.

Joseph Navari, who is currently teaching comparative history at Linfield College, designed and implemented a wide variety of international education programs for the University of California's Education Abroad Program, Linfield College, St. Cloud State University, and the University of Akron over a career of twenty years in international education.

William Nolting has been the director of overseas opportunities at the University of Michigan International Center since 1989. This office has frequently received the Council on Work Exchanges (COWEX) Award from CIEE as the leading U.S. university in work exchanges. Nolting was previously coordinator of international programs at Colgate University and codirected its Yugoslav Study Group. A member of NAFSA since 1985, he served as Region X SECUSSA representative (1988–89), on the Task Force on Financial Aid (1991–92), and as a member of NAFSA's COOP Grants Committee (1993–96). He is a member of the Advisory Committee to IAESTE and has been a contributing editor to Transitions Abroad since 1993. While a graduate student in Germany, he supported himself by working as a craftsman and interpreter.

John Pearson is the director of the Bechtel International Center and an assistant dean of students at Stanford University. Formerly, he was the assistant director for international education at the University of Tennessee-Knoxville. He was SECUSSA chair, 1995–96; a SECUSSA team member, 1989–92; chair of AACRAO Study Abroad Committee, 1991–92; and a member of the UK PIER workshop team (group leader for the study abroad chapter), 1990. Presently, he is the SECUSSA liaison to NAFSA's ANSWER project, and a member of advisory boards of Butler

474

University's Institute for Study Abroad, and AIFS Academic Programs Abroad. He has a B.A. in American studies from the University College of Wales, Swansea (1970), and an M.A. in American studies from the University of London (1971).

Ronald Pirog is associate director of off-campus studies and associate professor of German at Dickinson College in Carlisle, Pennsylvania. Formerly, he taught German language, literature, and culture in the United States and served as resident director of a study abroad program in Heidelberg (Germany). A member of NAFSA since 1987, he has been SECUSSA Region VIII representative and is coordinator of a NAFSA local area networking group. He has chaired and presented at workshops on the regional and national level. His overseas experience also includes undergraduate and graduate study at the University of Marburg (Germany) and postdoctoral research at the University of Heidelberg as well as extensive travel in Western Europe. On the Dickinson College campus he is responsible for advising and predeparture and reentry orientation programming.

Paul Primak is codirector for international programs for the Oregon State System of Higher Education. His program portfolio includes Denmark, Ecuador, Japan, Korea, Mexico, and Thailand. He previously served as the NAFSA field service representative from 1990–93. He has a B.A. in political science and has done graduate work in international studies and educational policy at the University of Oregon.

Joan A. Raducha is currently the director and assistant dean of international academic programs at the University of Wisconsin-Madison. She has a B.A. in anthropology, an M.A. in South Asian studies, and a Ph.D. in Buddhist studies from the University of Wisconsin-Madison and has published in the fields of early and medieval South Asian art and international education. She was the on-site director for the UW College Year in India program as well as a student in that program as an undergraduate. She is currently chair of the Whole World Committee, a subcommittee of SECUSSA.

Gary Rhodes has been the program coordinator at the University of Southern California Office of Overseas Studies since 1989. His doctoral dissertation at the University of Southern California was titled "Legal Issues and Higher Education: Implications for Study Abroad: Key Issues for Institutions and Administrators" (May 1994). He has presented, written, served as an expert witness, and been cited on issues related to liability, health and safety, and insurance. He has served as SECUSSA representative and membership representative for Region XII of NAFSA. He is currently on the NAFSA National Steering Committee for the Microcomputer Special Interest Group and is a member of the editorial board of *Frontiers: The Interdisciplinary Journal of Study Abroad.* He has been focusing his efforts on a World Wide Web project, developing a resource for administrators, students, faculty, and researchers interested in cooperation between colleges and universities around the world at http://www.usc.edu/dept/overseas/main.html. His own overseas experience includes educational development work in Cameroon as well as study in both Germany and France.

Thomas M. Ricks is director of international studies and adjunct associate professor of history at Villanova University. He holds a B.A. from the University of Notre Dame, and from Indiana University he earned an M.A. in Persian language and literature and a Ph.D. in Middle Eastern history. He has taught at many universities in the Middle East and in United States, and has directed faculty in Villanova's programs on the West Bank. Since 1986, Dr. Ricks has worked closely with NAFSA, participating in panels and workshops at national and regional conferences. Dr. Ricks is a member of the Center for Arab and Islamic Studies; CIEE's Review Panel for the Bowman Scholarships; CIEE's Academic Consortium Board; the National Fulbright Scholars Commission; the Whole World Committee; and the Editorial Board of Frontiers: The Interdisciplinary Journal for Study Abroad. He is also the president of the Pennsylvania Council for International Education. Dr. Ricks is a well-known author of many books and articles on Middle Eastern studies.

Tom Roberts is the director of the Institute for Study Abroad at Butler University. Formerly vice president and director of program development for the Institute for European Studies, he has served NAFSA as chair of the Lily von Klemperer Awards Committee, as founder and first chair of the SECUSSA Old Timers, as coeditor of Transcripts from Study Abroad Programs: A Workbook and Recording the Performance of U.S. Undergraduates at British Institutions, chair of SECUSSA (1986–87).

Rebecca Sibley has been employed in international education since 1975. She is currently a study abroad administrator at the University of Colorado-Boulder, vice president of the Alumni Association of the American Community School of Beirut, Lebanon, and co-chair of the School Improvement Team at Washington Bilingual School in Boulder, Colorado. She received a B.A. in Spanish and psychology from the University of Colorado, an M.A. in social and multicultural foundations of education, and a certificate in Hispanic studies from the Universidad Complutense de Madrid. A NAFSA member since 1979, she participated in the 1984 Baden-Württemberg seminar (Germany) and in the 1995 NAFSA travel seminar on experiential education in the developing world. She served as NAFSA's Region II SECUSSA representative, 1985–87; Region II newsletter editor, 1987–90; and Region II chair, 1992–93. In 1994 she was given an individual in-service training grant from NAFSA, and in 1994 she was the recipient of the Region II Bruce Tracy Award.

Kathleen Sideli is associate director for academic affairs at the Office of Overseas study at Indiana University-Bloomington. She is an active member and current co-chair of NAFSA's Lesbigay Special Interest Group. She regularly presents on a variety of topics at NAFSA's national and Region VI conferences and has maintained an active role in the field of computer applications for study abroad since the mid-1980s. She spent a number of years in Spain, first as a student and later as a study abroad administrator, and now routinely travels abroad to make site visits or review programs. She has a Ph.D. from Indiana University and teaches regularly as a part-time assistant professor in the department of Spanish and Portuguese, using a text of advanced Spanish grammar which she coauthored.

Mickey Hanzel Slind is currently an assistant director at the Institute for Study Abroad at Butler University, Indianapolis, Indiana. She travels for approximately 24 weeks a year on behalf of Butler programs and visits over 150 institutions annually. Since 1982, she has worked in all four study abroad professional tracks—as a study abroad adviser, program administrator, resident director, and program representative. She has served in various international education positions at Hamline University, St. Paul, Minnesota; the University of Minnesota; a national study abroad organization; and now with the Institute of Study Abroad. From 1994 to 1996 she was a member of NAFSA's Insurance Advisory Committee. She is a frequent presenter at regional and national conferences. In 1995 NAFSA presented Slind with its Lily von Klemperer Award for service and commitment to the field of study abroad.

Heidi Soneson is program director in the Global Campus at the University of Minnesota, where she is responsible for group programs in Europe and for the university's international exchange programs. Ms. Soneson has a master's degree in German from Indiana University and has studied and worked in England, Germany, and Kenya. She has served in the national leadership of NAFSA's Section on U.S. Students Abroad and has published and presented nationally and internationally on underrepresented disciplines in study abroad. Her current goal is to enhance and expand study abroad opportunities for students with disabilities.

Paula Spier is the retired dean of Antioch College's international programs. She continues to be active as a consultant, panelist, writer, and reviewer. She has served as executive coordinator for the CIEE Advisory Council on International Education Exchange (which produced the 1988 Educating for Global Competence), as chair of the Fulbright selection committee for the German exchange project, on the SECUSSA team, and on NAFSA's Board of Directors, as well as on numerous committees for Antioch and the Great Lakes Colleges Association. She has been honored with CIEE's Award for Service, NAFSA Region VI's Leo Dowling Award, and NAFSA's Life Membership Award.

Helen Stellmaker is coordinator of advising and student activities for international and off-campus studies at St. Olaf College in Northfield, Minnesota. She has been the Region IV SECUSSA representative (1994–96) and is on the Executive Board for American Association for Programs in Latin America and the Caribbean (AAPLAC). She has presented at numerous regional conferences and internationally in Costa Rica and Mexico.

Nancy Stubbs is associate director of study abroad programs at the University of Colorado-Boulder. She has spent 17 years in international education, first as finance officer and then as associate director. Her responsibilities have included budgeting and finance of study abroad, serving as liaison to the Office of Financial Aid, making all administrative arrangements for study abroad programs, recruiting, choosing, and orienting students, and advising students on all of the above. Nancy has two degrees from Boulder, a B.A. in music education and an M.A. in public administration. She has served on the Board of Directors at NAFSA and in regional and national positions representing study abroad professionals. She has some expertise in the use of financial aid for study abroad and has contributed to various publications on this and on models for organizing and operating study abroad offices.

Ellen Summerfield is director of international programs and professor of German at Linfield College (Oregon). Previously she taught at Middlebury College and directed Middlebury's graduate school in Mainz, Germany. She also served as assistant director of foreign study at Kalamazoo College. She holds a doctorate in German language and literature from the University of Connecticut and has published in the fields of German literature and multicultural education. Her most recent books are *Crossing Cultures through Film* and *Survival Kit for Multicultural Living* (Intercultural Press).

Ruth M. Sylte is the assistant director for outreach at LEXIA Exchange International in Palo Alto. Her previous positions have included working as a study abroad adviser at the University of California-Irvine and as the administrator of a field study center in Jerusalem. She earned her B.A. in political science and religion from Saint Olaf College, where she received her first exposure to computers in 1978 through a UNIX e-mail account. Today, she is an award-winning webmaster and frequent presenter on technology issues at international education conferences. She is currently the national chair of NAFSA's MicroSIG and a past list manager of SECUSS-L.

Beatrice Szekely is associate director of Cornell Abroad. In recent years, she has presented at NAFSA meetings and for BUTEX on "Redeparture: Study Abroad and Globalization," and has served on the New York State Task Force on International Education. Her early career was devoted to doctoral study and teaching in comparative education, specializing in education in the industrial nations, with particular attention to the former USSR.

Margaret Warpeha has coordinated the library and advising services at the University of Minnesota's International Study and Travel Center since 1979. She has presented Study Abroad 101 and other SECUSSA workshops at numerous NAFSA conferences. She studied abroad in Mexico and Spain, worked as a Peace Corps volunteer in Western Samoa, and has traveled in Asia, Africa, Latin America, and Europe.

Richard Warzecha is librarian and Internet specialist for the International Study and Travel Center at the University of Minnesota-Twin Cities. In addition to the center's main Web site, he created and maintains the Online Study Abroad Directory, the first Internet resource for researching study abroad options. Over the past few years, he has contributed his Internet expertise to regional and national NAFSA conferences. He is finishing a Ph.D. in philosophy at the University of Minnesota.

Henry Weaver is emeritus professor of chemistry and provost of Goshen College in Indiana, where he was interim president for the latter half of 1996. In fall 1995, he acted as interim dean of American University in

Bulgaria. From 1979 to 1991 he served as the deputy director of the University of California system's Education Abroad Program. He is the coauthor of Students Abroad: Strangers at Home.

Michael ("My") Yarabinec studied as a junior at the Universita di Pavia in Italy and did graduate research at the British Museum in London, England. He served in the U.S. Peace Corps in Morocco, worked for the French Cultural Services for five years in Paris, and worked for the French Consulate for three years in San Francisco. He has served as an international student adviser at the University of Southern California; an administrator for the Center of Middle Eastern Studies at the University of California-Berkeley; and as the campus relations officer for the California State University International Programs, where he was in charge of recruitment, publicity, and promotion of the CSU system's study abroad program. He is currently the coordinator of study abroad and international exchange programs at San Francisco State University.

 **Index**

Direct exchange model, 301–304
Director. See Academic director; Overseas leadership
Directory of Resources for International Cultural Exchanges, 14
Disabled students, 188–189, 198, 220–221
Disclaimer forms, 353, 367
Discrimination, 199–200
Diversity. See Disabled students; Ethnicity of education abroad students; Gay and lesbian students
Domestic work programs, 95
Duration of stay abroad, 150–152

E

EAIE. See European Association for International Education (EAIE)
Economic manager role. See Budget management
Education abroad advisory committee. See Advisory committee
Education abroad programs, developing. See Developing new overseas programs
Educational Associate, 13
Electronic mail (e-mail), 30, 119–120, 124–125, 288
  for promotion, 132
Emergencies, handling, 55–56, 140, 212–214, 367
Emergency Communications Network, 123
Emotional problems of students. See Mental health problems
Enrollment
  concurrent, 68
  on-site, 64–65
ERASMUS, 152
Ethnicity of education abroad students, 160–161
  increasing, 183–200
European Association for International Education (EAIE), 4
European Credit Transfer Scheme, 152
Evaluation. See Program evaluation
Examination, credit by, 60, 72
Exchange student model, 283–288. See also Direct exchange model
Experiential education, 60, 95–96, 173–175, 294

F

Facilities, 281, 286, 293, 297
Faculty development, 275, 282
Faculty-led programs. See Overseas leadership
Faculty support, securing, 30–31, 37–56, 59, 191–192, 259–260, 281,